COMPUTER FRAUD
AND
COUNTERMEASURES

COMPUTER FRAUD AND COUNTERMEASURES

LEONARD I. KRAUSS/AILEEN MACGAHAN

PRENTICE-HALL, INC., Englewood Cliffs, New Jersey 07632

52266

Library of Congress Cataloging in Publication Data

Krauss, Leonard I
    Computer fraud and countermeasures.

    Bibliography: p.
    Includes index.
    1. Computer crimes. 2. Electronic data
processing departments—Security measures.
3. Fraud. 4. Computers—Access control.
I. MacGahan, Aileen, joint author. II. Title.
HV6773.K7   364.1′63   78–13730
ISBN 0–13–164772–5

Editorial/production supervision
   and interior design by Linda Mihatov
Cover design by Edsal Enterprises
Manufacturing buyer: Cathie Lenard

Printed in the United States of America

10 9 8 7 6 5 4 3 2 1

PRENTICE-HALL INTERNATIONAL, INC., *London*
PRENTICE-HALL OF AUSTRALIA PTY. LIMITED, *Sydney*
PRENTICE-HALL OF CANADA, LTD., *Toronto*
PRENTICE-HALL OF INDIA PRIVATE LIMITED, *New Delhi*
PRENTICE-HALL OF JAPAN, INC., *Tokyo*
PRENTICE-HALL OF SOUTHEAST ASIA PTE. LTD., *Singapore*
WHITEHALL BOOKS LIMITED, *Wellington, New Zealand*

Contents

v

Section III

LOSS RECOVERY, LEGAL, AND INVESTIGATIVE CONSIDERATIONS

Section IV

IMPLEMENTING YOUR LOSS CONTROL PROGRAM

APPENDIXES

Preface

This book deals with computer fraud prevention, detection, deterrents, investigation, loss recovery, and risk management. The term "computer fraud" is our shorthand way of referring to *computer-assisted* or *computer-related* crimes. The people who commit these crimes may use the computer either directly or as a vehicle for deliberate misrepresentation or deception, usually to cover up the embezzlement or theft of money, goods, services, or information.

Avoiding the sensationalism that so often characterizes the current literature on the subject, this book is addressed to business executives, financial and administrative officers, data processing managers, systems analysts, auditors, corporate and computer security supervisors, law enforcement investigators, and others who are responsible for providing direction in coping with the risk of computer fraud.

Embodied in this book is the essential realization that your company is in business to do much more than protect its flanks against a possible computer rip-off. A part of this realization is that you cannot run a business properly if you treat employees and those with whom you deal as though they were all potential criminals. On the other hand, ignoring or giving lip service to what are known to be clear risks involving computers hardly qualifies as due diligence and reasonable care.

You need not refer to computer trade literature or even to business magazines to get the idea that a problem exists. For example, as this preface is being written, the current issue of *Time* magazine reports that computer crime is one of the fastest-growing industries in the United States. An FBI agent quoted in the article says, "This is the crime of the future." We hope that both *Time* and the FBI agent are wrong. But in case they are correct, you can do an effective job of staying ahead of the crooks and cheats by applying the principles and techniques covered in this book.

The book is divided into four main sections:

- *Section I—Understanding the Problem:*
  This section shows you how computer fraud occurs and explains how you should view the variables involved when establishing a system of fraud prevention safeguards.
- *Section II—Prevention, Detection, and Deterrents:*
  The chapters in this section detail methods, techniques, and approaches that you can use to reduce fraud risks and exposures. Here you will see how to evaluate your needs for basic as well as advanced types of security and control provisions. You will also gain insights to enable you to make the most effective use of the countermeasures cited.
- *Section III—Loss Recovery, Legal, and Investigative Considerations:*
  Covered in this section are the provisions you can expect to find in fidelity bonds; the new computer crime laws and ground rules about computer-based evidence; and tips and techniques involved in the investigation of computer fraud.
- *Section IV—Implementing Your Loss Control Program:*
  Successful implementation of a system of countermeasures requires a cooperative effort and some salesmanship. This section explains how to pull it together under a multidisciplinary approach. It shows you how to develop benefits for your program and discusses alternatives that you can use to overcome resistance to change and other human factors.

In short, we have sought to provide an understanding of the problem and to put you in a position to develop the best possible program optimized to meet the needs of your company. We have tried to present insights into practical problems and to offer practical solutions. And we have tried to save you time and money by providing ready-to-use approaches wherever possible. It is our hope, then, that this is a book you will want to both read and keep handy as a reference when you are establishing fraud controls and conducting investigations and audits.

Although nothing could be further from the truth, many people believe that the problem of computer fraud is limited to just a few situations. Among other things, this book will aid readers in identifying the potential areas for computer fraud in many different kinds of situations. Consider, for a moment, how your own company might be vulnerable to the following types of losses.

- *Theft of money in all forms.* This may involve paper currency, checks normally produced to pay legitimate debts, and checks received by the company in payment of debts to it. We shall explain how money that belongs to the company or is in its custody (a bank) can be wrongfully obtained by an employee or outsider, and the use of computers in such deception.
- *Theft of merchandise and inventory of all types.* The goods involved may be located anywhere (including in transit) and stored in every conceivable way: in retail stores, warehouses, tool cribs, storage tanks, refrigerators, yards (lumber, machinery, vehicles, gravel, etc.), elevators (grain commodities), vaults (precious metals, gems, narcotics, etc.), construction sites, grazing ranges (cattle), and so forth. The essential ingredient common to all such goods is that they are accounted for by computer systems. (Be careful not to restrict your thinking—a railroad lost over 100 boxcars in a computer fraud case where the stolen cars were repainted and sold.)
- *Theft of negotiable securities and instruments serving as the basis for the exchange of money and goods.* This would apply to securities, warehouse receipts, bills of lading, and similar items produced on your company's computer, as well as those that are accounted for by computer (an investment portfolio, pension fund holdings, etc.).
- *Theft of services of all types.* The service involved may be computer time or a host of other services, such as transportation for personal or business reasons (land, rail, air, sea, pipeline), medical or other individualized services, or services that may be provided by your company (construction, rebuilding, protection, repair, gas, electric, water, steam, hotel, etc.). This book explains how to establish appropriate safeguards to help prevent someone from obtaining these services without proper payment. It will also help you to determine whether your existing controls can deal with such risks.
- *Theft of data and software.* Although data and software can be physically stolen, more often it is a copy that is abstracted, so that the victim does not experience an actual physical shortage. Computer applications that have customer lists, certain

product information, proprietary programs that may be of value to a competitor (contract bidding, formulas, etc.), information that could be used for blackmail, or programs and data that pertain to national defense may be the objects of computer fraud. Perhaps the perpetrator's objective is to use the information to publicly embarrass your company or to hold the information for ransom. In determining what data or programs are sensitive, you will want to guard against accepting only the opinions of your data processing manager or controller. Top executives generally have a more accurate idea of what constitutes sensitive information. For example, a few data records from a mailing list obtained at random may be meaningless in terms of exposure. On the other hand, the *entire* mailing list or a customer profitability list may be of great value.

Misrepresentations for financial, personal, or political advantage. Crimes employing the computer to misrepresent might be termed *information crimes,* in the sense that someone acts (or fails to act) on the basis of fraudulent information, typically making a decision that would have been different had the true facts been known:

— A bank decides to grant a loan or a manufacturer decides to extend credit in a certain amount, based on fraudulent data about credit worthiness . . . *a credit fraud.*

— Individuals or companies decide to buy securities based on fraudulent data about sales, earnings, and assets of the company whose securities they are purchasing . . . *a securities fraud.*

— Terms and conditions of a corporate merger or acquisition are established on the basis of falsified computerized data.

— An employer decides to hire or a college decides to admit a person whose academic records are fraudulently shown on the computer records.

— Fraudulent health records enable a poor risk to obtain insurance coverage.

— Fraudulent police records enable a repeat offender to get away with a light sentence.

— Fraudulent engineering test data on a computer result in the acceptance or purchase of an inferior product.

Considering the scope of possible crimes, as outlined above, we could say that the vast majority are rational acts to achieve financial, personal, or political advantage. As more and more computer systems are used in connection with the areas discussed above, the greater the scope of the exposures becomes.

We are fast approaching the time when one out of every ten people in the work force will have a direct working relationship with computers. With the number of installed computers approaching the half-million mark and proliferating more rapidly as a result of mini-computers and microprocessors, there is not much doubt that computer fraud will grow proportionately. Although no one can know definitely, we speculate that computer fraud losses in the $1 billion range are not far away.

When looking at the risks and exposures, some people believe that computer fraud requires little more than traditional accounting controls, and they cite reported cases to support their conclusions. The problem with this is that for every computer fraud you read about in the newspapers, there are perhaps nine other cases that are unreported and ten more that remain undetected. So, in reality, you may only know about 5% of what is actually going on. And there is reason to believe that the reported cases that make up the 5% are not representative. We say this because so many of the reported cases employ fairly simple minded techniques—not the truly exotic manipulations that are possible on the computer. Yet, despite the simplicity of these frauds, most of them were detected by means that can be generally characterized as accidental. The smart perpetrators and their clever schemes await discovery, or so it would seem.

Although we know that the complexity of computer software provides great opportunities for the concealment of major crimes, the criminals employing just the relatively simple schemes have generated losses that are, on the average, 25 to 50 times as big as their non-computer counterparts.

The experts who say there is no totally effective way to stop computer fraud are wrong. One guaranteed method is to pull the plug on the computer. Since almost nobody will opt for this approach, you will undoubtedly be faced with the problem of using imperfect techniques to fend off the risks of computer fraud and provide reasonable care. Exactly what constitutes reasonable care in a computer environment defies absolute definition, although it is generally accepted that policies, procedures, and controls for the safeguarding of company assets should be responsive to the nature of the risks and exposures. The nature of the problem in the typical computer environment arises from the following properties:

- *Concentration of information.* Computer systems tend to centralize and integrate data files, making it easier for someone to obtain all the information needed to support a fraudulent scheme.
- *Lack of visible records.* The opportunity for concealment is

enhanced because the permanent record is not visible. At the same time, the possibility for detection through chance observation is reduced.

- *Programs and data can be altered without a trace.* Whereas manual manipulations of accounting records would often show evidence of tampering, which might be further investigated through handwriting analysis, there is nothing inherent in computer frauds that makes it necessary to leave "footprints."
- *Data can be made to disappear with extreme dispatch.* By pressing the right button on a computer console or keyboard, complete data files can be erased quickly to cover up a manipulation. The erasure can then be blamed simply on an operator or programmer error.
- *On-line systems often involve an efficiency versus control trade-off.* By entering transactions on-line, at their source, the several control steps that would otherwise be needed to have the data enter the system are bypassed.
- *Complexity.* Even fairly simple systems are quite complex in terms of the time and skill needed to understand exactly what applications programs are doing. After a time, people begin to accept the integrity of the systems without question, especially where the level of human intervention is designed to be minimal.
- *Difficulty of physically securing data files.* Unlike manual records and books of account, which are generally posted under control and locked up at night, computer records may be accessible to more people and be subject to much less control.
- *Concentration of functions.* Programmers and certain data-entry people are in a position to manipulate records fraudulently by the very nature of their jobs. Traditional separation-of-duties principles are ignored or overlooked.
- *Lack of control-oriented approach in systems designs.* The majority of computer systems designers and programmers are not knowledgeable about accounting controls and general principles of control. Audit trail provisions are frequently not worked into systems designs.
- *Technical personnel can circumvent key controls.* Even where a system design has built-in features to highlight exception conditions that can indicate a fraud, it is possible for a programmer or systems software specialist to patch up the program in order to make everything appear normal when, in fact, it is not.

To be sure, there are safeguards to deal with every one of the potential routes to compromise a system. These would cover the problem areas shown above and many others that were not mentioned (e.g., communications line tapping).

Another bright note serving to blemish the attractiveness of computer fraud is that computer power can be turned to the task of preventing and detecting it—provided the right people are alert to this possibility. For example, welfare-role match-ups are now under way in many parts of the country. Very simply, this finds welfare cheats by checking city and state employee payroll records against welfare-recipient rolls. It is done totally by computer, and, although it is admittedly a simple process, it would be an impractical exercise were it not for the economics of computer processing.

A word about language conventions

We explained earlier that we were using the term *computer fraud* to mean computer-assisted or computer-related fraud. We have also elected to use some other conventions to simplify the material. Often we will use the term *company* to mean any type of for-profit, not-for-profit, or government organization. Also, unless it can conveniently be avoided, we generally use the customary male expressions, where doing otherwise would have made the material sound awkward. For example, we shall usually refer to an embezzler as "he" rather than he/she. In these cases, the reader can mentally insert the expression or sex of his/her choice.

Although this book is designed to provide accurate and authoritative information on the subject matter covered, it is no substitute for legal, accounting, consulting, or other professional services. If objective advice or other expert assistance is required, the services of a competent professional person should be sought.

Leonard I. Krauss/Aileen MacGahan

Acknowledgements

This book, as most books, is the product of the authors' hard work, encouragement from friends and relatives, advice from professional colleagues, cooperative employers, kind people who attend to typing and provide other assistance, understanding publishers, and the patience of loved ones. In addition, the authors owe a special debt of gratitude to Gerry Drossman, who spent countless hours pouring over research materials, reviewing and revising sections of the manuscript, and serving as our critic. This book's quality has much to do with Gerry's dedication and unselfish interest. The book's shortcomings are the fault of its authors and no one else.

I

UNDERSTANDING THE PROBLEM

1

How It Happens

Using capsule case histories, this chapter is intended to give you insight into the means that have been used to perpetrate computer fraud. Each section contains one or more brief descriptions to give you a general idea of the situations to look out for. Since we are establishing the essential basis for particular types of fraudulent activity, we are going to avoid intricate details. For those of you who might wish to delve into such details, we recommend the 239-page *Report of the Trustee of Equity Funding Corporation of America*, an authoritative, well-written account of the biggest computer fraud so far discovered within the U.S. business community. Incidentally, the Trustee said that this was not a brilliant computer fraud, although the computer was used to generate fictitious printouts that were used to screen some aspects of the fraud. As you will see, there are few cases that we would consider to be brilliant computer frauds. The other brilliant frauds are going on undetected as you are reading these words.

In addition to the capsule cases, each section in this chapter ends with some key ideas on how the fraud might have been prevented or detected, or it raises some issues that should be considered in situations that can lead to computer fraud. The material in this chapter is divided into the following sections.

- Masquerading fraud.
- Computer fraud goes to the dogs.
- Inadequate audit procedures.
- Using computers to catch cheats.
- Internal control weaknesses.
- Delaying tactics.
- Providing too much information.
- Disbursement frauds.
- Price alterations and other fraudulent discounts.
- Ways to make your auditor prematurely gray.
- Wiretapping.
- The espionage connection.
- Another good reason to make your programmer take a vacation.
- The salami swindle.
- Hit-and-run computer frauds.
- Attacks from outside.
- Fraudulent debits.

Our objective for this chapter will have been accomplished to the extent that you come away with the idea that computer fraud can be perpetrated for a variety of reasons and in a variety of ways, by exploiting inadequate or nonexistent safeguards, and that a reasonable system of countermeasures can be established to provide reasonable protection.

MASQUERADING FRAUD

A Florida retiree is no longer receiving Medicare payments for his cancer treatments because a computer in Baltimore decided that he was dead. The man first learned of his own death when the computer sent him a form asking for the details of his passing. "I'm sorry to inconvenience you," the man wrote back, "but I'm still alive." Back came the computer with yet another request for information concerning his death. Meanwhile, the computer is continuing to deduct Medicare premiums from the man's Social Security checks.

On the brighter side, it appears that the same computer may have dispensed as much as $1 billion in Supplemental Security Income overpayments to the nation's aged and disabled. The error was traced to a faulty program. An official of Social Security was quoted as saying, "It's just one of those things that you couldn't believe would happen but did."

In Chicago, a woman named Mary applied for a Master Charge card, confident that her application would be approved. She owned her own home, had a savings account, had been employed at the same company for a number of years, and had established a good credit history with local merchants. Mary was quite surprised when her application was not approved and asked to see the records of the credit bureau that Master Charge had used to check her credit. The credit bureau's computer printout for Mary gave an incorrect previous address, erroneous employment information, and an overdue account at a store where Mary had never bought anything in her life.

If you asked most people about the significance of these three cases, especially people who know something about computers, they would say that these are just a few examples of carelessness or, in the vernacular, "computer screw-ups." We would like to suggest to you that in cases of this general nature (not necessarily these particular cases), there are fraud possibilities that people frequently fail to consider.

First, the appearance of "computer errors" is an ideal cover-up for computer fraud because nearly everyone knows and accepts the notion that computers make mistakes, sometimes big ones. Using this kind of deception, which we call the *masquerading fraud*, a perpetrator may have two choices of how to proceed. He can either create the error condition or work within one that already exists. Indeed, there have been cases where the very existence of true errors was of such a nature as to clearly demonstrate to a would-be perpetrator how the system could be ripped off.

Second, there is what we call the *tip-of-the-iceberg clue*. Simply put, this means that there may be much more wrong with the Chicago credit bureau's computer system controls and safeguards than just poor Mary's credit record. It could be that Mary's record got fouled up as a result of someone tampering with the system in an attempt to enter, or to change, other credit records. Again, there are documented cases of bankers granting loans based on credit bureau information that had been falsified on a computer.

Third is the notion of *opportunity assessment*. Let us suppose that there was simply a mistake in input data to the computer that thinks the Florida retiree is dead, and that the people in the Social Security office there are not adequately trained to correct the man's problem. Also, suppose that the overpayments resulted from a programmer error; after all, programmers are human and make mistakes. Assume, too, that Mary's problem happened as a result of a little slip-up during a data-entry operation. In other words, all incidents were just errors, nothing more. An opportunity assessment of these incidents might very well lead you to conclude that, although there may have been no fraud, the opportunity for fraud is much higher than it should be because the system of internal control failed to catch these errors. The message is simply this: There may be more to a computer "error" than meets the eye. Investigate, if there is any doubt at all, for possible masquerading fraud. Find out whether you are seeing the tip of the iceberg; make a fraud opportunity assessment.

COMPUTER FRAUD GOES TO THE DOGS

Several computer department and other employees of a Florida dog racing track allegedly conspired to siphon off $1 million in winnings over a five-year period. The fraudulent computer manipulation centered on the trifecta winners' pool. A winning trifecta wager calls for correctly predicting the first and second place dogs in three specific races. All trifecta wagers go into a pool which, after track and state fees are deducted, is divided among the winners. A winning bet of $2 will often have a payoff of several thousand dollars or more. For customary wagers on single races, the payoff amounts are constantly displayed on the track's tote board, so that bettors always have a fairly accurate estimate of the expected payoff. No such information was displayed for trifectas. The trifecta payoff was derived by the track's computer and displayed only after the completion of the last of the three races. The perpetrators took advantage of this fact in manipulating the system, after-the-fact, to issue additional winning tickets. Thus each legitimate winner received a lower payoff, since the pool had to be divided among more winners. The case came to light when a state auditor, investigating a very large trifecta payoff to one person, noted that an excessive number of winning trifecta tickets had been issued by the same machine. When the auditor started to probe, one of the conspirators reportedly confessed.

Here, then, is a case where total reliance was placed on the computer system. No manual controls or reconcilement procedures had to be circumvented. No losses were created that would eventually show up, as would be the case in many other instances of computer fraud. No complaints of the type that would arouse suspicion were possible, since a trifecta winner taking $3,000 home from the track would not only be delighted but also completely unaware that his take should have been considerably greater. This case points out the need for several types of countermeasures: *review procedures to find and eliminate system design flaws that permitted after-the-fact entries to be made; physical access restrictions to preclude manipulation of the programs and data and to limit system operation to appropriate personnel; and more vigilant internal auditing, in view of the high degree of reliance placed on computer-produced results.*

INADEQUATE AUDIT PROCEDURES

The data processing manager and a programmer were among those indicted in a $40 million scheme to mislead investors. In a fraud reminiscent of the Equity Funding scandal, the conspirators were reported to have generated phoney computer printouts that gave the appearance of inflated inventories and sales. The case came to light when company officials attempted to bring inventory back into line through a large writedown of inventory. Although auditors had previously missed the fact that $28 million of a reported $40 million inventory did not exist, they drew the line when company officials claimed to have destroyed $16 million in obsolete inventory at one warehouse on a Sunday afternoon.

The procedures used by this firm's external auditors to verify inventory were inadequate because they failed to identify the glaring discrepancy between actual and recorded inventory. If, in fact, the firm's record-keeping practices were so bad that inventory could not be verified, the auditors should have refused to certify the financial statements.

USING COMPUTERS TO CATCH CHEATS

In New York, following a computer match-up of welfare rolls and payroll master files, 42 state and city employees were arrested for collecting $250,000 in fraudulent welfare payments. In another drive to eliminate welfare cheaters, 12,000 cases were closed because the recipients could no longer be located.

Another computer put to work to identify fraudulent health insurance claims found: one doctor who removed the same set of tonsils six times in one year, another who first performed a hysterectomy on a patient and later put in a claim for an abortion, and a pharmacist who was dispensing to one customer 120 pills per day for about a year.

Government auditors and internal auditors should be alert to how the computer can be used to trace things and to locate inconsistencies. All too often, auditors fail to make the computer part of their routine audit procedures because of understaffing and lack of data processing qualifications.

INTERNAL CONTROL WEAKNESSES

A retired U.S. Army officer told the Senate's Committee on Government Operations of a 6-year fraud amounting to $17 million per year. This astronomical fraud reportedly involved a computer scheme to steal U.S. food and other supplies shipped to Korea. According to the officer, the system aided in the rip-off. One weakness cited was lack of an audit trail when goods were shipped from one point to another. Reportedly, when shipments were made, the inventory records went with the goods, so that, if a shipment were intercepted enroute, no record of its existence remained. In other instances the thieves reportedly used the system to learn what to steal and where the desired inventory was located.

The lack of a continuous record (known as an audit trail) of the supplies from their origin through ultimate consumption or distribution was a fundamental flaw in the system design. With an audit trail, thefts of this magnitude would not have continued undiscovered for 6 years. Unfortunately, many systems lack audit trails because computer professionals are, as a group, unfamiliar with internal control practices.

Internal controls and audit trails have long been a concern of the audit community. Internal auditors can help to alleviate the problem by reviewing a system design as it is evolving. If adequate controls and audit trails are not built in, the auditors should take strong exception, continually escalating their dialogue until corrective action is taken. All too often, auditors identify significant weaknesses only to drop matters if management takes no action.

DELAYING TACTICS

Two brothers, whose East Coast reinsurance firm had gone bankrupt, were charged with stealing more than $8 million in insurance premiums in what was called the largest fraud case ever brought in their state. According to the indictment, the brothers engaged in a scheme to delay for up to several months the necessary forwarding of premium payments from insurers to reinsurers. A series of tornados in the Midwest generated large claims and the scheme began to come apart. It was reported that the brothers tried to avoid discovery by telling insurance companies that payments were being delayed because of computer system changes.

Two New Jersey men were charged with swindling $150,000 from the New York City Finance Administration. According to the newspaper account of the incident, the mastermind of the caper was an outside consultant to the city employed by a major firm. The conspirators stole 30 checks destined for private firms that had done work for the city. Reportedly, the scheme continued for 4 months before one vendor complained that he had not been paid. The other vendors had not complained because they were used to delayed payments from the city.

These cases demonstrate why you, the reader, should *be suspicious of delays.* As long as victims accept delays as an excuse for nonpayment, perpetrators can continue their scheme. The extra time gives the perpetrator several options: taking more, absconding, or time to spend it all.

Repetitive, recurrent delays should be investigated to determine the cause. When investigating, *be alert to ways the delay could be exploited.*

PROVIDING TOO MUCH INFORMATION

After dinner one evening, a St. Louis man received a phone call from someone taking a "public opinion poll." The pollster made numerous inquiries concerning the man's background and finances, including the man's insurance company name and policy number. Unknown to the victim, the pollster was then able to obtain a check for the proceeds of a loan against the man's insurance policy which was recorded on a computer file.

Several months prior to the incident, a senior executive of the insurance company was informed by computer security experts that this kind of thing could happen because his company was providing too much information over the phone. The executive had told the experts that they were crazy to think such a thing could happen. The senior executive was fired within a month of the incident.

What this case illustrates is the ease with which outsiders can perpetrate fraud, based upon information given out to the public and to imposter customers as well. Prudent management should review the information content of routine disclosures from the standpoint of how that information could be used by a perpetrator. Following that review, which should be made periodically, management should set specific rules as to what information can be given out over the phone and what other information requires a written request and verification of the inquirer's identity before it can be disclosed.

DISBURSEMENT FRAUDS

An accountant employed by a fruit wholesaler made off with $1 million over a period of 6 years. The scheme used was a brilliant computer caper, discovered only because the perpetrator got tired of covering his tracks. The method used was to inflate prices on invoices by small amounts and then to disburse the extra money to any of 17 dummy vendors. Underlying the scheme was an environment in which fruit prices often varied widely. Because of these fluctuations, small amounts could be added to each of many purchases. To facilitate his scheme, the perpetrator developed a computer system that simulated his employer's accounting system. Using his own system, which he ran at a service bureau, he was able to determine which invoices could be inflated and by how much without attracting attention. The accountant then padded invoices accordingly and disbursed the extra amounts to fictitious vendors he had created. The fraud was so skillfully executed that the firm's external auditors never detected it. In fact, they were much impressed with the accounting system and inquired whether they could install it for other clients.

A major medical insurer was ripped off in a duplicate-claims scheme devised by a computer systems analyst and a claims supervisor. Working together, this duo discovered that the system would pay duplicate claims provided that the second time a claim was submitted it was at least 1 year old. After testing the scheme to make sure that it would work, the claims supervisor identified old claims that could be successfully resubmitted. The duplicate checks were sent to a mail drop, where they were picked up by the systems analyst and deposited to various fictitious bank accounts. The fraud came to light accidentally when the state department of health was investigating another matter and stumbled upon the fraud.

An electronics company accountant managed to embezzle $1 million in a 2-year period. The accountant was intimately familiar with the computer system for accounts payable because he had supervised its installation. Periodically, he would manipulate incoming documents in order to record more inventory than was actually received. Rather than paying the extra money to the vendor recorded on the sale, he would siphon it off and issue a check to a vendor account he had created.

A 25-year-old computer terminal operator arranged to receive pension checks under 30 different names. Her scheme was a simple one. When notice of a pensioner's death came in, she was supposed to enter it on the computer in order to terminate the payments. Instead of entering the death notices, she would enter an address change and send the check to a post office box. When auditors sent out letters to verify that the pensioners were still alive, the letters went to the fraudulent new addresses. It was a simple matter for the terminal operator to respond affirmatively.

Disbursement frauds have a number of common elements. First, they involve *deliberate overpayments* or additional payments, often for services or inventory not received. These overpayments are covered up by various means, such as inventory shortages that fall within *accepted tolerances*. In order to get cash out of the system, *dummy vendors or other payees* are set up in the computer. The computer *input is then juggled* to offset the overpayment.

Another common feature is the use of *post office box numbers and other special addresses*. The perpetrator or an accomplice *sets up a bank account* in the name of the fictitious vendor or payee and uses that account to cash the fraudulent disbursement checks.

PRICE ALTERATIONS AND OTHER FRAUDULENT DISCOUNTS	A retired pilot went into business buying and selling airplane parts. Our hero often did much of his buying from one parts vendor. In time, he struck up a friendship with the woman who operated the vendor's computer inventory terminal. The pilot and the terminal operator began meeting socially and, after the pilot had repeatedly wined and dined her, the woman agreed to help him in fraud. The fraud involved reclassifying valuable airplane parts as scrap or obsolete. The scrap and obsolete parts sell at a fraction of their original value. Whenever the pilot wanted to buy parts, he would first contact the computer terminal operator and tell her what he planned to buy.

She would designate the parts as scrap or obsolete. In one single transaction the pilot reportedly obtained parts worth $35,000 for a mere $1,100.

In another case, a systems analyst for a department store reportedly went into business for himself. He would buy expensive items such as refrigerators, televisions, and stereos on his charge account. When the paperwork came into the data center, he would designate the transaction as being subject to "special pricing." In one instance, he was reported to have been billed $3.98 for a new frost-free refrigerator. To avoid undue suspicion, he always paid his bills in a timely manner.

An office manager for a heating oil firm and a computer operator at one of the nation's largest petroleum refining companies were among those indicted in a scheme to bilk the refining company of 10 million gallons of heating oil through the manipulation of computer records. Reportedly, the operator would bill the heating oil company for less oil than was actually shipped. The office manager would then sell the extra oil privately and the two men would split the profit. The fraud was eventually discovered by verifying the physical inventory. The truly amazing thing about this case was that it continued for 6 years and amounted to $4 million before it was discovered.

A bakery salesman and a computer clerk worked out a plan whereby the bakery's computer billed the salesman for fewer baked goods than were actually sold. The two men then divided the money from the sale of the unbilled goods. The case came to light after another employee reported seeing an unauthorized person using the computer keyboard.

What these cases show is that the age-old practice of price alteration has joined the computer revolution. The new twist is that a computer maintains the records, and unauthorized discounts can get lost in a maze of automated entries. Another fact, illustrated by the second case, is the fact that crimes involving computerized price alterations can now be performed without external conspirators.

In order to catch the perpetrators, management should be alert to two tip-offs. First, there may be a *discrepancy in the physical inventory*. Another tip-off is *user adjustments*, which, upon examination, defy common sense. There are several ways in which a computer can be harnessed to detect suspicious adjustments. One means is to *program the computer to reject* transactions in which the special price deviates by more than a specified amount or percentage from the usual price. If outright rejection of transactions is inconvenient, the computer can be instructed to retain a record of such transactions on computer files for subsequent review and audit.

WAYS TO MAKE YOUR AUDITOR PREMATURELY GRAY

A chief teller in a New York savings bank embezzled $1.5 million in a 3-year period. Using his teller's terminal and his access to cash, he applied a variety of methods, including unauthorized transfers from inactive accounts, adjustments, and simple failure to enter transactions. The last method was by far the most difficult to detect.

When customers would make a sizable time deposit, the teller would fail to enter it and then pocket the cash. Later, when interest or maturities came due, he would reconstruct the account from records he maintained privately, covering the transaction with newly stolen money from other depositors. The scheme was so carefully executed that he was only discovered by accident when police raided a bookie whose records showed that the teller was a $30,000-a-day customer. In an ensuing investigation, the teller was brought to justice.

The debacle of unrecorded and unauthorized transactions can be averted by *system designs that enforce separation* of customer contact and adjustments. The computer can also be *programmed to extract transactions* against dormant accounts or significant adjustments for audit review.

WIRETAPPING

A $900,000 electronic-funds-transfer fraud involved two U.S. banks and two banks near the Italian–Swiss border. The perpetrators were monitoring funds transfers into one of the European banks from the two U.S. banks. When an attractive amount had accumulated, the perpetrators inserted instructions to transfer the balance to an account in another European bank. One of the U.S. banks discovered a wiretap in a routine inspection and alerted both the other U.S. bank and Interpol. The perpetrators were caught on their next heist.

This case could have involved even more dramatic amounts if one bank had not inspected for wiretaps. The incident could have been avoided entirely had the banks applied *encryption* to their telecommunications.

THE ESPIONAGE CONNECTION

XY Oil Company had a sophisticated seismic analysis system providing information necessary to make precise bids for tracts of land. They were always being beaten out on competitive bids against the QR Oil Company. Eventually, XY Oil hired a management consultant to tell them why they were always losing. The consultant learned that both XY Oil and QR Oil used the same computer service bureau where XY Oil ran its seismic analysis. QR had been using XY's system, obtaining the competitor's bid and then submitting one just a fraction higher.

Soviet agents were caught trying to bribe computer vendor engineers servicing a government installation. It developed that the service engineers always had lunch in the same restaurant as the Soviet agents. In the course of many lunches the agents were able to piece together enough of the conversation to realize that the customer reps had access to the computer installation they were trying to infiltrate. The Soviet agents offered a bribe and the service engineers reported it.

In another international computer espionage case, East German agents stole financial data on 3,000 West German businesses. The scheme was a simple one. The stolen data were stored on-line on a time-sharing computer. The agents opened an account with the time-sharing company under the name of a fictitious company. With a little experimentation and by asking a few well-thought-out questions of time-sharing employees, the spies were able to access the desired data.

A drug company learned by the industry "grapevine" that a competitor was about to patent a new miracle drug which would make several of its existing products obsolete. In an effort to obtain the exact formula, an original approach was tried that took advantage of the common business practice of selling excess computer capacity on a service-bureau basis. The competitor with the new drug had excess capacity available on a rental basis. The executives who were trying to steal the formula posed as employees of a small business that needed use of the computer for occasional runs. They came into the victim's offices at night and ran their program. What that program did was dump all the victim's on-line files to tape. Back in their own computer center, the executives browsed through the stolen files until they found what they were looking for. They then managed to patent the formula just a few days before the victim.

What these cases demonstrate is that *the espionage connection is a reality.* Many senior executives doubt that it is widespread—until they realize they have been victimized. Sometimes victims never know they have been "had."

Prudent managers should assume that competitors will actively seek means of obtaining business secrets. Secrets are often obtained from computerized programs and data. *Almost any confidential information has its use.* Consumer industries with guarded secrets, such as the design of new products, the timing of a promotion, the pricing of a bid, or the composition of a new product, are highly vulnerable.

Finally, management should realize that *a variety of methods can be employed.* These methods include bribery, posing as a potential customer for computer time, copying on-line files, and other methods limited only by one's imagination.

ANOTHER GOOD
REASON TO
MAKE YOUR
PROGRAMMER
TAKE A
VACATION

One of the most astonishing cases in the annals of computer crime involved the disappearance of 200 fully loaded freight cars belonging to a large railroad. Reportedly, programmers changed the routing instructions for the cars. As a result, the cars were rerouted to a remote location, where they were unloaded by conspirators. The computer records were then readjusted so that no trace existed of the missing cars. The "take" from this caper was $100,000.

An IRS programmer noticed the buildup of many unclaimed tax refunds. Judging this to be an undesirable waste, he instructed the computer, through program and file manipulations, to send the unclaimed refunds to a relative. This Robin Hood was caught when a real claimant appeared for his refund.

In another incident involving the IRS, a prison inmate was caught filing for false income tax refunds. Although actual access to the computer was never proved, a great deal of speculation existed. It seems that the prison had an inmate-rehabilitation program designed to teach inmates how to program a computer. The computer used for this training was shared by IRS and the prison, using terminals.

An Air Force programmer instructed a computer used for ordering fuel to issue payment checks for fuel not received. The checks were sent to company names he had invented and then he rigged the computer so that it would not miss the nonexisting fuel. His profit from this adventure was $100,000.

At a government welfare agency, a programmer noticed that when forwarding addresses were unknown, the computer continued to issue checks, pending receipt of new addresses. The programmer lined up several mailing addresses and then instructed the computer to send the extra checks to those addresses. Although neither the agency nor the amount of the loss was identified, other statistics relating to the welfare system suggest that the loss may have been very large. Reportedly, some 30% of the cases in which welfare replacement checks are requested involve some form of fraud. The fraud described in this case could certainly be part of that statistic.

At still another large federal agency, programmers were required to be on the premises at night when the payroll was being run. In the event of a program failure or a system crash, the programmers had to "patch" the program on the spot. We are anxiously awaiting news of a large fraud involving that system.

A programmer for a sales commission system created an individual named Zwana to be the last salesman on the file. For 3 years, the computer was instructed to round down every single commission computation and to add the rounding error to Zwana's account. When commission checks were printed by the computer, one for Zwana was among them. The scheme was discovered by accident when Zwana was selected to participate in a marketing promotion.

In Minneapolis, a programmer at a service bureau was assigned to develop a banking demand-deposit accounting system. Since the programmer had an account at the bank involved, he included a few extra lines in the program. Those extra lines instructed the computer to ignore any overdrafts in his personal account. The overdraft was discovered accidentally by a teller when a computer failure forced a temporary reversion to manual procedures. It took human judgment to catch this perpetrator.

The preceding cases illustrate only a few of the ways in which programmers can rip off a computer. Generically, the two things to look out for are *file modifications* effected by programmers, and *alterations to the processing flow of programmed decisions*. *File modifications* are used to create new payees, to change the recipient of a payment, and to erase evidence of manipulations. *Alterations to the processing flow of programmed decisions* are used to effect unauthorized inventory write-offs, inventory scrapping, reordering of stock, granting of credit, skipping of designated accounts, and transferring of incremental amounts from many accounts to a single fictitious account.

One reason to make your programmer take a vacation is that he is tired and needs a vacation. The other is to give yourself time to see what he has been up to.

THE SALAMI SWINDLE

A programmer responsible for an employee investment plan made off with an easy $400,000 simply by inserting a few extra lines of code into a program. Each month, a predetermined amount would be deducted from the paychecks of participating employees and invested by the employer in securities. The program in question computed the number of fractional shares each investor had bought. All the programmer did was slice off a small percentage of each participant's fractional shares and add them to his own account. Since the amounts taken from each individual were small and since the computation involved was complex, the perpetrator was able to continue ripping off his coworkers for some time before he was discovered.

Programmers have applied the salami swindle to their employer's payroll to raise their own paychecks. Sometimes the perpetrator subtracts small amounts from many paychecks and adds the total of those amounts to his own check. Because of the complexity of withholding-tax rates and the number of deductions involved, individuals seldom question differences of under $1.00 in their net pay. If the tactic is combined with a well-known change in withholding rates, there will be no suspicious sudden change for the victims to notice. Another popular variant on this scheme is for the programmer to round down in every instance in which a computation does not come out evenly and then accumulate the roundings in his own paycheck.

One brokerage firm deliberately applied a variation of this type of scheme against customers. Customers would call up their broker and place an order to buy and sell securities. The firm would then bill the customers for the security, plus commission and taxes. The company's scheme was to overcharge each customer by a small amount. The overcharge was programmed into the computerized billing program and duly applied to the bills. Few customers noticed the overcharge. Those that did were told that the brokerage house would check into the matter. After a reasonable interval, they were told that the computer had goofed and were asked to be patient while a correction was made. The customers were patient and the fraud continued for some time.

What these cases have in common is their reliance on a large number of relatively small amounts or *slices*—thus the name "salami swindle." Because the amounts taken from each account are so *small,* and the computations involved are *complex,* the *victims may find it difficult to verify the computations.* With all this natural camouflage, a salami swindle can only be uncovered through the use of special auditing techniques.

HIT-AND-RUN COMPUTER FRAUDS

One enterprising man instructed a computer to transfer $300,000 worth of securities into his account. This transfer was accomplished with an ordinary telephone connected by means of an acoustic coupler to a computer terminal located in his basement. From there, the perpetrator entered the transfer, awaited printing of a confirmation on his terminal, and then instructed the computer to erase all records of the transaction. He then sold the stock. Quite by coincidence, telephone company personnel were monitoring the call in a routine line check. Since the transmission seemed suspicious, they reported it and an investigation was begun. Early in the investigation the perpetrator was questioned. With that warning, the thief disappeared with his take. He is reportedly living under an assumed name somewhere in the Caribbean.

A businessman and his wife were traveling in the Orient. Running short on cash, they instructed their bank in the Midwest to wire them $10,000 through its computerized money-transfer system. A terminal operator in the bank sent $1 million instead of the requested amount. Before the bank discovered the discrepancy, the couple had spent all but $80,000 of the money. When the bank attempted to recover the loss, the couple offered to return $80,000. When the bank replied that it wanted the entire $990,000 back, the couple told them that they could either settle for $80,000 or that, too, would be spent. Meanwhile, the terminal operator (who could have been an accomplice) consistently maintained that he had just made an error. Lacking evidence and fearing bad publicity, the bank had to settle for $80,000 and write off a total of $910,000 as an error.

A major credit card company was victimized after a counterfeiting ring obtained a copy of the computerized customer master file. Using valid names and account numbers from the file, the ring counterfeited a large number of plastic cards. After accomplices signed the cards in their own handwriting, the cards were easily used to make fraudulent purchases. (In contrast to the problem of forging names on stolen cards, it is a simple matter to present a satisfactory signature if the thief has signed the card initially.) Similarly, since the customer names and account numbers were valid, merchant calls to obtain authorization for purchases did not arouse suspicion. The total take from the venture was more than $2 million.

A big-time swindler made off with more than $5 million through a series of fraudulent computer money transfers. Posing as a business tycoon, the perpetrator opened accounts in four major Swiss and U.S. banks. After maintaining a modest balance in two of the banks, he applied for loans to finance a factory he was building in the western United States. After approving the loans, the banks, as instructed, transferred the borrowed funds to the western bank. Meanwhile, the man had instructed the western bank to transfer the money to a Swiss bank account. The Swiss bank was then instructed to pay out the money as a down payment on extensive real estate holdings in the United States. Using the real estate as collateral, the tycoon next applied for and received a $5 million loan. The tycoon then disappeared without paying off either the loans or the mortgages on the real estate. Because of the speed with which computers can transfer large sums around the world, the total time to execute this heist was a mere 2 weeks.

The amounts taken in these cases were large. Even more unsettling were the *amount of getaway time* and the *ability of perpetrators to mobilize money without arousing suspicion.* Given the speed with which today's banking computers can transfer money to distant locations and a minimum getaway time of 2 weeks, the future of the hit-and-run computer criminal seems bright.

ATTACKS FROM OUTSIDE

A young electronics whiz used the local telephone company's computerized supply-ordering system to stock his own electronics supply house. His take from the venture was a neat $1 million. When he was finally caught, it was only because one of his own employees turned him in for failing to split the loot. How was this individual able to penetrate the computer's security and escape detection? First, the perpetrator posed as a reporter and interviewed company officials regarding the system. Then he obtained secret authorization codes required for system use from the company's trash. Armed with that information and a touch-tone telephone, the perpetrator placed orders for supplies with instructions to deliver them to out-of-the-way locations. He would then drive up at night in an old telephone company truck and pick up his order.

Two other precautions helped the perpetrator escape detection. One precaution was to steal only supplies he had ordered. Since these thefts would create shortages, the perpetrator's second precaution was to monitor the system to make sure that the amounts of each item he ordered were within the accepted tolerances. As a by-product of his monitoring activity, the perpetrator identified opportunities to sell the stolen goods back to his victim.

A computer operator was startled to see his computer console typewriter start itself up and begin printing him a message. Before signing off with the warning that "ZARF is with you again," the interloper blasted security weaknesses in the computer vendor's operating system, which had been called highly secure. ZARF is the trademark of a team of experts dedicated to uncovering weaknesses in the Air Force's computers. The approach of identifying security weaknesses through experimentation is known as a *penetration study*.

In another penetration study, Navy scientists broke the security of a computer, armed with only an ordinary telephone. This popular computer is a type used by government, civilian, and military agencies alike. One reporter refers to it as "Washington's dial-a-secret computer" because of the apparent ease with which it was cracked.

Besides the ease with which the computer's security was cracked, one other item in the penetration team's report is of interest. They reported that any file could have been selectively rewritten at will. In a business environment, the rewriting of a file could mean a big loss.

Unknown individuals made off with $2 million by exploiting a flaw in the nation's banking system. The scheme made use of the fact that certain information is magnetically encoded on checks so that they can be processed by computers. Among the magnetically preencoded information is a number enabling checks to be returned to the bank on which they are drawn (known as the bank routing symbol) and the customer's account number.

The perpetrators obtained checks from an East Coast bank and encoded them with the bank routing symbol of a West Coast bank. They then deposited the checks in the East Coast bank and its computer duly sent them on to the West Coast for payment. After 3 days, the East Coast bank automatically assumed that the checks had cleared and permitted the perpetrators to withdraw the funds.

Meanwhile, the West Coast bank's computer had rejected the checks because they appeared to be drawn on a closed account. Manual processing of the rejected checks led to the conclusion that they had been misrouted, since the East Coast bank's name was printed on the checks. The checks continued to ping pong back and forth between the West Coast and the East Coast for some time before someone got suspicious. By then, the perpetrators were gone.

Another bank case involved blank deposit slips that the bank provided for customers who wished to make deposits but did not have their personally encoded slips with them. The perpetrator stealthily removed blank deposit slips from the writing desk and replaced them with ones on which he had magnetically encoded his own account number.

Unsuspecting customers and tellers never noticed the alteration. For 3 days, customers making deposits with these slips were actually putting money into the perpetrator's account. After withdrawing $100,000, the thief disappeared. One reason he was able to escape is that deposit slips, like checks, are read automatically by computers designed to pick up the magnetic encoding.

A crime ring in Ohio bilked workman's compensation of $300,000 in phoney claims. Conspirators set up dummy companies with such addresses as post office box numbers, abandoned buildings, and empty lots. They registered these dummy companies with the state and appropriate records were set up on the workman's compensation computer files. The dummy companies were kept "alive" for 6 to 8 months each, and during that time anywhere from 5 to 15 fraudulent claims, averaging $8,000, were submitted for each "company." The computer obligingly paid all these claims.

These cases illustrate the number of methods outsiders can use to rip off your computer as well as the relative ease with which such schemes can be executed. Another point illustrated by these cases is that should an outsider find an exploitable means in your system's security, your chances of catching him are not good.

There are two types of flaws to watch out for, *design flaws* and *computer security weaknesses*. Design flaws are illustrated by the cases involving magnetically encoded checks and deposit slips. There was no check upon the number of daily deposits to the account (in the "deposit slip" case) or upon the number of times the check had been deposited (in the "check ping pong" case). There was also no cross check between the bank's name and the bank routing symbol or between the depositor's name and the magnetically encoded account number.

Computer security weaknesses are illustrated by the telephone company case and by the penetration studies. A widely held management fallacy is that, while opportunities exist in theory for penetrating on-line systems from outside, these loopholes are nearly impossible to exploit in practice. Nothing could be further from the truth.

Although the number of reported incidents have been few, penetration studies conducted by the military prove that loopholes exist

Case	Summary	Amount (thousands)	Time Frame (years)	Type of Scheme	Computer Manipulation	Fraudulent Debit	Job Position of Primary Perpetrator	Number of Perpetrators Inside/Outside	Means of Detection
1	Accountant at west coast department store set up phony vendors, purchases, and vouchers	$ 100	1.3	Disbursements	Unauthorized transactions added	Inventory	Accountant	1/-	Suspicious bank employee
2	Claims reviewer at insurance company prepared false claims payable to friends in a manner that would be paid automatically by the computer	$ 128	4	Fraudulent claims paid	Unauthorized transactions added	Expense	Claims clerk	1/22	Error made by greedy associate
3	Clerk at storage facility entered false information to computerized inventory system to mask theft of inventory. Shipments were then made without billing	$ 4,000	6	Inventory/ billing	Input transactions altered	Inventory	Computer terminal operator	1/13	Physical inventory shortage detected in audit
4	Warehouse employees manipulated computerized inventory system through unauthorized terminal entries to mask inventory thefts	$ 200	1.5	Inventory	Unauthorized terminal entries	None (inventory records changed as to location)	Warehouse employee(s)	"Several"	Suspicious wife of store manager
5	Accountant at metal fabricating company padded payroll, thereby extracting funds for own use	$ 100	3	Payroll	Unknown	Expense	Accountant	1/-	IRS investigation

#	Description	Amount	No.	Type	Transaction manipulation	Account affected	Position	Ratio	How discovered
6	Officer of London bank stole funds from inactive customer accounts	$ 290	5	Account transfers	Unauthorized addition and alteration of transactions	Customer accounts (liability)	Computer liaison officer	1/-	Unknown
7	Bank employee misused on line banking system to perpetrate large lapping fraud including unrecorded transactions, altered transactions, and unauthorized account transfers	$ 1,400	3	Lapping	Transactions altered, added, and withheld	Customer accounts (liability)	Teller supervisor	1/-	Gambling activities uncovered by police raid
8	Manufacturing company manager who had designed and installed automated accounting system used it to steal	$ 1,000	2	Disbursements (also billings fraud)	Transactions altered (also unauthorized transactions)	Inventory (also expense)	Operations manager	1/1	Suspicious associate
9	Customer representatives of large public utility, together with outside associate, erased customer receivables using computer error correction codes; received kickback from customer	$ 25 (probable losses much greater)	2	Accounts receivable collections	Unauthorized transactions	Expense (adjusting entry)	Customer service representative	2/1	Suspicious bank employee together with expanded type of scheme
10	Clerk in department store established phony purchases and vouchers paid to friend's company	$ 120	3	Disbursements	Unauthorized transactions	Inventory	Accounts clerk	1/1	Suspicious associate

Figure 1-1

Long-Running Computer Frauds. (After Brandt Allen, "The Biggest Computer Frauds: Lessons for CPA's," *Journal of Accountancy*, May 1977, p. 61. Copyright © 1977 by the American Institute of Certified Public Accountants, Inc.)

Case	Summary	Amount (thousands)	Time Frame (years)	Type of Scheme	Computer Manipulation	Fraudulent Debit	Job Position of Primary Perpetrator	Number of Perpetrators Inside/Outside	Means of Detection
11	Organized crime ring operated check-kiting fraud between two banks using computer room employees who altered deposit memos to record check deposits as available for immediate withdrawal	$ 900	4	Kiting (float fraud)	Transactions altered	(Timing)	VP-computer systems (also assistant branch manager)	2/3	Bank messenger failed to deliver checks on time
12	Accountant at large wholesaler established phony vendors through computerized accounting system that he operated	$ 1,000	4	Disbursements	Unauthorized transactions	Inventory	Controller	1/-	Gave up
13	Officer of brokerage house misappropriated company funds through computer system that he controlled	$ 277	3	Account transfers	Unauthorized transactions	Revenue account (interest earned)	VP-computer systems	1/-	Unknown
14	Partner at brokerage house transferred funds from firm's accounts to his own	$ 81	3	Account transfers	Unauthorized transactions	Expense (via adjusting entry)	Partner-head of computer system	1/-	Unknown
15	Director of publishing subsidiary manipulated computer system to add false sales and block recording of accounts payable—all to improve operating results, thereby securing a position on board of directors	$11,500	"Several years"	Padded sales (also unrecorded expense)	Program alterations (also file changes)	Receivables	Director of subsidiary	5/-	Unknown

Figure 1-1 (*Continued*)

in all systems and that knowledgeable perpetrators can easily exploit them. We think that the reason that more cases of this sort have not been discovered is not because these frauds are so hard to penetrate, but that instances are so hard to detect. There are undoubtedly many cases just waiting to be discovered.

FRAUDULENT DEBITS

Double-entry bookkeeping is still very much with us in computer systems. The idea is that for every account credit there must be a corresponding debit (and vice versa) to keep the books in balance. An out-of-balance condition triggers investigation as to the reason. So, as long as the books balance, there is no cause for concern . . . well, not quite.

In an award-winning article on computer fraud,[1] Brandt Allen advises readers to watch for the *fraudulent debit*. The reason behind that advice is that debits tend to remain on the company's books while credits tend to get lost in a company's financial accounting. To illustrate how this might be so, consider the following case.

Suppose that a larcenous employee wants to cover up a disbursement fraud by issuing disbursements for goods that were never received. The first step is to debit inventory for the amount to be stolen and credit accounts payable for the same amount. When the payables are processed, accounts payable gets debited for the payment and cash is credited. The result of that processing is to bury the original credit to accounts payable but to leave the debit to inventory intact.

As a result, inventory recorded on the computer will be greater than the physical count. This comparison should be made in any audit. If it is done, the auditor will find a discrepancy to investigate.

At that point, the auditor will have to go to the computer records to find out what is missing in the physical inventory. After noting the particular items involved in the discrepancy, the next step would be to examine transactions pertaining to those items. Here Brandt Allen's clue about the debit comes in handy.

If you are ever going to trace the shortage, you will have to start with the debits to inventory in order to locate the other entries. That debit will lead you to the original credit to accounts payable, thence to the offsetting debit to accounts payable and the final credit to cash. If you are lucky, you will find that the check to the recorded vendor is less than the amount credited to cash and debited to accounts payable. The check will be less if a second check was issued to a fictitious vendor in order to balance the credits to cash against the debits to accounts receivable.

[1] Brandt Allen, "The Biggest Computer Frauds: Lessons for CPA's," *The Journal of Accountancy*, May 1977.

At this point, you have a real clue, presuming of course that there was a discrepancy. If the check did not match the accounting transactions, there will be a discrepancy. Another possibility is that you may not find any supporting documentation. Either way, you now have a tangible situation to investigate.

The principle explained for disbursement frauds has broad applicability elsewhere, such as with accounts receivable, prepaid items such as rent and insurance, and fixed assets subject to depreciation. We believe that it would be useful for the reader to fill in the details. Figure 1-1 illustrates the fraudulent debits perpetrators used in some large and long-running computer frauds. It is a good starting place for analyzing sources of fraudulent debits and the means for tracing them.

2

Computer Fraud Theory and Its Practical Application

In Chapter 1 we explored various ways in which computer fraud has been carried out. Every case had elements of dishonesty on the part of the perpetrator, of opportunity permitting the fraud to occur, and of motive underlying the perpetrator's criminal acts. Subsequent chapters will cover the specifics of preventing, detecting, and deterring fraud, with little concern for the basic premises about fraud. Hence, between the coverage of "how it happens" and "what to do about it" we need to establish an understanding of the framework within which fraud occurs. This bridge is our theory of fraud, and we would like you to think of it as a theory that provides a mosaic into which fit the elements of a solution. As a working theory, it will help you formulate coherent action plans with a clear understanding of which variables you are attempting to deal with. Toward this end, this chapter covers the following topics:

- Theory of computer fraud.
- Dishonesty.
- Opportunities.
- Motives.
- Profile of a perpetrator.

In our theory of computer fraud, your company's probability of being a victim is a function of three variables: the dishonesty of the would-be perpetrator; the opportunity your company provides the potential perpetrator through having inadequate controls, preventive measures, and deterrents; and the would-be perpetrator's underlying motive for committing fraud.

The theory may be expressed by the following equation, which is meant as a conceptual representation:

$$CF_p = \frac{D \times O \times M}{1000}$$

where

CF_p = Probability of being a computer fraud victim (0.0–1.0)

D = dishonesty factor (0–10)

O = opportunity factor (0–10)

M = motive factor (0–10)

To illustrate how this concept works, let us suppose that we could determine values for each of the variables, in the range 0–10. A totally dishonest person would have a value D equal to 10. The opportunity that person has, if it were extremely good, would have a value O equal to 10. A very strong motive would have a value M equal to 10. Using these maximum values, the equation shows that

$$CF_p = \frac{10 \times 10 \times 10}{1000} = 1.0 \qquad \text{(a probability of 100\%)}$$

This value indicates that fraud is certain to occur. The opposite extreme would be where any of the variables (D, O, M) is 0. In other words, fraud would not occur if the person were totally honest, regardless of the opportunity or motive. Similarly, if there is no opportunity, the values of the other variables are irrelevant.

The theory is useful in that it expresses the concept that combinations of factors are important in coping with the risk of fraud. But, the theory will always remain a theory, because the real world rarely presents us with either 0 or 10 situations, even if we ignore the difficulty of quantifying the variables involved.

Company management will nevertheless need to weigh these variables in order to understand where conditions are most favorable to fraud as well as to make informed decisions about measures to control the risk of occurrence.

As we discuss the topics of dishonesty, opportunity, and motives in this chapter, it should become evident that the "human element" is by far the most significant and the most difficult to evaluate and control.

DISHONESTY   Some years ago, at an informal gathering, an experienced industrial security officer said that of the 15% of the general public that is not strictly honest, 5% would engage in a dishonest act if they believed there was no chance of being caught, 5% if there was a slight chance of being caught, and the remaining 5% if the odds of being caught were as high as 50%.

To put this in a context common to everyone, consider the problem of shoplifting in retail establishments. This results in enormous losses, which in some cases may be as much as a retailer's profit; if there were no shoplifting in a low-margin food store, for example, annual profits might double. The shoplifting is being done by people in the 15% group identified above. That group contains individuals from all walks of life: school kids, teachers, executives, clergymen, pilots, and computer operators, to name just a few. Realize, then, that on average, one of every seven customers you see in a retail establishment is a shoplifter. (Some retail security experts believe the proportion to be twice this number.)

Amateurs in retail store security positions have a great tendency to observe most closely those people they think look like shoplifters (often racial minorities) and may ignore the others altogether. This prejudiced outlook greatly reduces the effectiveness of any loss-prevention program.

Similarly, it is unwise to prejudge people who may be in a position to perpetrate a computer fraud. However, it does seem clear that there are many more people whose dishonesty goes no further than petty larceny than there are people who are prepared to commit felonies. Since the latter group represents a very small fraction of your employees, it makes little sense, and is quite counterproductive, for management to harbor a distrustful attitude. On the other hand, as we shall discuss throughout this book, a precautionary posture can be quite effective in turning back dishonest inclinations.

The table shown in Figure 2-1 is the result of a polygraph (lie detector) based study on attitudes about honesty and dishonesty. This "dishonesty test" clearly shows the attitudes of convicted felons as compared with those of a typical group of employment applicants. The messages that you should get from this table are that (1) there are a significant number of job applicants whose attitudes about dishonesty are such that they would not be suitable for employment in sensitive positions or positions of trust, and (2) there is no basis for racial prejudice with regard to dishonesty traits.

Category	Black			White		
	Sample Size	Mean Score	Standard Deviation	Sample Size	Mean Score	Standard Deviation
Felons	100	25.3	11.5	87	25.9	11.3
Employment applicants						
Total	233	47.1	11.9	797	47.7	12.1
Recommended	118	54.2	8.3	451	54.3	8.2
Not recommended	115	39.0	10.5	346	39.1	10.9

84% of the felonies were burgulary or theft. "Recommended" means passed polygraph interview without revealing any significant theft history. "Not recommended" means that significant theft history was validated. The mean score of 25 earned by the felons is at the first percentile for employment applicants (only 1 in 100 employment applicants earns a score this low or lower).

Figure 2-1

Comparison of Convicted Male Felons with Male Employment Applicants by Ethnic Group and by "Recommended/Not Recommended" for Employment. (After Philip Ash, "Convicted Felons' Attitudes Toward Theft," *Criminal Justice and Behavior*, Sage Publications, Inc., March 1974.)

Who embezzles? As we have indicated, dishonest tendencies cut across all socioeconomic groups. In an informal study of more than 50 incidents of fraud, we developed the material shown in Figure 2-2. These are reported embezzlement cases involving losses in excess of $100,000. The evidence in these incidents seemed fairly convincing, although there may not have been arrests, prosecutions, or convictions of the perpetrators. The right-hand column (L/I) is the loss-per-incident ratio. It shows, on a relative basis, how "profitable" the crimes were for each class of perpetrator.

Position of Perpetrators	% of Incidents	% of Losses	L/I
Top executives	9%	20%	2.22
EDP and support staff	19	22	1.16
Accounting staff	13	13	1.00
Treasurer	7	6	.86
Collusion	39	32	.82
Warehouse staff	13	7	.54
	100%	100%	

Figure 2-2

Perpetrators Who Profit Most

Occupation	% of Cases
Men:	
Branch manager*	18.3%
Salesman	17.4
Driver or delivery man	6.3
Union official (local)	5.6
Clerk	5.1
Bookkeeper	5.0
Executive	4.1
Women:	
Store clerk	21.8
Cashier	19.9
Bookkeeper	16.0
Branch manager*	7.7
Office clerk	6.4
Union or fraternity treasurer	5.1
Apartment manager	4.5

*Of retail stores, loan companies, insurance companies, and banks.

Figure 2-3

Occupations of Men and Women Embezzlers

From time to time United States Fidelity and Guarantee Company (Baltimore) compiles statistics on embezzlements, mostly in the United States and Canada. Although somewhat dated, the latest compilation, covers embezzlements of all magnitudes. The positions of 845 men and 156 women were analyzed. Figure 2-3 shows the occupations for the seven highest percentages. Over 80% of the embezzlers in the U.S. Fidelity and Guarantee study were employed 5 years or less. As for age distribution, one-third of the men were 29 or younger, and another one-third were in the 30–39 range. Just over half of the women were in the 29-and-under group, with one-fourth in the 30–39 range.

It is doubtful that the occupation or position ranks in Figures 2-2 and 2-3 will change much in the era of computer fraud. The frauds that were performed manually are likely to be carried out in an EDP environment. We already know that the loss-per-incident ratio is changing; it is progressing geometrically. For example, a typical embezzlement by a bank teller had been in the $10,000–$20,000 range. Now, with on-line computer terminals, the losses may run in the $500,000–$1,000,000 range and even higher. We also know that many EDP technical specialists are situated in positions where their peculations could produce an enormous loss-per-incident ratio.

White-collar crooks Although there have been indications that organized-crime interests have engaged in computer frauds, the vast majority have been perpetrated by white-collar employees. Perhaps you already know that computer fraud is one class of dishonest, illegal activity in a much broader field that has come to be known as white-collar crime. One good working definition of white-collar crime that appears in modern law-enforcement literature is attributable to Herbert Edelhertz of the Battelle Law and Justice Study Center:

> . . . an illegal act or series of acts committed by non-physical means and by concealment or guile, to obtain money or property, to avoid the payment or loss of money or property, or to obtain business or personal advantage.[1]

Later in this chapter, in the section "Profile of a Perpetrator," we will tie in white-collar criminal values with the other aspects of the computer fraud equation.

OPPORTUNITIES There is a notion, dating back at least 300 years, that *opportunity makes a thief*. Although this may not be entirely true, it most certainly identifies the most important variable in considering a course of action to prevent, detect, and deter computer fraud.

Opportunities to commit computer fraud exist, to some degree, in just about every company that uses EDP in its operations. Much of the remainder of this book is directed to the opportunity aspect of the fraud equation, for the simple reason that it is the ingredient over which management can exercise the greatest control.

Our definition of opportunities is somewhat expansive, in that we are looking at steps that you can take to help prevent, deter, and detect computer fraud.

The opportunities, which are discussed in overview form in this section, arise out of shortcomings in:

- Management policies.
- Administrative policies.
- Personnel policies.
- Internal controls.
- Computer security.
- EDP auditing.
- Strategy for integrating countermeasures.

[1] Herbert Edelhertz et al., *The Investigation of White-Collar Crime: A Manual for Law Enforcement Agencies*, prepared for the U.S. Department of Justice, Law Enforcement Assistance Administration (Washington, D.C.: Government Printing Office, 1977), p. 4.

One of the factors that a potential perpetrator of computer fraud may consider in assessing his opportunities to successfully commit computer fraud is the ethics or standards of conduct to which a company subscribes. Management's policies and conduct establish the moral climate in which employees work.

A company that expects every employee to act, in every instance, according to the highest standards, makes these standards known, and refuses to tolerate a compromise in standards is using management policy to optimum advantage in deterring fraud.

Today, when companies are being called upon to speak out about where they stand with respect to ethical behavior, we found it interesting that some large companies consider their corporate codes of conduct to be "for internal use only." Others were willing to tell us, in writing and in very clear terms, just where they stand on such matters as protection of assets, moonlighting, questionable payments, financial interests, insider information, gifts and entertainment, accurate reporting (product test reports, expense reports, financial reports, etc.), personal information about employees, competitive practices, purchasing practices, and operating within the letter and the spirit of antitrust laws.

Another aspect of management policy pertains to the setting and attainment of performance objectives. If either the policy or its implementation is faulty, employees might conclude that their tactics will not be questioned as long as sales, profits, or other objectives are met. Alternatively, they might feel that they are being exploited by being expected to accomplish unrealistic objectives operating within ethical bounds, while others in the company engage in unethical behavior. Under these conditions, individuals may feel justified to commit fraud.

The administrative policies that relate to computer fraud are those which cover the conduct of operations within the EDP department as well as within the user departments. Although administrative policies are usually established within the framework of management policies, they deal more specifically with the ground rules for day-to-day business operations. Opportunities to commit fraud may be evident to a potential perpetrator in situations where administrative policies are inappropriate, ill-conceived, or not adhered to. For example, administrative policies come into play in connection with the following:

- Vendor and customer complaints, where reported errors or discrepancies could be symptoms of ongoing frauds.
- Handling of exception items (such as manually prepared checks) and various kinds of adjustments (such as changing

a computerized perpetual inventory quantity to agree with a physical count), which could present an opportunity for fraud.

- Use of variance allowances (such as bad-debt loss, scrap, trade in, etc.), which cover up routine fraudulent activity.
- Excessive dependence on one EDP employee for a particular computer application (such as the programmer of the accounts payable system) could present opportunities for fraud.

The use of administrative policies to help prevent, deter, and detect fraud is sometimes a matter of simply extending or using procedures already in existence. As an example, a periodic review of complaints from vendors who reported late or missing payments could be made part of routine operations.

Personnel policies

Like administrative policies, personnel policies are something your company probably already has. Frequently, existing procedures can be used or enhanced to become an integral part of the company's efforts to reduce opportunities for computer fraud.

Personnel policies may have little impact on a would-be perpetrator's values about dishonesty and on many of his possible motives; however, they can be quite effective in holding the opportunity factor in the fraud equation to a minimum.

To clarify what may be a subtle point, we are saying that a company provides opportunity for fraud as a result of its failure to exercise reasonable care with respect to personnel matters:

- Weak preemployment screening and background checking procedures that enable an applicant, whose background shows him to be a significant security risk, to be employed in a sensitive position.
- Inadequate guidance, training, and orientation of supervisory personnel such that they fail to recognize and act on common problems (that could be signs of or could develop into fraud motives) exhibited by subordinates.
- Careless and/or insensitive handling of involuntary terminations that leave the terminee (a would-be perpetrator) in a position to seek redress through fraud.

Internal controls

One of the first events in a financial audit, which is performed to enable a certified public accountant to render an opinion on a company's financial statements, is the auditor's evaluation of the adequacy of the company's system of internal controls. This is done to help determine the degree of reliance that may be placed on the company's records and books of account, which are often computerized. The degree of reliance determination weighs heavily in the auditor's decisions about the nature and extent of auditing procedures and tests to be employed in the audit.

Auditors are especially attuned to control weaknesses that could lead to material inaccuracies in financial statements as a result of significant errors or fraud. Since situations that are prone to undetected errors may frequently provide opportunities for fraud, the internal controls of interest to the auditor are, for all practical purposes, identical to those we would recommend be employed to reduce the opportunity for fraud.

Most evaluations of internal controls are performed with the aid of checklists or questionnaires that contain hundreds of individual control items for such areas as:

- General (organization, accounting, internal auditing).
- EDP (data preparation/entry, operations, programming).
- Cash (receipts, disbursements, petty cash, bank reconciliations).
- Shipping, billing, and accounts receivable.
- Notes receivable and investments.
- Inventories (perpetual, retail, year-end).
- Property, plant, and equipment.
- Purchasing, receiving, and accounts payable.
- Payroll.

For specialized industries, such as banking, insurance, and securities brokerage, internal control reviews would be guided in part by specialized questionnaires (e.g., foreign exchange in banking).

In our previously mentioned informal study of frauds involving sizable losses, we found the relationship between incidents of fraud and losses to be as shown in Figure 2-4. As is quite clear here, the greatest number of incidents and largest fraud losses occur in those functional areas that pay out money. Needless to say, heavy emphasis should be placed on internal controls related to such areas.

Area	% of Incidents	% of Losses
Disbursements	44%	63%
Receipts	36	15
Inventory	8	9
Payroll	7	5
Other	5	8
	100%	100%

Figure 2-4

Fraud Areas and Losses

In this connection it is interesting to note that fraud investigators sometimes use the expression "follow the cash," meaning "trace the chain of events by seeing where the money went." A parallel notion in internal control is that of an audit trail, which enables any transaction to be followed through all processing steps, EDP and otherwise.

Computer security

The general topic of computer security is directed to questions about fire protection, backup, reliability, and other matters that may or may not have a direct bearing on limiting opportunities for fraud.

Our concern with computer security centers around those matters that have a direct bearing on fraud opportunities, although that may not be the exclusive reason for having that particular safeguard. For example, physical access controls are established to help prevent curious individuals, saboteurs, and potential perpetrators of fraud from gaining entry to sensitive areas.

The kinds of security measures that we feel have this direct bearing fall into the following categories:

- Physical access controls for data, programs, documentation, computer operations center, and terminals.
- User identification, authentication, and authorization methods to help ensure that people using the system are the ones permitted to do so, and that the functions they perform fall within previously established limits.
- Log maintenance and review functions for program changes, access authorization changes, security violation attempts, access to sensitive data elements, and other events whose history might provide early warning of possible frauds and enable reconstruction of events.
- Privacy transformations (encryption, scrambling, etc.) for sensitive data stored on computerized files and transmitted by way of telephone and/or other means of communications, to help protect data from being used for fraudulent purposes even though a would-be perpetrator is able to gain access to it (e.g., by using a telephone wiretap).
- Application controls designed into the system (for example, accounts payable) to help detect fraudulent transactions that might otherwise be processed normally, without arousing suspicion; also, features of applications whose sole purpose is to detect fraud (e.g., in bank demand deposit accounting, a kite suspect report or dormant account activity report).

There is generally no commonly respected or sharp dividing line between computer security and internal controls, especially on matters involving applications controls. The important thing is that there be no gap in the fraud controls at the point where one ends and the other begins, regardless of how that distinction is made.

EDP auditing

The mission of internal auditing, as we see it, should be broadly stated: to evaluate and identify opportunities to strengthen the company's planning, administration, and control functions. Within this mission, the internal auditor is concerned with the controls that safeguard against fraud.

An EDP auditor's mission is, of course, identical. The only difference is that of emphasis on EDP-related matters: EDP operations, applications, systems development, security, and internal controls of all types.

The EDP auditing function should neither adopt the posture of policing day-to-day operations, nor should it design controls and safeguards which it must inevitably evaluate. The keys to effective EDP auditing are: independence, competence, and top management commitment. A company provides opportunities for fraud by either not having an EDP audit function when its level of EDP activity is significant, or by compromising on independence, competence, or commitment.

Strategy for integrating countermeasures

You are right if you have already concluded that management policies, administrative policies, personnel policies, internal controls, computer security, and EDP auditing—as well as some areas we have not yet discussed (e.g., corporate security and law enforcement)—must be developed into a coherent strategy for preventing, deterring, and detecting computer fraud.

We have seen numerous instances where, as a result of poor communications and a lack of coordination, an almost absurd group of conditions coexist. One example is a company with an existing administrative policy with respect to handling proprietary information of certain types, where the policy was not reflected in either the internal control or the computer security standards and procedures, and whose EDP auditors were even unaware of the policy's existence. Often, but certainly not always, larger companies experience more situations of this type than do smaller ones.

At any rate, this may help explain why instances of computer fraud are not uncommon among companies that lack a coherent strategy, even though they may employ elaborate countermeasures. What happens is that the company overlooks something or relies too heavily upon a single countermeasure, or possibly has an inadequate internal auditing program.

Later in a discussion of considerations in a multidisciplinary prevention program, we shall discuss ways to bring multiple facets of the fraud prevention program into focus. Elsewhere, we shall touch on the need to coordinate particular countermeasures with other areas to help ensure that a given type of safeguard does the intended job in a consistent manner that conforms with what your company expects of it.

MOTIVES Motive, the third ingredient in the fraud equation, is the justification that exists in the mind of the perpetrator of a fraud. The motives for committing computer fraud do not differ perceptibly from those resulting in noncomputer fraud, regardless of whether the fraud is perpetrated by an employee, an outsider, or organized-crime interests. Motives may develop suddenly or may take a period of years to grow. It may be a critical combination of motives that actually triggers the fraudulent act.

We know that motives which are sufficient for a dishonest employee to defraud his employer (or other businesses and organizations) are very often insufficient justification for him to commit a fraud that would cause significant harm to his fellow employees and other human beings.

Finally, it seems that frauds by employees generally start on a small scale and grow to sizable proportions (this is especially evident in computer frauds) over a period of months or even years. It also appears that the motives have a way of developing strength in proportion to the size of the rip-off.

The categories of motives that show up most frequently in connection with computer fraud are:

- Avarice (pure greed).
- Desire for the "good life" and material possessions.
- Financial problems (arising from pressures to spend beyond one's means, gambling debts, family illness, children's college education, and many others).
- Ego gratification (the challenge of it).
- Charitable (take from the rich and give to the needy—the Robin Hood syndrome).
- Revenge or "getting even" (due to a grievance against the employer, being taken advantage of in financial dealings, losses suffered on investments in the company's and other securities, feeling cheated in terms of compensation, and other situations in which a lack of fair play is perceived).

In the study by U.S. Fidelity and Guaranty Company mentioned previously, there was an analysis of the "causative factors" behind the employee frauds committed by 845 men and 156 women. These factors, together with frequency percentages, are presented in Figure 2-5. Although there are a few motives that companies can try to prevent

36

MEN	
Living beyond one's means	24.8
Criminal character	13.5
Gambling	13.0%
Alcoholism related	10.1
Influenced by women who benefited	6.6
Irresponsible	4.0
Extravagance of spouse or children	3.9
Bad business management	2.9
Family illness	2.8
Accumulation of debts	2.8
Bad associates (being a dupe)	2.8
Grudge against employer	2.7
Other causes	10.1
	100.0%

WOMEN	
Living beyond one's means	19.8%
Family expenses	11.5
Extravagance of spouse or children	10.3
Criminal character	10.3
Influenced by men who benefited	9.0
Desire for new start elsewhere	5.1
Family illness	5.1
Alcoholism related	4.5
Own illness	3.8
Bad associates (being a dupe)	3.2
Mental problems	2.7
Grudge against employer	1.9
Other causes	12.8
	100.0%

Figure 2-5

Causative Factors for Employee Fraud

(some of those that are revengeful in nature), most are highly personal in nature.

The key to dealing with motives, to the extent that something can be done, is to make sure that supervisory personnel are alert to indications that employees may be having problems similar to those shown in Figure 2-5. The supervisor can then encourage the employee to seek appropriate counseling by competent specialists who may be retained by the company or are members of the personnel department. This aspect of the supervisor's job should be emphasized in training programs as well as in an expanded job description.

Here again your company may already have programs to assist

employees with family financial planning, and with drinking, gambling, and emotional problems.

PROFILE OF A PERPETRATOR

The majority of computer frauds have been committed by people who have not previously been involved in criminal activity. They are white-collar employees whose occupations put them in a position of trust, whether at a managerial level with direct control of company assets or at a technical level (computer or user), that involves the processing of data pertaining to company assets. David Plato, Supervising Examiner for Fidelity and Surety Claims, Fireman's Fund Insurance Company, summarizes his views on the perpetrator in the following way:

> What is an embezzler? Somebody who steals from a position of trust. He doesn't come in with a gun. He doesn't take the risks. He knows his employer. He knows that his employer trusts him. And he steals. He knows he's not taking a great risk. Some of the largest embezzlements do not end up with the perpetrator in jail.[2]

Some readers may be interested to know how the modern embezzler compares with his counterpart of the pre-World War II era, particularly since the trends seem to be validated by recent computer fraud incidents. The typical embezzler of Depression times, according to information developed by U.S. Fidelity and Guaranty Company, fit the following portrait. The typical embezzler of that era was a white-collar male, 36 years of age, with a wife and two children. He had a good education by the standards of those times, was not psychopathic or of criminal character, and did not live in a high-crime area. On the contrary, he lived comfortably, had a medium-price automobile, took occasional weekend trips, and had a 2-week vacation in the summer. He enjoyed a good time, had an occasional cocktail, was regarded as being sociable, and participated in community and civic functions. The typical embezzler's friends and wife concluded that he was earning over twice the actual amount of his salary, which was in the middle range. He lived in large and small towns in every state. His length of service was just over 5 years, and his employer regarded him as competent, hardworking, and with an above-average business reputation and future.

The modern embezzler is harder to depict. He is younger, earns much more money, is less often married, and has fewer dependents. His character and past record of employment is not quite as favorable. Generally, he has worked a shorter time for his employer. He is a product of the times, lives a faster-paced existence, and is harder

---

[2] *Crimes Against Business: A Management Perspective* (Washington, D.C.: U.S. Department of Commerce, May 1976), Seminar Transcript, p. 147.

to classify as a "regular sort of fellow." He is still a white-collar worker, falls prey to the same temptations, and fails his employer's trust under the same general circumstances: extended credit purchases and debt, loss of savings, reduction in income, gambling, living beyond his means, women, and so on. Often, his employer's supervision is lax. He is much less likely to confess voluntarily and much less likely to commit suicide than his counterpart of the Depression era.

Donn B. Parker of Stanford Research Institute, a leading historian on computer abuse, has developed findings from his work that tie in quite well with the characteristics of the modern-day embezzler, as described above. The essential points of Parker's findings,[3] based on 17 cases of computer fraud that he has examined in detail, are:

- Perpetrators are young (average age is 29, median age is 25, range is 18–46).
- Management and professional skills are predominant (70% were managers or highly experienced technical professionals).
- Violation of occupational trust was evident in 65% of the cases.
- Personal characteristics:
  - Viewed as highly desirable employees: reliable, trustworthy, bright, motivated.
  - Not special as a class, and not professional criminals who take pride in their crime (only one perpetrator, a 19-year-old programmer, had a prior conviction—a possession-of-marijuana misdemeanor).
  - Greatest fear was detection and having their illegal acts made known to family, friends, and fellow employees.

In considering the profile of a perpetrator, we can return to the fraud equation and reexamine the factors.

Dishonesty   Nothing has come to our attention that would indicate that people's basic values have changed with regard to dishonesty. We believe that the 15% group (or whatever that number really is) remains fairly constant.

Opportunities. We know that nonvisible computerized data records, and the complexity of the software that processes data, provides greater concealment opportunities than ever before. We also know that technical and supervisory personnel are in a position to exploit these concealment features to commit fraud, in the absence of appro-

[3] Donn B. Parker, *Computer Abuse Perpetrators and Vulnerabilities of Computer Systems*, a research report prepared for and supported in part by the National Science Foundation (Menlo Park, Calif.: Stanford Research Institute, 1975).

priate countermeasures to prevent, deter, and detect such exploitation. And, finally, because computers tend to concentrate the risk, the possibility for large-scale frauds to be perpetrated is much greater than ever before (magnitudes of 25 to 50 times those previously experienced).

Motives. It is doubtful that basic motives for computer fraud differ from those for noncomputer fraud. However, we believe that there are modern-day phenomena that are worth noting because they have an impact on the strength of a number of motives.

People are bombarded through the communications media, especially television, with advertising and entertainment that creates the impression that everyone is, or at least should be, enjoying all kinds of luxuries (travel to exotic places, expensive automobiles, vacation homes, etc.)

High rates of inflation silently rob employees, especially white-collar workers, of purchasing power. Earned income often does not keep pace with rapidly increasing costs of necessities—such as health care, housing, food, clothing, and transportation—not to mention discretionary expenditures that add enjoyment to living, such as sending the kids to camp and to college, vacation travel, recreation, a better automobile, and/or a boat.

Reasons for Stealing Choice	Number of Persons	Percentage of Total
Can afford it best, or has tremendous capital	69	67.7
Allows for it: raises prices, is insured	13	12.8
They cheat you; they're ruthless	8	7.8
Less chance of being caught	4	3.9
Provides the greatest opportunity	3	2.9
No reasons offered	5	4.9
TOTAL	102	100.0

This table is based on a forced choice stealing preference study involving 212 people. The resulting preferences as to the victim were distributed as follows: 102, chose to steal from large business (for the reasons shown above); 53, government; 10, small business; 9, large business or government; 5, any size business or government; 30, refused to steal; 3, would not answer question.

Figure 2-6

Primary Reasons for Preferring to Steal from Large Businesses. [After Erwin O. Smigel, "Public Attitudes Toward Stealing as Related to the Size of the Victim Organization," *Crimes Against Bureaucracy* (E. O. Smigel and H. L. Ross, eds.), Van Nostrand Reinhold Company, 1970, p. 23.]

The problem of "salary compression" is another factor that increases resentment of the type that intensifies fraud motives. Put simply, it means that the salaries of younger, new hirees, as compared with salaries of older, more experienced employees show a gap that has become increasingly smaller. At the same time, the older, more experienced employee may also observe that the top executives of his company are getting king-size increases and big bonuses.

Anti-establishment feelings need not take the form of a riot by college students. People from all walks of life see and hear about corruption in government, commercial bribery, illegal or questionable payments by companies (perhaps their employers), welfare cheats, and so on, and may develop feelings of resentment toward "the system." These may be combined with feelings that they or others are treated unfairly or with a lack of sensitivity by an employer.

Perhaps a combination of the factors just discussed could explain why, as shown in Figure 2-6, there is a definite preference for stealing from large companies—just the ones, incidentally, that are likely to be most dependent on computer-based systems.

Obviously, neither these factors nor any others justify criminal acts. They do, however, explain how motives may develop. This understanding is useful to a company in its efforts to safeguard its assets.

II

PREVENTION, DETECTION, AND DETERRENTS

3

Ethical
Business Conduct

A company should expect its directors, officers, and employees to observe the highest standards of integrity and fair play, and remain free of interests and relationships that could become detrimental to the company's interests. These expectations should be set forth, in writing, as standards, guidelines, or policies for business conduct. By having such standards and setting a personal example, management can reduce opportunities for employees to justify dishonesty to themselves. The implications of these matters are discussed in this chapter in the following major sections:

- Moral leadership.
- Communications channels.
- Enforcement of policies.

MORAL LEADERSHIP Management sets the moral climate of a company. The act of so doing may be active or passive, but every action management takes has an impact. Employees take their clues as to how to get ahead from the actions of top management. Every action can have an effect that works its way down through the company. Double standards, permissiveness, and laxity with regard to ethical behavior encourage dishonesty. Positive examples and enforcement of policies build respect and integrity.

> Corporations can and do create a moral tone that powerfully influences the thinking, conduct, values and even the personalities of the people who work for them. This tone is set by the men who run the company, and their corruption can quickly corrupt all else.[1]

Without presuming to chart out the proper scope for business ethics, we would like to point out a few areas for consideration. In particular, we would like to draw your attention to formal standards and representative actions.

Formal standards   One thing management should do to establish a favorable moral climate is to set formal standards for conduct. Means of communicating those standards will be discussed later. In terms of scope, the standards should cover prevailing and accepted business ethics but should avoid taking a stance on matters unrelated to the business.

Issues to address in formal standards are those accepted by the prevailing culture. While the issues change over time, examples of what is meant include:

- Gratuities from business contacts.
- Expense accounts.
- Practices affecting consumers.

Gratuities. Smooth business relations call for some level of personal involvement between vendor and customer representatives. While vendor and customer alike stand to gain from cooperation, the giving and receiving of gifts to further that cooperation constitutes a form of bribery. Your company should take a stance. An example of how one company chose to address the issue appeared in the Bristol-Myers Company's *Statement of Business Conduct* (September 1976):

> No employee may accept from any such organization [that might possibly conflict with the best interests of the company] any gratuitous payment, service, gift, or entertainment, except gifts and entertainment of a nominal value only, e.g., business lunch.

Expense accounts. Theoretically, expense accounts exist to cover the expenses incurred during the conduct of business. Interpretation of what constitutes an appropriate business expense can be a matter of policy or of interpretation. The area subject to interpretation

---

[1] Donald Moffit (ed.), *Swindled!* (Princeton, N.J.: Dow Jones & Company, 1976), p. 46.

should be narrow. The bounds of that area can be narrowed by various means: management policy statement, accounting policy, and supervisory scrutiny.

Sometimes, expense account abuses can become pervasive, as indicated in the following excerpt from a story in the September 10, 1977, issue of *The New York Times:*

> Auditors have uncovered new cases of apparent expense-account padding by officials of the Port Authority of New York and New Jersey. . . . An examination of records had disclosed that at least three or four top executives, in addition to the three already suspended for alleged padding, had billed the agency for apparently fictitious expenses. . . . Documented in the last three months have been patterns of private use of Port Authority helicopters, recreational overseas travel by authority officials and their wives, and other spending that was denounced as "lavish" and "extravagant."[2]

As a result of this publicity, employees of the Port Authority have now been exposed to the negative aspect of this situation. One can only hope that they will also be exposed to the harsh consequences that should befall any of those who are found guilty.

In a booklet for its employees entitled, *Business Conduct Guidelines,* IBM Corporation uses a discussion-type presentation to explain its position, which, in the example below, deals with accurate reporting:

> Almost every employee reports data of some kind. The engineer filling out a product test report; the salesman reporting on the status of an order; the scientist filling out an expense account; the customer engineer completing a call record—all are reporting information. All should do it accurately and honestly.
>
> Some forms of inaccurate reporting are illegal. Listing a fictitious expense on an expense account or petty cash card, for example, is illegal. You should list on your expense account everything you paid for on a trip that IBM is required to pay for, neither more, nor less. All reporting of information—whether sales results, hours worked or equal opportunity efforts—should be accurate and timely and should be a fair representation of all the facts. It should not be organized in any way that is intended to mislead or misinform the reader.

Practices affecting consumers. There is no faster way of alienating rank-and-file employees and customers than engaging in unethical practices that affect consumers. Some of the issues affecting consumers are shoddy products, false advertising, and price fixing.

Such practices have a way of becoming known. When they do, a company's moral reputation may be adversely affected for years to

[2] Ralph Blumenthal, "More Expense-Account Padding Reportedly Found at Port Agency," *The New York Times,* September 10, 1977, p. 29.

come. With that loss of reputation comes the conclusion on the part of employees that management is dishonest. That last conclusion leads to such ideas as: "only dishonest people get ahead in this company" and "it isn't really wrong to defraud this company because it makes money by dishonest means." Those kinds of thoughts enable individuals to justify dishonesty (to themselves).

Avoiding such practices is really a two-step problem. Top management must itself refuse to engage in such practices. Then, management must endeavor to see that employees and lower-level managers do not use such means to further their own careers. Means of preventing such practices include:

- Having a clear policy against them.
- Remaining alert to the symptoms that such practices may be in use.
- Investigation of suspected breaches of policy and dealing severely with individuals who are caught.

Representative actions

Nothing undermines formal policy more rapidly than hypocrisy. Avoiding hypocrisy means, among other things, that management lives up to the standards it sets and that it does not take a hard line against one group of unethical actions only to indulge in activities that are equally reprehensible. If top management gives the appearance of hypocrisy, employees will be quick to discount the formal policies.

Conduct of top management. The first consideration is the personal conduct of top management. While we are not suggesting that you go to your company's president and chairman of the board and tell them to clean up their act, we do recommend that you convey the idea that their actions set the example for the rest of the employees. Such individuals are aware of their leadership roles and will respond to tactful and well-timed reminders.

Other management conduct. A somewhat more difficult situation involves the actions of middle and lower-echelon management. By definition, top management has broad responsibility and cannot oversee each business activity that carefully, except on the basis of bottom-line results. The problem that arises is that individuals on the way up the corporate ladder may indulge in unethical practices and top management may be too far removed from the day-to-day details to perceive such practices.

Possible solutions. Most companies have a structure that resembles a pyramid. In other words, individuals at the top have contact with fewer employees than their subordinates do. Therefore, unethical practices by middle and lower echelons of management present a double bind. On the one hand, top management may be unaware of the unethical behavior of subordinates and, on the other, those subordinates are serving as bad examples to more individuals than top management is.

As we mentioned before, this is a difficult problem. Top management is well advised to maintain an awareness of the climate prevailing throughout the company. Some means of maintaining that awareness include:

- The grapevine.
- An open-door policy that encourages feedback from the rank and file.
- Observation of attitudes displayed in relatively public situations such as elevators and informal meetings.
- Close relations with the personnel department.
- Questioning the means used to achieve results.
- Staying alert to office politics and situations where, for example, managers steal ideas from each other or scheme to make the management of competitive departments look bad.

**COMMUNI-
CATIONS
CHANNELS**

A variety of channels for communicating management policy exist or can be created easily enough. Some of the channels to consider are:

- Policy manuals.
- Policy statements.
- The role of public relations.

Policy manuals

Unless your company is so small that top management can know and communicate directly with its employees, a policy manual is mandatory. The purpose of the manual is to get the policies directly and unequivocally in front of all managers and employees.

The trend nowadays is to have a corporate policy manual that brings together, in a single source, basic ethical principles for business dealings. Subjects covered may include: doing business with suppliers and reciprocity, product quality, competitive conduct, intercompany pricing, ownership and investment, hiring practices, political contributions and questionable payments, public responsibility, and matters that pertain directly to company internal affairs.

Objectives of policy manuals. The objective of a policy manual should be to communicate policies to all affected individuals in a formal manner.   By putting the policies in a permanent and written form, you are communicating the importance that top management attaches to its policy.   Another advantage of a written manual is that it serves as a reference.   If, upon first reading, a particular policy does not apply to an individual, chances are that the individual will not understand or remember it.   If the individual's responsibilities change or if the individual is contemplating an action on which the company might have a policy statement, existence of and access to a policy manual will serve to encourage the individual to refer to it.

Distribution and updating of policy manuals.   Policy manuals should be distributed to all managers.   To facilitate updating, a loose-leaf binder is desirable.   Care should be taken in the distribution of updates to see that all individuals receive copies and understand what to do with the updates.

In addition to the mechanics of updating manuals, ongoing attention should be given to keeping the manuals up to date through revisions.   A manual without updates that is several years old lacks credibility.   Employees may justifiably conclude that the manual was written and forgotten, inferring that top management does not take its contents seriously.

Every so often, perhaps every 3 years, it may be a good idea to issue new policy manuals and direct that the previous ones be discarded.   The new manual can serve to better consolidate and organize the updates that have taken effect since the previous reissue, and it provides an opportunity for management to reflect on the company's overall posture with respect to statements of policy.

When issuing new manuals, many companies include a reply form that is to be signed by the holder and returned to the corporate office.   Such a form will typically show the unique registration or control number that appears on the manual's title page and a statement that the holder acknowledges responsibility for familiarizing himself with the manual's contents.

Policy statements   In addition to policy manual updates, other periodic and ad hoc policy statements are desirable to clarify policy and to remind employees that top management is serious about its policies.   A few examples will clarify the role of policy statements.

Summaries.   More and more companies are developing summarized forms of policy manual contents that pertain to legal and ethical business practices.   Such summaries are distributed to all managerial and supervisory personnel, and in many cases to all employees.

Caterpillar Tractor Co. issued a 10-page *Code of Worldwide Business Conduct* covering just over a dozen subjects. IBM Corporation's *Business Conduct Guidelines* runs 32 pages and explains in plain language the company's position on broad guidelines (nine topics), marketplace (six topics), competitors, suppliers (four topics), and antitrust laws (five topics). Zenith Radio Corporation has a 12-page summary which it calls *Employee Code of Conduct*. Summaries of this general type are typically well written, brief, and to the point. They also avoid the rigid, dry legalese that one often associates with policy manuals.

Periodic reminders. Periodic reminders of policy should be distributed regarding policies that have particular applicability at a given time of year. One example is a company's policy regarding the acceptance of gratuities from vendors. Some companies have a practice of sending these reminders to both employees and vendors; in the latter case, the notice also requests that gifts not be offered. Because of the common practice of gift giving at Christmas time, an annual reminder in late November or early December is desirable.

Another policy that requires periodic reminders is one dealing with political activities and contributions. The time to remind employees of the policy is when election campaigns are beginning.

Ad hoc statements. Ad hoc reminders of policy are desirable whenever events bring a particular policy into the forefront. An example of such an event would be a scandal in your industry or in your company. If competitors are publically charged with price fixing, that is the time for top management to remind employees of its stance on the issue, or to take a stance if no relevant policy has been issued previously.

If your own company is involved in the scandal, management should still issue an ad hoc statement. If a policy existed prior to the scandal, management should remind employees of that policy and add that the offenders have been dealt with severely. If no policy existed prior to the scandal, management should issue a policy and should still deal severely with the individuals involved.

Another time when ad hoc statements are desirable is when lack of compliance becomes common. Unless there is some other reason for lack of compliance, it may have arisen simply because too little attention was given to the policy.

Speaking in front of employees. If your company has periodic seminars or assemblies of employees or managers, those occasions should be used by top management as opportunities to reaffirm policy. Policies that should be considered for discussion on those occasions include:

- Policies that are not being complied with.
- New policies that may require further explanation or discussion.
- Policies that are particularly timely.

Press releases. Certain circumstances may warrant public releases regarding company policy, such as the instance discussed previously in which the company is involved in a price-fixing scandal. If the company previously had a policy against that practice and if the individual responsible for the incident acted without the knowledge of management, a public statement or press release affirming management's policy is desirable.

Role of public relations

Many larger companies have public relations or corporate communications departments that handle external and sometimes internal communications. If your company has such a department, it should be acquainted with issues relating to computer and other forms of fraud so they will be taken into account in the timing and wording of relevant communications.

If your public relations department also handles internal communications, they are a possible candidate for writing and updating policy statements. Other possible candidates for that job are the personnel, financial, and administrative departments. Even if the public relations department is not responsible for policy statements, it should be informed as to the reasoning behind the policies so that this can be taken into account in issuing other communications.

ENFORCEMENT OF POLICIES

Compliance with prescribed management policy is enhanced when management makes serious efforts regarding enforcement. Appropriate efforts include:

- Demonstrating concern for compliance.
- Review for compliance.
- Disciplinary action for lack of compliance.

Demonstrating concern

Management demonstrates concern for compliance with policy when it conveys that concern directly and when it complies with its own policy. If management has one set of rules for employees and another set for itself, compliance is extremely unlikely. Similarly, if management closes its eyes to possible violations rather than investigating them, the expectation of compliance elsewhere is unrealistic.

Norman Jaspan, an investigator and consultant on asset-protection matters, has pointed out that employee dishonesty is a by-product of poor management. Asked about the underlying conditions, Jaspan stated:

> Failure to establish enforceable controls and procedures [and]
>
> Permissiveness and neglect by top management.[3]

Clearly, then, enforcement is a two-pronged proposition. It begins with having policies that can be enforced through procedural controls and is accompanied by vigorous follow-through on compliance. Both issues take on added significance in preparing successful claims to collect losses under a fidelity bond and in avoiding and defending lawsuits against company officers and directors where plaintiffs seek redress on the basis that the company failed to properly pursue evidence of dishonesty or other unethical acts.

**Review for
compliance**

Procedural controls should provide policy compliance feedback to management on routine business operations. For example, in the purchasing function, companies have adopted a checkoff sheet to accompany purchase requisitions which calls for entering certain information about how the purchasing decision was made. Not surprisingly, the information sought on the sheet bears a striking resemblance to matters covered in the company's purchasing policy.

Beyond routine compliance feedback, special reviews are desirable as part of the enforcement process. Such special reviews serve as an independent means for management to demonstrate its concern. They also provide information regarding noncompliance so that action can be taken if necessary. Compliance can be reviewed by spot checking and audits. For a review of compliance to be possible, clearly there must be some means of determining whether or not compliance exists.

Spot checking should be the responsibility of all levels of management for areas under their direct control. Top management cannot do all the checking, but it can review the results of spot checking by way of submitted reports. By holding all managers responsible for compliance and accountable for failures in areas under their direct control, top management can motivate lower levels of management to do an adequate job of spot checking.

Audits represent an independent means of checking for compliance. An internal or external auditor may take out your policy manual and systematically check for compliance. They may also evaluate policies, controls, and the adequacy of enforcement activities. By en-

---

[3] "Why Employees Steal," *U.S. News & World Report*, May 3, 1971, p. 81.

couraging all forms of comment on the part of your auditors and by reviewing their comments, you can receive feedback on more factors than just compliance with policy.

Disciplinary action

Appropriate disciplinary action in instances of noncompliance is essential to the viability of policy. By appropriate action we mean that you should deal with noncompliance severely, but the punishment should be commensurate with the offense. Disciplinary action should also be the same, regardless of who is responsible for the offense.

To put more bite into policies, many companies are returning to the older practice of discussing disciplinary action within the policy manual and as part of the more informal policy statements. At the same time, these policies also cover what to do if there is a question with regard to interpreting or deviating from a stated policy. The following items are indicative of how disciplinary action and questions are treated:

> Violation of the policies set forth in this manual will subject employees to disciplinary action, including suspension or termination of employment. Disciplinary action taken by the company in no way affects its right to take appropriate legal action, including turning over certain cases to public law enforcement agencies.
>
> An employee having a question about or needing an interpretation of policy, for an actual or proposed activity, shall bring the matter to the attention of his supervisor, who will arrange to have the question answered promptly and in confidence.

All defalcations should be considered to be grounds for dismissal. Legal prosecution is also strongly recommended. One of the strongest incentives to commit computer fraud is the belief that "even if they catch me, they won't do anything about it."

One veteran investigator who asked not to be identified claims that 85% of detected cases are not prosecuted and, of those that are, only 20% result in a conviction. That means that only 3% of detected cases result in conviction. With statistics like that, larcenous employees may presume that you, too, will not take action even if you catch them.

Time and time again, we hear of perpetrators who were caught saying that they watched others stealing before they began. Some of the others were caught and some were not. The ones who were caught were not prosecuted. With experience like that, there simply is not enough incentive for these people to be honest.

Punishment for other forms of noncompliance may not involve dismissal or legal prosecutions, but penalties should exist. Here, personnel policy can often be used as an enforcement vehicle. Minor infractions can often be punished through the performance evaluation process (i.e., low ratings on appropriate items).

Both the actual and potential effects of noncompliance should be considered. For example, the employee who is caught browsing through sensitive data, by means of computer terminal and "borrowed" password, should be severely reprimanded and his personnel record noted accordingly, even though no *apparent* harm was done.

4

Personnel Practices and Procedures

Computer fraud is a people problem. Since the majority of cases involve insiders, it is very important that employees be honest, reliable, and competent. Well-designed personnel practices can be very effective in identifying suitable personnel. They can also be effective in helping to ensure the integrity of the personnel and thereby reduce internal risks of computer fraud. The most important personnel practices and procedures include:

- Hiring procedures, especially preemployment screening.
- Policies on the nonuse/nondisclosure of confidential information.
- Vacation and job rotation policies.
- Channels for addressing grievances.
- Personnel review procedures.
- Employment termination practices.

HIRING PROCEDURES

If one examines the records of organizations that have suffered from theft, fraud, misuse of information, or sabotage at the hands of employees or ex-employees, probably better than 80% of these could have been prevented if the hiring practices of the organization had been more carefully thought out.[1]

The objective of hiring procedures is to identify competent and honest applicants. Meeting this objective requires the collection and verification of appropriate information about the applicant. The method for obtaining the necessary information is preemployment screening.

The most important aspects of preemployment screening of employment applicants are:

- The complete job description.
- The employment application.
- Matching applicants to available jobs.
- Interviews.
- Verification of the applicant's background and qualifications.
- Testing.
- Probationary period.

The complete job description

Clear, detailed, current job descriptions should exist for all activities, particularly for those activities related to data processing. The necessary components of a well-designed job description are identified in Figure 4-1. It is important to emphasize that a significant level of detail is necessary.

The job description should be prepared in advance of other hiring activities. If the position to be filled existed previously and there is an old job description, it should be updated before any of the other hiring steps are taken.

The employment application

All applicants should be required to fill out an application for employment prior to being interviewed. The contents of the application should include, but not be limited to, the items listed in Figure 4-2. Applicants should be asked to supply a copy of their birth certificate or citizenship papers, and military papers if applicable.

Applicants should be informed that thorough background and reference checks will be performed and that they may be required to submit to testing prior to being offered employment. The specific nature of the information to be collected about the applicant, the sources from which it will be obtained, and the means by which it will be gathered should be stated in plain language, along with the nature of any testing to be performed. The applicant should then be asked to sign a statement that he has read and understood the list of information to be collected, tests that may be used, and freely authorizes

[1] Dick H. Brandon, "Employees," in *Computer Security Handbook*, Douglas B. Hoyt, ed. (New York: Macmillan Publishing Co., Inc., 1973), p. 102.

1. Title

2. Position to whom the incumbent reports

3. Positions the incumbent supervises

4. Educational requirements of the job

5. Knowledge, experience, qualifications, skills, and abilities required

6. Duties, responsibilities, and authority of the job

7. Duties and responsibilities of the incumbent in the event of a security breach or disaster

8. Physical demands of the job

9. Physical areas and information (data) to which the incumbent has access

10. Physical areas and information to which the incumbent does not have access

11. Salary range

Figure 4-1

Components of a Job Description

the collection and testing activities. The signed statement will facilitate the collection and verification of information and will avoid violating the applicant's right to privacy. Should the applicant decline to sign the employment application, this should result in disqualifying the applicant from further employment consideration.

Matching applicants to available jobs

The information contained on the employment application and any other information that may have been provided orally, by letter, or by résumé should be used to identify open jobs for which the applicant appears qualified. The remaining steps in the hiring process should not be taken unless the applicant's qualifications match those required by available jobs.

It is particularly important to ensure that the applicant is qualified to perform the job for which he is being considered. Both underqualified and overqualified employees can present significant risks. They can be a negative influence on morale (both their own and their coworkers') and on controls.

The overqualified employee may try to improve his position by doing an exceptional job. If these efforts to attract attention do not result in recognition and advancement, frustration may develop and lead to resentment—resentment directed at the job, at coworkers and supervisors, at employers, and at the company. Eventually this re-

- Names
    - First, Middle, Last, Maiden name (if applicable)
    - Nicknames and other names used (either professionally, formally, or informally)
    - Was name ever legally changed? If so, what was name, to what was it changed, in what legal jurisdiction was it changed, and when?
- Date and place of birth
- Current and previous addresses for the past ten years (street, city, state, length of time)
- Telephone numbers (business, home, neighbor)
- Employment history (applicant should account for all time periods since leaving school; temporary and part-time jobs should be listed)
    - Company name and address
    - Employment and termination dates
    - Job title(s) and description of the nature of the job
    - Monthly or annual salary, or hourly wage
    - Name and title of immediate supervisor
    - Reason for leaving job (or seeking change)
    - References
- Military service, if applicable (current status, dates entered and discharged, type of last discharge, ranks on entering and at discharge)
- Education (primary and secondary schools, colleges, graduate schools, other formal education)
    - School name and address
    - Dates of attendance
    - Major field of study
    - Degree obtained, if applicable
    - Average grades
- Memberships and interests
- Personal references (three people who are not relatives of the applicant and who have known the applicant for at least five years)
    - Name and address
    - Business and position
    - Telephone number
- Health
- Credit references
- Fidelity bonding history (coverage refused or discontinued, explanation, reinstatement)
- Record of arrests and convictions, if any
- Signed acknowledgement that any falsification of information on the application will be grounds for dismissal if detected after employment, and authorizing the verification of all information on the application (should ask whether present employer may be contacted)

Figure 4-2

Some Suggested Components of an Application Form

sentment may turn to anger and to thoughts of retaliation, by embezzlement or by sabotage.

The overqualified individual may arouse resentment in his coworkers because he can perform the job better—with greater accuracy, in less time, and with less effort. He is more likely to feel indignant if his salary is comparable to that of his coworkers. He may also introduce problems with respect to controls, in the sense that they hamper him more than anyone else. As a result, he may be motivated to circumvent the controls or exploit their weaknesses.

An underqualified employee may create problems for his coworkers as well. They may become resentful of the fact that they must do more than their share of the work to make up for the individual's inability to perform adequately. They may feel indignation that the underqualified individual's salary is comparable to their own.

The underqualified employee is likely to produce substandard work. If his error rate is excessive, he may create a situation in which all the controls, both manual and computerized, are so overburdened with the additional work that they cease to be effective. Sufficient chaos may result to permit fraud perpetrated by other employees to be successful, especially if the manual input verification/authorization and output reconciliation procedures are affected or if the controls are relaxed.

Interviews

The interviewing process is often performed in several stages. Companies routinely seeing a large number of applicants often begin with a personnel department interview designed to weed out individuals who are obviously unsuitable for a given job. The advantage of this interview, from the standpoint of security, is that the prescribed hiring procedures are more likely to be followed than if performed elsewhere.

The next step is the interview with the applicant's prospective supervisor. During this interview, the applicant's suitability in terms of experience, skills, and temperament should be explored in depth. Attention should be paid to the applicant's reasons for leaving previous jobs, his fidelity bonding history, frequent changes of residence, and his job-related health/medical history. The applicant should be encouraged to talk about his education, employment history, interests, and hobbies. He should be asked about any arrests, convictions, or participation in illegal activities.

It is important to encourage the applicant to ask questions and express any concerns or reservations that he may have. These factors should be carefully analyzed as possible indicators of potential future problems.

The interviewer should try to assess the applicant's financial needs (mortgages, car loans, other outstanding loans, alimony and child-support payments, etc.) and should compare the applicant's apparent needs to the job salary and other sources of income that the applicant may have. If the financial needs appear to be significantly out of line with the salary to be offered, plus other sources of income, the applicant is a potential security risk. Similarly, the outside sources of income should be evaluated for possible conflicts with your company's interests. Or, if the applicant will be holding two jobs, there may be a performance problem while he is in your company's employ. If the risks in terms of the applicant's financial needs or in terms of outside financial interests and other jobs appear too great, it is probably advisable not to consider him for the job.

The interview is an important mechanism by which information about an applicant is collected. It is an opportunity that should be used to maximum advantage. All impressions of the applicant and his suitability should be carefully and completely recorded by the interviewer.

Verification

If the applicant has successfully completed all of the previous hiring steps, now is the time to verify the information you have gathered concerning the applicant. Most facts on the employment application should be carefully reviewed and verified for accuracy. The purpose of this review and verification is twofold: to determine the suitability of the individual for the job; and to determine if there are any problems in the applicant's background that may indicate potential risks. As much information as possible about the applicant should be collected.

This verification process may be conducted by the company's own personnel or by an outside agency. Regardless of who performs it, the cost of verifying the information is dependent on the extent of the investigation and on the time in which it must be completed. Numerous credit reporting firms, general security companies, and investigative agencies offer both limited and full background investigations (state law may require disclosure of the information sources to applicant). They prepare an impartial profile of the applicant from which an objective evaluation regarding the applicant's suitability can be made.

The methods of verifying the information include personal, face-to-face contact; telephone interviews; and letters requesting the desired information. The most effective way is face-to-face discussion; the least effective way is by means of written correspondence.

Employment history. The applicant's employment history should be closely reviewed. *All* time periods must be accounted for because gaps of even a month could indicate that the applicant served time in jail. Any time periods listed as "self-employment" require especially close attention.

Several employment-related references should be contacted. These references should be asked to discuss the applicant's job function and work competence, working relationships with coworkers and supervisors, job-related health/medical problems, absenteeism, habits, and honesty while in their employ. They should also be asked to identify the applicant's period of employment and to indicate if they would rehire the individual.

The applicant may request that his current employer not be contacted until after he has given notice to this employer. This reference must still be checked and should be checked before the employee begins to work for you. In fact, his employment with you should be contingent upon this check.

A situation to which the person checking the references must be particularly alert is one in which the applicant embezzled from a previous employer who is keeping the incident a secret. To uncover this situation the investigator must be very experienced, well trained, and extremely sensitive to facial expressions, physical reactions, vocal inflections, carefully worded ambiguities, and evasive responses.

Personal references. Although personal references are unlikely to give a negative picture of the applicant, they may provide an indication of whether or not the applicant has had serious problems in the past. Several personal references should be checked and should be asked to provide insights into the individual—his general health/medical problems, family difficulties, financial problems, habits, hobbies, interests, general ability, honesty, reliability, and educational record. The length of time they have known the individual should also be requested.

Other checks. The following information should be verified: date and place of birth, and previous addresses. A visit to the neighborhoods in which the individual lives and has lived can be very informative. It provides an opportunity for the investigator to talk to other people who know the individual. A review of the organizations in which the applicant is a member provides insights into the types of people with whom the applicant associates. Credit and insurance companies may give a reflection of the applicant's credit worthiness and thus of his financial position, reliability, and sense of responsibility. Military records, if applicable, may be checked for any problematic information. Educational records should be reviewed for indications of the applicant's competence, capability, and moral character. They should also be used to verify that the applicant did graduate when he said he did. Law-enforcement authorities in each location in which the applicant resided should be contacted to determine if the applicant has any type of criminal or law-enforcement record.

Discrepancies. Any discrepancies between the information furnished by the applicant and the information provided by the reference and background check should be noted and critically evaluated. They should be discussed with the applicant as well. An applicant who has deliberately misstated any facts on the application blank should not be considered for employment. If the person has already begun employment when the deliberate misstatement is discovered, serious consideration should be given to terminating him.

Testing

Numerous tests to assess basic intelligence, aptitude, attitude, and personality and to predict delinquent behavior exist and are used today in the screening of prospective employees. Two tests that we feel are particularly effective in the screening process will be discussed here. These are the polygraph test and honesty tests.

Polygraph test. The polygraph, or lie detector as it is more commonly known, is an electromechanical instrument that records physiological responses, such as changes in respiration, blood pressure, and pulse. As a screening test it is used as a verification technique. It provides the applicant with the opportunity to verify statements made during the interview and information provided on the application form. It may also be used to permit the applicant to establish that, if he made mistakes in the past, he has learned from them and is no longer making the same mistakes.

The test begins with a pretest interview conducted by the polygraphist. This interview concentrates on the applicant's background. The questions that will be asked during the polygraph test and the control questions (irrelevant questions with obvious answers) are then formulated by the polygraphist. The test questions concern only those items that have a definite bearing on the applicant's suitability for the job. The polygraph test includes questions concerning information on the application and questions about whether the individual has ever stolen anything from previous employers.

Although preemployment polygraph tests have proved effective and valid when administered by qualified polygraphists, various civil liberty groups, unions, and privacy-protection study commissions have urged the passage of a federal law that would prohibit polygraphing by employers of applicants as well as employees. Under the laws of some states, polygraphing is prohibited under certain circumstances. And, in general, the subject must volunteer to take the test, and the results of any such test may not be used as the sole basis for denying or terminating employment. One of the problems that has led to unfavorable attitudes toward polygraphing is that there is no certification program for polygraphists that would help ensure proper use of the tests and incorporate sanctions against those who misuse or abuse them. The tests can be somewhat expensive to administer and, considering the legal and other potential problems, companies would be well advised to engage the services of only the most experienced, professional polygraphists.

Honesty tests. The Reid Report (John E. Reid and Associates, Chicago) and The Stanton Survey (The Stanton Analysis Center, Chicago) are test/questionnaires given to prospective employees to evaluate their attitudes toward honesty. The combined experience of companies using these tests is that 35% to 50% of the applicants are considered to be high risks!

An honesty test is a pencil-and-paper exercise that takes an applicant 40 to 60 minutes to complete. Originally designed as a pre-polygraph test, it has shown itself to be almost as effective as the polygraph test and can be used in place of the polygraph. Among other things, it is effective at screening out potential risks—those individuals who have not yet committed a dishonest act but are likely to do so if given the opportunity or if the need arises.

The Reid Report, for example, consists of three sections. The first is a yes/no questionnaire that measures the individual's attitudes toward punishment for crimes involving theft as well as the individual's attitude and behavior relating to theft. The second section asks for detailed background information, similar to information provided on the employment application. The third section contains questions about the individual's own honesty. The completed report is analyzed by a member of J. E. Reid and Associates. A recommendation as to whether or not the applicant should be hired is provided to the employer.

The honesty test has not encountered the resistance that the polygraph test has. In fact, it appears to meet the Equal Employment Opportunity Commission "Guidelines" for employment testing, and is about one-fourth the cost of a polygraph test. At this writing, only the state of Minnesota outlaws honesty tests.

It should be noted that special versions of honesty tests, like the polygraph test, can be used to provide periodic testing of current employees as well as to investigate specific incidences of theft.

**Probationary
period**

As mentioned above, the objective of hiring procedures is to identify competent and honest applicants. Incompetent, unqualified, and dishonest applicants should not be considered for employment. Thorough preemployment screening procedures will help to identify such individuals; however, preemployment screening is not infallible. Some "unacceptable" applicants will filter through the screening.

What about people with criminal records? "The one time loser should not be discriminated against, and a prison sentence should not be held against a prospective employee. The one time loser may have learned his lesson the hard way and may be a trusted employee in the future."[2] The important considerations with respect to such applicants are that they have provided complete and accurate information on the employment application, thereby performing no errors of omission or commission; and that they impressed the trained interviewer with their honesty and integrity.

All applicants that are hired should be hired in a probationary status for a period of 30 to 90 days. Additional information about new employees will be available by way of birth certificates, citizenship papers, military records, and as the necessary employment forms are prepared, including health insurance forms, life insurance forms, tax-withholding forms, other employee-benefit forms, and bonding forms. If any discrepancies with the information collected during preemployment screening are detected, the employee should be questioned and, depending on his responses, perhaps fired.

The new employee should be given access only to those areas to which he must have access in order to perform his job at this initial stage. He should be restricted from entering any particularly sensitive areas. All his records, including his identification card or badge, should indicate his probationary status.

This probationary period provides management with the opportunity to complete the information-gathering and verification processes that were begun with the employment application. It also gives management the opportunity to watch the individual perform his job, to make sure the individual is competent, and to make sure that the individual is honest. If the probationary period proceeds with no problems, the individual is given permanent status.

NONUSE/NONDISCLOSURE OF CONFIDENTIAL INFORMATION

Every company has confidential information, trade secrets, and situations in which conflicts of interest can arise. Our discussion of ethical business conduct covered the latter considerations. Here, we are concerned more with recognizing the potential for the abuse and fraudulent use of computerized data and the establishment of policy directed at these matters.

As a personnel procedure, we suggest that all EDP department and user employees be required to sign a statement that explains the policy and acknowledges that they have read and understand the policy and will comply with it as a condition of employment. Noncompliance should result in prompt disciplinary action, including involuntary termination of employment.

If individuals are to be held responsible for unauthorized use or disclosure of confidential information, they should be told what is

[2] Martin S. Freedman, "A Primer on Fraud and Embezzlement," *Management Accounting*, October 1973, p. 37.

POLICY
CONFIDENTIAL INFORMATION
NON-USE/NON-DISCLOSURE AGREEMENT

In the normal conduct of business, officers and employees of the company have access to and deal with privileged information that belongs to the company and that the company considers to be sensitive or confidential.

Improper use or disclosure of such information can provide an unfair advantage to competitors of the company and certain investors in company securities, put the company at an actual or apparent disadvantage in terms of the conditions and pricing of purchases/leases/rentals of all kinds, result in an actual or apparent financial gain to employees/relatives/friends, jeopardize the company's negotiating position on agreements/contracts of all types, and may constitute a personal invasion of privacy. All such uses and disclosures of privileged information are prohibited during and following employment with the company, until such time as the information is made available to the general public.

Since it is impractical to state, in advance, all possible types of business dealings and situations where privileged information may come into play, employees are expected to use good judgment in complying with this policy. By way of illustration, not limitation, some types of confidential information are shown below:

- Customer names, addresses, sales data, engineering data, and specifications.
- Supplier names and prices of raw materials.
- Product cost, discount, profitability, and unpublished price data.
- Business plans pertaining to: new products, advertising and sales campaigns, mergers/acquisitions/joint ventures, real estate needs, plant closings, and layoffs.
- Computer system software, application programs, and security features.
- Trade secrets, formulas, proprietary processes, and research findings.
- Financial information: budgets, division performance, sales, profit and loss, balance sheet, earnings projections, and inventory data.
- All "insider information" which has not been released to the general public or investment community.
- Collective bargaining strategies and negotiation data.
- Shareholder names, addresses, and holdings.
- Personnel data such as: pay, performance, promotion, background, medical, names, and addresses.

The undersigned acknowledges that he has read and understands this policy, knows that compliance is a condition of employment, realizes that it is his obligation to obtain official authorization before using or disclosing confidential information, and understands that any failure to comply may result in immediate dismissal, in addition to legal action by the company and others.

Signed: _____ Date: _____

considered confidential and what is not. If confidential information is contained in computer printouts and other documents, those materials can be identified or stamped "Confidential." If information of a confidential or sensitive nature is stored in machine-readable form, its confidential status can be expressly indicated in a policy statement. Assigning the classification of "Confidential" indiscriminately can prove to be an enormous administrative burden or can result in little regard for anything with the designation.

We believe that it is a good idea to explicitly remind employees of their responsibilities with regard to confidential information through an annual "sign off" as well as at the time of employment. Figure 4-3 illustrates a form of policy statement that incorporates a sign off. At the same time, it contains enough examples so that employees will understand what is expected.

VACATION AND JOB ROTATION POLICIES

Vacation and job rotation policies are very important and can be very effective in deterring fraud because they both prevent any one employee from having exclusive control over any particular functions or applications. They also deter the potential perpetrator because the likelihood that the fraud will be detected increases greatly when the perpetrator's job is performed by another person, whether temporarily or permanently.

Vacation policies

You probably know individuals who never take vacations. Such individuals are hard workers who put in substantial overtime during the week, on weekends, and on holidays. These individuals are usually viewed by their employers as exceptionally motivated and reliable. Sometimes employers find such individuals to be indispensable and, in time, allow them to assume complete and exclusive responsibility for their function. They thereby become the only people who truly understand their job function in its entirety.

This situation is very undesirable, for several reasons. In addition to presenting substantial problems with respect to replacing the indispensable employee when he leaves the job or providing a temporary replacement if he should become ill or incapacitated, it presents a significant potential exposure to fraud. Perpetrators' schemes often require that the perpetrator be at work at all times in order to intercept certain input or output transactions or to prevent reconciliation discrepancies from being revealed. If the perpetrator were absent, discrepancies would appear immediately.

Recommended policy. All individuals in data processing-related positions should be required to take their vacations. At least two consecutive weeks of vacation are desirable. Ideally, the vacation period should include a month-end or quarter-end closing. During the individual's absence, discrepancies and problems must be resolved by the temporary replacement.

Bank regulators have long been aware of the fact that forced vacations facilitate the discovery of fraud. For nationally chartered banks, the Comptroller of the Currency requires all officers to be absent for at least 2 consecutive weeks. Enforcement of that rule is accomplished by requiring banks to provide the National Bank Examiners with a list of all officers who have not complied. Since the regulatory authorities are extremely likely to scrutinize the work of any officers on the list, and since they are empowered to remove bank management if its practices are unsound, instances of noncompliance are rare.

Benefits. Several benefits are realized by such a policy. The would-be perpetrator may be deterred because he knows that he must take his vacation and that his job will be performed by someone else during his absence. Requiring that vacations be taken often results in improved employee morale and in reduced fatigue and exhaustion, which also results in an improved error rate.

In order for a business to have a mandatory vacation policy and yet continue to function, people must be able to assume other people's jobs during their absence. This requires that an effective level of cross-training be conducted at all times. Besides reducing the risk of fraud, cross-training reduces the disruption experienced when employees terminate or are terminated, transferred, or promoted. It also prevents any one individual from becoming indispensable. Indispensable employees create problems for management control as well as for security.

Compliance. Compliance requires cross-training and active enforcement efforts. Maintenance and review of attendance records are required. Prior to year-end, individuals who have not taken their vacations should be identified. They and their supervisors must be reminded of the policy; they should be required to take their vacation before the end of the year.

Job rotation policies

Job rotation policies and vacation policies meet the same needs and have the same importance, benefits, and implications. They differ in one respect: vacations are scheduled in advance with the mutual consent of employee and supervisor; job rotation should be scheduled by management on a random basis so that the timing and new assignments are not known in advance. This difference is significant. Job rotation serves as an especially effective deterrent to the would-be perpetrator. He cannot plan to "wind down" or end his scheme in advance. Nor can he plan to cover his tracks since he has no time frame and no identified successor with which to plan.

Recommended policy. All jobs are rotated periodically. The timing of the rotation and the details of the rotation are not announced in advance. Individuals are expected to assume their new jobs immediately and to perform the functions of the job without calling on their predecessor. All questions and problems are addressed to their immediate supervisor.

> Rotation of assignment is particularly important for management and supervisory personnel. Experience indicates that, over a period of time, managers often become careless in their application of controls. A large number of embezzlements are perpetrated by very long-tenure supervisors, who had resisted reassignment or even promotion. On the other hand there was unusually high turnover among the individuals reporting to them.[3]

Benefits. Benefits include the reduced exposure to fraud, a reduction of the boredom experienced from the performance of repetitive tasks, and an effective cross-training program. The cross-training reduces, and almost eliminates, the disruption experienced when an individual terminates, is terminated, transferred, promoted, or is absent for whatever reason. It gives employees the feeling that they are being developed and that their opportunities for advancement are improved.

Rotation of duties can also be an effective alternative to proper separation of duties in situations where proper separation would result in overstaffing. With job rotation, many individuals will be performing the same function. No one individual will have the opportunity to perform a function continuously for a long period, thus reducing the amount of time during which embezzlement could be perpetrated. Rotation also means that successors will be reviewing the work of incumbents, thereby increasing both the perceived and actual chances of detecting fraudulent activity.

Compliance. Compliance requires substantial cross-training and a management commitment to the policy. It also requires active enforcement of all aspects of the policy, particularly the unpredictability with respect to timing and assignments.

[3] *Data Security Controls and Procedures—A Philosophy for DP Installations,* (White Plains, N.Y.: IBM Corporation, February 1976), p. 9.

CHANNELS FOR ADDRESSING GRIEVANCES

Grievances will arise, regardless of whether or not they are justified. Failure of management to address them in a timely fashion may lead to resentment on the part of employees. Procedures must define how employees should voice their grievances. The procedures must be designed in such a way that, by voicing grievances, employees will not jeopardize their position. The procedures must also define how and when management will respond.

Types of grievances

Sources of grievances and dissatisfaction are infinite. Some of the more common origins include:

- Performance evaluations.
- Compensation.
- Promotions.
- Disciplinary action taken by supervisors.
- Extra duties.
- Boredom.
- Personality clashes.
- Poor working conditions.
- Inadequate supervision.

Procedures for addressing grievances

Ideally, individuals should discuss grievances with their supervisor first; however, there are situations when an employee feels, for whatever reason, that he cannot discuss the problem with his supervisor. If that is the case, or if the discussion with the supervisor fails to yield a solution, the employee should not be thwarted in his attempt to air his problem. There should be an identifiable person or organization to which the employee can go and talk in confidence. Every employee must be made aware of the procedures to be followed and the people to be contacted if a problem or grievance should arise.

The mere existence of procedures for addressing grievances in no way assures the employee that grievances will be resolved in a manner acceptable to him. It does, however, assure him that his problem will be heard and evaluated, and that some action, or lack of action, will be taken. Some individuals may be more willing to accept a situation after having discussed it with someone they feel is impartial; others may not. If the individual absolutely cannot accept management's solution, he should be removed from the situation by transfer, reassignment, or, in the extreme case, termination.

PERSONNEL REVIEW PROCEDURES

Effective hiring procedures should ensure that the individuals hired are honest and competent; however, they will never be foolproof. Moreover, people change, their problems change, their needs change, and their motives change. Personnel practices that are effective necessitate continual observation and periodic rechecking of employees, particularly employees in sensitive positions (e.g., systems analysis, systems programming, applications and maintenance programming, operations). Supervisors should be trained to be very observant and sensitive to the needs, morale, and problems of the employees that report to them. These procedures should be clearly and concisely explained in a supervisors' handbook. In addition, mechanisms must be defined for dealing with problems that are detected; and the people that can be contacted for help in dealing with problems must be identified.

Periodic performance evaluations are another important aspect of personnel review procedures. They should, in fact, be an integral and formal personnel review practice. They provide the mechanism by which management acknowledges to its employees its understanding and appreciation of their individual contributions and accomplishments and rewards them. It also gives employees an understanding of their weaknesses and areas in which improvement is needed. The performance evaluation is another forum in which employees' problems can be addressed.

Supervisors' training

Supervisors must be trained to recognize problems and symptoms that could indicate that increased risks are developing. Danger signals assume many forms, including deteriorating morale; refusal of vacations, promotions, and job rotation; alcohol and drug abuse and gambling problems; and financial problems. Although supervisors cannot be expected to solve all problems or even to recognize all symptoms, they should be trained to be sensitive to their existence.

Supervisors should make an initial attempt to determine the exact nature and source of an employee's problem. It is their close working relationship with their employees that makes this possible. They may be able to encourage the employee to discuss the problem with them. On the other hand, they may be rebuffed by a troubled employee. All problems should be referred to the personnel department, where specialists who are either employees of the company or on retainer to the company can deal with the problem professionally and competently.

Deteriorating morale. Deteriorating morale and resentment may be exhibited by frequent employee grievances and complaints as well as by increased employee absenteeism and turnover. Morale may be adversely affected by dissatisfaction with salaries, promotions, recognition, working conditions, supervisors, and overall job conditions. Management must evaluate the complaints and grievances very carefully and determine where changes can be made.

If the morale problem can be isolated to one or two employees, the sources of the problems should be determined and specifically addressed. It may be desirable to transfer the employee to a less sensitive position until the problems are resolved.

Refusal of vacations, promotions, and job rotation. Refusal of vacations, promotions, and job rotation is a sign that a dangerous situation may exist. Employees who never take 2-week vacations, who never take any vacations, who refuse promotions and job rotation, or who are always at work when end-of-period closings are performed should be observed closely. These are all signals that fraud may be being perpetrated. The refusal of vacation, job rotation, and promotion should be prohibited as a matter of policy, and those policies should be strictly and uniformly enforced.

Alcohol, drug, gambling, and other personal problems. Symptoms of such problems may be very difficult to detect. If suspected, the employee should be encouraged to talk to personnel department specialists. The personnel department should also be notified and should encourage the employee to talk to them. Many companies sponsor programs designed to help personnel overcome drinking, drug, and gambling problems. Generally, the policy requires that if such a problem comes to light, the employee must participate in a company-sponsored program, get outside professional help, or else be terminated.

Financial problems. Financial problems may be manifested by constant borrowing, persistent calls by creditors, and excessive extravagances. A personnel counsellor may be able to help the individual to address his problem directly and to come up with a realistic solution. If the problem is a result of an unpredictable crisis, such as family problems or illness, the personnel counsellor may be able to help the employee get a salary advance or loan or help the employee obtain low-cost publicly sponsored health care. If the employee resists help and the problem is serious, the counsellor should refer the individual to a professional psychological counsellor and recommend to his supervisor that, if the individual is in a sensitive position, he be immediately transferred to a less vulnerable function.

Other potentially dangerous situations. Supervisors should carefully observe employees in very sensitive positions who have access to and control over input and output transactions, who can authorize transactions, and who have access to the assets of the company. They should also be observant of employees in positions that are not rotated or of employees performing functions in which the duties are not properly separated.

Periodic rechecking of personnel

It is advisable to periodically recheck employees in sensitive positions. The personnel department should conduct probing interviews of such employees and their supervisors on a routine basis. Extreme attention should be placed on keeping these employees' records complete and current. Changing financial needs, changing interests and habits, personal problems, attendance records, behavioral changes, personality clashes, and reported errors should all be recorded.

Performance evaluations

The importance of morale and a positive attitude on the part of the employee toward his employer has been emphasized. The performance evaluation performs a role with respect to this. It has several other benefits, also. It forces an assessment of all employees. Management is thus able to identify the capabilities of its employees. This is especially important because it provides management with the information necessary to determine the direction in which employees should be guided to enhance their opportunities for promotion. Employees, in turn, are reassured about management's concern for their future.

Fairness must be built into performance evaluations. The existence of a standard evaluation form with predetermined weighting factors will aid supervisors in performing evaluations as objectively as possible. Management should review the evaluations and discuss them with supervisors to verify the validity of poor or exceptional evaluations. Employees must have the opportunity to challenge their evaluations, as well. Personality conflicts are unavoidable; however, they have no relevance to a performance evaluation and must be put aside.

The contents of a performance evaluation should include a review of the job description and the duties actually assigned, and an evaluation of the employee's performance. The supervisor should also be asked to discuss the employee's attitude; aptitude; productivity; learning ability; maturity; working relationships; potential; and, readiness for promotion, increased responsibilities, salary increase, or need for additional training, transfer, reassignment, or termination.

A complete job description should be provided to the employee when he is hired; whenever he is promoted, transferred, or his job functions change; and when he is ready to have a performance evaluation. Copies of the job description should be forwarded to the personnel department and filed in the employee's file.

Timing. The regularity and timing of performance evaluations must be prescribed. They should be conducted annually, at a minimum, on the anniversary of the individual's employment. This makes the evaluation more personal and is easier on the supervisor because all evaluations do not have to be prepared at the same time.

They may also be conducted whenever there is about to be a change in an employee's supervisor.

Interview. The supervisor should discuss the evaluation with the employee. The supervisor should evaluate the employee's progress and discuss the employee's performance, complimenting the good, identifying the areas needing improvement, and suggesting ways to improve the stronger as well as the weaker areas. The employee should be encouraged to discuss his assessment of his progress, performance, and future. The employee should also be encouraged to talk about any problems he may have either with respect to the job or with respect to his personal life.

Supervisors' handbook

Supervisory personnel should be provided with a handbook that serves as a reference manual on all personnel-related issues and policies. Although supervisors should be expected to be knowledgeable regarding practices and procedures, the handbook serves as a reference and as a reminder.

The contents of the handbook must clearly define the company's policies and procedures with regard to hiring, promotions, terminations, employee performance evaluations, vacation and job rotation practices, sick time and other time off, and employee benefits. Guidelines for assigning, changing, and rotating employees' responsibilities, and suggestions for handling delicate matters such as personal problems, grievances, friction between employees, and other problems must also be spelled out.

The handbook must explicitly identify those statements which represent guidelines that supervisors may overlook at their discretion and those statements which are inflexible rules. The manual must be kept up to date. If new policies or procedures are established or if old policies and procedures are modified, the handbook must reflect the changes. If changes are not incorporated into the handbook in a timely manner, it will be difficult, if not impossible, to enforce any of the policies.

EMPLOYMENT TERMINATION PRACTICES

Termination of employment with the company occurs as a result of firing, layoff, resignation, retirement, or death. While this discussion focuses primarily on involuntary terminations of an employee through firing, it is important to keep in mind the fact that the procedures discussed are relevant and applicable to other terminations as well as transfers and promotions.

Terminations are unpleasant. Yet, they occur. Handling of these situations can have a significant impact on your company's exposure to computer fraud. Improper handling of terminations will increase your exposure significantly; careful handling and timing will reduce exposure.

Layoffs Layoffs are perhaps the most dangerous reason for terminations because the terminations appear to be very arbitrary and completely unrelated to performance, quality of work, competence, years of service, and honesty. For this reason they always have an adverse impact on morale, even among individuals in the same or other departments who are not affected. Unaffected individuals begin to fear for their security, wondering if they will be next. These fears contribute to the impression that loyalty to the company may not be justified, since employees are laid off in spite of long and satisfactory service. Such thinking may lead to resentment great enough to motivate acts of computer fraud and embezzlement.

Layoffs should be avoided whenever another means of reducing costs is available and whenever the reduction in manpower is expected to be short-term. We hasten to point out that accomplishing short-term cost reductions through the laying off of technical personnel is short-sighted because of the training investment in each individual, the difficulty and costs of trying to replace the individuals at a later date, and because of the risk introduced.

Layoffs may, however, be necessary. When layoffs cannot be avoided, they should be accomplished at one time and with great speed. Management should explain to the unaffected employees that there was no alternative. Those employees should also be given assurance, to the extent possible, that no further layoffs will occur or are anticipated.

How should the individuals to be laid off be selected? On the one hand, seniority considerations may give an impression of fairness and may result in retention of the most skilled and experienced personnel. However, this is not always true. If there is "deadwood" among the senior employees, terminating junior personnel will reduce the quality of the staff. Terminating junior personnel may also make it difficult to attract qualified entry-level personnel in the future. If, however, seniority is not observed and if terminations are based on performance evaluations and a realistic assessment of what is needed to keep the organization functioning, other problems may arise. Laying off individuals very close to retirement is likely to be viewed by all employees as unconscionable. The selection method depends on the conditions within the particular company. All aspects of the procedure must be seriously considered by management.

Defalcations Termination is absolutely mandatory whenever it comes to management's attention that an employee has embezzled regardless of the amount. The case for dismissing dishonest individuals is overwhelm-

75

ing. Once the facts become known, failure to terminate the employee may encourage him to continue embezzling, possibly more discreetly, with the notion that management may not do anything if he is caught.

> Statistics indicate the percentage of repeated transgressions by once-detected dishonest employees is sufficiently high to justify termination. Another important fact to be considered is that honest employees, whether they openly admit it or not, are pleased when a dishonest employee is detected and terminated. Knowledge of a transgression is normally wide-spread among employees. Employees with integrity tend to lose faith in management when the transgressor is not detected or, once detected, suffers no appropriate punishment. The moral fiber of many employees can be torn if honesty offers no rewards.[4]

Other employees may be encouraged to embezzle. In many companies there are individuals who will not embezzle simply because they fear the consequences of detection. If the consequences do not include immediate termination and criminal prosecution, these employees may feel that the risks involved in embezzling are worth taking. Failure to discharge and prosecute embezzlers has led to an upsurge in embezzlement and other dishonest acts by the same and other employees. Failure to dismiss and prosecute perpetrators can also adversely impact the costs of fidelity insurance, doubling and even tripling it.

Other involuntary terminations

Termination of employees may also become necessary due to deliberate misstatement of facts during preemployment screening, lack of adequate qualifications, incompetence, and serious morale, personal or behavioral problems. Termination is an extreme action. If the employee's problems do not relate to honesty, and the possibility of internal transfers exists, it may be safer from a security and personnel standpoint to try to reassign the individual before deciding to terminate him. When terminations occur, the morale of the remaining employees is often adversely affected. This is particularly true if the terminated individual is well liked or if the reason for termination is a personality clash with a supervisor. It is of utmost importance, however, that risks be reduced. If the employee has a problem of honesty or integrity, termination should be quick. If the employee has morale, personal, or behavioral problems, reassignment and restriction of physical and data access permissions must be immediate.

[4] B. E. Gorrill, *Effective Personnel Security Procedures* (Homewood, Ill.: Dow Jones–Irwin, Inc., 1974), p. 62.

Voluntary terminations

As soon as an employee notifies his supervisor that he intends to terminate, the personnel department should be informed. A final performance evaluation should be prepared by the supervisor. It should be reviewed by management and forwarded to the personnel department.

The personnel department should conduct an exit interview during which the terminating employee explains his reasons for leaving, whether he has accepted another job, and his impressions of the company. The interviewer must evaluate the reasons that the employee has given for terminating and determine if the employee is providing the real reasons. The employee should be encouraged to be as open and candid as possible. He may provide invaluable insights into potential or actual problem or risk situations.

Procedures

Forced terminations must be handled with extreme care. It is important that employees be removed from the data processing and computer areas prior to being given notice of their termination. Feelings of revenge because of having been terminated have often resulted in vandalism and destruction of data and equipment. "One procedure which has proved successful in regard to discharging employees is to have the individuals transferred to a nonsensitive job before they are given their discharge notices."[5] This may be effectively engineered in conjunction with a policy of job rotations, as outlined above.

Whenever an employee terminates or is terminated, regardless of the reasons, the following steps should be taken:

- All company identification, including badges, IDs, business cards, and business-related materials, should be collected.
- All keys, magnetic-strip cards, signature plates, and other indicators of authority should be collected. All sources of authority should be revoked.
- All relevant locks or codes, passwords, and access codes must be changed.
- All accounts should be settled (e.g., expense accounts, outstanding loans).
- Accounts over which the employee had control should be reconciled.
- Other members of the staff should be promptly informed of the termination.

[5] Jack F. Thorne, "Control of Computer Abuses," *The Journal of Accountancy*, October 1974, p. 46.

5

Administrative
and Internal Controls

The controls that will be discussed in this chapter are directed toward those procedures and practices that are performed as part of the day-to-day activities of the departments that use the data processing facilities. They are essentially the ground rules or procedures to be followed in the handling of data. The controls are general; they apply equally to all departments in the company. The controls are the responsibility of the company; they are not mandated by law or by any external commissions or governmental bodies. As such, it is management's responsibility to define, administer, monitor, and enforce them.

> Internal controls in the data processing environment pertain to the processing and recording of an organization's transactions and to resulting management reporting. They are the processes that ensure the accuracy and completeness of manual and automated transactions, records and reports, and the avoidance, detection and correction of errors. They encompass source document origination, authorization, processing, data processing record keeping and reporting, and the use of data processing records and reports in controlling an organization's activities.[1]

[1] *Systems Auditability and Control Study—Data Processing Control Practices Report* (Altamonte Springs, Fla.: The Institute of Internal Auditors, Inc., 1977), p. 19.

The purposes of these controls are wide-ranging:

- To ensure the completeness, accuracy, and integrity of the input data, whether they be routine input transactions, corrections of errors, adjustments, master file changes, or exception items.
- To ensure the timely and proper correction of errors.
- To detect, during the normal course of activities, any modifications to the input data, programs, or master files.

A comprehensive system of controls can be very effective in the prevention of fraud. The well-designed system of controls provides multiple points at which fraudulent or unauthorized transactions will be detected. It thereby makes it very difficult to successfully perpetrate fraud. Thus, the opportunity to perpetrate fraud is significantly reduced. Relating this to our theory of fraud, reducing the opportunity factor to a value close to zero reduces the probability that your company will be a victim of computer fraud.

The controls that will be addressed have been grouped in the following categories:

- Input controls.
- Processing controls.
- Output controls.
- Adjustment and error correction controls.

It is important to note that, although the controls have been grouped for discussion purposes, a system of controls requires that controls be enforced at all steps in the handling and processing of data.

The following areas or activities also play a prominent role in our system of controls and in the detection of fraud:

- Management reporting.
- Documentation.
- Monitoring customer complaints.
- Administration of programmed decisions.

These topics will be addressed after the control categories. A key control that encompasses all the controls cited above will be discussed first: Separation of duties and responsibilities.

Management should define its system of controls with the purposes and goals of the company as a whole in mind. The system must encompass all activities involved with the generation, processing, and dissemination of information. The controls must be strictly and uniformly enforced at all times. No lapses in control can be tolerated if the controls are to be effective in the prevention of fraud.

SEPARATION OF DUTIES AND RESPONSIBILITIES

The functions that must, if at all possible, be performed by, and be the responsibility of, different and distinct (identifiable) individuals are identified in Figure 5-1. This separation of duties and responsibilities is based on two very important concepts:

- No single individual must have responsibility for the complete processing of any transaction or group of transactions.
- The perpetration of fraud must require the collusion of at least two individuals.

The importance of this control, and of its underlying concepts, cannot be overemphasized.

All input transactions must be reviewed for accuracy and for legitimacy. This review should be performed by a responsible individual who is not involved in the preparation of those transactions. Because of the importance of adjustment and correction transactions and master file changes and because of their sensitivity and implications, it is critical that they be carefully reviewed and approved by a responsible individual different from the one who approves routine input transactions.

The functions that relate to the preparation and approval of in-

- Forms control
- Original source document preparation
- Original source document approval
- Preparation of adjustment and correction transactions
- Preparation of master file changes
- Approval of adjustments, corrections, and master file changes
- Calculation and logging of input control totals
- Output reconciliation
- Output distribution

Figure 5-1

Functions that Must be Performed by Different and Distinct Individuals

put transactions and those that relate to the distribution and reconciliation of output must also be separated. The purpose of output reconciliation is to verify that all authorized and approved input transactions, and *only* authorized and approved transactions, were processed and were processed correctly and completely. The person who performs this reconciliation cannot have any involvement in the preparation or approval of the input. If he does, he may have the opportunity not only to perpetrate fraud, by himself, but also to conceal it.

> There should be no way that a person could make an error or manipulation which would not be detected by some other person during the routine execution of that other person's responsibilities.[2]

With the proper separation of duties, an employee would be able to perpetrate fraud only by working in collusion with one or more employees. This can be very effective in deterring and even preventing fraud. It means that a dishonest employee will have to find other dishonest employees who are not only interested in perpetrating fraud but who are also in a position to be able to help effect and conceal the fraud. The chances of detecting the fraud then increase significantly. The greater the number of people involved, the greater the probability that one of them will make a mistake that reveals the fraudulent activities or that one will not be available at all times to perform the required manipulation.

INPUT CONTROLS

The purpose of input controls is to ensure the completeness, accuracy, and integrity of the input transactions from source document preparation and authorization through conversion to machine-readable form to data entry into the computer. If input controls are to fulfill their purpose, they must also explicitly address the prevention, detection, and correction of errors introduced during the processing of input transactions.

Before examining input controls in detail, an explanation of the key terms "completeness," "accuracy," and "integrity" is in order. Completeness implies entirety. *All* input transactions are captured at their source; *all* are converted into machine-readable form; and *all* are entered into the computer for processing. Accuracy means freedom from error, or correctness. Thus, the input transactions are captured correctly, are converted precisely, and are entered exactly as captured and converted. Integrity signifies a sound, unimpaired, and perfect condition. The input transactions that are captured, converted, and entered into the computer must be perfect. There must

---

[2] G. Hunter Jones, "DP Error and Fraud—And What You Can Do About It," *Price Waterhouse Review*, 1976, No. 2, p. 8.

be no additions to, changes to, or deletions of the input transactions at any step in their processing.

Input is particularly vulnerable to fraud because there are so many steps and people involved in capturing and recording it, approving it, entering it into machine-readable form, and submitting it for processing. It can be altered or manipulated at every step or between any two steps. Transactions may not be captured and recorded; or they may be captured and recorded twice. They may be captured or recorded improperly or incompletely. They may be lost, duplicated, or altered during collection, during or after approval, or before or during data entry.

Moreover, fraudulent input may be almost impossible to detect. It may be indistinguishable from legitimate transactions. This makes input particularly susceptible to fraud. Thus, particular care must be taken to minimize the potential perpetrator's opportunities to manipulate input transactions or introduce fraudulent input transactions and to maximize the probability that such fraudulent transactions will be detected.

Input controls will be examined in the following subsections:

- Source document preparation and approval.
- Data conversion and entry.
- Exception item handling.

Source document preparation and approval

Controls associated with source document preparation are summarized in Figure 5-2.

The objectives of such controls are to:

- Ensure that the input transaction information is captured and recorded in a timely and accurate fashion.
- Establish control totals for the batches of input transactions.
- Define the flow of the documents on which the input transaction information is recorded.

Input transaction information may be recorded in human-readable or machine-readable form. The controls discussed here relate to the preparation of human-readable documents. The controls associated with the recording of information in machine-readable form will be discussed briefly later in the subsection on data conversion and entry.

Authorize the types of transactions that can be prepared by each user department. Individual departments should be authorized by management to prepare and approve only those types of transactions

- Authorize the types of transactions that can be prepared and approved by each department or functional group within the organization

- Use specially designed input forms with preprinted information

- Use input forms with preprinted, sequential document numbers

- Use input forms with preprinted, copy indentification numbers and information

- Maintain tight control over all input forms

- Perform extensive batch control, including batching sensitive documents in separate batches, limiting the number of documents in each batch, computing several batch control totals for each batch, and using preprinted batch control forms with preprinted, sequential batch numbers

- Maintain logs for forms and batch control

- Require review and approval of all source documents and batches of source documents

- Comply with agreed-upon schedules for submission of batches for data conversion and entry

- Keep one copy in the user department of all source documents submitted for processing

- Retain source documents in accordance with defined source document retention policies and procedures

- Destroy source documents upon expiration of their retention period according to predetermined procedures based on their sensitivity

Figure 5-2

Source Document Preparation Controls

that are directly related to the functions and activities of that particular department. For example, the purchasing department should be authorized to prepare and approve purchasing-related transactions only. They must not be authorized to prepare and approve sales-related transactions, accounts receivable-related transactions, or any other nonpurchasing transactions. In effect, this control results in the proper separation of duties and responsibilities among the various departments and functional groups in the organization.

This control is especially important with regard to employees' personal transactions. For example, if an employee wants to purchase goods from the company, the appropriate sales transaction should only be prepared, approved, and submitted for processing by the sales department. The employee must not be able to effect his transactions through his own department unless his department is authorized to effect such transactions.

Use preprinted, specially designed input forms. Recording input transaction information on specially designed forms helps to ensure that the information is complete and accurate, especially if the forms identify the required information and specify its format and content. The individual pieces of information and the field size for each piece of information should be identified.

The input forms should contain preprinted information in those fields that remain constant or that change in a repetitive and predictable manner. Reducing the amount of information that should be coded reduces the errors that may be introduced.

Use input forms with preprinted sequential document numbers. Each input form should have a unique sequential document number preprinted on it. This document number serves two primary purposes:

- It establishes accountability for the source documents.
- It provides a way to identify and locate specific source documents.

The document number provides a means of accounting for all input documents. By sorting the documents into sequential order, it becomes immediately apparent which documents are missing, which documents have duplicate numbers, and which documents have altered or missing numbers. Such documents are suspect; they must be identified and investigated immediately.

The use of input forms with preprinted sequential document numbers provides accountability in another way as well. If the preparers of the documents are given a set of one or more documents on which to record the input transactions, they can be held responsible for all the documents in the set. A log, identifying the date, the preparer, and the range of document numbers on the documents given to the preparer, should be maintained. The preparer initials the forms control log to formally acknowledge receipt of the documents. The preparer should be required to account for each and every document assigned to him. Voided or ruined documents should never be discarded. Each document, or each copy of the document if it is a multiple-part form, must be clearly and indelibly marked as void and must be given to the person whose responsibility it is to maintain forms control. Missing documents should be reported to the forms controller as soon as their absence is detected. The forms controller should maintain a log of all voided and missing documents. The log identifies the documents by date, document number, responsible preparer, and problem (e.g., missing or voided).

Unique, sequential document numbers provide a means of identifying specific documents. They simplify the process of locating specific documents in the event that a question, discrepancy, customer complaint, or other problem or need arises. The responsible preparer is also identifiable. For this reason it is important that the document number be part of the transaction identification and be carried with the transaction throughout the processing cycle.

Use input forms with preprinted, copy identification and information numbers. Each copy of the input form should have a preprinted copy identification number along one side of each copy of the form. This is as important for one-part input forms as it is for multiple-part forms. For one-part forms, the copy number is "Copy 1 of 1." For two-part forms, the copy number on the top copy, or original, is "Copy 1 of 2"; the copy number on the duplicate, or second, copy is "Copy 2 of 2." The use of these copy identification numbers makes it possible for the person authorized to approve input documents to verify that the proper form was used to record the input transaction.

The copy number should be supplemented with information identifying the routing of the copy. Copy 1 should be designated "Original." The remaining copies should indicate the departments or functional groups to which each copy is sent. One copy would be the user department file copy. This copy identification information makes it possible for the person authorized to approve input documents to ensure that he is approving only the original copy of the document. It makes it possible for the data conversion and entry personnel to verify that they are working with the original or appropriate copy of the form. This control will prevent various copies of the same form from being processed at different times.

Use batch controls and preprinted batch control forms. Arrange completed source documents in batches. Separate batches should be assigned for each of the following: adjustment transactions, correction transactions, changes to the master files, transactions affecting employees' accounts, transactions with dollar or quantity amounts that fall outside predetermined limits, and any other transactions or types of transactions designated as sensitive. Limit the number of documents in a batch. Batches should not be allowed to become so large that calculation and reconciliation of batch control totals becomes unmanageable and difficult, if not impossible.

The batch control forms should have preprinted sequential batch numbers. They should identify the type of transactions in the batch, the date, the processing required, the path the batch should take for all subsequent processing steps, and the retention period. The control totals are recorded on the batch control form. The preparer of the form and the people who computed the control totals should initial the sheet.

The batch control totals should include:
- Number of documents in the batch.
- Sum of the document numbers.
- Totals of the dollar fields.
- Totals of the quantity fields.
- Totals of other significant fields (e.g., account numbers, part numbers).

The totals should be computed by two people working independently to ensure that the totals are correct.

A batch control log should be maintained. The batches should be identified by batch number and date. The following information about the batch should be recorded: type of transactions, retention period, preparer, control totals.

Effective batch controlling procedures simplify the reconciliation of batches that are out of balance and make it possible to verify the integrity of the batch of source documents at each step in the handling and processing of the batch. The path the batch should take can be predicted and the path the batch actually took can be traced. If any documents are lost or altered subsequent to batching, their loss or alteration would be identifiable.

Maintain logs. Several logs have been identified. The purposes of these logs are to maintain control and accountability and to provide a record or trail of the movement of the input transactions. The logs that have been discussed are identified in Figure 5-3.

Require approval of all source documents. All source documents should be reviewed by designated individuals whose responsibility it is to review and approve input transactions. It is of utmost importance that all input transactions undergo review.

Batches of routine input transactions should be examined, document by document. The approver should make sure that the appropriate copy of the input form is in the batch. He must not allow any documents to be processed if the original copy is not provided. If reproduced versions of the original copy are accepted, you are running the risk of either processing the same transaction two or more times or processing an altered version of the original transaction. Each document should be scanned for entries that are suspicious, illogical, unreasonable, or that simply do not seem right. If any entries on the document have been crossed out and corrected, the approver should validate the corrected entry and indicate that he has approved that entry by writing his initials right next to the entry. The document should be scanned to verify that the transaction is in the appropriate batch. The batch control totals should also be validated. Approval is indicated by the authorized person's signature either on the source documents or on the batch control form or on both.

Log	Contents
Input forms control	Date Document numbers assigned to the preparer Preparer's name Preparer's acknowledgement of receipt of documents
Voided/missing forms	Date Document number Responsible preparer Problem (i.e., missing/voided) Preparer's acknowledgement
Batch control	Date Batch number Type of transactions in batch Retention period Preparer's name Control totals Date and time the batch was actually submitted for data conversion and entry Discrepancy between actual and scheduled submission times Date and time the batch was received from date conversion and entry

Figure 5-3

Source Document Preparation Logs

All sensitive and nonroutine transactions should be batched in separate batches, by type of transaction. These transactions should be reviewed and approved one document at a time. The approver must make sure that the document is in the proper batch and that the original copy of the form, not a reproduced version of it, is provided. The entries on these transactions should be examined carefully. The approver should validate corrected entries and should initial them in such a way as to indicate the specific entry that he is approving. If that entry is subsequently changed, there must be no way to associate his initials with that alteration. The approver should sign each document to indicate his approval. After verifying the information and control totals on the batch control form, he should approve the batch by signing the batch control form.

Comply with established schedules. The user departments should be provided with schedules identifying the day or date and time that batches of input transactions are to be submitted for data conversion and entry and for processing. A supervisor in each department must ensure that the agreed-upon schedules are met. If the schedule is not met, he should ascertain the reasons for the delay and determine the appropriate corrective action to be taken.

The batch control log should be updated to reflect the time and date that the batch was approved and was submitted for data conversion and entry. Any discrepancies with the schedule, and the reasons for the discrepancies, should be noted.

Keep copies of all source documents. One copy of each source document and batch control form should be kept in the user department at all times. The purposes of this control are to:

- Make it possible to recreate the information if any documents are lost, destroyed, or manipulated once they leave the department.
- Make it possible to locate specific documents.

These copies of the source documents should be filed by batch.

The original source documents, after having been processed, should be filed sequentially by document number. This procedure will make it possible to locate specific documents quickly in the event that a question or problem arises. The voided forms are sorted into this file. It must be possible to account for all documents.

Retention periods for these documents should be clearly defined. The length of time the documents are retained is determined by considering appropriate legal requirements, company policy, and effective operating requirements. Depending on effective operating requirements, it may be necessary to store all the original source documents in the user department for the entire retention period. Alternatively, the documents may be moved to a secure, long-term storage location. Access to all source document files should be strictly controlled. Special procedures should be defined for the handling and storage of sensitive documents.

When the retention period has expired, the source documents are destroyed. The methods and procedures used to destroy the documents should be predetermined based upon their sensitivity. Special procedures are required for the destruction of sensitive documents to ensure that their contents are not compromised. The methods of destroying source documents include:

- Discarding.
- Shredding.
- Burning.
- Disposal using chemicals.

Data conversion and entry includes those processes and functions that are involved in the conversion of input transaction information into machine-readable format and in the transmittal of the machine-readable information to the data processing department. As mentioned above, input transaction information, once captured, may be recorded on a human-readable document or in machine-readable form. Our attention here is focused on the controls applicable to the conversion of the information into machine-readable form, regardless of whether or not it has been previously recorded on a human-readable document.

The controls associated with data conversion and entry should be designed to:

- Ensure that only complete, accurate, and approved input transaction information is converted into machine-readable form.
- Ensure that the conversion of the information is performed completely and accurately.
- Ensure that the input transaction information that is eventually processed by the computer is the complete, accurate, and approved information, and *only* the complete, accurate, and approved information, prepared and reviewed by the user department.

The conversion of input transaction information into machine-readable form should be performed as close as possible to the user department or to the area where the data are captured. If at all possible, it should be performed in the user department or at the source of origination. This will minimize the handling of the information, which in turn will reduce the chances of having transactions lost, duplicated, or altered.

The devices that may be employed to convert the information are:

- Keypunch.
- Key-to-tape or tape cassette.
- Key-to-disk or diskette.
- On-line entry, data-entry terminals.
- Optical character recognition.
- Magnetic-ink character recognition.

The advantages and disadvantages of the various devices will not be discussed. It is important to keep in mind, however, that regardless of the device used, the conversion process, similar to transaction information capture and recording, is primarily a human process. Therefore, it is very susceptible to human error, both accidental or unintentional, and intentional.

Input document conversion and entry controls. The recommended controls for the conversion and entry of source document information are essentially:

- Logging.
- Batch verification and balancing.
- Verification.

They are identified in Figure 5-4.

Upon receipt of a batch of input documents, the supervisor of the data conversion and entry function records its receipt in a data conversion/entry log (see Figure 5-5). The date and time the batch was received, the batch number, and the control totals on the batch control form are entered into the log.

The supervisor should have a schedule indicating when input documents are to be submitted for data conversion and entry by specific user departments. If the documents do not arrive as scheduled, the deviation is noted in the log. Any significant or repeated discrepancies should be brought to management's attention.

Once the batch has been logged into the data conversion/entry log, user department personnel must not be permitted to change any of the documents or any of the entries on the documents and on the batch control forms. In fact, no changes of any type must be permitted. Any changes made at this point in the processing of the documents are unauthorized and represent a serious breach of control. If changes must be made, they should be made according to controlled error correction procedures.

The batches are then reviewed. The number of documents in the batch are counted and the control totals are computed. If any discrepancies are detected in the control totals, the discrepancy is noted

---

- Maintain logs of batches received for data conversion/entry

- Maintain a schedule of when batches of input documents are due, and note when the batches are actually received

- Verify batch control totals

- Review the batch control forms and source documents for legibility and approval signatures; make sure the proper copy of the document has been submitted

- Verify, if possible, the results of key entry

- Mark processed documents "Entered"

Figure 5-4

Data Conversion/Entry Controls

Log	Contents
Data conversion/entry	Date Time the batch was received Batch number Control totals On schedule/deviation from schedule Problems (i.e., lack of approval signatures, batch balancing discrepancies, etc.) and action taken Key entry operator assigned Date and time key entry and verification were completed Date and time batch was returned to user department

Figure 5-5

Data Conversion/Entry Log

in the data conversion/entry log. The batch control sheet is reviewed for legibility and for appropriate approval.

The individual documents are scanned. The entries on the documents must be legible. Wherever entries were changed, the approver's initials should appear next to the corrected entry. The proper, original copy of the document should have been provided. Photocopied versions of the document should not be accepted. The proper approval signature should be present on all nonroutine and sensitive documents.

If any signatures are missing or suspect, if a photocopied version or incorrect copy of the form has been submitted, if any changes to entries have not been approved, or if any other problems are detected during the review of the documents and batch control form, the problems should be noted in the log along with any discrepancies in the batch control totals. A designated manager in the user department should be contacted immediately. The manager should investigate and resolve the problem before processing of the batch is allowed to continue. If the batch appears to be correct and approved, a key-entry operator is assigned to key the information. The name of the operator assigned is noted in the log.

If at all possible, the data entered by the key-entry operator should be verified in some manner. The purpose of the verification is to identify and correct any errors introduced during the keying of the information. Key verification, a process that requires a second operator to re-key the information from the source documents, may be in order. All the information or only fields containing critical information may be verified. There are problems associated with key

verification.   There is a cost involved in performing the keying twice
in terms of time and the number of operators needed.   A significant
problem may be introduced if the verification device automatically
replaces the information keyed originally with the information keyed
during verification whenever a discrepancy occurs.   Rather than being strengthened, in this situation control may be compromised, since
data may be altered or manipulated in an unauthorized manner during
the verification process.

Some key-entry devices are programmable or are connected to
minicomputers.   These devices may be able to provide batch balancing and data editing facilities as part of the data-entry process.   If
these devices are used, they should also be programmed to guide or
prompt the operator in keying the information.

Sight verification of the results of key entry may be adequate for
control purposes.   Regardless of which method of verification is
chosen, it is important that the keying and verification processes be
performed in accordance with predetermined, clearly established, and
uniformly enforced procedures.

The batches of source documents, after key entry, should be
marked "entered."   The data conversion/entry log should be updated to indicate that the batch has been entered and, if applicable,
verified.   The batches are returned to the user department.   The output of the key-entry process, if not an on-line file, is clearly labeled
and submitted to the data processing function with a transmittal
form.

Controls for data recorded directly in machine-readable format.
When data are captured and immediately recorded in machine-readable format, the intermediate step of source document preparation is
eliminated.   It may even be possible to eliminate human intervention
in the capturing and recording of the input transaction information.
Thus, the controls discussed above cannot be applied.

Input transaction information may be entered directly into a data-
entry terminal and recorded onto machine-readable media, such as
punched cards, punched paper tape, magnetic tape or tape cassettes,
or disks or diskettes.   The data-entry terminals may operate off-line,
simply recording the information and performing the most rudimen-
tary editing (e.g., validating user identification and passwords); or
they may operate on-line, performing data validation and editing.

Regardless of the type of data-entry device and the environment
in which it is operated, the only controls that exist with respect to
input preparation and entry are those that relate to access to the data-
entry device and to system controls relative to that device.   These
controls are discussed in detail in Chapter 8.   The only other input
control, if it can indeed be characterized as such, is the fact that the
source or origination of the transaction may be identifiable.   Subse-

quent manual and computerized processing of these transactions should be designed with greater controls to compensate for the lack of input control.

Exception item handling
Regardless of how carefully and well a system is designed, exceptional situations and unanticipated problems are bound to arise. If the system is to be effective and functional, these situations and problems must be handled in a timely manner. The critical concept that must always be kept in mind is that, regardless of the situation or problem, control should never be sacrificed.

If a system or application has not been designed to handle a particular transaction, the system or application must be corrected. It should, however, be corrected in accordance with existing program change procedures and controls. Exception-type transactions should be handled according to existing error correction and input preparation, approval, logging, and batching procedures and controls. They should be considered to be sensitive and, therefore, be batched separately and approved individually.

> Exceptions are the bane of control. Special transactions, unusual handlings, and irregular treatment are all dangerous and are frequently the avenues used by the embezzler. Continuous effort must be made to insist that each and every transaction, with no exceptions, go through controlled procedures.[3]

PROCESSING CONTROLS
Processing controls are those controls performed by the computer. The processing controls of concern here are those that:

- Verify that all the input transaction information that is expected has, in fact, been submitted for processing.
- Scan the data, checking for reasonableness.
- Make sure that the correct files are being accessed and updated.
- Check that the processing of information has been performed completely.
- Produce the appropriate and necessary reports and journals so that the user departments can review the processing and determine if it was performed properly, completely, and accurately and determine what, if any, errors or problems were encountered.

The essence of these controls is the validation of the input transactions and files, the validation of the processing of the information,

---

[3] Brandt Allen, "Computer Fraud," *Financial Executive*, May 1971, p. 42.

93

and the production of the necessary reports and listings. The controls will be discussed in the following subsections:

- Batch balancing.
- Data editing.
- Data validation.
- Reports and listings.

The batch balancing and data editing controls may be performed by the data-entry terminal, by a special editing routine that is executed before the application program, or by the application program itself. It is desirable to review the accuracy, completeness, and reasonableness of the input as early as possible, preferably before it is processed by the application program. The purpose is to prevent the application program from updating any files with incorrect information.

Batch balancing

Batch balancing is performed by the system to verify the integrity of the input information. The number of transactions in the batch are counted and the control totals are computed. The computed totals are compared with the control totals in the batch-control-form transaction. If there are any discrepancies, the entire batch should be written to an error suspense file. A listing of the batch-control-form transaction, and all transactions in the batch should be produced. The computer-computed totals should appear on the listing and the discrepancy highlighted. No subsequent processing of the batch is performed until the problem has been corrected. The discrepancy should be investigated by the user department and correcting transactions prepared, approved, and entered into the system.

Data editing

Input transaction information may be edited at several levels. Individual characters and fields in each input transaction may be checked. Individual input transactions may be tested. The batch of input transactions may be reviewed as a set of related transactions. The types of edits that may be performed are shown in Figure 5-6.

The entire batch of transactions should be edited. Editing must not stop as soon as the first error or problem is detected. If the edits do detect unacceptable or erroneous data in a transaction or among transactions, the transactions should not undergo additional processing. The entire transaction, the batch number, and processing date must be recorded in an error suspense file, where it will remain until the error or problem is corrected. The remainder of the batch may be processed. The batch control totals will have to be adjusted, how-

- Character and field edits

    1. Validity checks

        Tests for valid characters or types of characters (i.e., alphabetic, numeric, blank, special character, positive or negative sign)

        Tests for valid codes or values

        Tests for valid field sizes

        Tests for valid numeric signs

    2. Numeric quantity checks

        Reasonableness tests (Is the value normal or reasonable?)

        Range tests (Does the value fall within a given range of values?)

        Limit tests (Does the value fall outside of certain limits?)

        Specific value tests (Is the value a member of a set of specific values?)

        Absence tests (Is the value missing?)

    3. Field-specific checks

        Special tests unique to a given field, such as date tests and self-checking digit tests

- Transaction and batches of transactions edits

    1. Tests for completeness (Do all required fields have entries?)

    2. Tests for internal consistency (Are the fields within the transaction consistent with one another? If field A has an entry, does field B also have an entry?)

    3. Tests for external consistency (Are logical or expected combinations of transactions present in the batch?)

    4. Sequence tests (Are fields within the transaction or transactions in the batch properly sequenced?)

Figure 5-6

Data Edits

ever. Because the batch control totals must be made to balance at the end of the run, the totals for the rejected transactions must be available or able to be calculated.

One very important control with respect to data editing is that overriding of specific values or automatic correction of fields in error should never be permitted. Overriding of values and automatic correction bypass proper control procedures and can be used by a dishonest employee to perpetrate fraud.

An edit error report is produced as a result of the data editing. It lists all transactions that were written to the error suspense file with their batch number and the processing date.

Data validation Data validation is performed by the application program to ensure that processing is performed with the correct files and that processing is performed completely and properly. It involves the verification of file header label (record) information and file trailer label (record) information. The file name, file identification number, and creation date should be verified. If there is any discrepancy in this information, the run should be aborted. The batch of input transactions should be written to an error suspense file, and a report identifying the discrepancy should be produced.

If the file identification is proper, the processing of the input transactions is performed. Transactions that cannot be processed, because they cannot be matched with corresponding records in the file or because of some other problem, should be written to a suspense file for that particular application program. The application program should be programmed to produce reports identifying unposted transactions. When processing has been completed, the record counts and control totals for the files are verified. The expected effect of the processing on the record counts and control totals is compared with the recomputed record counts and control totals for the file. If a discrepancy is detected, the contents of the file should be listed and the discrepancy identified. A flag should be set in the file header or trailer record, indicating that the file may be in error.

In addition to verifying that the proper file is processed and that the processing appears to be complete, the integrity of the batch of input transactions should be verified; the batch control totals should be balanced after each processing step.

Reports and listings Several reports and listings have already been identified. They are produced as a result of errors having been detected during processing. Several other reports and listings should also be produced. The reports and listings are summarized in Figure 5-7.

These reports are used primarily by the user departments. Their purposes are:

- To provide an audit trail of all transactions submitted for processing.
- To identify transactions that were successfully processed.
- To highlight transactions of a sensitive or special nature that were successfully processed.
- To identify transactions or batches of transactions that were rejected and, therefore, not processed.

Figure 5-7 (*Opposite page*)

Routine Processing Reports

96

Report	Contents
Audit trail	Listing of all transactions submitted for processing and control totals (with indication as to whether individual transactions were accepted and processed or rejected) and all internally generated transactions (with indication of source of transaction)
Accepted transactions	Listing of all transactions that were processed, and control totals
Rejected transactions (edit error report)	Listing of transactions rejected during data editing (including batch number) and control totals, with identification of errors
Rejected batches	Listing of all transactions in a batch (including batch number) and control totals, for batches that failed batch balancing, with identification of discrepancies
Master file changes	Listing of all transactions that caused changes to the master files, and control totals
Adjustment and correction transactions	Listing of all adjustment and correction transactions that were processed, and control totals
Transactions affecting employees' accounts	Listing of all transactions that affected the accounts of employees, and control totals
Sensitive transactions	Listing of all transactions designated as sensitive that were processed, and control totals
Unprocessed transactions	Listing of all transactions (with batch number) that were not processed because file identification information could not be verified, and control totals, with identification of the problem
Unposted transactions	Listing of all transactions that were written to application suspense files
File in error	Listing of all records in a file where the control totals were not in balance after processing, and the expected and actual control totals

- Master file change transactions processed during the period

- Adjustment and correction transactions processed during the period

- Transactions affecting employees' accounts that were processed during the period

- Sensitive transactions processed during the period

- Transactions on the error and application suspense files at the end of the period, broken down by user department, identifying the errors associated with each transaction and the date the error was detected

- Suspense file analysis, including listings of the transactions on all the suspense files aged by date of original error, broken down by user department, identifying the errors associated with each transaction

- Suspense file analysis, including listings of the transactions on all the suspense files aged by date of original error, broken down by user department, identifying the error associated with each transaction

- Internally generated transactions processed during the period

Figure 5-8

Reports Produced on a Regular Basis

- To identify transactions that could not be processed (unposted transactions).
- To identify files that may be in error.

User departments as well as management may also require summary reports that are produced on a regular basis, such as weekly or monthly. These reports are essentially consolidations and summaries of the transactions processed during the period. Their purposes are to highlight those transactions of a special or sensitive nature that were processed during the period and to highlight both recurring and uncorrected errors. The reports are identified in Figure 5-8.

On a periodic basis, the entire contents of specific master files should be printed. This listing should be thoroughly reviewed and validated by the user department and management to ensure the file's accuracy and integrity.

The reports identified in Figures 5-7 and 5-8 are in no way meant to represent the only reports produced. These lists identify those reports that must be produced and reviewed to maintain good, effective administrative and internal control. Even then, the lists are illustrative of the types of reports required; they are not exhaustive. The role these reports play with regard to administrative and internal control is discussed in the next two sections of this chapter.

The purposes of output controls are to verify the accuracy and integrity of the information processed as well as to ensure that output is distributed to the appropriate authorized personnel only. Output controls must provide the means to verify that the transactions entered into the system were processed completely and properly, that only approved transactions were processed, and that only proper output is produced. These controls are designed to detect fraud committed during the earlier stages of input preparation and processing. However, output itself is susceptible to fraud. It, too, can be readily manipulated. Controls should be designed to detect output manipulation as well.

Output may assume many forms. The output reports and listings relating to administrative and internal controls were identified above. Other reports are used by management and user departments as a source of information and as the basis for preparing transactions, such as accounting entries. Still other output is used to transfer assets of the company (e.g., checks, savings bonds) or to effect future transactions (e.g., invoices).

Output controls will be addressed in the following subsections:

- Output distribution.
- Output reconciliation.
- Output retention.

The controls are summarized in Figure 5-9. The logs to be maintained are summarized in Figure 5-10.

Output
distribution

Output distribution controls must be designed to:

- Ensure that only authorized personnel receive the output.
- Ensure that the output received by authorized personnel is the proper output, is complete, and is received on time.
- Ensure that only the prespecified number of copies of the output is produced.

Output distribution controls are important for several reasons. Improper or untimely distribution could result in the misappropriation of negotiable documents and the compromise of confidential information. Important management decisions might be made without the proper information. In addition, inadequate distribution controls could prevent the detection and resolution of both intentional, and unintentional, errors.

Use forms with preprinted copy identification numbers. All output forms should have preprinted copy numbers in one corner or along one side of each copy and page of the form. This is as im-

- Use output forms with preprinted copy identification numbers on each copy and page

- Use output forms with preprinted, sequential numbers on each page or document

- Print sequential page or form numbers on all output

- Provide output distribution instructions to the data processing department, and keep them current

- Provide an output distribution schedule to user department personnel authorized to receive output

- Reconcile computer-generated control totals with input control totals

- Compare the audit trail with the original source documents

- Verify, review, and approve transactions appearing in the audit trail for which no original source documents are prepared, e.g. certain transactions from on-line terminals

- Compare all sensitive and special transaction listings with the original source documents on a transaction-by-transaction and document-by-document basis

- Review and validate all internally-generated transactions on a transaction-by-transaction basis

- Verify the output documents produced:
  - Validate the actual number of documents produced with the computer-generated number
  - Verify the control totals
  - Validate the number of copies produced
  - Verify that all documents have proper, unique document numbers and that no documents are missing
  - Review the documents for reasonableness and verify important calculations
  - Investigate unreasonable documents and documents whose amounts fall outside of predetermined limits

- Review the output reports for usefulness

- Retain the output documents in accordance with established document retention procedures

- Dispose of expired documents in a timely and appropriate manner

- Maintain logs of output document numbers, voided or missing documents, and requests for additional copies of output reports

Figure 5-9

Output Controls

Log	Content

Additional copies of output	Date
	Request form number
	Reason for the request
	Identification of output and
	    processing date
	Number of additional copies
	    requested
	Approval

Output document control	Date of processing
	Form number description
	Preprinted number of first and
	    last document printed
	Number of documents printed
	Control totals
	Document numbers of all
	    missing documents and
	    action taken
	Date received

Output delivery	Scheduled day or date and
	    time of delivery
	Identification of output
	Actual day, date, and time of
	    delivery

Output reconciliation	Date of processing
	Identification of output
	Batch number
	Computer generated batch
	    control totals
	Input batch control totals
	Reason for discrepancies, if
	    applicable, and action
	    taken

Voided/missing output documents	Date of processing Document number Problem (missing/voided) Action taken
File verification	Date File identification File control totals Problems detected during review and action taken Reviewer's name

Figure 5-10

Output Control Logs

portant for one-part forms as it is for multiple-part forms. The copy number for one-part forms is "Copy 1 of 1." For two-part forms, the copy number on the top copy, or original, is "Copy 1 of 2"; the copy number on the duplicate or second copy is "Copy 2 of 2."

By using forms with preprinted copy numbers such as these, those authorized to receive and reconcile the output can easily detect if the wrong number of copies were produced because the wrong multiple-part paper was used. Thus, this control provides one means of ensuring that the proper number of copies of the output were produced. As important as it is, especially for sensitive and negotiable documents and reports, it is not sufficient in and of itself, since it will not detect situations where the same output is printed twice.

Computer operations should be held accountable for producing output using proper multiple-part forms. If the wrong number of copies are printed, the operations supervisor should account for the distribution of any additional copies that may have been produced, as well as the authorized set of copies. In order to exercise this accountability, the operator's run instructions for the particular program must clearly specify the multiple-part form on which the output is produced. Requests for additional copies of a given output should be made in accordance with formal request procedures. The request should be prepared in writing; it must be authorized and approved. It should also be noted in the logs maintained by the department making the request and in the logs maintained by the data processing department.

Management should be alerted immediately whenever the wrong number of copies of sensitive documents or reports are produced.

User forms with preprinted sequential numbers. All particularly sensitive output documents (e.g., negotiable instruments, checks and saving bonds, orders, and invoices) should be printed on forms containing preprinted sequential numbers. As with input forms, the preprinted sequential number on the output forms provides a means of accounting for all the forms. This is especially important with respect to output forms because some output, such as checks, are used to effect a transfer of the company's assets, and other output, such as invoices, are used to trigger actions and transactions that affect the company's assets.

Extremely tight control must be exercised over all forms of such a sensitive nature. Logs showing the use of these forms should be maintained in the operations area, forms control area, and user department. User department logs should identify the date of processing, the form number or description, the preprinted numbers of the first and last form printed, the number of forms printed, and the control totals. If any forms are missing or if there is any gap between the first form number of this processing run and the last form number of the previous processing run, the numbers of the missing forms should be noted and investigative action taken immediately. Management should be alerted.

Print sequential page or form numbers on all output. Computer-generated sequential numbers should be printed on all pages of output produced. The purpose of this control is to ensure that no pages of the output are lost. For particularly sensitive or negotiable output documents, this control augments the control provided by the use of preprinted sequential numbers. The difference between the first and last preprinted sequential numbers must equal the difference between the first and last computer-generated numbers. The computer-generated numbers should be scanned to make sure that no numbers are missing or duplicated.

Provide output distribution instructions to the data processing department. The data processing department should be supplied with output distribution instructions for each program or system. These instructions identify each output report, document, or form; the output form number and description on which the output is to be printed; the number of copies of the output that should be produced; and the person authorized to receive each copy. The output distribution function must make sure that each copy of the output is delivered to the authorized person only. The authorized person should be required to acknowledge receipt of the output in writing.

It is very important that the instructions be kept current. New instructions must be issued whenever the number of copies of output is changed and whenever the person authorized to receive the output is changed. A special form with preprinted sequential document numbers should be used for the output distribution instructions. The form must be reviewed and approved by appropriate personnel in the user department. A copy of the form must be retained by the user department.

Provide an output distribution schedule to all personnel authorized to receive output. All personnel authorized to receive output should be provided with a schedule indicating when (day or date and time) output should be delivered. If the output is not received in a timely manner, user department management should be notified. Authorized personnel should maintain logs identifying the output and when it is scheduled to be delivered. They should note the day or date and time when it is actually delivered. Consistent discrepancies between actual and scheduled delivery should be brought to management's attention.

The purposes of output reconciliation are:

- To verify that the integrity of the input transactions was not compromised or lost during processing.
- To verify that processing was performed completely and accurately.
- To verify the accuracy of the output produced.

Output reconciliation should be performed as soon as the output is received in order to ensure the timely detection and correction of errors.

Reconcile control totals. Computer-generated control totals should be compared with the control totals computed during input preparation. If any discrepancy between the control totals is detected, the reason for the discrepancy should be determined, corrective action taken, and the reason for the discrepancy noted.

Verify the audit trail. The audit trail produced by the system should be compared with the original source documents to ensure the integrity of the source document information. If the computer-generated control totals and input control totals are in balance, sampling may be used in place of verifying each transaction individually. It is important, however, that the verification be performed both from the audit trail to the original source document and from the source document to the audit trail.

If the computer-generated control totals and input control totals are not in balance, it may be necessary to compare all the transactions in the audit trail with the original source documents. Make sure that all the audit trail transactions and all the original source documents are involved in the comparisons.

The verification of the audit trail is critical for those applications or systems where input is captured and recorded directly into machine-readable format and no original source document is prepared. The audit trail is the first human-readable version of the input transaction to be produced. It should be reviewed transaction by transaction. The person responsible for these transactions should approve each transaction, verify the control totals, and sign the document. Adjusting and correcting entries for these transactions should be prepared, reviewed, approved, and submitted for processing in a very timely manner.

Verify all sensitive and special transactions. The listings of master-file changes, adjustment and correction transactions affecting employees' accounts, and sensitive transactions should be compared with the original source documents on a transaction-by-transaction basis.

Again, it is important to make sure that all the transactions identified in the listings and all the original source documents are involved in the comparisons.

Validate all internally generated transactions. Review and validate the internally generated transactions on a transaction-by-transaction basis. Invalid or improper internally generated transactions are a sign that the program or system may not be functioning properly. Therefore, the occurrence of such improper transactions requires investigation. Corrective action may involve program modification procedures.

Verify the output documents produced. The actual number of documents produced should be compared with the computer-generated number of documents produced and the control totals for the output documents should be verified. Make sure that the proper number of copies of the output documents were produced. The preprinted and computer-printed sequential numbers on the output documents should also be verified to ensure that no documents are missing and that no documents have duplicate or improper numbers. Review the documents for reasonableness and verify important calculations. Documents that appear to be unreasonable or whose dollar or quantity amounts are outside predetermined limits should be investigated. If the documents are found to be in error, the error must be corrected, the document voided, and the cause of the error determined. Action should be taken to correct and remove the cause of the error. A log of voided documents should be maintained.

Validate file listings. Whenever listings of files are produced, the contents of the file should be carefully reviewed, record by record. It is important to verify that the records are valid (i.e., that they represent valid accounts, inventory items, vendors, etc.) and that the fields within the records appear reasonable.

Review the reports produced. The reports produced by a given program or system should be reviewed for usefulness on a periodic basis. Consideration should be given to eliminating those reports that are not needed and are not used. The information on the report and the format of the report should be studied to determine if additional or different information is needed and if the information should be presented differently.

Maintain logs. The logs that should be maintained are identified in Figure 5-10. The purposes of these logs are to provide forms control and to maintain output controls.

Retention periods for the previous output reports, listings, and copies of output documents should be clearly defined and documented. As with input document retention, the length of time output is retained must be determined by considering appropriate legal requirements, company policy, and effective operating requirements. Secure retention facilities will have to be provided for all output of a sensitive or confidential nature. Access to this output must be strictly controlled.

When the retention period has expired, all copies of the output should be destroyed. The methods and procedures used to destroy the documents are predetermined based upon their sensitivity and confidentiality. Special procedures are required for the disposal of sensitive documents to ensure that their contents are not compromised and that all copies of the output are destroyed appropriately. The methods of disposing of output documents include:

- Discarding.
- Shredding.
- Burning.
- Disposal using chemicals.

ADJUSTMENT AND ERROR CORRECTION CONTROLS Error correction and adjustment transactions are input transactions that correct previously rejected transactions or batches of transactions and that correct information in the data and master files. Thus, they are prepared because an error was detected during processing, during output reconciliation, or during routine work performance. The problem already exists. It must now be corrected as quickly, accurately, and properly as possible.

Because error correction and adjustment transactions are initiated in reaction to an existing problem situation, they are often not subjected to appropriate and adequate control procedures. They, therefore, provide an opportunity for the dishonest employee to perpetrate fraud by preparing and submitting improper or fictitious transactions. In the absence of adequate controls, such fraudulent transactions may never be detected.

Error correction and adjustment transactions should be handled in accordance with the input controls discussed earlier in this chapter. In fact, they must undergo especially stringent controls. The controls should be designed to:

- Ensure that all transactions and batches rejected during processing are corrected and resubmitted for processing in a timely manner.
- Ensure that all errors detected during output reconciliation are corrected and resubmitted for processing in a timely manner.

- Ensure that the correction transactions are proper, accurate, and complete.

In addition, the controls should make it possible to review and analyze the errors in order to identify and eliminate the causes of the errors.

The controls are addressed in the following subsections:

- Error detection.
- Error correction and resubmission.
- Error analysis.

Error detection

The most critical elements in the detection of errors are the processing reports produced. These reports are identified in Figures 5-7 and 5-8. The reports identify errors or problems detected by the system. They also make it possible for employees, supervisory, and managerial personnel responsible for output reconciliation and review to identify errors or problems that were not detected by the system during processing.

Because error detection is so dependent on output, it is extremely important that output distribution controls be strictly adhered to.

Error correction and resubmission

Once the errors or problems have been identified through the thorough review of output reports, the appropriate corrective action must be determined and performed. Adjustments and correction transactions should be subjected to the controls established for all input transactions. Those controls were discussed above in the "Input Controls" section and are not reiterated here. What is discussed are those controls that relate solely to adjustments and error correction transactions.

Logging of all errors. Information relating to rejected transactions and batches should be recorded in an error control log. The original source document or batch is identified by document or batch number and preparation date. The date of processing when the transaction or batch was rejected is also identified. A description of the error is noted.

An adjustment control log should also be maintained of all errors or problems identified during output reconciliation and review. Whenever possible the original source document that was in error or that caused the problem should be identified by number and preparation date. The date of the processing run that produced the output report that made it possible to identify the problem is noted and the error or problem is described.

When the adjustment or correction transaction has been prepared,

Log	Contents
Error control	Original source document or batch number of rejected transaction or batch and preparation date
	Date of processing
	Description of the error
	Error correction source document number
	Preparation date of error correction transaction
	Correction processing date
Adjustment control	Original source document number and preparation date, if identifiable and if applicable
	Date of processing run that produced the report that made it possible to detect the problem
	Description of the error
	Source document number of the adjustment transaction
	Preparation date of adjustment transaction
	Adjustment processing date

Figure 5-11

Adjustment and Error Correction Logs

its number and the preparation date should be recorded in the appropriate log next to the entry identifying the corresponding error.

The purposes of these logs are to provide a record of the errors and problems and to monitor the submission of adjustments and correcting entries. The logs are summarized in Figure 5-11.

Monitoring of error correction. The correction of errors and problems should be monitored by designated supervisory personnel to ensure that all errors and problems are corrected in a timely manner. The information required to perform this control is available in several places:

- Error control log.
- Adjustment control log.
- Rejected transaction report.
- Rejected batches report.
- Unposted transactions report.
- Adjustment and correction transactions report.
- Suspense file reports.

The error control log identifies all transactions and batches rejected during processing. It should be reconciled with the reports of rejected and unposted transactions and rejected batches to make sure that entries exist in the log for all entries identified in the reports.

The adjustment and correction transactions report should be reconciled with the error and adjustment control logs to ensure that the adjustment and correction transactions were actually processed. The date of the processing run should be entered into the logs next to the entry identifying the error. If there are any transactions identified in the report that cannot be matched with corresponding entries in the logs, those transactions must be identified and investigated. The reason for the discrepancies must be established. The source documents for those transactions must be reviewed for proper preparation and approval in order to verify that all controls were adhered to at all times.

The error and adjustment control logs should be scanned to identify those entries for which no corrective action has been taken. The reasons for the delay in their correction should be determined and the problems causing the delay resolved. The suspense file reports, particularly the aged suspense file transaction report will also help to identify unresolved errors that were detected during processing. Every effort must be made to correct all unresolved errors and problems in a timely manner.

Error analysis

Errors and problems should be corrected as soon as possible. However, errors cannot be forgotten once they have been corrected because they may be an indication that problems exist within the organization. The types of problems that may be manifested by errors and the need for adjustments and error correction include:

- Inadequate adherence to and enforcement of control procedures.
- Inadequate control procedures.
- Improper or unauthorized preparation and submission of input transactions.
- Inadequate training of personnel.

Errors should be analyzed in terms of their sources, nature, frequency, and timing. The analysis should be designed to identify the problems that are causing the errors. Once the problems have been identified, action should be taken to correct the problems and to prevent the errors from recurring. Perhaps the controls are not enforced. A renewed effort to enforce the controls may be necessary. The problem could be that the controls are not adequate or not appropriate. A redefinition of the controls may be in order. Employees may not understand the controls, or they may not be adequately trained or competent to perform their jobs. In this case, additional training is called for. The problem could also be that employees are attempting to perpetrate fraud, and their fraudulent transactions are creating errors or the need for adjustments. *In any investigative effort you should, of course, always be alert that this is a distinct possibility.*

MANAGEMENT REPORTING

In addition to the routine operations reports and special reports requested by management, reports of an internal control nature should also be provided to management. These reports highlight sensitive and nonroutine transactions and identify problem areas. The primary purpose of these reports is to alert management to the possibility that fraud is being perpetrated.

The management reports that are produced as a result of computer processing were identified in Figure 5-8. Additional reports that should be produced by the user departments on a regular basis include, but are not limited to:

- Analysis of missed schedules in the following areas:
  —Source document preparation.
  —Data conversion and entry.
  —Output delivery.
- Voided and missing input documents.
- Voided and missing output documents.
- Requests for additional copies of output.
- Improper output production (e.g., wrong multiple-part forms).
- File verification results.
- Error analysis reports (errors and adjustments).
- Batches rejected by data conversion and entry, and the reasons for their rejection.
- Customer complaint analysis reports.

DOCUMENTATION

In order to enforce administrative and internal controls, employees must be aware of the controls and of the procedures they are expected to follow. The documentation that must be prepared, maintained, and provided to all employees involved with the handling of data is identified in Figure 5-12. This documentation should explicitly describe the controls relating to the various procedures.

Figure 5-12 (*Opposite page*)

Documentation Relating to Administrative and Internal Controls

110

Input Source Document Procedures

- Identification of authorized types of transactions
- Forms control procedures
- Source document preparation instructions, including identification and explanation of valid codes
- Batching instructions, including identification of batch control totals
- Source document approval procedures
- Identification of the flow of each copy of the source document
- Logging procedures and the review procedures for the logs
- Schedules for source document preparation and submission
- Source document filing procedures
- Source document retention procedures
- Procedures for handling sensitive and nonroutine transactions

Data Conversion/Entry Procedures

- Logging procedures and the review procedures for the logs
- Procedures for reviewing documents for acceptability
- Procedures to be followed in the event that input documents are determined to be unacceptable
- Key entry instructions
- Verification instructions
- Schedules for receipt of source documents and for submission to data processing
- Data processing transmittal form preparation instructions
- Procedures for receiving batches of input documents from the user departments and for returning keyed batches to the user departments

Output Distribution Procedures

- Specification of the multiple-part forms on which output for each each application is to be printed (in operator's run instructions)
- Procedures for requesting additional copies of output reports
- Output distribution instructions (for data processing department)
- Output distribution schedules

Output Reconciliation Procedures

- Logging procedures and the review procedures for the logs
- Procedures for reconciling output
- Procedures for reviewing output reports and documents
- Procedures for requesting adjustment transactions
- Output forms control procedures
- Output document filing procedures
- Output document retention procedures
- File verification procedures

Adjustment and Error Correction Procedures

- Logging procedures and the review procedures for the logs
- Adjustment and error correction procedures
- Adjustment and error correction monitoring procedures
- Error analysis procedures

Management Reporting

- Identification of reports required and due dates

Customer complaints play a very important role in the detection of fraud as well as in the detection of problematic situations in which fraud could prosper. Complaints, particularly those relating to errors in accounts or monthly statements, or failure to receive goods, are an indication that control problems exist. In essence, customer complaints are a means of error detection. They are a control mechanism external to the system. They indicate that errors are being processed through the system that are not being caught by any of the internal controls.

The source of the problem could be:

- Inadequate employee training.
- Inadequate internal controls.
- Unenforced internal controls or a loss of control.
- Misapplied controls.
- Improper recording of transaction information onto source documents or onto machine-readable media.

The problem is manifesting itself in the existence of erroneous transactions that may be inadvertently and unintentionally prepared and processed, or that may be intentionally and fraudulently prepared and processed.

Customer complaints should be handled in accordance with the adjustment and error correction and analysis controls discussed above. The error in the customer's account already exists. Thus, an adjustment transaction is required to correct it. The person authorized to initiate this adjustment transaction should not be authorized to initiate other types of input transactions. Once initiated, in accordance with input controls, this transaction should be subjected to all the controls, special handling procedures, and monitoring that apply to all adjustment transactions.

All customer complaints should be recorded in a customer complaint log. The following information should be recorded for each complaint:

- Date.
- Customer's name, address, and telephone number.
- Customer's account number.
- Description of the complaint.
- Name of the person recording the complaint.
- Action taken.
- Source document number of the adjustment transaction.
- Preparation date of adjustment transaction.
- Preparer's name.
- Adjustment processing date.

The log should be reviewed on a regular basis and an analysis the complaints, similar to the error analysis described above performed.

Programmed decisions are decisions that particular systems and applications programs are programmed to make in specific situations when an explicitly defined set of conditions exists. The system essentially makes the decision and takes the appropriate action without requiring preparation and submission of input transactions. The types of programmed decisions that are often incorporated into systems include:

- Loss allowances, including bad-debt allowances, inventory scrapping, differences between book and physical inventory, spoilage, breakage, off-grade inventory items, defective inventory items.
- Account write-offs.
- Floor limits on credit transactions.

Our specific concern here is the relationship between programmed decisions and fraud.

Loss allowances and account write-offs are accounting procedures that reflect a recognition that losses are unavoidable. The need, with respect to such procedures, is to control the amount of losses without overburdening management by requiring the investigation of each and every occurrence of a loss. Only those losses that exceed a predetermined amount are investigated. Programmed decisions are one method of implementing the control of losses.

The problem with respect to loss allowances and programmed decisions is that they can be used to perpetrate fraud if the decision criteria are known. The perpetrator must merely make sure that his actions remain within the defined limits. He can be relatively certain that his actions will be undetected and can be even more certain that they will not be investigated.

Programmed decisions are necessary to ensure efficient functioning of any system. Effective controls can be implemented to limit their vulnerability to fraud. These controls are:

- Periodic spot checks of loss transactions.
- Unscheduled and unannounced changes of the defined limits and predetermined criteria that make up the programmed decisions.
- Logging of all transactions processed by the programmed decision and a periodic review and analysis of the frequency, source, and nature of such transactions.

6

Computer Security and Controls

Computer security controls can be very effective in protecting you from computer fraud and embezzlement by reducing the opportunities for someone to perpetrate fraud and by significantly increasing the likelihood that fraudulent activities will be detected. The purposes of computer security controls are to protect against the unauthorized use of all data processing resources, unauthorized access to and modification of data files and software, and the misuse of authorized activities.

The controls relate to the physical security of the data processing department and of the areas within the data processing department; to the security of the data files, programs, and system software; and to the human interaction with the data files, programs, and system software. The controls that will be discussed in this chapter include:

- Physical access controls.
- Segregation and rotation of duties.
- System development and maintenance controls.
- Physical access controls.
- Library controls.
- System integrity.

114

- Operations controls.

- Supplies controls.

Before beginning the discussion of computer security controls, it is important to note that many of the measures that protect against fraud fall within both computer security and communications and data base systems. Because we have one chapter for computer security and one for communications and data base systems, it was necessary to determine where the overlapping controls should be discussed. To avoid repeating ourselves, we used the following criterion to determine where to discuss the overlapping controls: if the controls became relevant and pertinent as a result of developments in communications and data base systems, they are discussed in Chapter 7; otherwise, they are discussed in this chapter.

PHYSICAL ACCESS CONTROLS

The purpose of physical access controls is to protect the resources of the data processing department, which include both confidential and sensitive information and assets of your company, by preventing unauthorized access to them. If the potential perpetrator of fraud cannot gain access to the data files, programs, documentation, computer equipment, and sensitive forms, his ability to misuse them is limited. Physical access controls should be designed to allow access to authorized personnel only and to deny access to all other personnel.

There are essentially three levels of access controls:

- Perimeter controls.
- Access controls to the data processing department.
- Access controls within the data processing department.

Perimeter controls

Perimeter controls relate to the prevention and detection of unauthorized access to the building housing your data processing department. Although these controls will not be discussed here because they are outside the scope of the book, various intrusion detection and prevention methods and devices have been identified in Figure 6-1.

Access controls to the data processing department

Access to the data processing department, including those areas identified in Figure 6-2 and all data processing department offices and work areas, must be strictly controlled. Only those non-data-processing-department people who have a legitimate and necessary reason for being in the data processing department should be allowed entry, and, even then, their access to the various areas in the department must be controlled.

115

Property

- Fences (possibly equipped with barbed wire or vibration sensors)

- Extensive outside lighting (particularly for entrances and parking lots)

- Intrusion detection devices—infrared or microwave beams

- Outside patrol forces (possibly equipped with vehicles, radios, or dogs)

- Closed-circuit television (for entrances and parking lots)

Building

- Windows glazed with break-resistant glass or plastic (possibly equipped with sensors)

- Air conditioning louvers covered with heavy-gauge screens

- Entrance door controls
  - Screening by guards or other responsible persons
  - Conventional or pick resistant locks and keys
  - Electronic key systems or badge reading locks
  - Electronic combination locks
  - Mechanical dial or push-button combination locks
  - Physical characteristic locks (hand geometry, fingerprint, voice)
  - Closed circuit television
  - Alarm system

- Electromechanical intrusion detection devices
  - Metallic foil tape on windows
  - Magnetic or mechanical contact switches on doors and windows
  - Mercury switches on doors and windows that tilt
  - Vibration detectors
  - Wire lacing and screening on doors, floors, walls, and ceilings
  - Taut wire across air ducts or utility tunnels
  - Photo-electric beams

Figure 6-1

Examples of Perimeter Controls

The recommended access controls are discussed below. They are summarized in Figure 6-3. Various methods and devices for controlling access are identified in Figure 6-4.

Eliminate nonessential doors to the data processing department. All doors and entry points to the data processing department that are not essential for safety purposes (to permit safe evacuation of the premises in an emergency) should be eliminated or blocked. The number of entry points must be limited to control access.

Set up one designated entry (access control) point. The entry

- Input/output area

- Data conversion area

- Libraries
    - Data
    - Program (including applications and system software)
    - Documentation

- Computer room

- Programmer, system design, and system analysis areas

- Communications equipment area

- Computer maintenance area

- Supplies area

- Telephone closet

Figure 6-2

Data Processing Department Areas Requiring Controlled Access

point to the data processing department should be set up in the direct path of all traffic flow into and out of the department. A receptionist or guard should be stationed at the entry point during all hours that the department is working. At all other times, entry to the department by anyone other than authorized department employees should

- Eliminate nonessential doors to the data processing department

- Set up one designated entry point to the data processing department, where access is controlled

- Control use of essential doors (emergency exits) to the department

- Equip after-hours entry and exit points with access control mechanisms

- Define and enforce visitor controls for all non-data-processing department employees

- Provide data processing department employees with an identification card

- Involve data processing department personnel in access control

- Have security guards tour the data processing department looking for unescorted visitors and suspicious activities

- Check all briefcases, bags, and packages carried into and out of the data processing department

Figure 6-3

Access Controls to the Data Processing Department

- Fire exits with alarms

- Entrance door controls
  - Screening by guards or other responsible person
  - Conventional or pick-resistant locks and keys
  - Electronic key systems or badge reading locks
  - Electronic combination locks
  - Mechanical dial or push-button combination locks
  - Physical characteristic locks (hand geometry, fingerprint, voice)
  - Closed circuit televisions
  - Alarm systems

- Panic-bars with alarms on doors not to be used as entrances (outside doorknob removed)

- Closed-circuit televisions

- Motion picture and single exposure sequence cameras

- Intrusion detection devices
  - Photoelectric or infrared beams across walls, ceilings, windows, entrances
  - Photometric systems
  - Sonic and ultrasonic motion detection systems
  - Microwave motion detection systems
  - Audio detection systems
  - Vibration detection systems
  - Electromagnetic or electrostatic proximity systems (capacitance detectors)

- Guards assigned to fixed posts and roving

- Internal partitions

- Alert, security-conscious data processing employees

Figure 6-4

Access Control Methods for Access to the Data Processing Department

not be possible. The entry point should be equipped with a telephone call director so that the receptionist or guard can let department employees know when visitors have arrived. It should also be equipped with a mechanism for summoning help in the event that a problem or emergency arises.

Control use of all essential doors to the department. Entry to and exit from the department should be by means of the designated entry point. All other doors to the department should be kept locked at all times. It may be desirable to remove the door knobs from the outside of the doors wherever possible. These doors should be equipped with panic bars on the inside to permit easy evacuation in the event of an emergency. They should also be alarmed so that all exits through those doors alert security guards and department employees. This should prevent, or at least deter, the unauthorized removal or theft of data processing department resources, including files, documentation, program listings, output, or other information and records.

Equip after-hours entry and exit points with access control mechanisms. The entry and exit points to the department used by authorized department employees should be kept locked. Access control mechanisms, such as pick-resistant locks, badge-reading locks, combination locks, or physical characteristic locks, should be used to limit access to authorized department personnel only.

Enforce visitor controls. By visitors, we mean all people, including company employees, who are not employees of the data processing department. All visitors should be required to show positive identification to the receptionist or guard at the designated entry point to the department. They should sign a visitors' register, indicating the date and time of their arrival, their name and company, the nature of their visit, and the person whom they wish to see. They should be provided with a numbered visitor's badge that they must wear while in the department; the badge number should also be recorded in the register.

Visitors should be escorted at all times by a data processing department employee. They should not be allowed to roam around the department unescorted. Department employees should be instructed to watch for visitors who are unescorted, regardless of whether or not they are wearing the visitor's badge, and should politely ask them to identify themselves and their reason for being in the department.

Upon departure, visitors must be required to sign out in the visitors' register and to surrender their badge. It is desirable to have the receptionist or guard inspect visitors' briefcases or other bags and packages upon entry and exit to deter unauthorized removal of department resources.

Provide data processing department employees with an identification card. Department employees should all be provided with an identification card to facilitate their entry into the department. The identification card may be coded, such as by color or letter, to indicate those areas within the data processing department which the employee is authorized to enter. These cards may also serve as keys to badge-reading locks if card-controlled access mechanisms are used in the department.

Involve data processing department personnel in access control. Effective security procedures require continuous observation and the cooperation of all employees. Department employees should be encouraged to be watchful for unescorted visitors and for any unusual or suspicious actions or occurrences. They should be instructed to immediately inform management or security whenever they detect anything out of the ordinary.

Additional access control. It may be advisable to have security guards periodically tour the data processing department checking for unescorted visitors with or without a visitor's badge and for any suspicious activities.

Department employees' briefcases and other bags and packages should be inspected upon exit from the department to discourage them from removing department resources unless they have explicit, written authorization to do so.

Access controls within the data processing department

Within the data processing department, access to critical areas must be restricted to visitors as well as department employees. These critical areas, identified in Figure 6-2, should either be occupied by a department employee authorized to be in the area or be locked (and unoccupied). Unauthorized people must be denied access. It may be desirable to station guards at the entrances to these critical areas or to install card-controlled access systems to restrict access. Such access controls are essential if the integrity of the system, programs, and data are to be preserved. Let us look at some of these areas and the implications of uncontrolled access to them.

Program, data, and documentation libraries. The librarians should be the only people that have access to these libraries. It is very important to restrict access to the libraries to programmers, analysts, and operators as well as visitors, because the contents of the libraries are so valuable and vulnerable to misuse, fraud, sabotage, and theft. Programmers and analysts are capable of modifying programs; however, if they are not permitted in the libraries, they will not have access to the programs or to the data. Operators have access to the computers. If they are given access to the libraries, they also have access to the programs and data. They are thus given the opportunity to run and possibly modify whatever programs and data they want. Therefore, unless very strict control over access to the libraries is enforced at all times, your company will be left wide open to fraud.

Computer room. Access to the computer room should be limited to operations personnel. "*Nobody* and *nothing* should be permitted into the computer room unless they or it needs to be there then."[1]

[1] Harold Weiss, "Computer Security—An Overview," *Datamation*, January 1974, p. 45.

120

The computer room is the only area where the programs, data, and computer equipment are all brought together. Extremely tight control is necessary if the integrity and confidentiality of the data and programs are to be preserved. Programmers and analysts should not be permitted in the computer room, except perhaps under the most carefully controlled conditions. They must never be permitted in the computer room alone. Programmers and analysts know how to modify programs. They also know, or can determine, the data input formats. If they have direct access to the computer they can introduce unauthorized and fraudulent modifications to the programs and data, and they can create and process fraudulent input transactions. They essentially have "carte blanche" to do whatever they want. This is an intolerable situation if the perpetration of fraud is to be controlled.

Intrusion detection

In addition to controlling access to the data processing department and to critical areas in the department, it is often desirable to detect intrusions into various areas when those areas are unoccupied. Figure 6-4 identifies various methods of detecting intrusions. These systems should be installed in such a way that, when activated, the department or company's security guard is immediately alerted to the fact that an intrusion has occurred and the location of the intrusion.

SEGREGATION AND ROTATION OF DUTIES

First, and foremost, the data processing department must be an independent organizational entity. It must be completely independent of all the user departments or other units for which it processes information. Data processing department personnel should be prohibited from having authority, responsibilities, and duties in any other department. They should be prohibited from making master-file changes, from establishing and correcting control totals, and from initiating or authorizing any transactions whatsoever. This separation of department responsibilities is absolutely mandatory if proper controls and security are to be effective in the prevention, detection, and determent of fraud.

Within the data processing department, the functions that, for control purposes, should be performed by different individuals are identified in Figure 6-5.

The reasons for requiring this segregation of duties are many:

- To prevent unauthorized and fraudulent use of the computer, data, and programs.
- To prevent unauthorized and fraudulent modification and manipulation of data and programs.

121

```
• Input control

• Data conversion/entry

• Library management and maintenance

• Job scheduling

• Job setup

• Computer operations

• Output control and distribution

• Applications design

• Applications programming

• Maintenance programming

• Systems analysis and design

• Systems programming

• Data definition

• Program testing
```

Figure 6-5

Recommended Segregation of Duties Within the Data Processing Department

- To prevent unauthorized and fraudulent modification of data during normal processing.
- To ensure the validity, integrity, and accuracy of applications and systems software during design, programming, testing, and implementation.

As with the separation of duties and responsibilities for administrative and internal control, the segregation of duties in the data processing department must be designed to ensure that the perpetration of fraud requires the collusion of at least two individuals.

All input transactions, including correcting entries, adjustments, and master-file changes, should be initiated by the appropriate, authorized user department and subjected to the controls identified in Chapter 8.

Programmers should never be allowed to operate the computer, even during program testing. This is particularly important during second and third shifts, on weekends, and on holidays. Programmers know how the programs function, what the controls are, and what the input data formats are. By permitting them to operate the computer, they are essentially being given unlimited access to the programs and the data files. They can fraudulently modify the program and data files. They can input fraudulent transactions that circumvent the controls or even transactions that comply with the controls.

Operators should not have access to the program and data libraries. In addition, operators should not examine input transactions nor reconcile output. Their job must be limited to operating the computers if the proper segregation of duties is to be effective in reducing the opportunities for the perpetration of fraud.

Segregating the programming and maintenance functions reduces the probability that unauthorized program changes will be made. It also makes it possible to maintain tight control over program changes.

In addition to maintaining a strict segregation of duties, it is recommended that duties be rotated on a random basis so that programmers do not always work on the same programs, operators do not always run the same jobs, and data conversion/entry personnel do not always work on the same transactions. The practice of duty rotation acts as a deterrent to the perpetration of fraud and to collusion. If a person knows that he will not be working on or running a particular job for a long time, he is less likely to go to the trouble of manipulating the job or program. He also knows that his chances of getting caught are increased when someone else takes over working on or running the job. Collusion is difficult because the people involved in the fraud will not always be in a position to perpetrate the fraud. Thus, more willing people must be brought into the fraud. As the number of people involved increases, the likelihood that the fraud will be revealed also increases. And there is always the probability that the person who has assumed the duties of a perpetrator will not go along with the fraud.

SYSTEM DEVELOPMENT AND MAINTENANCE CONTROLS

Applications systems development and maintenance controls must be carefully designed, implemented, and continually enforced. These controls are an integral part of an effective system of controls to prevent, deter, and detect fraud. The controls that will be discussed are especially important because the opportunity to implement fraud and embezzlement, and thus the ability to commit fraud and embezzlement, will exist during system development and maintenance unless proper and effective controls are observed.

The purposes of system development and maintenance controls can be summarized as follows:

- To ensure that adequate controls are incorporated into the design of the new or modified system.
- To ensure that the implementation of fraud during system development and maintenance will be detected before the system becomes operational.
- To ensure that the new or modified system performs all the

functions that it is supposed to perform; performs them accurately, completely, and reliably; and does not perform anything other than those functions.

- To ensure that the controls designed into the system function accurately, completely, and reliably; and that the controls cannot be bypassed.
- To ensure that the integrity of the controls and of the system will be preserved once the new or modified system becomes operational.

In order for many of the controls to be effective, the user departments and internal auditors must be directly and closely involved in the process of development and maintenance of applications systems.

For discussion purposes, we have divided this section into six subsections:

- System specification and design controls.
- Programming controls.
- Program/system change controls.
- Program/system testing.
- Program/system cataloging.
- File-conversion controls.

The controls discussed in this section are summarized in Figure 6-6.

System specification and design controls

System specification and design controls should be designed to ensure the development of effective and adequately controlled systems. The output of this phase of the system development cycle is comprised of the functional and programming, or technical, specifications for the system.

Require user department and internal audit department approval of system development projects. Before a system development project is undertaken, the project should be reviewed, authorized, and approved in writing by the appropriate user department and the internal audit department. The user department and internal audit department will have to be very involved in the system development process, including system design, testing, and implementation. They must, therefore, be aware of and approve all system development projects before such projects are begun.

Require user department and internal audit department involvement in the system specification and design phase of the project. The user department and internal audit department should be involved in

System Specifications and Design Controls

- Require user department and internal audit department approval of system development projects

- Require user department and internal audit department involvement in the systems specifications and design phase of the project

- Require user department and internal audit department approval of detailed user specifications

- Require the preparation of detailed technical specifications and of a detailed plan for the development of the system

Programming Controls

- Establish comprehensive programming standards

- Require adherence to the programming standards (even if the programming is contracted out to a software house)

- Divide the system into smaller units for programming purposes

- Perform an in-depth review of each unit of the system

- Establish documentation standards and require adherence to them

- Require the preparation of appropriate documentation

Program/System Change Controls

- Use a pre-printed formal change request form with pre-printed sequential form numbers

- Set up a change control committee

- Require user department and data processing department authorization of all requests for changes

- Maintain a log of all requests for program/system changes

- Establish formal procedures by which programmers can gain access to source code program listing

- Establish formal procedures by which a copy of the source version of a production program can be catalogued in the program testing library

- Be wary of program patches, as opposed to source code modifications

- Maintain adequate security for the program being modified

- Perform an in-depth review of the modified program/system

- Update all documentation

- Maintain logs of all program/system modifications

- File copies of the change request forms

- Document formal program/system change procedures

Figure 6-6

System Development and Maintenance Controls

Program/System Testing

- Set up an independent system testing group
- Involve the user department
- Design comprehensive test data
- Prohibit the use of live data files and data bases during system testing
- Perform parallel testing, whenever possible, and thoroughly investigate unexpected differences in results
- Review nonprinted outputs
- Verify that all statements are executed at least once
- Test two or more cycles of the program or system
- Test the entire system
- Require user department approval of the system test
- File test data and test results with the program documentation
- Document program/system testing standards and procedures

Program/System Cataloging

- Use a pre-printed catalog control form with a pre-printed sequential form number
- Require all the necessary approvals
- Inform all the appropriate people that the catalog has been changed and disseminate the new or updated documentation
- Maintain logs of all catalog changes
- File copies of the catalog change forms
- Document formal catalog change procedures

File Conversion Controls

- Establish formal procedures by which programmers can gain access to the data documentation
- Establish formal procedures by which a copy of the data files and data bases can be made (the live data files and data bases should never be used)
- Compute records counts, control, and hash totals for the files being converted and for the converted version of the file, compare the results, and thoroughly investigate any discrepancies
- Compare selected records from the original file to the corresponding records in the converted file, and from the converted file to the corresponding records in the original file

Figure 6-6 *Continued*

File Conversion Controls (continued)

- Maintain adequate security for the files being converted

- Perform an in-depth review of the converted data files

- Update the data documentation

- Test the converted data files and data bases with the new or modified system

- Require all the necessary approvals before cataloging the converted file

- Catalog the resulting approved data files and data bases

Figure 6-6 *Continued*

the specification and design phase of the project in order to ensure that the system designed complies with acceptable accounting policies, accounting and applications controls, and with record keeping and other procedures prescribed by taxing authorities and regulatory agencies. They should also ensure that the system is designed with management's objectives in mind. It is of utmost importance that the user department specify (with internal audit department review) what is needed in terms of accounting policies, decision rules, controls, and procedures and regulations that must be followed.

Require user department and internal audit department approval of detailed user specifications. Systems analysts must, in the course of designing a new system, prepare a detailed user specifications manual fully describing the new system. Figure 6-7 identifies what should be included in the user specification manual. This manual must be carefully reviewed by both the user department and internal audit department. Necessary changes to the specifications must be communicated to the systems analysts. When the user department and the internal audit department are satisfied that the specifications are accurate and complete and meet their needs, they must indicate their approval in writing. Then, and only then, can the system development process proceed.

Require the preparation of detailed technical specifications and of a detailed plan for the development of the system. These documents will guide the programming, file conversion, user training, and testing of the system being developed. The detailed technical specifications should divide the system into modules or segments for programming purposes. Each module or segment should be documented in detail, with processing logic, processing specifications, and file specifications

- Description of system

- Data element identification and description

- Identification and description of input data elements

- Preliminary design of input source document or format

- Identification and description of output data elements

- Description of output documents and output reports (formats and controls)

- Flowchart of manual aspects of system

- Flowchart of automated aspects of system

- Identification and description of files (input, output, master, temporary), with record layouts and data element descriptions for each file

- Detailed description of processing to be performed, including
  - Identification of the possible codes and values of the data elements and the specific processing to be performed for each code or value
  - Processing logic

- Detailed description of controls (input, processing, and output)

- Discussion of system design constraints

- Management summary, including benefits to be realized from new system

Figure 6-7

Contents of User Specifications Manual

clearly identified. These technical specifications will be used to guide, control, and review the programmers' work.

Programming controls

Programming controls should be designed to ensure that the program or system that is produced conforms to the detailed technical specifications prepared during the system specification and design phase. It must also conform to an established set of programming standards. The controls must be designed to prevent, or deter, and to detect frauds that are programmed into the system. The output of the programming phase of the system development project includes the program or system and the documentation.

Establish programming standards and require adherence to them. Programming standards should define the programming languages and techniques to be used for all applications systems programmed.

They should also define the controls that must be incorporated in all systems. For systems that will process information of a sensitive or confidential nature, the standards must identify the specific controls that must be included (such as elimination of all residual information on scratch files or in work spaces). In addition, those programming techniques and instructions that should not be used must be explicitly identified. For example, applications programs must never be allowed to operate in supervisory state. Applications programmers should never be allowed to write their own input and output or data base management routines (macros). The standard systems software should handle all input, output, data file accesses, and data base management. Programming standards should thus direct the programmer by telling him what tools and techniques he may and must not use.

The standards will, if properly defined and continually adhered to, help to ensure the security of computer system, including the applications programs and systems, operating systems software, and data files. In fact, the standards should apply to all applications systems, regardless of whether the system is programmed by your own programmers or the system is contracted to a software house for development. Your programming standards should be included as part of the system specifications given to the contractor. We also recommend that you evaluate applications packages that you are considering purchasing with your programming standards always in mind.

Divide the system into smaller units for programming purposes. The system under development should be divided into segments or modules. The segments or modules should be assigned to several different programmers. This control, of dividing up the programming responsibility, serves two very important purposes: it implements a separation of responsibilities; and it makes it possible to review and inspect the resulting system more effectively.

The separation of programming responsibilities makes it very difficult for the dishonest programmer to program fraud into the system because he does not have control or even detailed knowledge of all parts of the systems. Thus, he must work in collusion with other programmers if he is to be successful in building fraud into the system. The importance of this control is increased when you realize that, if fraud is successfully built into a system, none of the other controls and control areas (e.g., input, output, programmed controls) may be able to prevent the fraud from being perpetrated. The programmer may not need access to the programs, input transactions, output, or data files to perpetrate the fraud.

The division of the system into smaller units also increases the opportunities for detecting such programmed fraud. The units can be analyzed and reviewed in much greater detail by the control group or managerial personnel responsible for the review. Each unit can be reviewed for hard-to-follow, apparently unused, or inexplicable code that could be used to perpetrate fraud.

Perform an in-depth review of each unit of the system. Each unit of the system should be studied in depth to ensure that the programming standards are observed, that the programming logic is good, that the appropriate controls have been properly incorporated, that the unit meets the technical design requirements, and that there is no suspicious, hard-to-follow, unused, or unexplained code in the unit. This control can be effective in deterring programming fraud because it increases the probability that the fraud will be detected. By ensuring that the appropriate controls are in place and functioning, fraud perpetrated by manipulation of input transactions, data files, or output may also be deterred or prevented, since it, too, is likely to be detected.

Establish documentation standards and require adherence to them. Documentation standards should identify the documentation that must be produced for all systems developed. It should also define the contents and the format of the documentation.

Require the preparation of appropriate documentation. The documentation that should be prepared for all operational systems includes: system testing instructions, file conversion instructions, operator run instructions, output handling and distribution instructions, complete systems documentation, and complete users' instructions.

**Program/system
change controls**

The need for system modifications, or changes to operational programs, cannot be avoided. Bugs or discrepancies in the operational system may be discovered; programming logic or decision tables may have to be changed because procedures or requirements of regulatory agencies change; and processing or output reports may have to be modified as management's need for information evolves. In addition, it may be desirable to modify systems to take advantage of new hardware and software developments or to make them operate more efficiently.

The purpose of program/system change controls is to maintain the integrity of the system. The introduction of unauthorized and potentially fraudulent changes to tested and approved systems should not be possible. Because of the exposure to fraud, errors, and control problems whenever a system is modified, program change controls must be clearly documented and enforced at all times.

Use a preprinted formal change request form. All requests for system modifications should be made on a standard change request

PROGRAM CHANGE REQUEST FORM	Control No. XXXXX

Requestor (Name, Title & Dept.) | **Request Date**

Program (Number & Name) | **System (Number & Name)**

Functions of this program

Reason for change (attach additional sheets, if necessary)

Detailed explanation of change (attach examples, if necessary)

Effects of change on related data and programs

Estimate of effort, time, & cost to make change | **Desired effective date for change**

User departments that rely on program to be changed

Authorizations (Name, Title, Dept., & Date)	Test results approvals (Name, Title, Dept., & Date)
User(s)	User(s)
Data Processing Dept.	Data Processing Dept.
Change Control Committee	Change Control Committee
Other	Other

Programmer Assigned (Name & Date)	Due Date	Actual Date

Notes

Figure 6-8

Program Change Request Form

form. An example of one such form is shown in Figure 6-8. The kind of information that should be provided is identified on the form. Enough information must be included so that the request for change can be evaluated and can be scheduled for implementation. There may not be enough space on the form to fully describe the needed change. A detailed description of the change should be provided on separate sheets of paper attached to the form.

The change request form should include a preprinted sequential number so that control of the forms can be maintained. A batch of forms should be provided to each of the user departments as well as to the data processing department. Records should be kept of the form numbers assigned to each department.

Set up a change control committee. A committee, consisting of user department representatives, data processing department managerial personnel (e.g., operations manager, systems analysis and design manager, programming manager), and internal EDP auditors, should be assigned responsibility for reviewing, evaluating, approving, and scheduling system modifications. This committee should also be responsible for ensuring compliance with program change controls and procedures. The committee's authorization and approval should be required before the modified system can be placed in the program residence file and thus can be used for production runs.

Require authorization of all requests for changes. Regardless of how small or insignificant the change might be, the implementation of the change exposes the system to the same control problems, errors, and potential for fraud as does a major system change. Therefore, all requests for changes must be authorized, in writing, by appropriate designated user department managerial personnel. User department authorization is required regardless of whether the request is initiated by user department personnel, data processing department personnel, or personnel of any other department. The appropriate user department managerial personnel should be aware of all changes to any systems or programs on which they rely.

In addition to user department authorization, data processing department management should authorize, in writing, the request for a system modification. This second authorization should be made after the request has been authorized by the appropriate user department and after the request has been reviewed, evaluated, and approved by the change control committee.

Maintain a log of all requests for program/system changes. A log of all requests for changes should be maintained to provide a

| Control Number | Request Date | Request Initiator | | User Department Authorization | | System/ Program | Description of Change | Change Control Auth. Date | Implementation Date | | Comments |
		Name	Department	Name	Department				Sched.	Actual	

PROGRAM CHANGE REQUEST LOG

Figure 6-9

Program Change Request Log

133

history of such requests. The information that should be recorded is identified in Figure 6-9.

Establish formal procedures by which programmers may gain access to listings of program source code. The only time that programmers should have access to the source coding for a particular production, or operational, program is when they have been authorized to make a change to that program. Thus, very carefully controlled procedures must be established to ensure that the programmers can access the source coding when, and only when, they have the appropriate authorization to do so. It is very important to prevent programmers from accessing production program source coding, except under controlled conditions, if your exposure to spurious and potentially fraudulent program changes is to be minimized.

The change control committee should provide the documentation librarian with a copy of the change control request form, which also identifies the programmer assigned to make the change. The programmer can then request the program listing and documentation from the documentation librarian and sign the library log, acknowledging that he received it.

Establish formal procedures by which a copy of the source version of a production program may be cataloged in the program testing library. The programmer will need access to the source code version of the production program which he has been assigned to modify. A controlled procedure must be established to request that a copy of the source coding be cataloged in the testing library. A catalog control form identifying the program and the programmer assigned, and referencing the change request form should be used. Authorization by the change control committee should also be required. Programmers must not be permitted to request catalog changes on their own if the integrity of the programs and data files are to be preserved.

Be wary of program patches. Patches to production programs, instead of source code modifications of production programs, often provide the programmer with the opportunity to implement fraud. Patches are very difficult to review and control. They should never be permitted when sensitive or critical programs or programs requiring security are involved. Changes to such programs should require source code modifications and recompilation of the source code.

If program patches are permitted, a study of the software that performs the patching should be conducted. Not all "patching" software provides an audit trail or printed record identifying that a modification has been made. Thus, an unauthorized, and possibly fraudulent, modification could be made and might never be detected. The source code version of the program would not reflect the change. This is a dangerous situation that should be remedied immediately.

Maintain adequate security for the program being modified. It is very important to ensure that adequate security is provided for the program being modified. The programmer assigned to program the modification must not leave copies of the program lying around, exposed to unauthorized access by other programmers or other people in the area. The copies of the program should be kept in a secure location and disposed of in an appropriate manner when the modification has been completed.

Perform an in-depth review of the modified program/system. When the programmer has completed his work and is satisfied that the modified system is accurate, appropriate, complete, and correct, he should submit a listing of the modified system to the change control committee. Someone on the committee, or a person designated by the committee, should study the system in depth. This study is similar to the study conducted for all new system development projects. The purpose of the in-depth review is to ensure that the appropriate modifications were made; that the programming standards were observed; that the programming logic is good; that the appropriate controls were properly incorporated; that there is no suspicious, hard-to-follow, unused, or unexplained code in the system; and that portions of the program or system that were not affected by the particular modification were not modified or manipulated in any way. It is very important that the entire program or system, not just the modified portion of it, be studied if the programmer had access to the entire program or system when programming the modification. The programmer could have built fraud into an entirely different section of the program or system while properly programming the modification.

Update all documentation. All system, program, system operating, and user documentation must be updated to reflect the modification. The change control committee should review the updated documentation for adequacy, accuracy, and completeness.

Maintain logs of all program/system modifications. A log of all modifications should be set up and maintained for each program within each system and for each system. The logs should identify the change request form number, the new version number of the program/system, the changes made, the reasons for the change, the date the new version became operational, and the programmer responsible for the change. These logs will provide a history of the program or system and will make it possible to trace the changes and to fix responsibility for the changes in the event that a problem arises.

File copies of the change request forms. Once the modified system has been completely tested and has become the operational version of the system, and the change request form has been updated to indicate that the change has been effected, the completed change request form must be filed. One copy should be filed sequentially, by form number, with all other change request forms. Another copy should be filed with the program/system documentation.

Document formal program/system change procedures. To ensure that the procedures for requesting, authorizing, programming, and approving program/system changes are followed consistently, the procedures must be clearly and completely documented. The documentation should be disseminated to all data processing department personnel and appropriate user department personnel.

Program/system testing

Before any system or program can become the operational, or production, system, it should undergo extensive and comprehensive testing. This testing should be performed for both new and modified programs and systems. The purposes of such testing are:

- To ensure that the system functions in accordance with user requirements.
- To ensure that the system meets data processing department operational standards.
- To ensure that the controls function reliably, accurately, and completely.
- To ensure that the system does exactly what it is supposed to do, and, that it does not do anything more or less than what it is supposed to do.
- To ensure that the system functions reliably, accurately, and completely.

Although system testing will not be able to guarantee that the system is well designed, perfect, and completely free of errors, well-designed system tests and testing procedures can go a long way toward ensuring that the processing and controls are effective, accurate, and complete, and that the system will operate predictably and reliably. System testing also provides the opportunity for data processing and user department personnel and internal auditors to see and study the system in its finished form before it actually is implemented as the production system.

From the standpoint of detection and prevention of fraud, comprehensive system testing provides the opportunity for the user department and internal auditors to exercise the system exhaustively and to see how the system handles invalid, inappropriate, or potentially fraudulent transactions and transactions that violate the controls.

Set up an independent system testing group. An independent testing group, consisting of appropriate user department management, internal auditors, and data processing department personnel, should be set up and charged with the responsibility of preparing test data and test cases and of reviewing the results of the tests. The programmer or programmers responsible for programming the new or modified system should not be involved. These programmers have already performed sufficient testing to satisfy themselves that the system functions the way they feel it should. If they have built fraud into the system, or have not implemented all the required controls, their involvement in this phase of testing gives them the ability to ensure that the test data and test cases are prepared in such a way that the fraud or control weaknesses will not be detected. In fact, no programmers at all should be members of the system testing group. They should not know how the test data and test cases are determined nor what the testing group looks for and is concerned with. If they have this knowledge, they may be able to program fraud or control weaknesses into their programs in a way that they know will not be detected by the testing.

Involve the user department. The user department should be heavily involved in the program/system testing. They should specify the test data and test cases to be run, compare the test results to predetermined results, make sure that the system handles accurately and completely all the situations that may occur, and they must eventually sign off on the system and approve it for production runs. The user department should also review all the system outputs, in detail, to ensure that they understand how each field in the output is generated, what the error messages mean, and how to correct each error. *Users must be confident that they understand the system so that they will not be reluctant to challenge questionable processing or output results.*

Design comprehensive test data. The test data and test cases should include all valid combinations of data and cases, data and cases designed to violate the edits and controls in all conceivable ways, and all conceivable invalid combinations of data and cases. The test data and cases must be designed "to exercise the application system for errors of omission and errors of commission, i.e., the applications system should perform all functions it is intended to do and no more."[2] They should also be designed to test that rounding and

[2] *Systems Auditability and Control Study—Data Processing Control Practices Report* (Altamonte Springs, Fla.: The Institute of Internal Auditors, Inc., 1977), p. 104.

137

truncation of arithmetic data elements and arithmetic overflow conditions are handled properly.

Designing comprehensive test data is not an easy task. Those responsible for designing the test data may be assisted in performing this task by a number of program products known as test data generators. Test data generators are typically designed to generate large volumes of test data.

> Since, in most cases, the [test data generator] program packages generate a wide variety of data combinations, they will often create tests that would be overlooked by the average human who attempts to derive tests. Everyone will agree that it is impossible to test all logic paths and data combinations in a moderately complex system. However, even if a test does not guarantee 100 percent coverage, a well designed test is vital in assuring that the system will handle the usual mix of transactions. The test data generator programs increase the use of testing and provide a broad coverage of data types and combinations, both valid and invalid.[3]

Various test data generators available today are identified in Appendix H.

Prohibit the use of live data files and data bases during system testing. Although it may be desirable to use actual data to test the system, provided that the data are not sensitive or confidential, the live data files and data bases should never be used or updated during system testing, either by the programmers or by the testing group. Specially prepared, duplicate copies of the data should be made and used for the system testing. The system has not been thoroughly tested and approved; therefore, any changes made to the data are unauthorized, inappropriate, and probably incorrect. If the programmers have access to the live data, they essentially are being given the opportunity to modify and manipulate the data any way they wish. This may provide them with the opportunity to perpetrate fraud.

Perform parallel testing. Whenever possible, the new or modified program or system should be run in parallel with the program or system which it was designed to replace. This is to provide the testing group and user department with the opportunity to compare the results produced by the new or modified program/system to the results produced by the existing program/system and to identify discrepancies.

It is interesting to note that in one computer fraud case the

---

[3] Donald L. Adams, "A Survey of Test Data Generators," *EDPACS*, April 1973, p. 6.

parallel testing of a new system with the system it was designed to replace actually exposed a computer-assisted fraud. Fraud had been successfully built into the existing system. When the differences in the results produced by the parallel test were investigated, the new system was determined to be processing transactions correctly while the existing system was fraudulently manipulating the transactions. This case highlights the necessity of thoroughly investigating any unexpected differences between predicted and test results. Such differences should not be overlooked or ignored.

Review nonprinted outputs. Not all outputs of the system are necessarily printed during the routine functioning of the system. Such outputs should, however, be carefully reviewed during system testing; therefore, they should be included in the printed audit trails and other printed outputs during system testing. These "invisible" outputs are particularly vulnerable to undetected errors, manipulation, and fraud precisely because they are not routinely printed and subjected to output controls.

Verify that all statements are executed at least once. Testing of new or modified programs/systems should include verification that all statements are executed at least once. Any statements that are not executed should be reviewed carefully to determine why they were never executed, under what conditions they would be executed, why they were included in the program, and if they are necessary. The testing group should carefully examine such statements because the statements might have been included to facilitate the perpetration of fraud under specific conditions known only to the programmer or to facilitate the perpetration of fraud by replacing seemingly innocuous code with an unauthorized and fraudulent program patch.

Test two or more cycles of the system. To ensure that the updating and error correction capabilities of the system function properly and completely, two or more cycles of the system must be tested. This testing will also serve to further verify the adequacy and accuracy of the controls built into the system, and to ensure that any frauds or manipulations in the system will be detected before the system becomes operational.

Test the entire system. Even if a modification involves a change to only a small part of the system, or to only one program in a much larger system, the entire system should be tested to ensure that the change is compatible with the entire system. Again it is necessary to review the nonprinted outputs and to test more than one cycle to verify that nothing unexpected occurs and that the integrity of the entire system has been preserved. As mentioned earlier, even the smallest and most insignificant program change exposes the entire program and system to possible manipulation and fraud.

Require user department approval of the system test. When the user department has reviewed all the test results, including the printed and nonprinted outputs; is satisfied that the system functions reliably, completely, accurately, and properly; and is confident of their ability to use and understand the system, they should indicate their approval, in writing. Any subsequent changes to the system should be performed in accordance with documented program/system change control procedures.

File test data and test results with the program documentation. The test data and the test results should be filed with the program documentation. If a problem should develop with the program for any reason, the test data and results may be invaluable in the investigation of the problem. In addition, the test data should be analyzed to determine why the problem was not detected during testing. It may be possible to identify additional types of tests or test cases to be incorporated in all future testing.

The test data and test results should be kept as secure as the program listing and program documentation, since they provide insights into the functioning of the system as well as into the way the tests are designed.

Document program/system testing standards and procedures. To ensure that system testing is performed completely and uniformly for all new and modified systems, the testing standards to be met and procedure to be followed should be documented in detail. Inadequate, incomplete, or nonexistent documentation will result in ineffective system testing and in the possibility of production systems with inadequate controls and built-in frauds.

Program/system cataloging

Only those new and modified programs and systems that have been thoroughly documented, reviewed, and tested, and that have been approved by the change control committee (modified programs only), testing group, user department, internal audit department, and data processing department should be cataloged in the production program/system library or libraries. The production program/system library contains those programs/systems that are authorized for production use. Programs/systems that are not resident in the production library should not be permitted to process live data. Thus, stringent controls are needed to ensure that only those programs and systems having *all* the necessary approvals are cataloged for production use. The controls relating to production systems and programs will be discussed in the next section of this chapter. Let us take a look at the cataloging controls here.

Use a preprinted catalog control form with a preprinted sequential form number. A new or modified program/system is placed and cataloged in the production library by the computer operators who execute the appropriate utility or system support program. They should only perform the cataloging when all the necessary approvals to do so have been given. A preprinted catalog control form identifying the program/system in the testing library; identifying the name, version number, and other information required to catalog the program/system in the production library; and containing the necessary approvals should be used to authorize the execution of the utility program and the cataloging of the program/system. Operators should be required to check the approvals on the form to make sure that all are present.

Require the necessary approvals. As mentioned above, the change control committee (for modifications to programs/systems), testing group, user department, internal audit department, and data processing department should all approve, in writing, the cataloging of the new or modified program/system in the production library.

Inform the appropriate people that the cataloging has been performed. All those people who approved the cataloging, as well as all the people who will use the new or modified program/system, and the librarian must be informed that the program/system has been cataloged. They should also be given copies of the new or updated documentation.

Maintain logs of all catalog changes. A log should be maintained. It should identify the date the catalog change occurred, the operator performing the change, the program/system in the testing library, and the program/system in the production library. It should reference the change request form (for program changes) and the catalog control form. These logs will provide a history of all changes to the program/system catalogs and will facilitate the tracing of catalog changes if a problem should arise.

File copies of the catalog control forms. One copy of the catalog control form should be filed sequentially, by form number, with all the other catalog control forms. Another copy should be filed with the program/system documentation.

Document formal catalog change procedures. To ensure that the procedures are understood, and are followed consistently and uniformly, the procedures should be clearly and completely documented. This documentation should be provided to all people involved in the catalog change process.

File conversion controls

Whenever a new system is designed or an existing system is modified, the data files processed by the new or modified system may also have to undergo conversion or may have to be created. Many of the program change controls, program/system testing controls, and program/system cataloging controls discussed above apply to the conversion of data files. These controls will not be discussed again here. They have been identified in Figure 6-6 under the heading "File Conversion Controls."

Additional precautions are necessary. The integrity of the data files and data bases must be maintained. Therefore, record counts and a series of control totals and hash totals of all important numeric fields should be computed for both the file being converted (regardless of whether it is in a journal or ledger, or is in machine-readable format) and the converted version of the file. All discrepancies between the record counts and control and hash totals must be thoroughly investigated.

Comparisons of selected records from the original file to the corresponding records in the converted file, and from the converted file to the original file, should be made.

Precautions must also be taken to prevent the compromise and unauthorized modification of confidential and sensitive data files. The exposure to fraud during file conversion is significant and all possible safeguards should be taken.

PRODUCTION SYSTEM AND PROGRAM CONTROLS

The production libraries contain the application programs and systems that are used for the processing of the input data and data files. These programs and systems generate the output and reports on which management and user departments rely. Only those programs that have been thoroughly documented, reviewed, tested, approved, and authorized should be in the production libraries. Effective system development and maintenance controls will help to ensure that inappropriate or improper programs are not placed into production. We must now be concerned about maintaining the integrity of the production programs as well as of the production libraries.

Unauthorized modification of the production programs and libraries can have serious effects, including the manipulation of the programs for fraudulent purposes. Ineffective production system and program controls may provide the opportunity for the dishonest programmer to implement the fraud that he intended to program into the system but was prevented from doing because the system development and maintenance controls were so effective.

142

Figure 6-10

Production System and Program Controls

The controls that relate to the integrity of the production libraries will be discussed here. Additional controls that relate to the production programs will be discussed later in this chapter and in Chapter 7. The controls are summarized in Figure 6-10.

The controls

Prohibit processing of live data by programs and systems not resident in the production libraries. Only those programs and systems resident in the production libraries must be used to process live data. The programs and systems in the production libraries have been thoroughly reviewed, documented, tested, and approved for production runs. The controls associated with programs and systems in the production library were discussed in the system development and maintenance controls section of this chapter.

Programs not resident in the production libraries have not been approved for production runs. Allowing such programs to process live data exposes you to all kinds of problems, including incorrect, improper, unauthorized, and fraudulent processing and changes to your data files; exposure of confidential and sensitive data files and

143

programs; and the loss of the live data. The integrity of your entire computer system could be jeopardized.

Maintain an up-to-date inventory list of all production programs and systems. An inventory list of all production programs and systems should be maintained. In addition to identifying the program or system, it should identify the date the program or system was originally cataloged as a new production program, the dates it was recataloged, and the expiration date of the program or system. If possible, the inventory should also indicate the length of contiguous storage required for the program or system.

Compare the production libraries' directories to the inventory list on a regular and surprise basis. The actual contents of the libraries should be compared to your inventory list on a regular and surprise basis. If there are any discrepancies between the lists, an investigation should be undertaken immediately to determine why the discrepancies exist. They may be an indication that the procedures for maintaining the inventories or for cataloging production programs are not being followed, or they may be an indication that the libraries or programs are being manipulated.

Compare the production libraries' directories to previous directories on a regular and frequent basis. The production libraries' directories should be compared to a previous day's directories on a regular basis. If program patches are permitted, or if there is a great deal of activity in the libraries, perhaps this comparison should be performed daily. Be sure to check the contiguous storage requirements of individual programs. Whereas this check does not ensure that programs have not been patched, since the patch may have replaced an equal amount of existing code, it is an easy and fast way to detect problems.

Maintain logs of all changes to the production libraries. Whenever a change is made to the contents of the production libraries, the change should be recorded in a production catalog control log. As discussed earlier in this chapter, the following should be recorded: the date the change occurred, the operator performing the change, the library and the identification of the program before the change, the library and the identification of the program after the change, the catalog control form identification number, and any other pertinent information.

Modify your system software to produce daily reports of all changes to the production libraries. All changes to the production libraries should be logged by the operating system software and a daily report of such changes should be produced. The report should be compared to the production catalog control log on a daily basis. If any discrepancies are discovered, they could indicate that production programs or the production libraries are being manipulated and should be investigated immediately. The file of catalog control forms or the documentation for the particular program being investigated should be checked for a valid catalog control form with appropriate approval signatures.

Use a program/system version numbering scheme. All programs in the production library should have a version number associated with them. Each time the program is modified, its version number should be changed to reflect the modification. Whenever the program is executed, the version number should be printed on the console log along with the name of the program. It is also desirable to include the program name and version number on all printed reports produced by the program. This will help keep track of program changes and will alert management and users to program changes as well as to execution of the wrong version of a program.

Establish program and system naming conventions. The names of the production programs and systems should provide an indication of the relationships among the programs or of the logical groupings of programs. Programs whose names do not comply with the established conventions should be investigated.

Establish instruction counts for source code programs and byte counts for object code programs. Instruction counts for source code programs and byte counts for object code programs should be established whenever a new system is developed and approved for production processing and whenever an existing system is modified and approved for production processing. On a periodic, spot check basis, the number of instructions actually in the source code program and the number of bytes actually in the object code program should be computed and should be compared with the latest approved counts. For sensitive programs and programs requiring a great deal of security, the latest approved counts may be kept in secured data files and the actual counts may be computed and compared to the approved counts each time the program is run.

It is important to note, however, that this control may not be sufficient in and of itself. It will only detect unauthorized modifications and program patches that result in a change in the number of instructions or bytes in a program. It will not detect such unauthorized changes if they do not affect the number of instructions or bytes.

Perform periodic comparisons of the programs in the production libraries to those actually approved. This is, perhaps, the most difficult control to actually perform. It is also the surest way to determine if production programs have been manipulated. It is relatively simple, albeit very time-consuming, to compare the source code for a particular production program to the approved and authorized program listing. However, the source code version of the production program is not the version that is being executed. Thus, determining that the source code is the same as the approved program listing does not ensure that the production program has not been manipulated or patched. The only way to verify that a production program has not been tampered with is to compile the approved source code program listing and to compare the resulting object code, byte by byte, to the production program. This comparison would be laborious and extremely time-consuming without the use of software designed for making such comparisons.

Compute and compare hash totals of production library programs. Another effective way to determine if production programs have been manipulated is to compute hash totals of the program object code. On a regular, and frequent, basis the hash totals should be recomputed and compared to the hash totals computed when the program was cataloged in the production library. If there are any discrepancies between the hash totals, there is a good probability that the production program has been manipulated. An investigation should be undertaken as soon as possible.

LIBRARY CONTROLS The data processing department library is the repository for data processing media, such as tapes and disks. We are expanding the concept, and contents, of the library to include all documentation. Thus, the library (or libraries) houses all the data files; the source and object code program files; master copies of all the programs, systems, and systems software; the source code program listings; all the data, program, systems, and systems software documentation; and the operating instructions or manuals for the operational, or production, programs and systems. The library must not only provide a physical storage location for these items; it must also provide for their security. In addition to identifying and describing the controls needed to provide adequate security for the data, programs, and documentation, we will discuss the implications of the lack of good controls as they relate to the perpetration of fraud. The controls are summarized in Figure 6-11.

The purposes of library controls are:

- To ensure the security and integrity of the data, programs, systems, and documentation.

- To prevent unauthorized access to, modification of, manipulation of, and misuse of the data, programs, systems, and documentation.

The controls discussed here relate primarily to physical access, modification, manipulation, and misuse of the data, programs, systems, and documentation from within the data processing department, either by department employees or by visitors. Controls relating to access to the data, programs, and systems by authorized and unauthorized users of the computer system will be discussed in depth in Chapter 7 as well as in other sections of this chapter.

The controls   *Physically separate the library.* In order to provide security for the tapes, disks, and documentation, the library (or libraries) must be physically separated from the other functions performed by the data processing department. It should be surrounded by impenetrable walls, ceiling, and floor. Physical access controls, discussed earlier in this chapter, should be employed to provide physical security and control over unauthorized access. Unless the library is physically secure, there is no way to prevent unauthorized access to and misuse of the tapes, disks, and documentation.

We have already discussed some of the dangers of uncontrolled access to the tapes and disks; however, let's summarize them here. Data files, including files containing sensitive and confidential information, may be copied or printed. The copies or listings may then be sold to your competitors; to companies contemplating entering your line of business; to investors or potential investors; to credit bureaus; to direct mail outfits; to people interested in blackmailing you, your employees, or your customers; to your creditors; or to people interested in defrauding you. The list of people or organizations who would be interested in the information stored in your data files is limitless. Take a moment to think about that information and then identify some of the people and organizations, or types of people and organizations, that would like to have the information and the uses to which it may be put.

If any of your user access information, such as passwords, personal identification numbers, account numbers, authorization codes or tables, encryption keys or encryption algorithms, is stored in data files on tapes or disks, the security and integrity of your entire system may be compromised if the file is copied or printed.

Program and system files, as well as data files, may also be printed or copied. Your program and system files may be as interesting to your competitors or potential competitors as your data files. Listings of data files may be used by perpetrators of fraud to identify those records or fields they want to manipulate. They may also be used to identify the format of the files and records, thereby making modifica-

- Physically separate and secure the tape, disk, and documentation libraries from the other functions performed by the data processing department

- Restrict access to the tape, disk, and documentation libraries

- Require all tapes, disks, and documentation to be stored in the libraries when not in use

- Provide the librarians with a list of personnel authorized to access specific files and documentation, and keep the list current

- Maintain a library log of all tapes, disks, and documentation removed from and returned to the libraries

- Review the library log on a regular basis

- Maintain a media maintenance log

- Maintain an up-to-date inventory list of all tapes, disks, and documentation

- Maintain a complete, up-to-date inventory list of all data, program, and system files

- Institute procedures to prevent the unauthorized removal of tapes, disks, and documentation from the data processing department

- Institute procedures to prevent the unauthorized introduction of tapes, disks, and documentation into the data processing department

- Require the use of external labels on all tapes and disks

- Require the use of internal labels

- Require the use of internal volume and file identification and control information labels (and the checking of such labels by the operating system software and production programs)

- Conduct regular and surprise inspections of the libraries

- Conduct regular tests of the accuracy of the external labels

- Maintain an up-to-date inventory of all items stored in an off-site storage location

- Institute procedures to ensure that adequate security is provided for all items stored in the off-site storage location and when transported to and from the off-site storage location

- Store critical data and program files and their documentation in locked vaults or safes

- Conduct regular and surprise inspections of the contents of program and data files

- Institute procedures to ensure that adequate security is provided for your data and program files whenever they are sent to a service bureau or other company for processing

Figure 6-11

Library Controls

- Degauss, or in some other way obliterate, confidential information on tapes and disks before they are sent out for recertification and for cleaning

- Degauss, or in some other way obliterate, scratch tapes and disks whenever they have been used in the processing of confidential information

- Document the library procedures and the librarians' duties

Figure 6-11 *Continued*

tion of the information easier to accomplish. Listings of program and system files make it possible for perpetrators to identify the controls in the programs and systems. They can then determine how to circumvent, disable, or modify the controls. They can also see how the program or system functions and can determine how to change the programs or systems to incorporate their fraud directly into the system.

Uncontrolled access to the tapes and disks may also allow the perpetrator to manipulate and modify the program, system, and data files, or to create new tapes and disks with modified information and to substitute the bogus files for the proper, accurate files.

Uncontrolled access to the documentation presents many of the same risks as access to the program, system, and data files. The system controls, the way the system or program functions, and the format of the files and records in the files can all be determined from the documentation. Thus, the physical security of the documentation is as important as the physical security of the tapes and disks.

Assign control of the library to librarians. One or more employees should be given the responsibility for the custody, maintenance, and recordkeeping of the tapes, disks, and documentation. The librarians should be responsible for maintaining control of everything stored in the library and for performing the necessary control procedures. Unless someone is designated as being responsible for the library, it is unlikely that the proper control and security procedures will be observed.

Restrict access to the tape, disk, and documentation libraries. Access should be limited to the librarians who are responsible for maintaining the libraries. Computer operators and systems and programming personnel must not be permitted access to the libraries if the integrity of the data, programs, and systems software is to be preserved.

Require all tapes, disks, and documentation to be stored in the libraries. In order to provide the needed security, all tapes, disks, and documentation must be stored in the libraries when not in use. If any items are allowed to be stored elsewhere, it becomes very difficult to ensure their integrity. It also becomes difficult to keep track of such items. If enough items are stored out of the libraries, it becomes difficult, if not impossible, to keep track of and to provide adequate security for all the items. The library controls would become ineffective.

Provide the librarians with a list of personnel authorized to access specific files and documentation. The librarians must know who is authorized to physically access specific files and documentation. They should not rely solely on their own judgment, on the particular situation, or on the say-so or assertion of any individual. This list may be organized by the security levels of the various files and documentation; or it may be organized by individual files and documentation. The list must be kept up to date. Whenever there is a termination, a change in one or more employees' responsibilities, or a change in access authorization, the list must be immediately updated to reflect the change. Without such a list the librarians cannot be expected to maintain adequate and effective access control.

Maintain a library log of all tapes, disks, and documentation removed from and returned to the libraries. Every time a tape, disk, or documentation manual is removed from the library, even when it is released to operations for a production run, an entry should be made in the library log. The following information should be recorded: tape, disk, or document identification; date and time released; the person to whom the item was released; the reason the item was released; date and time when the item is to be returned.

When the item is returned to the library, the date and time it was actually returned should be noted in the log. The log should be reviewed by the librarians several times during the day. If there are any items that are late in being returned, the person to whom the item was released should be contacted. Items must never be released overnight or for extended periods, unless they are released to an off-site storage location for backup purposes.

It is very important that the librarians know where all tapes, disks, and documentation are at all times. These items must only be released to authorized individuals and, even then, only for authorized or approved purposes. Tapes, disks, and documentation must only be released to operations personnel when the production and/or test schedule indicates that the particular items are needed. Documentation must only be released to systems and programming personnel when they have written approval, from the change committee or data processing department management, to access the information. There is almost no acceptable reason to release tapes or disks to systems and programming personnel. There is no benefit, either to the personnel or to the organization, to be gained by anyone having physical possession of a tape or disk.

Review the library log on a regular basis. The library log should be reviewed by data processing department management to ensure that tapes, disks, and documentation are issued to only authorized personnel and that they are promptly returned after being used. The release of any items to unauthorized personnel, the release of any items to authorized personnel for suspicious or unauthorized purposes, the release of any items overnight or for extended periods, the late return of items, and any other suspicious conditions, such as patterns of the release of items to particular personnel or of continual late return of items by particular personnel, should be immediately and completely investigated. Such incidences or patterns could be an indication that fraud is being perpetrated.

Maintain a media maintenance log. The media maintenance log should identify when and how particular tapes and disks are maintained. This log should be reviewed periodically to ensure that the media are properly maintained.

Maintain an inventory list of all tapes, disks, and documentation. A complete inventory of all tapes, disks, and documentation should be maintained by the librarian. The inventory list should identify the storage location in the library of each item. Items sent to an off-site storage location should be so designated. It is critical that this inventory be updated continuously because it is very important in the control of the tapes, disks, and documentation, and in the identification and investigation of missing and extra items.

Maintain a complete inventory of all files. An inventory of all program and data files should be maintained. The data file inventory should identify for each file the reels or packs on which the file resides, the creation date, the identification of program that created the file, the retention period, the expiration or release date, the generation number, the identification of the transaction files that updated the file, and an indication of its security classification. The program file inventory should identify for each production file the reel or pack on which the program resides, the creation date, the modification dates, the change request form number for each modification, the version number of each modification, the catalog control form number for the original program or system and for all modifications, and an indication of its security classification.

Institute procedures to prevent the unauthorized removal of tapes, disks, and documentation from the data processing department. Strict procedures to prevent the removal of tapes, disks, and documentation from the data processing department should be instituted and followed. Such procedures will probably necessitate inspection by the receptionist or security guard of all packages, bags, and briefcases that are carried or sent out of the data processing department. Special release forms for the removal of tapes, disks, and documentation to an off-site storage location should be signed by the librarian and authorized by appropriate data processing department management. The release form should identify all the items being removed. The receptionist or security guard should verify the identity and authority of the person transporting the items and should compare the list with the items being removed to ensure that only the items authorized to be removed are, in fact, being removed.

Institute procedures to prevent the unauthorized introduction of tapes, disks, and documentation into the data processing department. Strict procedures should be implemented to prevent introduction of items into the data processing department. Thus, it will probably be necessary for the receptionist or security guard to inspect all packages, bags, and briefcases being carried into or sent to the department. Such tapes, disks, and documentation could be modified or manipulated versions of existing items that are intended to replace the accurate versions or are to be used in the place of accurate versions. Whenever items are being returned to the library from an off-site storage location, the receptionist or security guard should be provided with a list identifying each item. The list should be signed by the librarian and authorized by appropriate data processing department management. The receptionist should positively identify the person returning the items, and should verify each item being returned against the list, initialing the items on the list as each item is checked.

Require the use of external labels on all tapes and disks. All tapes and disks should have external labels identifying the reel or pack. Tape files should have labels containing the following information in addition to the tape or reel identification number: file name, creation date, retention period, expiration date, reel number (for multi-reel files), density and number of tracks, dates cleaned, and date recertified. It may also be desirable to identify the job that created the file and the job (or jobs) for which the file is an input file.

Require the use of internal labels. Internal labels, in the form of tape and disk identification records and file header and trailer records, should be required for all volumes and all data files, regardless of whether these files are on tapes or on disks. The header and trailer records should contain identification of the file, the creation date, the retention period, record counts, control totals, and other control information.

The operating system should be designed to issue mount messages for the tapes and removable disks. It should also check the tape and disk identification labels to verify that the appropriate tape or disk was mounted before permitting processing of the information on the volume.

All production or operational programs should be required to check the internal labels both before and after processing and to update the appropriate control totals after processing. As discussed in Chapter 8, if any discrepancies between control totals are detected by the program, they must be identified in the output reports. A complete listing of the file should be provided to the appropriate user department so that the discrepancy can be thoroughly investigated and corrected. Label checking should never be bypassed.

Conduct regular and surprise inspections of the library. On both a regular and a surprise basis, data processing department management should compare the contents of the library to the inventory list. Any extra items found in the library that are not on the inventory should be investigated immediately. An extra set of tapes may constitute an extra set of books, in much the same way that a manual fraud would require a double set of books. If extra tapes are found, a partial listing of their contents should be made. The internal label should be compared with the external label and with the inventory list. The record formats and fields should also be examined to determine if they match the record formats and fields of a tape that is on the inventory list. These steps should provide some indication of whether or not the extra tapes contain a second set of particular files. It is also necessary to determine when and how these extra tapes were used. Thus, the creation date on the external label should be checked against the library log to find out if the tape was released to and returned from operations on or about that date. The library log should also be reviewed for a few years prior to the creation date to see if the tape was used before the creation date. Console logs should also be reviewed for the appearance of that tape as an input or output file for particular programs.

If items identified on the inventory list are not found in the library, the library log should be reviewed to determine when and to whom the item was last released. If the item is late being returned, the reason for the delay should be ascertained. If the library log indicates that the item is not currently released, the person to whom the item was last released must be determined and an investigation undertaken. Again, it will be necessary to review the console logs to find out when the tapes or disks were used. Although these investigations are time-consuming and very involved, they are necessary if you are to be successful in detecting and deterring fraud.

Conduct regular tests of the accuracy of the external labels. The internal labels on your tapes should be compared with the external labels on a regular basis for a random sample of tapes to ensure that they are the same and that a bogus file has not been substituted for the proper, accurate file.

Maintain an up-to-date inventory of all items stored in an off-site storage location. An inventory of all items in an off-site storage location should be maintained. On a regular and surprise basis, the items actually in the off-site location should be checked against the inventory list. The existence of extra items or the absence of items could be an indication that some manipulation or fraud has taken or is taking place. Investigations identified above for library inventory discrepancies should be undertaken immediately.

Institute procedures to ensure that adequate security is provided for all items stored in the off-site storage location. The tapes, disks, and documentation stored off-site are as vulnerable, if not more so, to exposure, unauthorized access and use, and manipulation as the tapes, disks, and documentation stored in your library. Steps should be taken to ensure that adequate security is provided to all items stored off-site. Periodic security reviews of the off-site storage locations should be conducted. The security of the items during transportation to and from the off-site location must also be carefully studied and evaluated.

Store critical data and program files and their documentation in vaults or safes. For particularly critical or sensitive data and program files, additional security may be appropriate. Such files and their documentation should be stored in vaults or safes in the library. These vaults and safes must be locked, along with the door to the library, whenever the librarian is not in the library.

Conduct regular and surprise inspections of the contents of the files. On a regular and surprise basis, the contents of the program and data files should be checked to ensure that the files are complete, accurate, and contain no unauthorized or spurious entries. User departments may be given the responsibility of verifying the accuracy and integrity of their respective data files. Data processing department management should be responsible for the verification of the program files.

Institute procedures to ensure that adequate security is provided for your data and program files whenever they are sent to a service bureau or other company for processing. Many companies go to great lengths to preserve the confidentiality and integrity of their program and data files. However, when they send their files to a service bureau to be processed or to be reproduced on computer output microfilm, they take no steps to ensure that the service bureau will provide adequate security and protect the confidentiality and integrity of the information.

Degauss, or in some other way obliterate, confidential information on tapes and disks before they are sent out for recertification and for cleaning. The contents of files on tapes and disks are vulnerable to exposure to large numbers of people when the tapes and disks are sent to a service bureau or other company for recertification or for cleaning. To protect the confidentiality of the files, the tapes and disks should be degaussed or overwritten so that their contents are obliterated.

Degauss, or in some other way obliterate, scratch tapes and disks whenever they have been used in the processing of confidential information. Extend the controls to your scratch tapes. Don't forget that confidential information could be made available to unauthorized people whenever scratch tapes and disks are used during the processing of confidential information.

Document the library procedures and the librarian's duties. To ensure that the librarians know their responsibilities and the procedures that they are to follow, the responsibilities and procedures must be clearly and completely documented. This documentation will make it possible for data processing department management to enforce the procedures since the librarians and management know what the required procedures and responsibilities are. It will also facilitate the cross-training of the librarians, if there are librarians for prime, second, and third shifts, as well as the training of new librarians. The document should include the following procedures: procedures for handling new tapes and disks, including logging and labeling; setup procedures for production runs; logging procedures; log and inventory maintenance and review; tape and disk maintenance procedures; off-site storage procedures, including choosing items to be sent; sending and receiving procedures; assignment of scratch and test tapes and disks; sensitive and confidential tape and disk procedures; security procedures; and other pertinent information.

<table>
<tr><td>Library management aids</td><td>The librarian may be aided by the use of tape and disk management systems. Some of the library management systems available today are identified in Appendix H. Such systems typically provide inventory information and tape and file maintenance information. They also produce many reports, including physical inventories, file inventories, scratch tape inventories, file expiration and retention information, job setup information, and tape status and activity information.</td></tr>
</table>

SYSTEM INTEGRITY   The subject matter of this section of our chapter on computer security addresses the need to maintain the integrity of the system software, including the operating system and system support, or utility, programs, and of all programs and systems, and their work areas, while they are executing. This section, with its emphasis on isolation techniques, is the first part of a much broader and comprehensive discussion of access controls, and authentication and protection mechanisms. The remainder of the discussion will be found in Chapter 7.

Programs that are being executed must be isolated from one another. Their work areas and files must be protected. The reason for this isolation and protection is to prevent the programs, work areas, and files from being destroyed, modified, or compromised by other programs or users of the system. The destruction, modification, or compromise may be the result of an inadvertent and undetected programming error, or of an error or flaw in the operating system. It may also be the result of a deliberate attempt of another user to perpetrate fraud.

Because the security features to prevent programs and users from interfering with one another have traditionally been incorporated into the operating system, it is also necessary to protect the operating system. Users and programs must be prevented from bypassing the operating system, thereby bypassing all the controls built into it, and from capturing the operating system, thereby subverting the controls.

Isolation of the system software   The basic, and most common, mechanism for isolating the system software is the system state bit, a hardware flip-flop mechanism. The system state bit determines whether the program is executing in supervisor, or privileged, state or in user or problem program (nonprivileged) state. The operating system runs in supervisor state; the system state bit is "on." User programs run in problem program state; the system state bit is "off." Some of the more modern systems have more than two system states. There is still only one problem program state, however, there may be multiple privileged states.

User programs must rely on the supervisor to perform privileged instructions, instructions that can only be executed in supervisor state. Privileged instructions are used to allocate system resources to applications programs, to perform I/O operations, and to establish and maintain user, program, and file access controls. If a program operating in nonprivileged state tries to execute a privileged instruction, control of the system is automatically turned over to the operating system.

Security of the system software

The system design and maintenance controls, discussed earlier in this chapter and summarized in Figure 6-6, apply to the design and maintenance of the system software as well as the applications programs and systems. They will not be reiterated here. Many of the production system and program controls are also applicable. It is very important to compare the current system software to the latest approved version on a frequent basis to ensure that no unauthorized modifications were made.

To provide additional security to the system software it may be desirable to place the system software in its own hardware, in a separate minicomputer or microprocessor. Thus, if a perpetrator manages to take control of the processing computer, the operating system would not be compromised, modified, or destroyed. Implementing the system software, or those parts of the system software that establish and maintain the security controls, in microcode may provide the best protection. Microcode cannot be modified nearly as easily as object code, and in some instances it cannot be modified at all.

Control of the system programmers

The system programmers may present the greatest threat to the integrity of your system since they know how the system software functions, what weaknesses and holes exist in system software, how to take advantage of the weaknesses and holes in the software, and how to modify or manipulate the system software. Their actions should, therefore, be carefully monitored and controlled.

System software is generally modified by patching, which, as discussed earlier, may pose serious security problems. In order to overcome this problem, the program change and testing controls should be implemented, and the actual change to the system software should be password-controlled. Two passwords should be required to modify the system software. The first password might be the system programmer's password; the second should be the password of the system programming manager or other designated data processing department manager who is authorizing the change. Both people should be required to enter their passwords independently and secretly, and both should be present while the change is being made.

System programmers should be encouraged to enumerate all weaknesses and holes in the system software and to identify the exposures resulting from the weaknesses and holes. It may be desirable to reward them in some way in order to further encourage them to bring the weaknesses and holes to your attention rather than to take advantage of the problems themselves.

Isolation
mechanisms

In addition to the system state bit described above, there are several other isolation mechanisms which we will identify and describe briefly here. These all exist to prevent executing programs from interfering with one another.

Memory bounds registers. The memory bounds registers are hardware registers. Two such registers are assigned to each program before it is executed. The operating system loads these registers with memory addresses. One address is the base address, which is the lowest memory address that the program can access. The other address is the bound address, which may be either the highest memory address that the program can access or the number of memory locations beyond the base address that the program can access. Each memory reference by the executing program is checked with the memory bounds registers before it is performed. If the reference falls within the set memory bounds, it is performed. If it does not, the reference check automatically transfers control to the operating system.

Hardware locks and keys. Memory is divided into fixed-size blocks. The operating system assigns a key to each executing program by setting the value of the key in a hardware register associated with the program. The operating system also sets the hardware registers (locks) associated with the blocks of memory assigned to the program. Whenever the executing program references a memory location, the program's key is compared to the applicable memory block's lock. If they are equal, the reference is performed. If they are not, control is automatically turned over to the operating system.

Paging. Memory is divided into fixed-size blocks called pages. The operating system maintains page tables for each user program. The page tables are used to translate virtual memory addresses into

158

actual physical memory addresses. Whenever an executing program references a memory location, the virtual address is translated into the physical address and the physical address is tested to determine whether or not the physical address is within a page assigned to the program at that particular time. If it is, the reference is processed. If it is not, control is automatically turned over to the operating system.

Others. There are several other isolation mechanisms, including compartmentization, segmentation, capabilities, and rings of protection. These will be discussed in Chapter 7.

Potential problem areas

There are many ways in which fraud can be perpetrated. Let us look at some of them and then identify some of the recommended controls. It should be recognized that most of the widely used operating systems were designed when the emphasis was on function and performance, before security became a major concern. Thus, they are not well equipped to deal with the problems and threats that exist today. There is now a heavy emphasis on developing secure system software.

Sensitive residue. In some operating systems, service routines control I/O and use buffers supplied by the program. If the system software does not "clean out" the buffer before returning control to the program, some sensitive system information may be made available to the program. This problem is more complex in systems that permit asynchronous I/O and processing, since such systems make it possible for the program to copy the information from the buffer as the buffer is being cleaned. They permit concurrent access to memory by both the I/O routines and by the processor.

Sensitive or confidential information may be left in main memory or on secondary storage when the system crashes or when a program terminates normally or abnormally. Unless the system software or program obliterates the information by writing over it, the information may be available to a subsequent user or program. This problem is particularly dangerous when temporary disk files containing sensitive or confidential data are not erased.

After a system crash, there may be a tremendous amount of sensitive residue in main memory or on secondary storage. Short of writing over all main memory and all temporary storage, which would be very expensive, the operating system would need a complete inventory of all programs, files, and work areas at the time the system crashed in order to limit the amount of "erasing" that had to be done.

Unless action is taken by the system software or by the programs themselves, a tremendous amount of confidential information may be made available to unauthorized users.

Physical I/O.   I/O is generally initiated by the program and carried out by the system software.   The system software, unless under the control of a perpetrator, is generally not concerned with the contents of the data.   A person who wants to commit fraud, however, may be able to bypass some of the security controls built into the system software by using the physical I/O capability.

Recovery and checkpoint/restart.   In addition to the problem of sensitive residue, recovering from a system failure by restarting a program at the last checkpoint reached may present a security problem.   The program status recorded at that checkpoint may be manipulated before the program is restarted.   Since the system status bit is stored at the checkpoint, a perpetrator of fraud may change the system status bit, thereby causing the program to restart in privileged status with access to all privileged instructions.

This opportunity may also exist when user-supplied error routines are used to recover from an error that would generally cause the program to end abnormally.   The error routine is given access to the program status information at the time the error occurred. Since the system status bit is often part of the program status information, the perpetrator may be able to change the system status bit before restarting the program.

System support, or utility, programs.   System support programs and other system software should be controlled by the same security controls built into the operating system as the applications programs. However, this is often not the case.   These programs can frequently be used to access any programs and files.   Thus, they may be used by unauthorized people to gain access to sensitive and confidential information.

The controls   The controls are summarized in Figure 6-12.   This list is by no means complete.   Many more controls will be discussed in Chapter 7.

**OPERATIONS
CONTROLS**   Operations controls relate to the computer operators' activities and to the running or operation of the computer equipment.   The purpose of these controls is to reduce the likelihood that fraud will be perpetrated in the computer room by increasing the probability that the fraud will be detected.   Several of the controls have been discussed elsewhere in this chapter.   We will only summarize them here, in Figure 6-13.

- Perform periodic penetration tests or similar analyses of your system software to determine if it is possible for:
    - Applications programs to access areas of memory outside their assigned area
    - Applications programs to get into the supervisor (executive) state
    - Applications programs to execute their own input/output instructions
    - Applications programs to read or overlay the operating system (executive)
    - Utility programs to access programs and data without proper authorization
    - Applications programs to get into the supervisor state by chaining calls to the operating system, or other means used to "confuse" the operating system

- Compare current system software to carefully checked master versions on a regular basis and whenever the current system software has been modified

- Maintain an inventory of all system software, including vendor identification, update and change information, and responsible system programmers

- Store operating system and job accounting parameters, and program patches in a protected library (they should be automatically called in at IPL time)

- Institute procedures to review updates to the systems software supplied by the vendor to help insure that the updates are necessary, valid, and appropriate

- Institute procedures to test updates to the systems software

- Protect the systems software from all unauthorized access

- Store sensitive utility programs in a protected library segregated from other utility programs

- Protect sensitive utility programs from unauthorized access

- Implement the security software in microcode whenever possible

- Implement methods to automatically erase sensitive memory residue after a system crash and after an application program terminates (either normally or abnormally)

- Implement program/system change controls and program/system testing controls identified in Figure 6-6

- Require the use of two passwords to modify the system software and observation of the modification process by a second technical specialist

- Insure that at least two system programmers are trained in the maintenance of system software and that each gains hands-on experience

- Prevent system programmers from accessing the production and test program libraries

Figure 6-12

System Software Integrity Controls and Safeguards

- Prohibit the operators from having access to the program, data, and documentation libraries
- Limit the operators' responsibilities to those directly related to the operation of the computer equipment
- Prohibit anyone other than the operators from operating the computer equipment
- Prohibit anyone other than the operators and operations personnel from having access to the computer room
- Prohibit the operators from initiating or correcting any transactions, adjustments, or master file entries
- Rotate the operators among the shifts and rotate their responsibilities
- Maintain tight control over the console logs
- Review the console logs frequently, at least daily
- Investigate all job reruns and operator interventions
- Require all programs to be run under the control of an operating system that automatically logs their use, without exception, on the console log
- Require the preparation of operators' logs
- Compare the operators' log to the authorized run list or production schedule
- Establish standard run times for each production program and compare actual run times to the standard, where possible
- Prohibit operators from making program modifications
- Prohibit operators from working alone
- Read, log, and review data processing equipment usage meters
- Account for all computer time
- Maintain output logs
- Destroy carbon paper from output containing sensitive or confidential information
- Prepare complete operating instructions for all production programs
- Shield the computing equipment and connecting cables
- Prepare comprehensive management reports
- Remove all sensitive and confidential data, remove the system disk, and return them to the library whenever the equipment is being serviced
- Institute effective controls and procedures for facsimile check signing operations and for the handling of spoiled and voided checks
- Make use of system performance measurement aids

Figure 6-13

Operations Controls

The controls   *Maintain tight control over console logs.* The console logs should provide a record of all jobs processed, of all operator activities, and of anything done to the system. The logs are invaluable in determining everything that was done to or with the system. They are, thus, invaluable in the detection of fraud. Every rerun, authorized or unauthorized, is recorded. Every program run, scheduled or unscheduled, and the actual run time for each program is recorded. Every file processed, authorized or unauthorized, proper or improper, is identified. Every operator intervention, including overrides and halts, is logged. The console logs provide a tremendous amount of information, and must, therefore, be protected against alteration or manipulation.

There are several ways to protect the integrity of the console logs. The console logs should be produced on paper with preprinted sequential page numbers. The operators should be required to account for each and every page at the end of each shift. Prenumbered console pages will prevent an operator from advancing the console paper to a clean page when performing an unauthorized or fraudulent act, removing that page from the log, and destroying it.

Each entry on the console log should be numbered sequentially. This will prevent an operator from inserting a blank piece of paper in the console, in front of the console log, having the improper action recorded on the extra paper, and destroying the paper, thereby leaving the console log seemingly intact.

Numbering both the console log pages and the entries can be effective in controlling operators' activities provided that the console logs are reviewed at the end of every shift, or, at a minimum, once a day, to ensure that all pages and all entries have been accounted for. The operators must be held accountable. If any pages or entries are missing, an investigation should be undertaken without delay.

If especially sensitive information is processed frequently, or if numbered pages and numbered entries cannot be provided, it may be desirable to install an additional console and to lock that console in another room, inaccessible to the operators, so that alteration or manipulation of the logs is impossible.

Review the console logs. The console logs should be reviewed by appropriate and responsible supervisory or managerial personnel at the end of each shift or once a day. The purpose of this review is to make sure that no pages of the log are missing, that no entries are missing, and that there are no unexplained time gaps. The review should also include a check for improper operating procedures, suspicious reruns, unauthorized runs, and improper or unauthorized operator interventions, such as overrides and halts. All suspicious entries or improper actions should be investigated since they indicate potentially serious problems and possibly fraud.

Investigate all reruns and operator interventions. All reruns and all operator interventions, such as overrides, interrupts, halts, and restarts, should be investigated in a timely manner. A detailed explanation of each such occurrence should be provided. In addition, the occurrences of reruns and operator interventions should be charted to determine if there are any patterns emerging. The individual occurrences or patterns of occurrences could be an indication that fraud is being perpetrated by the computer operators.

It may be desirable to require authorization, by the operations manager, for all reruns and restarts. A perpetrator might rerun a program to produce a second set of output, or to introduce additional or fraudulent data. He might stop an executing program to prevent it from processing all the data. He also might stop an executing program, with the intention of restarting it at a checkpoint or at the beginning after he has altered the data. The opportunities to perpetrate fraud are almost limitless; therefore, all operator interventions and all reruns must be reviewed very carefully if you are to be successful in deterring and detecting fraud.

Require all programs to be run under the control of an operating system that automatically logs their use, without exception, on the console log. It must be possible to identify each and every program that is run to verify that the runs were authorized. If it is possible to run jobs in such a way as to prevent a record of the run from being generated, it will be very difficult to determine if unauthorized processing is being performed and to identify the files, data, and programs involved. Fraudulent processing would be difficult, if not impossible, to discover.

Require the preparation of operators' logs. Operators should be required to prepare written logs identifying the jobs run and showing the date, setup time, processing start and stop times, processing status (such as normal, rerun, test), and any relevant comments for each job. They should also be required to initial each entry on the log.

The operators' logs should also reflect all equipment malfunctions, idle time, and downtime. A carefully prepared and detailed explanation should be included for each malfunction or incidence of idle or downtime. The operations supervisors or managers should review all such entries for completeness and accuracy and should initial each entry to indicate that it was reviewed.

Compare the operators' logs to the authorized run list or production schedule. The operators' logs should be compared to the au-

164

thorized run list or production schedule daily. This comparison will identify unauthorized processing of programs and data. All unauthorized runs should be investigated. The occurrence of unauthorized runs should be charted by date and time. A chart will help to highlight patterns of unauthorized processing, and will, therefore, highlight when the problems are occurring and who is responsible for the problems.

Establish standard run times for each production program and compare actual run times to the standard. Standard run times for each production program should be established. The standard run time should be developed by running each production program with a representative or average number of transactions and mix of transaction types. The actual run times, as recorded on the console log, should then be compared to the standard run times on a regular and frequent basis. Significant deviations between actual and standard run times should be investigated. They may indicate that unauthorized processing took place.

Prohibit operators from making program modifications. The controls discussed in the section "Program/System Change Controls" must be followed at all times to ensure the integrity of the programs and systems. Operators must never be permitted to make program modifications of any kind. They must be strictly prohibited from patching programs from the console. Permitting operators to change or patch programs is a serious breach of the recommended segregation of duties. It provides an opportunity for the operators to perpetrate an almost unlimited number of frauds.

Prohibit operators from working alone. Whenever possible, two or more operators should be working during each shift. If two operators are not present, the operations manager should be present in the computer room. The purpose of this control is to require collusion if fraud is to be perpetrated successfully. As discussed in Chapter 5, requiring collusion can be a deterrent to fraud and an aid in its detection. One operator would have to seek the cooperation of another operator if he is to perpetrate fraud; and the more people that are involved in the fraud, the more likely it is to be detected. If this control is combined with frequent rotation of operators, the deterrent effect can be further enhanced.

Read, log, and review data processing equipment use meters. Use of the data processing equipment should be recorded in a log at the beginning and end of each shift. This log should be reviewed regularly for possible unauthorized use of equipment. By charting the usage, in addition to reviewing it, patterns of usage may be discovered. Such patterns could reflect unauthorized and possibly fraudulent usage of the equipment.

The actual usage of the equipment should be reconciled with the planned usage. Discrepancies or variances between the actual and planned usage should be investigated in a very timely manner. This control will be an aid in the detection of unauthorized and fraudulent processing. If it is performed regularly, it can be an effective deterrent to fraud.

Comparative usage reports should be prepared showing actual (metered) usage; planned usage; and variances between actual and planned usage, actual usage for this time period and actual usage for the previous time period, and actual usage for this time period and actual usage for the same time period last year. The data processing department director should review these reports very carefully.

Account for all computer time. The total CPU time allocated to processing production programs and developing and testing new programs should be compared to the total CPU time used, as recorded on the CPU meter. Significant variances between allocated and actual times should be investigated to ensure that unauthorized or fraudulent processing did not take place.

Maintain output logs. All output produced should be reflected in an output log. The computer operator or person responsible for the handling and distribution of output should record the following information: date, time, quantity in pages, number of copies, method of delivery, delivery person, and the person and department to whom delivery is to be made. These logs will provide a record of all output produced and will provide a means of reconciling and charting the use of forms supplies.

A catalog or other listing of all computer-generated reports indicating the number of copies to be produced and the distribution for each copy must be maintained by the data processing department. This will help to ensure that the appropriate number of copies are produced and that they are properly distributed.

Destroy carbon paper from output containing sensitive or confidential information. The carbon paper from multiple-part, continuous-form printouts contains the information printed on the computer-generated report. It can be read. To protect the confidentiality of the information, the carbon paper should be destroyed by burning or shredding as soon as possible after the output has been decollated. It must not be thrown out intact.

Prepare operating instructions for all production programs. The operating instructions for production programs should contain all the information needed to run the programs and none else. It should identify all console messages, error messages, and halt or "abnormal end" messages, and should explain, in detail, each message and the action to be taken. It should also identify the equipment to be used, the input transactions, the data files, the output forms, the handling and distribution of the output, and any other required information. It should not contain program listings or identification of the programmed controls.

The operating instructions must be complete enough so that the operators can run the programs independently, without having to seek the assistance of the programmers. It should not contain enough information to allow the operators to manipulate the input transactions, files, programs, or processing and thereby perpetrate fraud.

All new and revised operating instructions should be reviewed and approved by the operations manager. The review is to verify that the instructions are complete, understandable, and leave little room for confusion and error.

Shield the computing equipment and connecting cables. If you are processing extremely sensitive and confidential information, you should consider taking steps to shield the central processing systems and connecting cables to prevent the emission of signals that could be picked up by "bugs" planted by espionage agents.

Other controls

Reports should be prepared for management review. The reports should identify unscheduled runs, uncompleted runs (with an explanation of each), completed runs, nonproductive machine time (with an explanation of each occurrence of equipment malfunctions and downtime), equipment usage (charts and statistics), operator interventions (with an explanation of each occurrence), and deviations between actual and standard run times for production programs.

Whenever the computer equipment is being worked on, regardless of whether it is to perform preventive maintenance or it is to correct a malfunction, an operator should be present. All sensitive and confidential information should be removed from the equipment and returned to the library. The system disk, containing all or portions of the operating system, should also be removed from the disk drive to prevent compromise of the operating system and of the controls built into the operating system. If it is not possible to remove the system disk, consideration should be given to obliterating its contents when the equipment is being serviced and to restoring the information after the servicing has been completed.

Controls should be instituted to provide additional security for facsimile-check-signing operations. Procedures must be specified for the handling of spoiled checks and checks to be voided.

Some of the controls discussed above could be performed in an automated manner through the use of system performance measurement software. Appendix H contains a list of some of the software packages that are currently available. Whenever such software is used, its output should be cross-checked with actual equipment meter readings, console logs, and any other available information.

The importance of accounting for all equipment usage cannot be overemphasized. It is an invaluable method for detecting computer fraud.

> Every use of the computer whether it be to test a program, run a job or copy a file is recorded by the system measurement facility. This tool alone would have helped to detect over half the reported computer frauds.[4]

**SUPPLIES
CONTROLS**

The blank and preprinted output forms and input media are also resources of the data processing department. As such they, too, require protection. The necessary controls include the following:

- Account for the use of punched cards, paper tape, blank output forms, preprinted forms, multipart output forms, console paper, and all other input and output media.
- Reconcile the actual use of input and output media with the planned use and investigate significant variances (unauthorized numbers of copies of output may be being produced).
- Maintain tight forms control over checks and other official or important forms.
- Store preprinted forms, such as checks and other official or important forms, in vaults or safes.

[4] Marshall Romney, "Fraud and EDP," *The CPA Journal*, November 1976, p. 26.

7

Communications and Data Base Systems Safeguards

Neither the objectives of computer fraud nor the fundamental aspects of the underlying manipulations and deceptions differ much in data base/data communications (DB/DC) systems versus non-DB/DC systems.

What does distinguish DB/DC systems and make them worth considering as a class are the special security problems attendant to having *multiple users accessing centralized data through terminal devices at remote locations linked to a central computer system via telephone lines or other communications links.*

The teller terminal in banking may enable any teller to update all accounts in the data base, regardless of the branch offices to which the accounts are assigned. Accordingly, the bank gives the customer the advantage (and itself the competitive feature) of "any branch—any teller" banking services. Some readers will remember that, in times past, bank customers had to go to their assigned branch and (if it was a large branch) go to a particular teller serving customers whose last names were in a certain range (A through E) to make a savings account transaction (particularly a withdrawal).

Before the era of computerized airlines reservations systems with their DB/DC capabilities, the job of making a reservation was a time-consuming, cumbersome chore for the customer as well as the airline.

In manufacturing, insurance, securities brokerage, public utilities, and many other industries (not to mention education, law enforcement, and other government services) it has become commonplace to see DB/DC systems putting managers, staff, and customers in touch with information and processing capabilities they need to conduct business. Dozens, hundreds, thousands, and even tens of thousands of people (users of an automated teller machine) may be users of such DB/DC systems.

It would take more than the space contained in this book to extol the virtues of particular DB/DC systems, just as it would take more than the available space to discuss their particular security and control vulnerabilities. The key to understanding the vulnerabilities is recognizing that you are dealing, in relative terms, with a large population of users, massive amounts of data, many communications links, and perhaps a vast array of functions. This translates into a large number of possible places where the security of the system and integrity of the data may be compromised for fraudulent purposes.

In this chapter we will explain the latest techniques and safeguards to protect against compromises of DB/DC systems. They are covered in these sections:

- Terminal physical security considerations.
- User identification and authentication.
- Authorization.
- Surveillance.
- RACF—example of a specific data/software security system.
- Communications line safeguards.
- Encryption systems.
- On-line program development.
- Data base integrity.
- Administrative considerations.

TERMINAL PHYSICAL SECURITY CONSIDERATIONS

In remotely accessible computer systems, the terminals may be teletypewriters, keyboard/displays, minicomputers or intelligent terminals, remote job entry stations, automated teller machines, or any other type. Because they are the machines through which data are entered and output is received, and can be used to perpetrate computer fraud, their physical security deserves consideration. In this section we will briefly discuss:

- Terminal access controls.
- Terminal control features.

All terminals, of every type, have at least one thing in common—
the need to be protected against sabotage or unauthorized use. Although the principles for determining proper physical location, and
the procedures for restricting access are essentially the same as those
that apply to the central computer facility, the problems of remote
terminals are even more difficult. Isolated locations, inadequate
supervision and user access by more people all increase the likelihood
of compromised security.[1]

Access to the terminals should be restricted whenever possible.
It is particularly important to restrict access to terminals that are
used to access or update sensitive data files, data bases, and programs.
Access to such terminals should be limited only to people authorized
to use the terminals. If certain terminals are designated for on-line
program development only, they, too, should be secured against
unauthorized use. It may be desirable to isolate such terminals in
locked rooms to which only authorized users have keys.

There are many control features that are or may be built into the
terminal itself to enhance security. We will only discuss some of the
more common features here.

The terminal may be equipped with a lock that, in the absence of
the proper key, prevents the terminal from being used. Keys are provided only to authorized users of the terminal. There are two problems with this feature. Keys may be lost, stolen, or duplicated; and
locks may be picked or bypassed. If a key is lost or stolen, or is
suspected to have been duplicated, it may be necessary to rekey the
lock and issue new keys to the authorized users. It may also be
necessary to rekey the lock if a previously authorized user's authorization is removed or changed, because requiring the return of the key
in no way assures that the key was not duplicated prior to its return.

With regard to picking or bypassing a terminal lock, many of the
locks and installations we see can be readily defeated by an amateur
locksmith. If one of your important fraud prevention measures relies
on terminal locks, you would be well advised to get the opinion of a
master locksmith on the extent to which the locks are *manipulation-
resistant*. Also, note whether electrical contacts on the terminal lock
could be easily bypassed with a *jumper wire,* by opening the terminal
cabinet or tilting the terminal on edge to expose its internal wiring.

Terminals may be equipped with magnetic card or badge readers.
A legitimate card or badge must be inserted into the reader in order
to activate the terminal. The cards or badges are distributed to authorized users only. Such cards or badges usually serve another purpose in addition to activating the terminal. They often play a role in

[1] Seymour Bosworth, "Hardware Elements of Security," *Computer Security
Handbook* (New York: Macmillan Information, 1973), p. 56.

the identification and authentication of the user, as we will see in the next section.

The keyboard of the terminal may be locked by the computer system whenever the system suspects that an unauthorized person is trying to access the system, or an authorized user is trying to access, change, or enter information he is not authorized to access, change, or enter. Thus, the person would be prevented from further breaching the security of the system, at least until the terminal was unlocked by the appropriate security officer.

A terminal may have its own identification by which it is able to positively identify itself to the computer system. The security code for the terminal identification is generally hard-wired (installed in the circuitry where it is protected against tampering) in the terminal. This feature is particularly important if the terminal is not in a secure location; if the terminal is used to access sensitive data files, data bases, or programs; or if the communications network uses public dial-up or switching equipment (anyone from anywhere can dial up the system). The problem of positively identifying terminals is that, if a terminal should malfunction or break, another terminal cannot either replace it or be used in its place without a time delay.

A terminal might be equipped with a mechanism for checking messages transmitted to it, to be sure that the messages were routed properly, before displaying or printing the information. This mechanism goes hand in hand with the terminal identification feature. It is important in the same situations and has the same drawbacks.

Terminals should have a facility by which the user can prevent information that is entered from being displayed or printed. This facility may be either automatic or manual, in that a user is required to press a special key. This facility is very important for user identification and authentication, and will be discussed below.

Terminals may be equipped with the capability of enciphering and deciphering cryptographic information. This is a particularly important feature in a remotely accessible computer system that maintains sensitive information. This will be discussed later in this chapter.

USER IDENTIFICATION AND AUTHENTICATION

The computer system in a remotely accessible computer system environment must identify, in a positive manner, each user. Establishing the identity of the user is usually a two-step process involving two fundamental notions:

- *Identification*—the process by which the user identifies himself to the computer system.
- *Authentication*—the process by which the user offers proof to the computer system that he is who he claims to be.

The user generally *identifies* himself to the computer system by entering his name, employee number, or account number, or by inserting a card or badge that contains his name, employee number, or account number into a card or badge reader. This identification, however, is insufficient for the computer system to identify the user in a positive manner. The computer system must be reasonably satisfied that the user is who he claims to be; therefore, it must verify the authenticity of the identification.

There are three general bases on which the identity of the user may be established and authenticated:

- Something known by the user, such as his employee number, password, or secret code.
- Something possessed by the user, such as an encoded card or badge, or a key.
- Something about the user, such as his fingerprint or hand, his voice, or his signature.

Let us examine each of these three bases and identify their strengths and weaknesses.

Something known by the user

The user may both identify himself and authenticate his identity by something he knows. He typically *identifies* himself by his name, his employee number, or his account number. He may *authenticate* his identity by something else that he knows. The methods that may be used to authenticate a user's identity by something known are:

- Reusable passwords.
- Once-only codes.
- Limited-use passwords.
- Question-and-answer sequences.

Reusable passwords. The most commonly used method for authenticating the identity of a user is the password. In consumer-oriented electronic funds transfer systems (EFTS), the password is referred to as a personal identification number (PIN) or code (PIC). The user enters his password after having identified himself to the system by entering his name, employee number, or account number. With EFTS, the PIN/PIC is usually entered after the user has identified himself by supplying an encoded plastic card.

The disadvantage of a password is that something known by an authorized user of the computer system may become known to another person who is not authorized to use the system. That other person may then be able to impersonate the authorized user and, thus, be able to perpetrate fraud. There are several ways to minimize this risk and the resulting exposure:

1. The importance of keeping the password secret and secure should be impressed upon all users. They should be told not to leave their passwords lying around where they can be observed by others. In fact, they should be discouraged from writing them down. They should be encouraged to destroy any paper containing the password in such a way that another person cannot learn the password by retrieving the paper from the trash. They should be encouraged not to divulge their password to anyone.

2. The password should be sufficiently short so that it can be memorized. Passwords are generally four to eight alphanumeric characters. As mentioned above, it should not have to be written down to be remembered. Perpetrators of fraud know the obvious and not-so-obvious places where passwords are recorded, such as on paper in a desk drawer or in a wallet, on a desk calendar, on tape stuck underneath the desk or terminal or on the desk drawer, or scratched onto the terminal. On the other hand, the password must not be too short. The degree of security of the password is a function of the possible number of combinations from which it is chosen. For example, if the password is two numeric characters, there are 100 possible combinations. If it is two alphanumeric characters, there are 1,296 possible combinations. If it is four alphabetic characters, and all possible combinations are used (i.e., the password does not have to be pronounceable or a valid English word), there are 456,976 possible combinations. If it is four alphanumeric characters, there are 1,679,616 possible combinations. The more possible combinations, the more difficult it would be for a perpetrator to guess the right one.

3. The password should be fairly random. It should not be something that can be determined easily, such as a person's name or nickname, the name of an immediate family member, a person's birthdate, or the city in which the person resides.

4. The password should be unique for each user. This serves two very important purposes. It reduces the likelihood that the password will become known to other people who are not authorized to use the system or to use that particular password. And, it fixes responsibility on the user if his password is used by an unauthorized person. This would discourage a user from allowing another to use his password because he, the user, would be held accountable.

5. The password should not be printed or displayed when entered into the terminal. If it is not possible to suppress the printing or display, the password should be concealed by over- or under-printed characters. Embedding special nonprinting characters in the password will also help to conceal the password. Concealing the password

when it is entered will make it difficult for a perpetrator to secretly observe the password as it is entered.

6.   The password should never be printed on output reports.

7.   The password should be changed periodically and whenever a compromise of the password is suspected. This will minimize the exposure resulting from the compromise of a password. In time-sharing systems, users generally change their own passwords. In data base systems, it is more common to find that the passwords are changed centrally, for all users, at the same time. Although this ensures that the passwords are changed, it introduces an additional risk of compromise because the new passwords must be distributed to the users. This risk can be minimized. If the users know what day the new passwords are being distributed, they can be instructed to notify the appropriate person if they do not receive the new password, or if the transmittal (i.e., envelope or mailer) appears to have been tampered with or opened. They can also be required to positively acknowledge receipt of the password by signing and returning a turnaround document that accompanied the password.

What should the system do if a user enters an incorrect password? Realizing that everyone makes mistakes, the system should give the user a second chance. If the second entry is also incorrect, the system might:

1.   Give the user one last chance to enter the correct password.

2.   Lock the terminal keyboard in such a way that it can only be unlocked by an appropriately authorized individual.

3.   Refuse to give the user another chance for a period of time, such as 1 minute. This will thwart any schemes to guess a password that are based on high-speed trial and error.

4.   Keep the user trying, and prevent him from accessing any sensitive data and from performing any unauthorized activities if he should guess the password, while alerting the appropriate security officer at the particular terminal location to the attempted penetration of the system. In this way, the perpetrator may be caught red-handed.

Regardless of the action taken by the system, the system should, at a minimum, inform the person at the central security control location (the computer security officer) of the attempted penetration.

We have already identified several ways that a perpetrator might learn an authorized user's password:

- Finding it written down.
- Finding it printed on terminal paper or output reports.
- Observing the user entering it.

- Intercepting the distribution of new passwords.
- Guessing it.
- Being told what it is by the user.

There are other ways as well:

- The perpetrator might learn it by tapping the communications lines.
- The perpetrator might learn it by penetrating the operating system and accessing the file of passwords.
- The perpetrator might use a piggyback penetration scheme. He might insert a minicomputer into the communications lines and intercept the user's sign-on. The minicomputer would return the expected system responses to the user until the user enters his password. Then the minicomputer would respond with an innocuous message (i.e., that the system has failed) and would disconnect the user.

These last three exposures may be controlled by encrypting the password during transmission and by encrypting the file of passwords. The subject of encryption will be discussed later in this chapter.

Once-only codes. Once-only codes are essentially passwords; however, they become invalid as soon as they are used once. Thus, if they are observed being entered, they cannot be used again. Once-only code schemes are implemented in one of two ways. A user may be issued a new code or password whenever he uses the one that he has. Alternatively, a user may be supplied with a list of passwords that must be used in succession. The user must be instructed not to mark off the passwords as they are used so that it will not be apparent which password is to be used next.

There are advantages and disadvantages to single once-only codes and lists of once-only codes. The advantage of single once-only codes is that they do not have to be written down. The disadvantage is that they are vulnerable to exposure during distribution. In addition, in an environment in which the system is accessed frequently by users, the need to get a new code before each access is time-consuming and cumbersome.

The advantages of lists of once-only codes are that the risk of exposure during distribution, and the time involved in distribution, are significantly decreased. The disadvantage is that the codes are written down. Unless the user keeps the list secure, it may fall into the hands of a perpetrator. If a user has not marked off the codes he has used, the perpetrator has only a finite number of passwords from which to choose. The odds of guessing the proper code are significantly increased, especially if the system gives him three chances to enter the correct code. It may be desirable to invalidate the current list as soon as one incorrect password is entered and to issue a new list. Although this will prevent trial-and-error schemes, it does not take into account the fact that an authorized user is bound to make a mistake entering the code at one time or another.

Limited-use passwords. The advantages of reusable passwords and once-only codes may be combined by associating expiration dates or maximum number of uses with a password. For example, the password may expire on the tenth day of the following month. Or, the password may expire after it has been used 17 times. The password can be memorized; it need not be written down. The password must be changed periodically, thereby limiting the amount of exposure if the password should be compromised. Moreover, if a usage count is implemented, or if expiration dates are staggered, new passwords are not distributed to all users at the same time. This may serve to reduce the risk of exposure during distribution because a perpetrator might not be able to find out the distribution date.

Question-and-answer sequences. Question-and-answer sequences are another method to authenticate the identity of a user. This method does not use passwords or codes at all. The user is asked a series of personal questions, to which only he presumably knows the correct answers. The questions may pertain to the user's family (e.g., names, birth dates, birthplaces, anniversaries, etc.), to the user's background (e.g., former addresses, schools attended, teachers' names, etc.), to the user's interests and hobbies, or to the user's preferences (e.g., favorite color, favorite food, etc.). The disadvantage of question-and-answer sequences is that they significantly slow down the sign-on procedure and may become very tedious to the frequent user. It is desirable to maintain a file of questions and then to randomly select a few questions to ask during a particular sign-on. The number of questions asked depends upon several factors, including the time involved in signing onto the system. It also depends on the number of possible answers to the questions and the ease with which a perpetrator may successfully guess the answers. Yes/no and either/or questions are much easier to guess than such questions as "What elementary school did you attend?" or "Where (in what city) was your mother born?" The benefit of asking different sets of questions at each sign-on is that it would be difficult for a perpetrator to learn the correct answers by observing one, or even a few, sign-on sessions.

Because the question-and-answer technique relies on factual information that is somewhat likely to be known by others (friends, coworkers, people with access to personnel and credit records, dossiers, etc.) it should not be used as a sole basis for authentication, and should be avoided in high-security applications.

Something possessed by the user

The user may be given an encoded card or badge, a key, or some other physical item by which to identify himself or to authenticate his identity. Typically, such items are used to establish the identity of a user, and a password, code, or PIN is used for authentication of the identity.

Encoded cards or badges are particularly appropriate in situations where several users share a terminal. Each user is supplied with his own card or badge. The terminal is equipped with a reading station into which the card or badge is inserted. Some terminals may be designed to accept only specific cards or badges. Such terminals, thus, have internal lists of the authorized cards or badges; the lists may be changed by the security officer as authorized users change. Other terminals simply read the card or badge and the computer system establishes the identity of the user.

Keys are appropriate when a single user is assigned *exclusive* use of a terminal for a fixed period of time.

The disadvantage of cards, badges, and keys is that they may be lost, stolen, or duplicated. They may even be stolen, duplicated, and returned without leaving a trace. Keys and locks have an additional disadvantage: locks may be picked. If a card or badge is lost, or suspected to have been duplicated, a new card or badge must be issued and the list of authorized cards or badges must be changed to reflect the change of cards. If a key is lost, stolen, or suspected to have been duplicated, a new key must be issued and the lock must be re-keyed.

If there is a change in authorized users, and cards or badges are used, only the list of authorized cards or badges need be changed. However, if keys are used, the lock may have to be rekeyed.

Optically encoded cards may be the least secure of all physical items because the coding is visible. Magnetically encoded cards may be the most secure because they are the most difficult to duplicate.

Something about the user

Developmental efforts are currently focused on perfecting ways to authenticate the identity of a user by the user's personal and behavioral characteristics. It should be noted that personal and behavioral characteristics are not used to establish the identity of a user. They are used for *authentication*. The characteristics receiving the most attention are:

- Fingerprints, including pattern and distinctive marking recognition.

178

- Hands, including the shape or translucency of the hand, the length of the fingers, and the curvature of the fingertips.
- Signature patterns.
- Signature analysis, including the velocity, acceleration, and pressure characteristics exhibited whenever a person signs his name.
- Voice recognition.

Other characteristics, such as footprints, ear features, and dental features, are also being studied.

The key considerations with regard to the effectiveness of these characteristics for identification validation are their ability to be copied or forged, the ability of a perpetrator to obtain and enter a copy of an authorized person's characteristics (i.e., a copy of the signature or a thin, skinlike glove with an authorized user's fingerprints), and the degree of interpersonal and intrapersonal variations of each characteristic.

Interpersonal variations are the variations of a particular characteristic from one individual to another. Intrapersonal variations are the variations of a particular characteristic exhibited by one individual. A person's voice or signature may be affected by several factors, including his health, emotional condition, stress, or physical condition. A person's fingerprints or hand may be affected by injuries. The degree of intrapersonal variations necessitates the incorporation of tolerances into the recognition process. As the tolerances are increased, the chances of one individual impersonating another also increase. Thus, the probability of a perpetrator successfully gaining access to the system is increased.

AUTHORIZATION

Modern computer systems have innumerable advantages over their predecessors, one of which is the ability of users to share data and programs. This sharing must be controlled if the integrity and confidentiality of the data and programs are to be preserved. Permission must be granted to authorized users of the system, and to production programs, to access the data and programs and to perform some functions (such as execute, read, copy, write, or modify) or combinations of functions. This permission is commonly referred to as *authorization*. Authorization is granted by user management to specific users or groups of users. Authorization must be implemented or enforced by the security software of the computer system. This section will introduce various ways to specify and implement authorization. The section is divided into the following subsections:

- Authorization principles.
- Authorization specification.
- Authorization implementation approaches.

As we shall soon see, there are several methods for specifying and implementing authorization. Regardless of the approach, or approaches, employed, there are several principles that should be established to ensure that the approach is effective in controlling unauthorized or fraudulent actions.

1. Authorization should not be confused with user identification and authentication. User identification and authentication is the procedure by which the user establishes and authenticates his identity and the computer system determines whether or not he is a legitimate user of the computer system. Authorization is performed after user identification and authentication. It is the procedure by which the computer system determines whether or not the user has been given the explicit right (has been authorized) to perform certain actions, such as entering specific types of transactions; executing, reading, or modifying specific programs; or, reading, modifying, or copying specific data. Authorization is also the procedure by which the computer system determines whether or not particular production programs and system software programs have been authorized to access other production or system programs, and data.

2. The system must be able to determine whether or not the user's, or the program's, actions are authorized. Thus, some mechanism for identifying the actions that a user or program is authorized to perform must be established and implemented.

3. Each and every access to every data file, data base, program, or component thereof should be checked for proper authorization. The security system, whether it is part of the operating system, part of the data base management system, or an independent system, must determine whether or not each access is authorized. Furthermore, it must determine whether or not the functions to be performed are authorized. It is not enough to determine the authorization upon the first access only since a perpetrator's strategy may be to try to hide unauthorized actions among authorized and benign actions.

4. The security system must be able to enforce the authorization rules in all environments, in static, unchanging environments as well as in dynamic environments where authorizations may change quickly and frequently. It must not be possible to confuse the security system (e.g., by chaining so many calls to the security system that it ceases to function properly), thereby causing it to lose control, if the system is to be effective. Systems that can be confused, and penetrated, in dynamic environments have been exploited by perpetrators of fraud. If the security system can be penetrated, the system and all its resources (data and programs) may be completely vulnerable to exposure, compromise, unauthorized modification, and possibly destruction. Even if the environment is static, situations may arise

that require changes to authorizations to be effected quickly. Such a situation might arise if an employee is suspected of perpetrating fraud, or if an employee is suddenly terminated or transferred. The system must be able to accommodate such changes.

5.   Every user and program should use only those resources that must be used to do the particular job at hand. Just because a user or program may be authorized to access several system resources (system software, production or test programs, data) and to perform several functions (read, write, modify, execute) on those resources, he, or it, should not invoke all the authorizations if only one or two particular authorizations are necessary at the time. Only those portions of the system that must be exposed should be exposed.

6.   The default condition must always be a denial of access. In other words, unless a user, terminal, or program has explicit authorization to enter a particular type of transaction, or, to access a particular data file, data base, or program, or component thereof, *and* to perform the requested function on the item, the requested transaction, or the access and the function must be denied. The user must also be denied any instructions or prompts that relate to the requested action. Some computer systems tend to view users, terminals, and programs as benign, and to permit access to system resources even if the user, terminal, or program was not explicitly authorized. This is not an acceptable method of operation. It exposes you to disclosure, compromise, unauthorized or fraudulent modification, and destruction of your data and programs.

7.   Users' actions must be monitored and users must be held accountable for their actions. Furthermore, users must know that their actions are being monitored and that they will be held accountable for all unauthorized actions performed either by them or in their name (using their identification and authorization). Knowing that there is a high probability that they will be caught if they do anything wrong or unauthorized, or if they allow something wrong or unauthorized to be done in their name, is a very effective deterrent to fraud.

8.   Regardless of the approach used to implement authorizations, it is of utmost importance that the tables or files containing the authorizations be tightly secured against browsing (reading through the tables or files) and modification by anyone other than the computer security officer. It is also critically important that *all* changes of authorizations be carefully reviewed and monitored by management.

Authorization specification   The specification of authorizations involves three elements:

- •   Resources (protected objects).
- •   Functions (actions/operations).
- •   Subjects (system users).

These three elements must be specified, regardless of the approach used to implement authorization.

Resources, or protected objects. The resources, or protected objects, are the types of transactions, the data, and the programs available in your computer system. Authorization may be granted at one or more of the following levels:

- Entire data file, data base, or program.
- Particular group items within the data base.
- Particular records or categories of records within the data base or data file.
- Particular data fields or categories of data fields within the data base or data file.
- Particular bits within the data fields of a data base or data file.
- Particular data fields or records within the data base or data file, depending upon the value of the particular data field or of another data field.
- Particular data fields or records within the data base or data file, depending upon the number of records or fields that meet the selection criteria.
- Particular transactions or types of transactions.

Thus, a user may be authorized to access the entire data file or data base; or he may be authorized to access only particular components of the data file or data base. This access to particular components of the data file or data base may be dependent upon the value of the particular component or the value of some other component. For example, a user may be able to access the entire payroll file or data base, or only the payroll records of all employees in his department. Or, he may only be able to access the payroll records of employees in his department whose annual salary is less than $20,000. Or, he may be able to access the payroll records of employees in his department whose annual salary is less than $20,000, only if there are at least five employees in that category.

Functions. Whereas access to the protected objects may be granted at one or more of the above-mentioned levels, the functions that the user, or subject, may be authorized to perform may be restricted. The user, program, or terminal may be authorized to perform one or more of the following functions on the protected objects:

- Read.
- Execute.
- Update (add or delete particular records or fields).
- Modify (change particular records or fields).

- Print or copy.
- Enter (input particular transaction types).

The authorization for performing these functions may also be dependent upon the time of day, the time or day during an accounting period, the terminal used, the values of particular data fields, or the number of records or fields that meet the selection criteria.

Subjects. The subjects are the users, the programs, and the terminals used. The subjects are the initiators of the request to perform a specific function on specified protected objects. The subjects may be:

- Individual users.
- Categories, or groups, of users.
- Individual terminals, or groups of terminals (i.e., by location).
- Individual programs (system software and production).
- Categories of programs (system software and production).

Authorization implementation approaches The relationships among the protected objects, functions, and subjects must, in some way, be made available to the computer security system. There are numerous ways to implement authorizations. We will examine a few of the more common ones here:

- Data and program stratification.
- User compartmentalization.
- User security profiles.
- User security codes.
- Terminal security codes.
- Transaction authorization tables.
- Record-type authorization tables.
- User/record-type authorization tables.
- Passwords.
- Access control lists.

It is important to remember that, as authorizations become more detailed and refined, the authorization mechanisms become increasingly complex. Several involved calculations may be necessary to implement authorizations based upon particular data values or upon numbers of items meeting selection criteria.

Data and program stratification. The data and programs may be stratified, or classified, by the degree of security to be provided to them. All data and programs of a confidential and extremely sensitive nature might be one class. Another class might contain confidential data and programs. The number of strata, or classes, defined is dependent upon the number of security levels defined for the data and programs.

This stratification may be carried over to computer memory. The hardware implementation of stratification is referred to as "rings of protection." Memory is divided into segments. Each segment is assigned to one, and only one, ring. Thus, hardware isolation may be provided to the various strata of data and programs.

User compartmentalization. Users may be compartmentalized, or grouped, according to the access privileges afforded to them. The compartments may contain one user identification, or hundreds. The number of compartments or groups defined depends upon the variety of access privileges that are permitted for individual users. All users of a given group have the same access privileges.

Compartmentalization has also been used to define organizational groupings. Each compartment thus contains the user identifications for all users in one department or in one area within a department. Each compartment would then be stratified according to the various levels of access privileges of the users in the group.

As with stratification, compartmentalization may have a hardware isolation counterpart which involves subdividing memory into sections with different access privileges.

User security profiles. A security profile may be established for each user. It typically contains user identification information, including employee number, department number, and the user's access privileges. In systems employing compartmentalization, the profile might, or might not, contain the user's access privileges. It would, however, indicate the compartment of which he is a member.

User security codes. Users may be assigned security codes. The access privileges might then be defined in terms of the security codes. If each user is assigned one security code, the code might be defined in his profile. The user might also be required to enter his security code during sign-on as an additional identification authentication mechanism.

Alternatively, users may be assigned two or more security codes depending upon the types of work they are to perform. The security code entered during sign-on would have to be validated to ensure that the user is authorized to use that code. This multiple-security-code concept is a variation of compartmentalization, in which users may belong to multiple groups. The user authorization tables might use the security codes as the subjects.

Terminal security codes. Terminals might also be assigned security codes. The terminals' security codes are generally defined in terminal profile tables or files. Security codes for a particular terminal might be used to:

- Define the types of transactions and types of actions that can be performed using that terminal.
- Define the users authorized to use that terminal.
- Define the types of information that may be sent to that terminal.

The terminal security code might serve as a limiting factor in the sense that, if the user's authorization is greater than the terminal's, the user may be limited to using the terminal's authorization rather than his own. Figure 7-1 depicts a user sign-on in which the user is assigned a once-only security code. The terminal identification is used to identify the terminal and identify the users authorized to use the terminal.

Transaction authorization tables. Authorization tables define the relationships between subjects, protected objects, and functions. A simple transaction authorization table is depicted in Figure 7-2. The subjects are the users, identified by their user identification numbers. The protected objects are the available types of transactions. The functions are represented by a single bit: 0 (entry is not authorized) and 1 (entry is authorized). Thus, there is one entry for each user, specifying whether or not the user is authorized to enter the particular type of transaction.

Record-type authorization tables. Another type of authorization table is depicted in Figure 7-3. In this table the subjects are the individual users, who are identified by their employee numbers. The protected objects are the various types of records. Three bits are used to specify the functions that the particular user is authorized to perform on the specific type of record. The first bit indicates whether or not he is authorized to read the particular type of record. The second bit indicates whether or not he is authorized to modify the particular type of record. The third bit indicates whether or not he is capable of modifying the particular type of record. He may be authorized to modify the particular type of record, as a function of his position in the organization. However, he may not be capable of modifying the particular type of record until he has received additional training, has spent a minimum amount of time in the position, or has gained more experience.

User/record-type authorization tables. We have looked at two relatively simple authorization tables. Let us now take a look at a more complex authorization table. Implementation of authorization

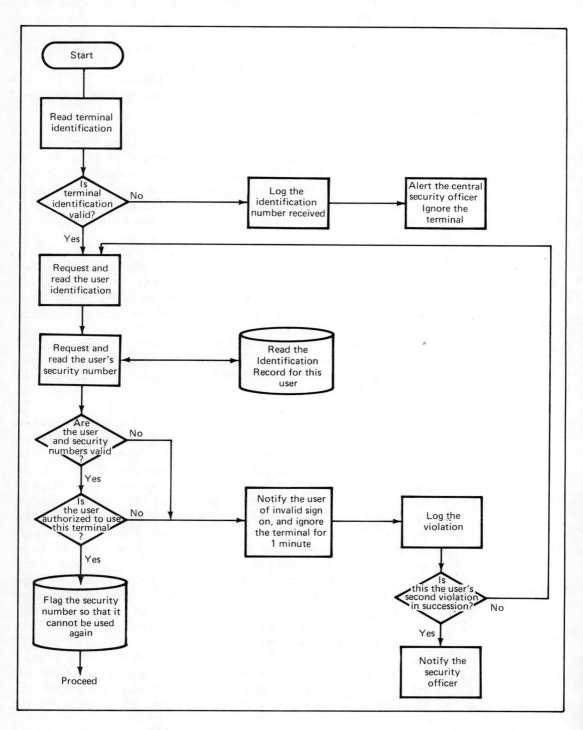

Figure 7-1 (*Opposite page*)

Sign-On Using Terminal Identification Verification and Once-Only Security Code. (After James Martin, *Security, Accuracy, and Privacy in Computer Systems,* 1973, p. 181 by permission of Prentice-Hall, Inc.)

may, in some cases, be best handled by setting up multiple authorization tables. One such approach is depicted in Figure 7-4. In this figure there are two authorization tables: one for the user and one for the data.

The user authorization table is essentially a user security profile. It contains one entry for each user and defines each user's security

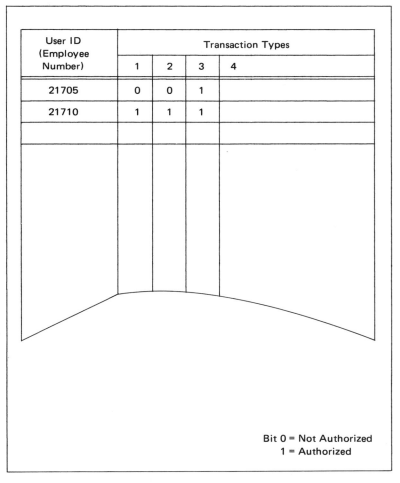

Figure 7-2

Simple Transaction Authorization Table

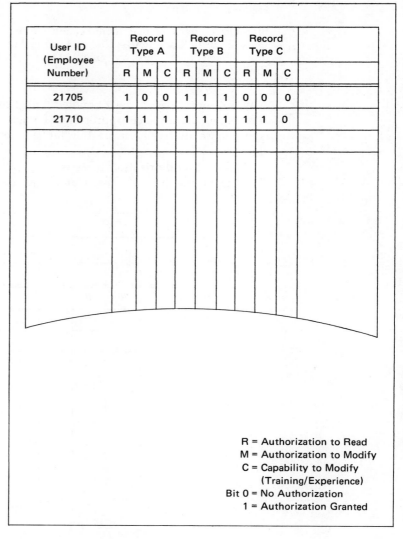

User ID (Employee Number)	Record Type A			Record Type B			Record Type C			
	R	M	C	R	M	C	R	M	C	
21705	1	0	0	1	1	1	0	0	0	
21710	1	1	1	1	1	1	1	1	0	

R = Authorization to Read
M = Authorization to Modify
C = Capability to Modify (Training/Experience)
Bit 0 = No Authorization
1 = Authorization Granted

Figure 7-3

Record-Type Authorization Table

code, the group of terminals each user is authorized to use, and the user group, or compartment, to which each user is a member. The computer security system may be able to verify that the user is authorized to use a particular security code and to use a particular group of terminals. It can determine the user's compartment, or group, from the user authorization table.

The subjects in the data authorization table are the user groups

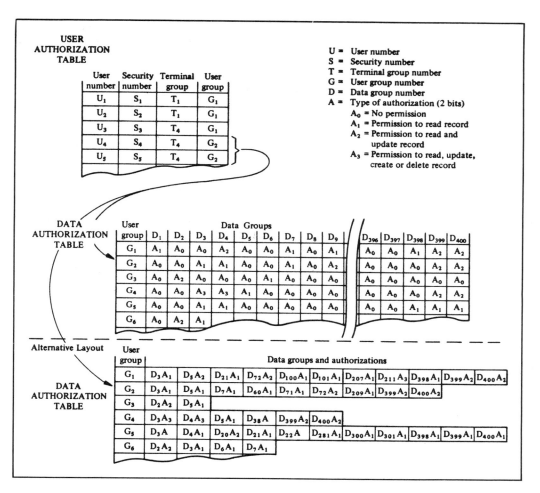

Figure 7-4

User/Data Group Authorization Tables. (After James Martin, *Security, Accuracy, and Privacy in Computer Systems*, 1973, p. 166 by permission of Prentice-Hall, Inc.)

instead of the individual users. The protected objects are the various categories of records, referred to in the figure as "data groups." Each user group's authorization with respect to each record category, or data group, is represented by two bits: 00, no permission; 01, permission to read only; 10, permission to read and modify; 11, permission to read, modify, and create and delete records.

Each time the user requests a particular record, the system must determine the user's user group from the user authorization table. It must then determine the user group's authorization with respect to the particular type of record in the data authorization table.

The alternative layout for the data authorization table represents the situation in which each user group is only authorized to access a small subset of the available record types. Each entry identifies the protected object, record type that the user group may access, and the functions that may be performed on the particular record type.

Passwords. Program and data files may be password-protected. A user or a program wishing to access a particular file might have to supply the proper password. Files may be protected by multiple passwords. Each password may have access privileges associated with it. Therefore, the password supplied by the user or the program might define the functions that can be performed on the file. Users and programs would be given only the password that corresponded to the privileges afforded to them.

The disadvantage of the password protection is that the passwords must be communicated to the authorized users. They are thus vulnerable to exposure during distribution. Each user might be given a unique password rather than giving users with the same access privileges the same password. This provides more security because each user can be held accountable for actions performed using his password. Users would, therefore, be less likely to divulge their passwords to others.

Access control lists. Files may be labeled with lists of users authorized to access them and their access privileges. Each time a user tries to access a file, the access control list for the particular file is scanned to determine if the user is authorized to access the file and if he is authorized to perform the function he is requesting. Files may be segmented, and each segment may have its own access control list. Access control lists may be used in conjunction with user compartmentalization, security profiles, and password protection.

SURVEILLANCE Methods for detecting possible security violations must be implemented in communications and data base systems. Effective methods of detecting security violations will deter many people who are considering violating the security of a system and its data because there is a good probability that they will be caught. In addition to acting as a deterrent, effective detection will make it possible to identify some of the weaknesses in the security system. Such weaknesses can then be corrected. There are basically two types of surveillance:

- Real-time surveillance, in which immediate action may be taken.
- Logging, or after-the-fact surveillance.

The following checks can be made in real time:

- Invalid user identification.
- Invalid user identification authentication.
- Invalid security code, or security code inconsistent with user identification, if user supplies his security code.
- Unauthorized terminal identification.
- Authorized terminal used by unauthorized user.
- Unauthorized request to process, read, or modify programs or data.
- Unauthorized transaction type entered (unauthorized user and/or unauthorized terminal).
- Maximum number of invalid or incorrect entries made, or actions taken.

As discussed earlier in this chapter, when suspicious situations are detected it may be necessary, or desirable, to take immediate defensive action. In other situations, recognizing that everyone occasionally makes misakes, it may be desirable to give the person a second chance, and possibly a third, before taking action. For instance, depending upon the method of authentication used, you might want to give the user three chances to enter his password correctly before taking action. On the other hand, you might want to take action as soon as two unauthorized data access attempts have been made in a row, or during a given terminal session. Regardless of the situation, all such errors and violations, including the first, should be logged.

There are many different actions that may be taken:

- The terminal keyboard may be locked by the system.
- The terminal may be disconnected from the system.
- The system may refuse to process any further requests for sensitive data or programs.
- The system may institute a time delay, of perhaps 1 minute, before accepting any additional input from the terminal.
- The system may, or should, notify the local security officer of the problem.
- The system may, or should, inform the computer security officer at the central control station.

A combination of these actions may, and in many cases, should occur. For instance, whenever a terminal is disconnected or its keyboard is locked, and whenever the system institutes a time delay, or refuses to accept input or requests for sensitive data and programs, the local security officer should be immediately informed. He should be the only person that can unlock a locked keyboard or reconnect a disconnected terminal.

The purpose of the action taken may be to prevent the user from accessing the system or to prevent the user from trying to violate the security of the system and its data by schemes based on high-speed trial-and-error techniques. The purpose may also be to keep the user trying, without allowing him to violate security, while informing the local security officer that an attempt is under way. The local security officer may be able to apprehend the perpetrator in the act of attempting to penetrate the system.

Another type of surveillance that may be categorized as a real-time check involves the printing of the password or authentication usage count on the terminal after user identification and authentication have been completed. The user might know that the last time he entered his password the usage count was, say, 17. If it is now 19 or 20, he should suspect that someone had used his password and should immediately notify the local and the central security officers. Automatic teller machines, used in an EFTS environment, frequently issue transaction receipts that contain a transaction count or countdown (i.e., number of uses remaining) if a limit is placed on the number of times the machine may be used with a particular magnetically encoded card.

A similar type of surveillance check would be if a single once-only code was rejected, or if the next sequential once-only code on a list was rejected. Regardless of the exact nature of the situation, any time an authorized user is unable to complete his identification and authentication, he should immediately notify the local and central security officers.

Logging

Logging is every bit as important as real-time surveillance because logs make it possible to identify patterns of attempted security violations and identify weaknesses in the security system. They also provide an audit trail in the event that an unauthorized activity occurred that was not detected by the security system. Let us identify some of the more important logs that should be produced by the system.

1. All attempts, both valid and invalid, to access the system should be logged. The following information should be recorded: date, time of day, terminal identification, user identification, and an indication of whether the attempt was valid or invalid. If the attempt was valid, the nature of the access and the sign-off time should also be recorded.

This log provides an audit trail which may prove invaluable in investigating unauthorized activity that is detected after it has occurred. For example, suppose a masterfile record had been changed improperly. One log might identify dates and times the masterfile was updated. Using information from this log and our terminal audit trail, it may be possible to pinpoint the user identification (userID) and terminal used to perform the unauthorized change.

The log will also help to identify vulnerable userID's, vulnerable terminals, and the vulnerable times of day. Invalid access attempts for a particular userID may indicate that the user's identification and authentication were partially compromised. The user may have lost his card, badge, or key; or his card, badge, or key may have been stolen, duplicated, and returned without his knowledge. The user's list of once-only codes may have been compromised. The log will identify the userID with a problem. The action to be taken depends upon the nature of the problem. It may involve issuing a new card, badge, key, single once-only code, or list of once-only codes, and invalidating the current one. It may involve providing additional training to the user in the use and security of his identification and authentication.

If a particular terminal is the subject of frequent or numerous invalid access attempts, it may be necessary to strengthen the physical security of the terminal. If there are particular times of day when many, or more, invalid access attempts occur, the conditions at that time of day should be studied and corrective action taken.

2. All requests, both authorized and unauthorized, for protected objects (programs, data, and transactions) should be logged. The date, time of day, user identification, terminal identification, the particular protected object accessed, and the nature of the access should be recorded.

Authorized actions should be reviewed regularly to ensure that the authorization is proper and that the authorized actions are appropriate. It may be possible to detect if users are taking improper advantage of their authorization or if users are performing actions that are authorized but are not appropriate given the time of year or the particular job they have been assigned. It may also be possible to detect if the authorizations have been fraudulently manipulated, or if a user's identification, authentication, and authorization have been compromised, either unbeknown to the valid and authorized user, or with his knowledge.

Unauthorized actions should be reviewed and analyzed in depth. The purpose is to identify the transaction types, data, and programs that are being "attacked," the userID being used, the terminal being used, and the vulnerable times of day and periods during the year. All individual actions and all patterns of actions should be thoroughly investigated to determine the causes of the problems, the reasons for the problems, the exact nature of the problems, and the accountable or responsible people involved.

3. All modifications of sensitive data and programs should be logged. The following information should be recorded: date, time of day, user identification, terminal identification, the particular pro-

tected object that was modified, and a "before" and "after" image of the protected object.

This log should be reviewed in detail. Each entry should be reviewed for appropriateness, authorization, and accuracy. If any inappropriate, improper, unauthorized, or inaccurate modifications are detected, they should be investigated immediately and corrective action taken. Again it is necessary to analyze the individual entries as well as the patterns of inappropriate, improper, and unauthorized modifications. The "before" and "after" images will facilitate the review, will make it possible to identify faulty processing, and will make reconstruction or restoration of the protected object easier to perform.

4. Listings of all security-procedure violations should be prepared daily. The listings should contain an analysis of the violations and summary statistics (such as the number of violations and errors committed by each user, at each terminal, on each type of protected object, on particular protected objects) that would highlight unusual and suspicious activities and patterns of activities.

5. Histories of security-procedure violations should be maintained. Summaries and statistics relating to the types of violations committed, when the violations were committed (most vulnerable time of day, week, or month for all violations and for specific types of violations), who committed the violations, and many others should be prepared. Such statistics and summaries will highlight patterns of unauthorized activities over a period of time. Patterns may emerge that might not otherwise be suspected or detected.

6. Daily and historical listings and logs of all changes to user identifications, authentications, authorizations, security codes, file passwords, and the like should be prepared. The listings and logs should be scrutinized by authorized management to ensure that all such changes were proper, appropriate, authorized, and performed by authorized personnel. Any suspicious, unauthorized, improper, and inappropriate changes must be investigated immediately. Patterns of suspicious, unauthorized, improper, and inappropriate changes must also be investigated.

All *temporary* authorizations (ones granted in special situations when access to particular protected objects is needed but the authorized user or terminal is not available) must be logged. In addition, such temporary authorizations must be carefully administered and closely monitored.

The security of the logs must be preserved. This is equally true when they are on-line, when they are being processed, when they are being printed and distributed, and when they are in the possession of the authorized security officers and of management. When they are on the system they must receive higher security than the most sensitive data files, data bases, and programs. When they are in hard-copy form, they must receive the same attention as the most confidential reports. They must not be left lying around on desks or in unlocked cabinets. They should be kept under lock and key. They should not be thrown out with the trash. They should be shredded or burned prior to disposal.

RACF—EXAMPLE OF A SPECIFIC DATA/SOFTWARE SECURITY SYSTEM

IBM's Resource Access Control Facility (RACF) is one example of a data/software security system that provides user identification and authentication, authorization, and surveillance controls. SECURE (a product of Boole & Babbage Inc., Sunnyvale, Calif.) is another such system. Figure 7-5 presents an overview of RACF.

We will discuss briefly the RACF features in the following areas:

- User identification and authentication.
- Authorization.
- Surveillance.

User identification and authentication

RACF performs user identification by userID and authentication by password.

Authorization

RACF maintains security profiles for each user, for each group of users who have the same access authorizations, and for each protected data file. The security profiles are maintained on a direct access device, labeled "RACF Data Set" in Figure 7-5. The profiles contain the attributes of the user, group of users, and protected data file, as well as the authorization specification (function, such as read or modify; and protected object) for each protected data file. Thus, the users are explicitly authorized to access particular data files and to perform specific functions on those data files.

Surveillance

RACF logs all authorized and unauthorized attempts to access the system and to access particular data files. This logging is performed by recording all system and data accesses in the SMF (System Management Facilities) Data Set. (The SMF Data Set typically contains job accounting and system utilization information.) RACF also records, on the security console, all unauthorized attempts to access the system, and all authorized and unauthorized attempts to access protected data files.

COMMUNICATIONS LINE SAFEGUARDS

Communications lines, whether they are dial-up, leased, or satellite or radio microwave links, are vulnerable to penetration and interception. It is difficult, if not impossible, to physically secure the communications lines. There are, however, steps that can be taken to reduce the exposure. This section has been divided into two subsections:

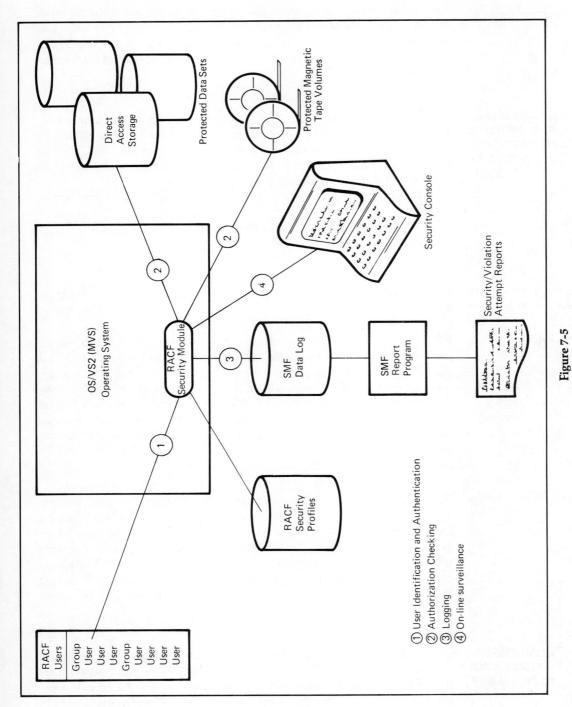

Figure 7-5

Overview of IBM's RACF Functions

① User Identification and Authentication
② Authorization Checking
③ Logging
④ On-line surveillance

• Threats and penetration techniques.
• Controls and safeguards.

We will identify some of the more common threats and penetration techniques and will discuss some of the available controls and safeguards to prevent the penetration and minimize the exposure resulting from penetration.

Threats and penetration techniques

The perpetrator's ability to successfully penetrate a communications network depends on several factors, including his technical knowledge of both telecommunications and the system he is attempting to penetrate, and his access to or possession of the necessary interception, penetration, and monitoring equipment.

The more common penetration techniques are:

• Masquerading.
• Eavesdropping.
• Piggybacking.
• Between lines.
• Line grabbing.

Masquerading. A perpetrator may pretend to be an authorized user and may attempt to gain access to a computer system and its data as that user. The perpetrator would have had to obtain the user's identification and authentication information by some means in order to perform this technique.

Eavesdropping. This involves tapping or cutting in on a communications line, or on a satellite or radio (terrestrial) microwave link. It is often referred to as "passive" infiltration. It is passive in the sense that the perpetrator only listens (or records), but does not interfere with the transmission.

Piggybacking. The perpetrator inserts a special terminal into the communications line, then intercepts the transmission between the user and the computer system. The perpetrator may intercept the user's input and modify it, or completely replace it before sending it to the computer system. The perpetrator typically transmits an error message to the user indicating that the system is not available or has gone "down." This technique is often referred to as "active" infiltration.

Between lines. The perpetrator inserts a special terminal into the communications line. The perpetrator then accesses the system whenever the authorized user is connected to the computer but is inactive. During any particular terminal session (i.e., the time period during which an authorized user is signed onto the system) there will be short periods of time during which the authorized user will not be actively sending and receiving information. It is during such periods of inactivity that the perpetrator goes to work, taking advantage of the communications line that has already been established.

Line grabbing. The perpetrator inserts a special terminal into the communications line. He eavesdrops on the line until the authorized user signs off the terminal. The perpetrator intercepts the user's sign-off, preventing the message from reaching the system. He transmits the expected system sign-off message to the user. Then he uses the line he "grabbed" from the authorized user to access the system.

Controls and safeguards

The controls and safeguards that exist in a communications environment are:

- Physical security.
- Encryption.
- Authentication checks.
- Transaction serial numbering and "time stamping."
- Automatic terminal disconnect.
- Wiretap and bug checks.
- Call-back procedures.
- Others, including user identification and authentication, terminal identification, and authorization.

Physical security. It is virtually impossible to physically secure public communications lines and microwave communications. However, there are some steps that can, and should, be taken. These steps should be taken in addition to physically securing your data processing installation and terminal locations.

There are only certain points in a communications network where wiretapping is not extremely difficult. One of the best places from a perpetrator's standpoint is your telephone closet. You frequently make the job easy for the wiretapper by prominently labeling your data communications lines. You should, therefore, physically secure your telephone closet and carefully restrict access to it.

Communications lines that exist solely on your own property should be buried in metal conduits in concrete-filled trenches. This will inhibit wiretapping by making the communications lines inaccessible to the wiretapper.

Encryption. Encryption is the process of transforming the data transmitted over the communications and microwave links to render it unintelligible during transmission. The transformation may be accomplished by transposition of the characters in the data or message (scrambling), substitution of the characters with other characters or groups of characters, or logical, arithmetic, and algebraic manipulations of the characters in the data or message. Encryption may provide the only secure way to protect your passwords and data during transmission, especially where microwave communications links are used. Encryption will be discussed at length in the next section.

Authentication checks. A code may be inserted into each message sent to and from the computer system that would in some way provide authentication to the user and the computer system that messages were not being intercepted, rerouted, or introduced by an illegal, intervening terminal. The code may be a sequential message number or it may be generated using an algorithm driven by characters of the previous message.

Transaction serial numbering and "time stamping." With this technique, the computer assigns a unique sequential identification number (and also, in some systems, a date and time of day) to each transaction received from terminals (and also, in some systems, the before-and-after version of the data base records affected by the transactions). Often, the terminal operator will also have this identifier displayed on his terminal. The transactions with their appended serial numbers are recorded, as they occur, on a tape or disk known as a transaction log or journal. The process of number tagging and logging is sometimes called "journalizing."

Journalizing serves a number of purposes. One common use is in reestablishing system operations after a failure, where the journal is used to determine the last transaction processed before the failure. The journal is also used to aid in the analysis of system errors and suspicious events and, in this sense, is part of the audit trail for on-line systems. Some on-line systems perform what is called a "memo-posting" or "shadow-posting" function, which updates a *copy* of the master file or data base during daytime on-line operations. At night, during batch operations, the original (actual) master file or data base is updated, often using the journal as a source of transactions and the before-and-after records as a control feature (for comparison). In one computer fraud, it was this journalizing feature that helped track down discrepancies between the on-line results (which had been manipulated) and those derived in the batch system.

Automatic terminal disconnect. The computer system software, using the hardware clock or timing mechanism, should automatically disconnect a terminal from the computer system after a predetermined period of inactivity. Users should not, however, rely on this feature. They should disconnect the terminal themselves when they have finished their session. This feature is important because it prevents an unauthorized user from accessing the system by using a terminal or communications line already connected to the system that has been abandoned by the authorized user.

Wiretap and bug checks. On a periodic basis and whenever there are any suspicious occurrences, experts should be called in to examine your telephone closet and test communications lines for the presence of wiretaps or bugs.

Call-back procedures. Call-back procedures are, in a sense, an authentication scheme in which the computer system verifies that the user is, in fact, who and where he says he is. The user signs onto the system and enters his user identification and authentication. The computer system establishes the user's identification and terminal location. It then disconnects the user and "calls back" the identified terminal. *The communication line established by the computer system (not the user) is the one actually used for the terminal session,* the purpose being to ensure that the user is at an authorized terminal in an authorized terminal location. It is a particularly useful safeguard in a communications environment that uses dial-up rather than or in addition to leased lines, because the user could be calling the system from any location, authorized or unauthorized.

Call-back procedures may be implemented in other ways as well. For example, the user may sign onto the computer system and the computer system may call him back using a separate line, without disconnecting him, to verify that he is, in fact, accessing the system. The user would respond by actuating a switch on the terminal.

Others. There are other controls that will not be discussed here because they were discussed earlier in this chapter. Among these are:

- Identification and authentication, especially techniques that make masquerading difficult.
- Terminal identification, especially when used as one aspect of authorization specification.
- Authorization, especially techniques such as password-protected data and programs, where an additional "layer" of security is provided. With such techniques, knowing or having an authorized user's identification and authentication does not give you access to all the protected objects the user is authorized to access. The passwords securing the protected objects must also be known.

ENCRYPTION SYSTEMS Data transmitted over communications lines and over radio and satellite microwave communications links, and data stored within the computer system are vulnerable to unauthorized and fraudulent access, use, and modification. We have discussed in this chapter and in previous chapters ways to protect data stored on your system. Encryption techniques, used in conjunction with the other controls discussed, can provide additional security for your data and data bases. In a data communications environment, where there is very little, if anything, you can do to secure the communications lines and microwave links, encryption may provide the only practical way to protect your data.

Encryption is, in essence, the transformation of a message or of data for the purpose of rendering it unintelligible. The transformation may be effected, as we shall soon see, by *transposition* (changing the order of the characters in the message or the data), by *substitution* (replacement of the characters in the message or the data with one or more different characters), and by *arithmetic, algebraic, and logical manipulation* of the message or the data.

The elements involved in encryption are the original version of the message or data, known as *plaintext or cleartext;* the transformed version of the message or data, known as *ciphertext;* the *algorithm,* or the method by which the message or data is transformed; and, the *key,* a pattern of characters or bits that serves as a secret parameter in the encryption and decryption processes. We will talk about these elements in more depth throughout the remainder of this section.

Our discussion of encryption will be divided into the following topics:

- Types of encryption.
- Types of encryption systems.
- Data Encryption Standard.
- Encryption implementation.
- Cryptanalysis.
- Generation, administration, and distribution of keys.

Types of encryption There are two basic types of encryption:

- Reversible encryption.
- Irreversible encryption.

Reversible encryption. In a data communications environment, the sending location, which may be a terminal or a computer, encrypts, or encodes, the data and transmits them to the receiving location. The receiving location decrypts, or decodes, the ciphertext, thereby returning it to its original form. Reversible encryption, therefore, involves the encryption of plaintext into ciphertext and the decryption of ciphertext into plaintext.

Irreversible encryption. Irreversible encryption involves only the encryption of plaintext into ciphertext. The ciphertext cannot be decrypted. Irreversible encryption is useful for protecting security profile data, such as passwords and PINs used to authenticate a user's identity in data communications and consumer-oriented EFTS environments. Even if a perpetrator was able to penetrate the computer security system and gain access to the user identification and authentication files, he still would be unable to masquerade or gain access to the system as an authorized user. The terminals used in this type of encryption environment require that the data be entered in its original (plaintext) form.

Types of encryption systems

There are several different types of encryption systems. For illustrative purposes, we will identify a few of them here and will discuss their strengths and weaknesses. The encryption systems that will be discussed are:

- Transposition.
- Monoalphabetic substitutions.
- Polyalphabetic substitutions.
- Codebook substitutions.
- Vernam system.

Transposition. Transposition involves the rearrangement of the characters in the data or message according to some predetermined rule. The same characters appear in both the plaintext and the ciphertext; however, they appear in different positions. The number of characters in the plaintext and the ciphertext is the same. This type of transformation is often called "scrambling." Because there is such a great relationship between the plaintext and ciphertext, transposition is *not* an effective way of securing data.

Monoalphabetic substitutions. Monoalphabetic substitutions involve the replacement of each character in the data or message by a corresponding character in the cipher alphabet. There is, thus, a one-to-one correspondence between the letters in the plaintext alphabet and the letters in the cipher alphabet. An example of monoalphabetic substitution is presented in Figure 7-6. Encryption is performed by finding each character of the plaintext in the plaintext alphabet and finding the corresponding character in the cipher alphabet. Thus, PASSWORD becomes OZHHDLQC. Decryption is performed by locating the characters of the ciphertext in the cipher alphabet and finding the corresponding characters in the plaintext alphabet.

```
Plaintext Alphabet:     A B C D E F G H I  J K L M N O P Q R S T U V W X  Y Z
Cipher Alphabet:        Z A X C V E T G R I P K M N L O J Q H S F U D W B Y

Sample Encryption:
    Plaintext:          P A S S W O R D
    Ciphertext:         O Z H H D L Q C

Sample Decryption:
    Ciphertext:         H V X Q V S
    Plaintext:          S E C R E T
```

Figure 7-6

Monoalphabetic Substitution

Monoalphabetic substitutions use only one cipher alphabet for encryption and decryption. Monoalphabetic substitution is *not* a secure encryption system. Because there is a one-to-one correspondence between the plaintext alphabet and the cipher alphabet and because English, as well as most other languages, is highly redundant, it is easy for an amateur cryptanalyst (codebreaker) to decrypt the ciphertext. The method used to break the code involves performing frequency analyses on the individual characters, pairs (bigrams) and trios (trigrams) of characters in the ciphertext. The results of the frequency analyses are compared to frequency analyses of the occurrence of individual characters and pairs of characters in the English language. Such frequency analyses are readily available. An expert cryptanalyst can break a monoalphabetic system with a single message containing 40 to 60 characters.[2]

Polyalphabetic substitutions. Polyalphabetic substitutions differ from monoalphabetic substitutions in that they use two or more cipher alphabets in a predetermined pattern to perform the encryption and decryption. Thus, if two cipher alphabets are used, the odd characters (i.e., first, third, fifth, . . .) of the plaintext might be encrypted using the first cipher alphabet, and the even characters (i.e., second, fourth, sixth, . . .) might be encrypted using the second cipher alphabet. Figure 7-7 illustrates a polyalphabetic substitution using four cipher alphabets.

In the figure, the "P" is encrypted using the first cipher alphabet, the "A" using the second, the "S" using the third, the "S" using the fourth, the "W" using the first, the "O" using the second, and so on. Thus, PASSWORD becomes ROVWYCUH.

The standard method of breaking a polyalphabetic substitution code involves deducing the number of cipher alphabets used and then

[2] David Kahn, *The Codebreakers* (New York: The Macmillan Publishing Co., Inc., 1967), p. 213.

```
Plaintext Alphabet:      A B C D E F G H I J K L M N O P Q R S T U V W X Y Z

Cipher Alphabet 1:       C D E F G H I J K L M N O P Q R S T U V W X Y Z A B

Cipher Alphabet 2:       O P Q R S T U V W X Y Z A B C D E F G H I J K L M N

Cipher Alphabet 3:       D E F G H I J K L M N O P Q R S T U V W X Y Z A B C

Cipher Alphabet 4:       E F G H I J K L M N O P Q R S T U V W X Y Z A B C D

Sample Encryption:
   Plaintext:            P A S S W O R D
   Ciphertext:          R O V W Y C U H
```

Figure 7-7

Polyalphabetic Substitution

performing the frequency analyses, described for monoalphabetic substitution, on the characters believed to be encrypted using the same cipher alphabet (the first and fifth characters, second and sixth characters, etc., in our example). An experienced cryptanalyst would need 40 to 60 characters of ciphertext for each cipher alphabet.[3] Thus, he would need 160 to 240 characters of ciphertext to break our code. Polyalphabetic substitution, although more secure than monoalphabetic substitution, is nonetheless *not* a very secure encryption system.

Codebook substitutions. Codebook substitutions involve the use of a codebook or dictionary which relates the plaintext elements (characters, words, phrases) to the ciphertext elements, referred to as codegroups. Codebook substitutions generally operate on elements of the plaintext that are variable in length, such as syllables, words, phrases, or sentences. Each element of the plaintext is looked up in the codebook or dictionary to determine its codegroup, the corresponding ciphertext element. An example of a portion of a codebook is shown in Figure 7-8.

There are several disadvantages to codebook substitutions. One disadvantage is that, as with monoalphabetic and polyalphabetic substitutions, codebook substitutions are vulnerable to analysis by experienced cryptanalysts. Another is that the codebook may be compromised, which means that the encryption system has been compromised. This is particularly true if the codebooks are in printed form. Thus, new codebooks might have to be issued very frequently. If the codebook is stored on the computer system, it is still vulnerable to compromise. In addition, either the plaintext–ciphertext combina-

[3] David Kahn, *The Codebreakers* (New York: The Macmillan Publishing Co., Inc., 1967), p. 213.

Codegroup	Plaintext
3964	Emplacing
1563	Employ
7260	En-
8808	Enable
3043	Enabled
0012	Enabled to

Figure 7-8

Portion of a Codebook. [After David Kahn, *The Codebreakers* (New York: The MacMillan Publishing Co., Inc., 1967), p. 213.]

tions would have to be very limited or the codebook would require a tremendous amount of storage space and the codebook look-up would be time-consuming.

Vernam system. The Vernam system is a *key-additive* system. The key is a string of 0s and 1s. The key is added, using modulo-2 (exclusive-or) addition, to the bit pattern of the plaintext, thereby producing the ciphertext. To decrypt the ciphertext, the same key is added, modulo-2, to the ciphertext. This is illustrated in Figure 7-9.

The key may be a sequence of random numbers, pseudo-random numbers, or characters. It may be a *block cipher*, meaning that a sin-

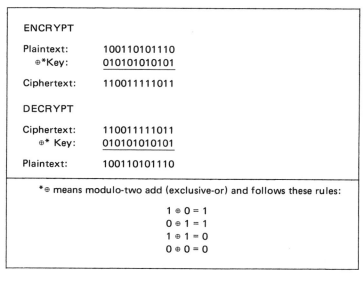

Figure 7-9

Key Additive Encryption

gle block, or quantity, of plaintext is enciphered into a single block of output. Figure 7-9 used a block cipher of 12 bits. If the plaintext were 24 bits long, our block cipher would have been added, modulo-2, to the first 12 bits of the plaintext, and to the second 12 bits of the plaintext. The key may also be a *stream cipher*, meaning that the string of bits (bit stream) is very long and the entire string is added, one bit at a time, modulo-2, to the plaintext, without requiring repetition of the key. We will discuss key generation later in this section.

The degree of security provided by key-additive encryption is dependent upon the randomness and the security of the key. We will have more to say about this later.

Data encryption standard

The National Bureau of Standards adopted a standard encryption algorithm in November 1976. The encryption algorithm was developed and patented by IBM and is called the Data Encryption Standard (DES). DES is a reversible encryption system; the sending location encrypts the data or message, and the receiving location decrypts the ciphertext.

How it works. DES uses a recirculating block product cipher. The key consists of 64 bits, 56 bits for the key and 8 bits for parity checking. The DES algorithm enciphers a block of 64 bits at one time, thus the key is designated as a block cipher. DES is not a simple key-additive encryption system, as the Vernam system. Rather, it uses a complex algorithm involving the following steps:

1. The plaintext block of 64 bits is subjected to an "initial permutation," which, in essence, is a transposition of the bits according to a predetermined rule.
2. The permuted plaintext is then subjected to a rather involved key-dependent computation, involving several more permutations of the input as well as of the key, modulo-2 arithmetic, and table look-ups. This process is repeated 16 times. It produces what is referred to as the *preoutput*, a 64-bit block.
3. The preoutput is subjected to a final permutation, transposition, which is the inverse of the initial permutation.

Degree of security. DES is highly secure but not unbreakable. The security of DES is totally dependent upon the security of the 64-bit key. The algorithm has been published in numerous publications. Just how secure DES actually is has been the subject of some controversy. The *controversy* revolves around whether or not the size of the key is adequate for security purposes.

Whitfield Diffie and Martin Hellman, of Stanford University, contend that the length of the key should be increased, perhaps doubled. They maintain that a machine capable of "breaking" the key could be built for approximately $20 million.[4] The method used to break the key would be brute force, that is, trying every possible combination of 56 bits (with 8 parity bits). Whereas $20 million may *not* be cost-effective for most criminally motivated individuals, it may, however, be cost-effective to some organizations, such as the major intelligence agencies. "[The] major intelligence agencies possess the financial resources and the interest to build such a machine."[5]

Diffie and Hellman's concerns go another step. "More seriously, in about 10 years' time, the rapidly decreasing cost in computation will bring the machine's cost down to the $200,000 range, and the cost per solution down to the $50 range. The standard will then be almost totally insecure."[6] The current cost per solution (i.e., cost to find one key, assuming that the key is changed daily) is estimated to be $5,000.

Some others, who agree with Diffie and Hellman's suggestion that the key is too short to provide adequate security, feel that the plaintext should be double-encrypted (i.e., encrypted twice with two different 64 bit keys). This double encryption would essentially provide the same level of security as doubling the size of the key. Doubling the size of the key would result in a cost per solution of 2×10^{25}.[7]

Those who feel that DES provides the necessary level of security counter their opponents' arguments on the following grounds: (1) $20 million would be very difficult to obtain; therefore, the method for breaking the key is cost-prohibitive; (2) the accumulation of the necessary LSI chips to build the machine would arouse suspicion; and (3) there would be difficulties with component reliability, cooling, and obtaining sufficient electrical power to run the machine which would doom the effort.[8]

The National Bureau of Standards (NBS), while committed to DES, nevertheless realizes that technological advances may impair the security provided by DES. They expressed the following qualification:

> The protection provided by this algorithm against potential new threats will be reviewed within five years to assess its adequacy. In

[4] David Kahn, "Tapping Computers," *The New York Times*, April 3, 1976, p. 27.

[5] Whitfield Diffie and Martin E. Hellman, "Exhaustive Cryptanalysis of the NBS Data Encryption Standard," *Computer* (published by the IEEE Computer Society), June 1977, p. 74.

[6] Ibid.

[7] Ibid., p. 75.

[8] Paul Meissner, ed., *Report on the Workshop on Estimation of Significant Advances in Computer Technology* (Washington, D.C.: U.S. Department of Commerce, 1976), pp. 7, 11.

addition, both the standard and possible threats reducing the security provided through the use of this standard will undergo continual review by NBS and other cognizant Federal organizations. The new technology available at that time will be evaluated to determine its impact on the standard. In addition, the awareness of any breakthrough in technology or any mathematical weakness of the algorithm will cause NBS to reevaluate this standard and provide necessary revisions.[9]

We feel that the controversy about DES has been useful in the sense that it has made people aware of several important considerations about encryption systems in general—*key length, and the importance of randomly generating and protecting access to the keys.* We would also acknowledge that there are national security systems that involve intelligence data for which DES would not be suitable. However, for the vast majority of commercial and governmental systems, DES should provide an appropriate level of protection and avoid the problems that would arise from the incompatibility of competing systems. Few technical developments in the EDP world are viewed as having extraordinarily long lives, and we would remind our readers to expect a need to change some years in the future, as indicated in the NBS statement above. The master system breaker who is able to execute successfully a large-scale fraud will gain his knowledge to do so by exploiting a variety of security and control weaknesses that are far more vulnerable than DES.

There is no question but that the proper administration of the key, discussed later in this section, will go a long way to making DES "unbreakable" in practice, if not in theory.

> The cryptographic algorithm . . . transforms a 64 bit binary value into a unique 64 bit binary value based on a 56 bit variable. If the complete 64 bit input is used (i.e., none of the input bits should be predetermined from block to block) and if the 56 bit variable is randomly chosen, no technique other than trying all possible keys using known input and output for the DES will guarantee finding the chosen key. As there are over 70,000,000,000,000,000 (seventy quadrillion) possible keys of 56 bits, the feasibility of deriving a particular key in this way is extremely unlikely in typical threat environments. Moreover, if the key is changed frequently, the risk of this event is greatly diminished. However, users should be aware that it is theoretically possible to derive the key in fewer trials (with a correspondingly lower probability of success depending on the number of keys tried) and should be cautioned to change the key as often as practical. Users must change the key and provide it a high

[9] "Data Encryption Standard," *Federal Information Processing Standards Publication 46* (Washington, D.C.: National Bureau of Standards, January 1977), p. 4.

level of protection in order to minimize the potential risks of its un-authorized computation or acquisition.[10]

Encryption
implementation
Encryption systems may be implemented in software and hardware. Various systems are available commercially, including vendor-pro-prietary systems, and DES. The commercially available software encryption systems vary in terms of processing overhead and system degradation.

Hardware encryption systems are also commercially available. DES may be implemented in hardware, as well as in software. The encryption system is typically contained on an electronic "chip."

> The nearly 14,000 electronic logic elements needed to implement the data encryption algorithm (DES) may be contained in such a chip which is less than .635 centimeter (¼ inch) on each side. The costs of producing this piece of electronic hardware may be as low as $10 after the initial costs of production have been recovered.[11]

Hardware encryption systems are incorporated into a number of special-purpose terminals. Microprocessors containing the encryp-tion system may be appended to certain terminals. Encryption de-vices may also be inserted at modem interfaces. We will examine two of these here:

- Link encryption.
- End-to-end encryption.

Link encryption. The encryption devices are placed at the modem interfaces. Encryption and decryption is performed in a manner that is transparent to the receiving and sending stations.

> Link encryption is adequate for protecting against wiretapping, but in a network it does not guard against misrouting. In a network which contains a routing (switching) function, this switch handles cleartext, and if a message sent from A to B is misrouted by the switch to C, the message is as intelligible to the user at C because it had been reencrypted using the key that deciphers the encryption at that sta-tion.[12]

Thus, link encryption will not provide protection against inten-tional or unintentional misrouting in a switching network.

[10] "Data Encryption Standard," *Federal Information Processing Standards Publication 46* (Washington, D.C.: National Bureau of Standards, January 1977), p. 4.

[11] Dennis K. Branstad, "Data Protection Through Cryptography," *Dimensions/ NBS*, September 1975, p. 196.

[12] David J. Sykes, "Protecting Data by Encryption," *Datamation*, August 1976, p. 81.

End-to-end encryption.   Performed with either hardware or software, end-to-end encryption involves encryption performed by the sending station and decryption performed by the receiving location. The encrypted message can only be decrypted by a receiving location that has the appropriate key.   Thus, the message is protected if it is inadvertantly or deliberately misrouted.

Cryptanalysis   Cryptanalysis is the process of analyzing encrypted messages for the purpose of recovering the original (plaintext) message without using the means available to the legitimate recipient.   Cryptanalysis is thus the penetration of the encryption system.   The perpetrator is known as the cryptanalyst.

We are bringing this subject up to warn you that, without proper administration and a good encryption system, encryption may provide a false sense of security.   The greatest threat to encryption systems is human ingenuity and diligence, particularly the human ingenuity and diligence of the experienced cryptanalyst.   History has shown that, if an encryption system can be broken, it will eventually be broken. This is not meant to imply that encryption is any less important as a security measure.   The emphasis is on "eventually."   It is, however, meant to alert you to the fact that not all encryption techniques provide the same degree of security, and that proper administration of your encryption system is of the utmost importance in preserving the security it provides.   You cannot simply implement an encryption system and then ignore it because you assume that you are protected.

The most important elements of cryptanalysis, for the purposes of this discussion, are the length of the intercepted message, available computational resources, time, and the work factor.   The longer the ciphertext message that the cryptanalyst has to work with, the greater the probability that he will be able to break the system.   If the intercepted ciphertext is too short, an expert cryptanalyst, with sophisticated resources and an abundance of time, may never be able to break the code.   Work factor relates to the amount of effort, time, and resources required to break the code.   If the work factor is very high, meaning that a tremendous amount of human and computational resources are needed to break the system, the system is considered to be strong.

How do we assess the strength of our current or prospective encryption system?   There are several ways:

1.   Experts in the field of cryptanalysis should be consulted whenever you decide to design your own encryption system.

2.   Experts in the field of cryptanalysis should be asked to validate your current, new, or prospective encryption system.   They will be able to tell you, after extensive analysis, whether or not your system is very difficult to break.   Thus, they will tell you what the

210

relative work factor is. They will not be able to determine if penetration of your system is absolutely impossible.

3. In most encryption systems the algorithm remains fairly constant. The key is the crucial variable. If you have a strong, secure encryption system, the cryptanalyst should be able to know the algorithm, to have a plaintext message and its corresponding ciphertext, and still not be able to break the code. The work factor then relates to the effort and resources expended to derive the key. You can significantly increase the work factor by decreasing the amount of time that is available to the cryptanalyst. You decrease the amount of time that is available to the cryptanalyst by changing the key on a regular basis. Since the key is the crucial element, if it is generated properly and is distributed and maintained in a very secure manner, then every time it is changed, the cryptanalyst must start the analysis from ground zero.

Generation, administration, and distribution of the keys

As mentioned earlier, the strength of, and the security provided by, an encryption system is often dependent upon the security of the key. Let us now take a look at:

- Key generation considerations.
- Key administration considerations.
- Key distribution considerations.

Key generation considerations. It is generally acknowledged that whenever the key size (the number of bits that make up the key) is equal to, or greater than, the input size (the number of bits that make up the plaintext input), it is possible to construct an encryption system that is "unbreakable" in practice, if not in theory. Each bit of the key is used once, and only once, to encipher each bit of the input. This type of key is referred to as a stream cipher, a once-only key, or a one-time tape key.

A once-only key may be produced on paper tape, magnetic tape, or a disk. The medium on which the key is produced is dependent upon the equipment at the receiving and sending locations in the communications environment. All the receiving and sending locations must have a copy of the appropriate key and the encryption algorithm in order to encrypt the plaintext to be transmitted and to decrypt the ciphertext that is received.

Such once-only keys or stream ciphers are not practical in all situations. Thus, a block cipher or periodic key may be used. This key enciphers a block of input equal to the size of the key. The same key is used over and over to encipher a plaintext message.

Regardless of whether an "infinite" stream cipher (once-only key) or a "finite" block cipher is used, *the single most important consideration in generating the key is that it be as nearly random as possible.* There must be no predictable relationship among the bits of the key.

Pseudo-random-number generators are often used to generate the key. Not all pseudo-random-number generators are equally effective in generating numbers that appear to be truly random. Therefore, extreme care should be taken when choosing a pseudo-random-number generator.

The initial *seed* used to start the pseudo-random-number generator may be derived (through selection of certain characters, computation, etc.) from the user's authentication password, from the user's identification, from message length, or from any number of constant or variable values. The initial seed has to either be communicated to or be determined in some way by the receiving location.

The pseudo-random-number generator is a method of key generation using software. Keys may also be generated by hardware, using linear shift registers and a series of exclusive-or and transposition operations, or by special cryptographic hardware. Again, the overriding consideration is that the bit pattern of the key be as nearly random as possible.

Key administration considerations. The need to change the keys periodically has been discussed throughout this section. Changing of the keys in a controlled and regular manner can effectively make your encryption system unbreakable. For example, if it would take an experienced cryptanalyst one year or more to determine your key, and you change the keys quarterly, the cryptanalyst could make no practical use of the keys. Thus, the recommended frequency of changing keys is partially based on the estimated work factor associated with breaking the key.

Another consideration is the potential loss resulting from a compromised key. In some national and international EFTS environments, where large-dollar-value money movements are involved, the potential loss may be extremely great. In such environments it may be desirable to change the key as often as once or twice each day. The potential loss need not be a direct loss. It may also be the loss or compromise of data. Thus, the data requirements may necessitate a very frequent changing of the key. The key must also be changed whenever it is suspected to have been compromised.

Key distribution considerations. Utmost care must be taken when distributing keys to ensure that the key is not compromised or exposed during distribution. Depending on the equipment used, the key may be produced on paper tape, magnetic tape, disk, plug-in module, magnetically encoded card, or almost any other available medium. They may be sent by registered mail or transported by company courier. Depending on the equipment used, they may also be transmitted through the communications network.

Whenever the key is distributed, regardless of the method of distribution, utmost security precautions must be taken. It may be desirable to transmit multiple keys and to indicate which key is to be used at another time. Alternatively, it may be desirable to send bit streams to two different people at different times. Each bit stream is loaded into the encryption device and the modulo-2 addition of the bit streams produces the actual key.

If the equipment in the communications environment has been equipped with key generation hardware or software, it is frequently necessary to distribute the seed for the generation algorithm. Again, distribution may be by registered mail, by company courier, or by transmission through the communications network. And, again, utmost security precautions are necessary. It may be desirable to distribute multiple seeds at one time, and, at another time, an indication of which seed is to be used.

In systems that are terminal-security rather than user-security oriented, the *down line loading* of the new key may be accomplished by transmitting the new key encrypted by the current key. Of course, once a perpetrator discovers one key, he can readily obtain the others. A way to reduce the odds of such a compromise is to transmit new keys *encrypted by a key that is only used for this purpose.* Since this special-purpose key is used much less often than the one employed for routine transmission, the cryptanalyst would be faced with a much higher work factor in trying to break the system.

If, in any of the methods of key or seed distribution we have discussed, the transmittal appears to have been tampered with, the computer security officer should be notified immediately. Depending on the circumstances, it may be necessary to regenerate and redistribute the keys or seeds.

Concluding remarks. In this section, we have introduced a number of concepts that are of fundamental importance in the generation, administration, and distribution of keys for encryption systems. It should be evident that detailed procedures and controls must be fashioned to suit the particular characteristics of a given application. It should also be evident that casual attitudes and carelessness cannot be tolerated under any circumstances. Perhaps the following equation will aid readers in remaining mindful of these warnings.

$$\begin{array}{l}\text{Carelessness in the Generation,} \\ \text{Administration, and Distribution} \\ \text{of Keys for an Encryption System}\end{array} = \begin{array}{l}\text{Massive Chaos,} \\ \text{Compromise of Security,} \\ \text{or Both}\end{array}$$

**ON-LINE
PROGRAM
DEVELOPMENT**

On-line program development should be subjected to all the controls identified in the "System Development and Maintenance Controls" section of Chapter 6. In an on-line environment there are additional considerations to be kept in mind.

1.   On-line program development efforts must be prevented from compromising the data stored in the system and the production program libraries.   Therefore, on-line programmers' activities must be controlled by the authorization system that controls the actions of all users of the system.   On-line programmers should be restricted from accessing live data files, data bases, and production libraries. If, as a general rule, they are authorized to access particular protected objects, such authorization should be removed before on-line program development begins.

2.   Specific terminals should be designated as program development terminals.   Such terminals should not be authorized to access the data files, data bases, and production libraries.   These specific terminals, and only these terminals, should be used for on-line program development and testing.

3.   The security system should be able to distinguish between the execution of a program under development and of a production program.   The program under development should be restricted from accessing live data files, data bases, and production libraries.

4.   As discussed in Chapter 6, program testing must not be performed using live data.   This control is equally important if the program testing is performed on-line.   If "live" data or data bases must be used to test the program, a temporary subset of the data should be created.   Care must be taken to prevent sensitive data from being incorporated into such temporary subsets.   The temporary subset of the data file or data base must be obliterated when program testing has been completed.

The essence of these controls is to prevent the unauthorized access to the data files, data bases, and production program libraries.   The protected objects must be carefully secured against unauthorized modification, destruction, and disclosure.   Thus, the actions of the on-line programmer should be restricted at every possible point—in terms of user authorization, terminal authorization, and development program authorization.   The actions of the on-line programmer must also be subjected to the same surveillance as are the actions of the users of the system.

DATA BASE INTEGRITY

The data base management system software and the data in the data base must be protected against unauthorized and fraudulent access, modification, and disclosure.   There are essentially two different "types" of controls that relate to data base integrity:

- Controls to maintain the integrity.
- Auditing.

We will discuss each of these types of controls here.

We have already discussed many of the controls to maintain data base integrity in this and previous chapters. These controls fall into the following categories:

- Authorization.
- Processing controls.
- Adjustment and error correction controls.
- Output controls.
- System development and maintenance controls.
- Production system and program controls.
- Library controls.
- System integrity.
- Operations controls.
- Surveillance.
- Others.

We will point out those aspects of the controls in each category that are particularly appropriate to data base integrity. We will also discuss aspects that may have changed as a result of the use of data bases. We will not, however, identify all the controls that remained intact.

Authorization. Authorization is the mechanism by which users are permitted or denied access to particular data bases or particular data elements within the data base. Authorization, in addition to specifying access permission, also specifies the functions (i.e., read, write, modify, etc.) that can be performed on the particular data elements. Thus, authorization is the mechanism by which access to, modification of, disclosure of, and destruction of a data base is controlled.

Processing controls. Data editing controls, such as validity checks, reasonableness tests, range tests, and limit tests should be performed on the data in the data base whenever the data base is updated to ensure that the data are reasonable.

In addition, audit trails should be produced. The audit trails should contain a listing of all transactions submitted for processing. The user's identification, terminal identification, date, time, and an indication of whether or not the transaction was authorized, and whether or not the transaction was processed should all be identified on the audit trail. A journal should also be produced. It should identify the user, the terminal, the date and time, the transaction, and a "before" and "after" image of the particular component of the data base that was updated.

On a regular basis, validity checks, reasonableness tests, range tests, and limit tests should be performed on the data elements within

215

the data base. Listings of "exception" conditions, of data elements that do not pass the tests, should be produced. On a regular basis the contents of the data base should be printed so that the appropriate portions can be reviewed by responsible management. Utmost care must be taken to ensure that the data are not compromised as their integrity is reviewed.

Adjustment and error correction controls. The adjustment and error-correction controls discussed in Chapter 5 apply equally well to data bases. It is very important that adjustments and error corrections be handled in a timely and *very controlled* manner.

Output controls. The output controls discussed in Chapter 5 apply. Care should be taken by the users to protect the confidentiality of the data with which they are working. Terminal printouts should not be left lying around, nor should they be thrown out in the trash. Users should also be careful that their terminal session is not observed by an unauthorized individual.

System development and maintenance controls. The system development and maintenance controls discussed in Chapter 6 apply. In addition, the on-line program development controls discussed earlier in this chapter are necessary.

The programmer, when developing a new program or modifying an existing program, should only be given the relevant information for those particular data elements in the data base which his program must process. There is no need for him to know the structure of the entire data base.

System development must include the additional step of requesting the authorizations necessary for a particular program or system that has been tested, accepted, and approved, to access other production programs and data in the data files and data bases. The procedures for requesting such authorization should be formalized and should require the use of preprinted sequentially numbered authorization request forms.

The data base administrator must be involved in all system development and maintenance projects involving the data bases to ensure that new production programs or modifications to existing production programs do not affect other production programs' ability to process the necessary data in the data base.

Production system and program controls. The data base administrator should be responsible for all changes to the data base software library. He should, on a regular basis, review the library to ensure that no unauthorized changes were made.

Library controls. The library controls discussed in Chapter 6 apply regardless of whether the data are in a data file or data base, on a magnetic tape, or disk. When not in active use, the disks containing the data bases should be stored in the library (such as overnight and on weekends). If the disks are to be sent out to be refurbished, the data bases should be obliterated prior to doing so.

System integrity. The system integrity discussion in Chapter 6 applies here as well.

Operations controls. The operations controls discussed in Chapter 6 apply. The operators' actions must be monitored. In addition, in larger data base and communications systems, there may be a network control center where engineers are performing equipment and line tests and monitoring the network and where programmers may be changing the polling lists and patching the communications software monitors. Their actions too, must be monitored.

Surveillance. The real-time surveillance and the logging discussed earlier in this chapter are directed toward ensuring data base integrity.

Others. There are several other controls that relate specifically to data base integrity:

1. If authorization control is performed by the data base management system (DBMS), controls must be established to prevent all accesses to the data bases whenever the DBMS or other security software is not operational. It may be necessary to physically remove the disk from the drive or to, in some way preclude use of the drive. Without a functioning DBMS or security software, the data base is vulnerable to uncontrolled, unauthorized, and fraudulent modification, disclosure, and destruction.

2. System utility programs should not be authorized to access, in any way, the data bases. Whenever such programs must access the data bases (i.e., for back-up purposes), a temporary authorization should be granted. The processing of data bases by utility programs must be very carefully controlled.

3. The console logs should be reviewed by the data base administrator to ensure that the data bases were not accessed when the DBMS was not operational and that the utility programs that accessed the data bases were given proper temporary authorization.

Auditing   Auditing, in addition to the controls and safeguards identified above, plays a key role in ensuring data base integrity. The EDP audit techniques that are applicable to data base integrity, and the role of the EDP auditor with respect to data base integrity, are discussed in more detail in Chapter 8. We will identify some of the applicable techniques here:

- Sampling.
- Integrated test facility.
- System control audit review files.
- Tracing.
- Others.

Sampling. Sampling involves the random selection of data elements for inspection purposes. The intent of the sampling techniques is to uncover errors in the data base and to estimate the extent of erroneous data.

Integrated test facility. The integrated test facility (ITF) allows the auditor to add "dummy" records to the data base and to process test transactions against the "dummy" records. The test transactions are included with the live data during a normal processing run. Thus, ITF enables the auditor to monitor the processing performed by production programs and to verify that processing is being performed properly.

System Control Audit Review Files. System Control Audit Review Files (SCARF) allow the auditor to monitor the processing of data by allowing him to incorporate auditor-designed tests within the production program. The auditor's tests and SCARF data collection are performed on the processed data during the normal production run and the results are written in an audit review file.

Tracing. Tracing allows the auditor to tag specific, live input transactions and to monitor the tagged transactions as they are being processed by the production program.

Others. The internal EDP auditor should perform pointer reference validity checks to verify that the pointers in the data base records point to valid and appropriate records and that all the pointers, or links, in chained files and data bases exist.

**ADMINISTRATIVE
CONSIDERATIONS**

To ensure that the controls and safeguards are effective in preventing, deterring, or detecting unauthorized or fraudulent systems, data, and program access and modification, the controls and safeguards must be administered and audited carefully and continually. We will discuss the administrative and audit considerations in the following subsections:

- The role of the data base administrator.
- The role of the computer security officer.
- The role of the local security officers.
- Administration of user identification and authentication.
- Administration of authorization.
- Administration of surveillance.

The role of the data base administrator

Data bases are used by many departments and are processed by numerous production programs. It is, therefore, necessary that someone be responsible for the data bases and that someone coordinate the activities that affect the data bases. This, in essence, is the role of the data base administrator.

The data base administrator may be responsible for the design of the data base, the data base organization, and the data definitions. He is responsible for controlling and coordinating the use of the data bases by the various users and the production programs. He is also responsible for designing and implementing procedures to ensure that the integrity of the data bases is maintained.

Depending upon the variety of data base users and your company's management philosophy, the data base administrator may review and approve all requests for authorizations. On the other hand, user management or others may control authorizations.

The role of the computer security officer

The computer security officer is responsible for overall computer security. In terms of our discussion in this chapter, he may be the only person who has access to the authorization mechanisms, and who can change users', terminals', and programs' authorizations to access and perform specific functions on the data and programs.

The computer security officer is responsible for investigating all security violations and for reviewing the surveillance logs to ensure that the security system is functioning properly and to detect emerging patterns of security violations. He is responsible for doing everything he can to enhance the security of the system and maintain it at a prudent level.

The role of local security officers

Local security officers are responsible for maintaining physical and administrative security in their particular locations. They are typically located in places with terminals. They are responsible for investigating all security violations that occurred in their locations and for being alert to security violation attempts. If a terminal keyboard is locked by the system, as a result of suspected security violation attempts, the local security officer is responsible for investigating the attempt and unlocking the terminal. If there are any terminals in his location reserved for special use, such as on-line programming or sensitive data and transaction processing, he is responsible for ensuring that such terminals are used by authorized people to perform only the special function.

User management, users, the computer security officer, and others may be responsible for the administration of user identification and authentication:

1. User management must identify the users whom they have authorized to use the terminals. This may be performed with the assistance of the computer security officer, who may explain the implications of authorizing an employee to access the computer system.

2. Users are responsible for properly protecting their user identification and authentication mechanism (i.e., something known, something possessed, or something about the user) against possible compromise. Users are also responsible for notifying the computer security officer whenever they suspect that their user identification or authentication may have been compromised.

3. The computer security officer is responsible for making sure that users understand the need to protect the security of their user identification and authentication. He is responsible for maintaining the user identification and authentication files; for secure distribution of any cards, badges, keys, or passwords; for changing passwords regularly, if passwords are used; and for following up on all security violation attempts that involved user identification and authentication.

4. The EDP auditor should, through observation and interviews, check on compliance with security regulations. He should be concerned that the user identification and authentication be handled in a secure manner by the user and the computer security officer, that the user properly understand the need to secure the information or object, and that the distribution of the information or object be secure.

The responsibility for the administration of authorization may lie with user management, the data base administrator, or the computer security officer.

It is often the responsibility (even if the duties are delegated) of user top management to designate which employees can enter particular transaction types, and which can read, write, or modify particular data files, data bases, and execute programs.

However, it is the computer security officer's responsibility to ensure that management has a clear understanding of what it is they are actually doing or delegating, and of the implications of the authorization decisions. The computer security officer might help management understand authorization by preparing written instructions for them and conducting meetings and informal discussions with them. If the computer security officer, during his review of the security log, begins to suspect that the ground rules for designating authorization are being disregarded, he should bring the matter to top management's attention.

Administration of surveillance

Surveillance is everyone's responsibility. We have discussed, in this chapter and, in fact, throughout the book, how logs and violation reports can be generated. If these logs and reports are not reviewed and attempted security violations are not investigated, their purpose has been defeated. It is essentially the responsibility of the computer security officer and the internal EDP auditor to verify that proper review and follow-up are carried out.

8

EDP Internal Audit
Functions
and Techniques

A strong EDP internal audit program can be one of the most effective countermeasures a company has in its total system of safeguards to prevent, detect, and deter computer fraud. There is no way of knowing the extent to which EDP auditing discourages would-be perpetrators from committing fraud in the first place, but we believe the impact to be quite significant. While the EDP auditor himself does not prevent computer frauds, his recommendations to management about strengthening EDP security and applications controls are often directed to the prevention aspect.

With regard to the auditor's role in detecting computer fraud, more than a few experts in the EDP security field have leveled severe criticisms at the EDP internal audit community for their failure to detect significant ongoing computer frauds. Viewing these criticisms with the advantage of hindsight, it seems to us that there is at least some justification for this position. In an attempt to explain why auditors have failed to detect ongoing computer frauds, the same critics will suggest that the EDP auditor lacks the appropriate training and tools to do an effective job in this area. It is hard to argue with this position, but we feel that the critics, and the auditors themselves, are missing the essential ingredient.

The essential ingredient of the auditor's ability to systematically, rather than haphazardly, detect ongoing frauds is a frame of mind which assumes that fraud exists and brings to bear examination techniques geared to find it. This approach should be used in combination with the one most EDP internal auditors traditionally use. The more traditional approach calls for the EDP auditor to examine the company's EDP safeguards and application controls, comment on their adequacy, provide recommendations for strengthening them, and sample some of the computerized data to determine its accuracy. Using this combination of approaches, the EDP internal auditor can be more confident in his conclusions about the adequacy of safeguards to prevent fraud.

In this chapter we plan to discuss the functions of the EDP internal auditor in helping his company protect itself against fraud. We will also present some of the important techniques the auditor can employ in conducting an evaluation of EDP security and application controls designed to prevent and detect fraud. The major topics we will be covering are:

- Systems development auditing.

- EDP security auditing.

- Application control auditing.

- Financial records auditing.

- EDP auditing methods and techniques.

- EDP auditor qualifications.

- EDP audit organization and planning.

While this chapter will emphasize the EDP internal auditor's role as it pertains to fraud, readers should be aware that EDP auditors are typically concerned with a number of other areas that may have little if any effect on the prevention and detection of computer fraud. In addition to dealing with fraud controls, EDP auditors are typically concerned with the effectiveness, efficiency, and productivity of the EDP department and computer applications. The auditor may recommend that the company use better procedures for EDP feasibility studies. He may point out where the company can save money on things like computer forms. He may show his company how savings can be achieved through modern data-entry methods. He may review EDP project planning and control practices, and recommend that specific techniques and approaches be adopted to improve the company's performance in this area. These, then, are but a handful of the numerous other aspects of the EDP internal auditor's job that we recognize as being important but which are not directly pertinent to his responsibilities in matters relating to computer fraud controls.

SYSTEMS DEVELOPMENT AUDITING The ideal time for EDP internal auditors to recommend changes and extensions to the system for fraud control purposes is during the development of the system. When a system is being specified, designed, programmed, and tested, it is usually less expensive and easier to build in the needed controls and safeguards than to wait until the system becomes operational, at which time introducing control features can become difficult as well as expensive. Moreover, controls and safeguards introduced after the fact are frequently of a makeshift nature and are not entirely responsive to what would be desirable to have a properly controlled system.

In the *system development life cycle,* a number of distinct steps are involved which include the definition of the problem and analysis of systems requirements, the design and programming of the system, and implementation of (or conversion to) the system. These activities involve a series of steps defined in a manner that a given company finds best suited to its way of developing systems. One set of steps is as follows:

1. Discussion and problem analysis.
2. General problem definition.
3. Functional requirements analysis.
4. Functional specification review.
5. System design.
6. System design quality assurance.
7. System review and user concurrence.
8. Programming.
9. Integrated system testing.
10. System checkout in parallel.
11. Conversion.
12. Operations follow-up.
13. Post-conversion evaluation.

The EDP internal auditor may be involved in all these steps, with particular emphasis on steps 4 through 10. By interacting with the people who are specifying, designing, programming, and testing the system, the auditor is able to review system controls and safeguards, and to recommend appropriate changes and additions as the project moves forward.

We believe that it is important for the auditor to review and make recommendations as to controls to ensure an adequate level of fraud protection. However, he should avoid the actual specification and design of such controls. We would also advise against having the EDP internal auditor become a member of the project team, where he could find himself inadvertently designing actual controls. In so doing, the auditor may jeopardize or appear to jeopardize his independence and objectivity such that (1) future EDP internal audits of the operational system can be challenged in the sense that the auditor is reviewing his own work or the work of the audit department, and (2) the EDP internal auditor could wind up as a convenient scapegoat for the systems development people if all does not function as expected when the system becomes operational.

System design review
The EDP auditor will need to understand the functions and capabilities of the system and have an appreciation of the degree to which the system may be exposed to fraud. As we have discussed elsewhere in this book, a system that disburses funds is always a high-exposure system. Other systems, depending upon the purpose for which they are designed, may represent less of a risk in terms of fraud, or perhaps practically none at all. It goes without saying that the emphasis on fraud control should be addressed to those areas that the auditor selects as being most critical.

In evaluating the adequacy of system design from a fraud control standpoint, the auditor will need to understand what *responsibilities for data integrity* (transaction authorization, edit list reviews, error correction) will fall into the user's area of responsibility. The adequacy of the design in terms of the system's ability to impose certain controls on user activities will be an important consideration.

The auditor will want to understand how, in the case of an on-line/data base system, users are to be identified as to their *authorization to use the system* and which functions they are permitted to perform. With regard to data elements, the auditor should satisfy himself that appropriate controls over their *access and modification* are provided in the system design. Beyond this, the system's ability to *detect tampering and unauthorized access* should be evaluated in terms of its adequacy. For example, the auditor will want to learn whether provisions have been made to record all transactions in the form of a log or a journal, so that a *chain of events* could be reconstructed, if needed, to facilitate the investigation of a suspected fraud.

The auditor must closely examine the whole area of *input controls* that are provided in the system design. This would include the establishment of initiation, review, and authorization procedures. It would also consider the adequacy of any batch balancing and input validation and editing specifications. The system design should be developed to the point where the auditor can comment on the provisions and need for such things as: coded validation tables, check digits, range and reasonableness tests, validity tests for invalid combinations and missing data, cryptographic techniques for on-line/data base system designs, and so forth.

Of special interest will be the *exception reports and alerts* that the system design provides when data are found to be inaccurate or

225

invalid, and when the system detects tampering or unauthorized attempted accesses to data elements. In reviewing these matters the auditor will want to consider whether the reporting is practical from the standpoint of those who are expected to respond to it and take action, whether the reports be in the form of alerts on a user terminal or security officer's output device, listings, exception reports, dormant activity reports, special reports of credits and adjustments, questionable activity reporting such as a kite suspect report, and so forth. For all such reporting, the auditor will want to make recommendations that enhance the possibility for these safeguards and control measures to serve their intended purpose. For example, the EDP auditor may recommend that some type of history be maintained on tampering attempts and that some form of exception reporting be instituted which considers the number of invalid attempts and the history of past attempts, rather than having the system print out, every day, a complete listing of everyone who failed to enter his password correctly the first time. Here, the objective would be to present control and security information in a manner that someone can reasonably be expected to review carefully and act on as necessary. Conversely, if someone has to look through a foot-high stack of computer printout to find a handful of exceptions, the experienced auditor will recognize that this will probably fail to provide the anticipated control (because of human inability or a deterioration of interest in coping with an impractical situation).

The auditor should also review the system design to see whether *maximum advantage is being made of the computer to take over control and security functions* that would otherwise be imposed on users or systems operations personnel. Out of this type of appraisal would come auditor recommendations to avoid dependence on human interaction and performance to the extent that it can reasonably be done. Here, again, the knowledgeable auditor will bring his experience and understanding to bear, in the sense that he knows that *people-based controls are the ones most likely to fail, deteriorate, be subjected to compromise, or end up being ineffective simply because people were not instructed or do not know what is expected of them.*

Finally, the auditor will want to satisfy himself as to the *adequacy of the specifications* that have been developed for the programming personnel, since there is always a risk that the system design will not be properly interpreted in all respects when it is time for the programmers to commence programming work. To reduce the risk of design features not being incorporated as intended, the auditor will want to see that programmers are being given specifications which follow accepted standards, are understandable, and which can be conveniently referenced if there is any question about whether a program is being developed as reflected in the system design.

Programming
audits

Programming, as we are using the term here, involves the logical design of the program, coding of the program in a language such as COBOL, testing the program, and documenting the program. Some installations have coders who are responsible for writing programming code but not for the design of the program. Also, some installations use documentation specialists or technical writers to document the program. For our purposes, we will assume that the programmer does these things, since this is the most common practice and really does not affect the EDP auditor's role in conducting a review.

The programmer will start with a properly prepared specification from the system designer which describes the inputs to the program, outputs it is to produce, and the processing requirements for the data. When the programmer develops the logic of the program to accomplish the desired processing, he may inadvertently make logical errors of the type that may not be detected in testing. The more inexperienced the programmer is, the more likely it is that he will make logical errors. For example, the specifications may state that the program is receiving as input, transaction types A, B, and C. The inexperienced programmer may, in his program logic, make positive tests for A and B and otherwise assume that the transaction type is C. This is a bad assumption and a flaw in the logic.

A programmer intending to perpetrate fraud through the program once it becomes operational can put "trap doors" into the logic to facilitate the fraud. The trap door may work in conjunction with open-ended logic to sense an otherwise unauthorized transaction and shunt it off to be specially processed by extraneous program code that has been placed in the program to facilitate the fraud. The programmer could also insert *excess code* which has no function for authorized processing but which he could replace with fraudulent coding at a later date. His purpose in putting these "holes" in the program during its development might be based on the knowledge that the auditor will later perform an audit to determine whether the size of the program has changed.

If the programmer, in entering bogus coding at a later date, stays within the hole space he has provided, the auditor would not be able to detect a change in program size.

To preclude processing logic errors that can be used to cover up a fraud as well as extraneous coding and holes left in the logic for the entry of fraudulent code at a later date, the auditor should concern himself with the adequacy of programmer supervision and *provisions for program logic reviews*. A logic review is typically performed by a more senior programmer than the one who is developing the program in question. In performing the logic review, the reviewer will study the logic or coding of the program to determine whether the original programmer has met the original specifications and whether the logic is sound. In going through this process, the reviewer will be able to detect problems and questionable practices within the program coding. The reviewer's job is somewhat easier in an EDP installation that has adopted what is known as *structured design* and *structured programming* practices which have the effect of making the programs modularized and easier to analyze.

If the auditor is satisfied that logic reviews are being carried out effectively, he may wish to simply make some random spot checks of logic on his own. However, where an installation does not follow the logic review practice, the auditor may want to recommend that it be adopted and, in the meantime, take on the logic review job for at least the most sensitive programs.

Many EDP departments have *programming standards* that call for the use of certain coding conventions, formats for data and instruction names, use of preprogrammed logic that is common to a number of programs, prohibition against the use of certain options in the programming language, comments to be placed within the program coding to explain the processing and logical steps, forms and formats for the preparation of program documentation, and more. As a general rule, a feature common to all the standards is that their use will enable another qualified programmer to follow what is being done with relative ease. This is certainly important in an investigation of suspected fraud where someone is trying to understand the processing steps involved and whether a program has been compromised. Some standards may contribute directly to fraud control objectives, while others introduce consistency that makes the anomalies often involved in fraud difficult to disguise. Additionally, a properly documented program can greatly reduce what may otherwise turn out to be *excessive continuing dependency on the original programmer* or another person who ends up being the only one who understands the idiosyncrasies of the program. The latter condition can greatly increase the opportunity for fraud, in the sense that no one else is capable of reviewing the assigned programmer's work without an enormous amount of effort and study.

If the company does not have standards of the type just discussed, the auditor will want to recommend that such standards be developed or acquired from outside sources. If the standards exist, the auditor's role during systems development will be to *monitor adherence* to them. This is a job that the auditor will probably want to perform on a sampling basis for systems that are comprised of a large number of programs. However, the auditor should be certain to examine the compliance to standards for programs, such as major posting programs, which are especially vulnerable to manipulations for fraudulent purposes.

In order to *test or "debug" a program*, a set of test data must be provided to the programmer or he must create it himself. The

EDP internal auditor should look into the testing aspect from a couple of angles. First, the auditor will want to satisfy himself that the programmer is using an *adequate set of test data*, meaning that the data fully exercise all the features for which the program has been designed, including error conditions. A *test data generator* can be put to good use here, in that it eliminates the need to laboriously produce by hand a reasonable set of test data. By giving a test data generator the proper parameters, it can generate a large amount of test data that gives better assurance that all the program's logic is "exercised." Second, if the programmer is using actual data from existing computer records to test his program, the auditor will want to check to be sure that the programmer is not using data that is not supposed to be seen by the programmer, such as payroll information, and that he is *not using* the live *operational version of the data file* which he might either manipulate or obliterate. A copy, never the original, should be used.

The auditor should satisfy himself on the basis of evidence of test results shown him by the programmer that an *adequate amount of testing* has been performed for individual programs. It is also a good idea for the auditor to actually observe some of this testing. The final step before a system goes into live operations is a system test and/or a parallel test. In this kind of testing the entire system (all programs) is run using a comprehensive set of test data or live data taken from an existing system that is to be replaced by the new one. This kind of testing is especially important in that it proves the workability of the entire system, whereas individual program testing only proves the workability of a particular program. The fact that all programs work on a unit test basis does not necessarily mean that they will work together as a system. Accordingly, the auditor's role in *system and parallel testing* is vitally important, since this is the last time that errors and faults can be detected and corrected before they do real harm.

The auditor should satisfy himself that an adequate set of test data has been made up or, in the case of parallel operations, that the sample is representative and sufficiently large. He will also want to be sure that users are heavily involved in verifying the results produced by the system. The *user verification* should be evidenced by a sign-off procedure, but the auditor should assure himself that the sign-off is not merely a perfunctory chore on the part of the user.

At this stage of testing, the auditor may wish to apply his *audit software* to the computer files that are being used and generated by the new system. This will serve as an additional check on the test results and, at the same time, will provide the auditor with some good insights into how well his audit software will function when the system becomes operational.

The auditor may have previously requested that certain features be built into the original system design to serve EDP auditing objectives. Later in this chapter we will discuss some of these techniques used for *audit monitoring,* such as the integrated test facility, transaction selection, embedded audit data collection, and extended records. If any of these features have been specified, the auditor will, of course, want to be sure that they are functioning as expected during the system test or parallel testing operation. Since some of these features will be very relevant to fraud detection objectives, the auditor should make every attempt to begin using them during the final testing phase to assure himself that they are performing to expectations and that manipulations that might be attempted during testing do not escape his attention.

As the system is coming together in anticipation of system or parallel testing, *user instruction manuals* will have been prepared and classroom and/or on-the-job training will be conducted for users. The EDP internal auditor will want to examine these user instructions and evaluate whether they adequately address users' needs and whether they incorporate effective instructions to the user that emphasize responsibilities for controlling input and output in the interest of preventing and detecting fraud. Likewise, any *training* that is given to users should also stress user responsibilities for acting on information that is suspicious or bringing to the auditor's attention any situation in which irregularities might be symptoms that a manipulation has or is taking place.

Throughout the system development process, the EDP auditor will want to be *formulating an audit plan* for the new system and making determinations as to what audit software and other resources are needed to do an effective auditing job. For example, the auditor may recognize early in the game that the new system utilizes data communications/data base techniques that are foreign to the company's prior EDP environment. This may mandate the auditor to see that appropriate members of the audit staff receive the necessary training in these new areas or that persons who possess the requisite skills are added to the staff. It goes without saying that the entire matter of the *auditability of the system* should be addressed throughout all aspects of its development.

Immediately after the system goes into live operation, the auditor will want to be especially watchful for any program bugs and user errors that require "quick fixes" to the system. Systems people and programmers will have a natural tendency to want to make such *fixes on the spot, skipping customary program change controls.* Control considerations that are affected in altering a previously established user procedure may also be overlooked. A programmer, user, or computer operator could exploit the emergency situation to perpetrate fraud if it becomes a case where good control practices are thrown out the window in the interest of making a rapid fix. In such a situation, the auditor will generally want to avoid becoming a stumbling block to having corrective action take place. However, he should sharply increase his *surveillance and monitoring* of the actions being taken and watch closely for any suspicious conditions. Readers will recognize that there are genuine emergency situations that must be accommodated with some sacrifice of preventive control. However, if emergencies become the routine rather than the exception, the auditor should make recommendations to cope with the underlying problems, because effective control and auditing tends to be impractical, if not impossible, in a situation where crises and chaos are the normal mode of operation.

EDP SECURITY AUDITING

The scope of an EDP security audit can be far-reaching, extending to safeguards and controls in the following areas:

- Personnel practices and policies.
- Physical access to hardware, data, and programs.
- Data file library procedures.
- Operating procedures and controls.
- Documentation standards.
- Change controls for applications and systems software.
- Data base/data communications technical controls.

The auditor would be examining the adequacy of controls in the areas listed above and making selective checks on compliance. Such checks on compliance would not be intended to demonstrate that particular computer applications have adequate safeguards, but rather to provide a basis for commenting on the adequacy of the *general system of safeguards for computer security*. In-depth reviews of particular applications are considered as separate from the computer security auditing we are now discussing.

Since we have discussed each of the preceding computer security topics in some detail elsewhere in the book, the following sections are intended to point out some of the key controls and safeguards that the auditor should note as they pertain to the prevention and detection of fraud.

Personnel practices and policies

The idea behind examining personnel practices and policies is to evaluate their adequacy in preventing the company from employing someone who is or may become a security risk. Further, it examines the organization and working relationships between people to assess whether they are consistent with overall fraud control principles.

Preemployment screening and background verification will be of interest to the auditor from the standpoint that adequate procedures in this area can help the company avoid the blunder of hiring someone with a record of fraud or whose financial and other problems may make the candidate undesirable for employment in any sensitive position.

With regard to organization and job functions, the auditor will want to make inquiries and note whether responsibilities are divided such that fraud would *require* collusion between at least two individuals. The auditor should see that programmers are not performing EDP operations functions or engaging in accounting activities, and vice versa.

The auditor should note whether a job rotation procedure is in effect to help prevent overdependence on particular individuals for particular functions. The auditor should also note what controls are in effect to control overtime work and to enforce policies that call for employees to take at least one consecutive week of vacation.

Also, the EDP auditor should determine whether termination procedures are in line with good practices, in that they call for the recovery of company property, identification cards, keys, and so forth. In the case of an involuntary termination, in particular, the auditor should determine that such individuals are not permitted to remain on the premises after they have been discharged.

Physical access to hardware, data, and programs

The EDP auditor's examination of physical access safeguards will be concerned with controls to deal with access by employees, visitors, and intruders. In the case of employees, there should be several layers of security access controls, such that only those people authorized to be in particular areas can, in fact, gain access to them.

For example, programmers should not be permitted into the computer operations areas or have access to user terminals. Computer operators should not be permitted to enter the data file library. Visitors should be escorted. Controls should be established to define and limit the access privileges granted to maintenance personnel, contractors, and outside consultants.

The auditor should note whether access to program listings and documentation is controlled on a strict "need to know" basis. He should also note whether data files and programs are kept under lock and key, and that access to them is properly logged.

Among other things, the EDP auditor should assess the adequacy of safeguards to prevent and detect intrusion: guard and watchman activities, effectiveness of surveillance devices such as closed-circuit television and intrusion detection alarms, and whether the use and construction of safes, vaults, and secure areas is consistent with the degree of protection needed in the circumstances.

The auditor should also evaluate access controls for computer printouts before, during, and after distribution. Controls over the access to sensitive computer forms, such as continuous-form checks, warehouse receipts, negotiable instruments, and so forth, should also be noted.

Data file library procedures

Some types of fraudulent manipulations may call for the perpetrator to have access to the company's tape and disk library in order to accomplish an irregular master-file update or to switch data files. The auditor will be interested in physical access control provisions, as mentioned above. He should also evaluate the adequacy of library procedures.

For example, the auditor should determine whether library procedures have been established and are enforced for all operations shifts. There should be an inventory list of tapes and disks showing location in the library, serial number, application name and number, creation and expiration dates, and the name of the data file. The listing, among other things, can be used to conduct periodic physical verifications of the contents of the library. Any variances noted may be an indication of fraudulent use of the data, and an investigation should be made as to the explanation.

The data librarian should maintain a log of data files issued and received and follow up on any delays in having data files returned on a timely basis. The auditor should note whether all data files are stored in the library, including so-called "programmer test data tapes."

If magnetic tapes and disks are sent to an outside service for reconditioning or if they are to be discarded, the auditor should satisfy himself that steps are taken to erase such files so that outsiders cannot print out the records.

Operating procedures and controls

The EDP auditor should check to see that appropriate operations logs are maintained and reviewed to detect any suspicious runs or reruns and possible unauthorized use of the system. The auditor should note whether computer job scheduling procedures provide for adequate follow-up if there are delays in starting or completing jobs, excessive or questionable use of the system or program testing, and to preclude the submission and running of unauthorized programs.

The auditor should note whether operating instructions provide adequate information to operators on a "need to know" basis.

If data entry or keypunching functions are performed within operations, the auditor should inquire as to the adequacy of controls over the integrity of input, such as batch balancing and subsequent quality and completeness controls.

233

There are a number of different types of documentation, including:

- Specifications resulting from systems analysis activities.
- System-level documentation describing the design of the system and overall flow of information.
- Program documentation, describing the logic and coding of programs, which is employed when troubleshooting program bugs and during program maintenance activities.
- Operations documentation describing the procedures and steps involved in running the system: shows what actions are to be taken under various exception or error conditions, provides instructions for data preparation, gives information pertaining to the distribution of output, specifies certain security precautions, and so on.
- User instructions, which include directions as to the collection and preparation of data, the use of edit and balancing lists, terminal operating procedures, and scheduling and work submission instructions.

The EDP auditor's chief interest in documentation is to see that it is prepared according to adequate standards and that it is sufficiently descriptive to preclude excessive dependence on any one individual for interpretation. Also, the auditor's appraisal should consider whether the documentation is clear enough to preclude errors of misunderstanding and to describe what action should be taken when errors and exceptions arise. Access controls for documentation are also evaluated.

The auditor should consider whether the documentation would be useful in an investigation of a suspected fraud, or whether, because it is out of date or poorly prepared, its usefulness for this purpose would be doubtful.

New programs and changes to existing programs should be specifically authorized on a form designed for this purpose and should not be permitted on any other basis. The change procedure should require adequate testing of any changes made, reviews of test results, and some kind of verification that the changes made do no more and no less than what was originally authorized. The EDP auditor should satisfy himself that the change control procedures are adequate and that they are being complied with. The auditor should also note whether the on-line library of production programs is adequately safeguarded, such that the addition of new or revised production programs can only be accomplished under adequately controlled conditions.

Part of the audit procedure should examine any use of interactive program development terminals to ensure that production programs are protected from unauthorized manipulation through such means. Additionally, the auditor should concern himself with the activity of systems programmers and satisfy himself that changes to the operating system, communications monitor, data-access modules, and utility programs are adequately supervised from a security and control standpoint.

Data base/data communications technical controls

The EDP auditor will want to review the methods by which the on-line terminal user is required to identify himself—whether by passwords, security codes, machine-sensible badge, physical characteristic (hand geometry, voice pattern, fingerprint), question-and-answer interrogation, or a combination of these means. The auditor should satisfy himself that the implementation of these safeguards is such that the desired level of security is achieved. For example, if passwords are used, they should be administered in a controlled manner and otherwise protected by those who are required to use them.

The auditor should also note whether terminals used for sensitive work are in secure areas to which access is limited to authorized operators. Also, any tampering attempts should be logged, and the auditor should satisfy himself that these logs are being reviewed for security violations.

In the area of data base usage, the auditor should evaluate the adequacy of controls on particular users as to: the transaction types they are permitted to use, the processes and programs they are authorized to invoke, and the items or categories of data that can be read and updated by the user.

The auditor should note whether an adequate log or journal is being maintained of terminal and data base usage, and whether it is of such a nature as to make it useful for the investigation of a suspected fraud perpetrated through the on-line system or data base. The auditor may wish to consider whether cryptographic techniques would be desirable for particular data bases or communications, or, if they are already implemented, whether they are being administered in a secure manner. For example, the auditor would want to review the administration of encryption keys and their means of distribution. Similarly, for passwords and data base access authorizations, the auditor should satisfy himself as to the adequacy of administrative controls and operational follow through.

In general, the areas of inquiry for data communications/data base systems include:

- *Identification*—the means by which the users and system identify themselves to one another (e.g., by means of an employee number).

- *Authentication*—the means by which identification is validated—the user is who he says he is (e.g., by means of a password).

- *Authorization*—the means by which users (and systems) are permitted access to and use of only those data and functions for which they have authorization (e.g., to update pay rates).

- *Surveillance*—the means by which a system detects and records access to and uses of the system, especially attempted unauthorized access to data and use of functions (e.g., an attempt to browse through payroll records).

- *Administration and maintenance*—the role and responsibilities of, and controls over the manager or administrator of the data base, communications network, authorization function, surveillance function, and systems programming activities for the software.

**APPLICATION
CONTROL
AUDITING**

Applications auditing is done for operational systems. Such systems may or may not have undergone audit involvement in their development, as discussed earlier in this chapter. Further, the results of an application audit can be misleading if computer security and controls, as discussed previously, are not maintained at a satisfactory level. With these considerations in mind, the auditor will want to select one or more applications, especially those which are more likely to be targets of fraud, for a detailed application audit. As shown in Figure 8-1, various situations might arise that create concern about particular applications.

Typically, the larger part of an application audit takes place in the system user environment. Here, the auditor is concerned with controls to prevent and detect frauds resulting from input manipulations as well as the misuse or manipulation of system outputs. The audit concepts that we shall discuss below are generally pertinent to batch as well as to on-line/data base systems. However, it should be recognized that the specific areas of inquiry depend a great deal on the particular application under review. Pension fund systems, accounts payable, accounts receivable, demand-deposit accounting, insurance policy loan, welfare, warranty parts and service reimbursement, inventory accounting, payroll, freight payment, credit authorization, and many other such systems that may be vehicles for fraudulent activity have particular characteristics and user procedures that the auditor must examine in a systematic, step-by-step manner.

Situation	Concern About Application Safeguards
A commercial bank installing an on-line commercial loan application package it has purchased from a software house.	The senior vice president of operations is painfully aware of the many sizeable embezzlements that have occurred in the commercial loan area, and wonders whether the new system may open up even more avenues for defrauding his bank.
A manufacturer of automotive products that can be moved readily on the "black market" is installing an inventory management system for a totally automated warehouse.	Inventory thefts are nothing new to this company. But the president wonders whether the new computerized system will enable a heist of a grand scale to be concealed until its discovery results in a material loss and his ending up unemployed.
A protection services firm developing a system to allocate manpower and prepare the payroll for guards, watchmen, and others working under many different time and compensation arrangements.	The firm's outside auditor learns about the new system, which he will have to review in next year's audit, and reminds the firm's chief financial officer about opportunities for payroll padding frauds.
An insurance company is trying to, at last, accomodate the complexities and exceptions of group insurance in a new, highly flexible system.	The company's executive in charge of group lines knows that premium billings and receipts are for large dollar amounts and that group claim frauds have always been a problem. Will the new system expose the company even more than the old systems?
A university making cost-cutting changes in its student registration and grading system that will call for the use of display terminals with data entry keyboards.	The university is having financial problems as it is. The last thing it needs is a scandal about registration and grading frauds that could have been foreseen and precluded.
A distributer of consumer appliances has just computerized its purchase order preparation procedures, which completes the "loop" with its accounts payable system.	The distributer recently fired its Northeast marketing director for a fraud that involved drop shipments that bypassed home office purchasing procedures. The newly hired controller now worries whether a parallel situation, with some new twist, could be concealed under the automated purchase order system.
A sizeable retail chain has been successfully using point-of-sale terminals for several years. Because of a power failure, the stores in the outlying cities had to use their terminals in an off-line mode. When the power was restored, and all transactions entered, the chain discovered a number of significant shortages.	The chain's auditor and several of the computer people, based on their knowledge of the system, think that someone took advantage of some control weakness that only existed in off-line terminal operations to defraud the company.

Figure 8-1

Sampling of Situations and Concerns About Application Safeguards

An application control audit, although it stresses input and output on the users side, also traces the controls through the data processing activities performed on the computer and can involve detailed examinations of documentation and program code. The audit is concerned with the adequacy as well as the adherence to appropriate safeguards. Like systems development auditing, the application audit results in recommendations to strengthen controls and to help ensure compliance at the desired level. Several of the appendixes to this book list or otherwise illustrate the types of controls to look for.

In the following two sections we will discuss some of the key points that the application audit should cover.

Input controls   The auditor will want to follow all the steps and associated controls from the point at which data are originated or initiated, recorded, formatted, coded, and finally entered into the computer system by means of a terminal or other data-conversion device.

The auditor should look for a definition of responsibilities for those individuals in the user areas who prepare and process input. He should determine whether they understand their responsibilities and whether appropriate written instructions are provided. Controls that place limits on who can initiate and authorize input transactions should be evaluated. The auditor should question whether the separation of duties is adequate, such that different individuals originate input, authorize it, and then perform review and reconciliation functions based on computer output. Also, the auditor should see whether job-rotation practices are in effect and whether vacations and other personnel policies and practices are at an adequate level and adhered to, as verified by compliance testing.

Various amount, item, hash, and other control totals should be maintained, depending upon the particular type of system. Procedures should be in effect to check on the completeness of processing, correctness of input, and for the correction of errors. The auditor should satisfy himself that the administrative and internal controls relative to input processing meet adequate standards and are followed for routine as well as exception processing conditions.

The auditor should satisfy himself that an adequate audit trail is being maintained throughout the user processing of input. The use of prenumbered and precoded forms, sequential numbering of transactions, and some type of manual posting procedure may be necessary or desirable in a situation where a fraud investigation might necessitate tracing the sequence of events employed in the manipulation scheme.

Access controls to sensitive input forms, source documents that are the basis of input, and output reports containing sensitive information should be noted by the auditor during an application control audit.

As a first step, the auditor will need to understand what outputs are produced by the system and their intended uses. With this understanding, he can evaluate whether they are formatted, coded, sorted, summarized, extracted, and otherwise presented in a form that is supportive of their intended use. An exception report that is designed to call a user's attention to some possible irregularity or error, but which is too voluminous to be used in any practical sense, should be noted and commented on by the auditor in the sense that it defeats a control objective.

The reported information may be used for error correction, and the auditor should evaluate whether the level of error detection and the manner in which it is reported is in line with control principles. The auditor should also look for indications on outputs of run-to-run totals, reporting of balancing and differences, and some presentation of items held in a suspense file and aging information pertaining to them.

Outputs containing or displaying sensitive information should be controlled strictly on a "need to know" basis, and access to data elements, computer records, and reports of this nature should be under appropriate control. The controls in effect should be verified by the auditor during the application review.

The records management policy and procedure should see to it that source documents, output reports, and other significant records are maintained under secure conditions and in an orderly manner, so as to facilitate their usefulness in any future investigation of irregularity or suspected fraud.

Deliberate entry of unauthorized or invalid transactions For certain reasons, maybe just to prove a point, the auditor may wish to perform certain *counter-control testing*. Simply put, this involves the entry of erroneous, invalid, or unauthorized input by the auditor and his observance of what action is taken by the user. Depending on the application being audited, the auditor can submit types of transactions that would be useful in perpetrating a fraud. For example, in an accounts receivable system, the auditor could set up a dummy customer account, then initiate a large unauthorized credit transaction to the account and observe what actions are taken by the user. Or, in an accounts payable system, the auditor could try to get a duplicate invoice through the system to see whether it would be paid twice. In banking, insurance, welfare, and many other systems, there are many possibilities for counter-control testing.

As a general rule, this type of testing should be minimized.

239

Where it is employed, the auditor must be careful not to disrupt the system and not to exploit his privileges as an auditor to demonstrate a system weakness. If the auditor fails to use good sense and proceeds to try to make fools of the auditees, he will engender their ill will for years to come. For example, if the auditor is admitted to a secure area with the understanding that he is performing an audit but then proceeds to engage in some counter-control testing, the test will prove little and end up being distasteful to those who are cooperating with the auditor. On the other hand, if the auditor is able to gain entry and perform counter-control testing on a basis that in no way depends on his audit, the test can be useful in proving a point to management or to users.

FINANCIAL RECORDS AUDITING

The audit of computerized financial accounting data may or may not be based on the auditor's findings in an application control review. Financial records may be periodically selected by the auditors for verification and confirmation. On the other hand, an application control review may have revealed some control weakness, the effect of which the auditor wishes to verify through an audit of financial records. For example, the auditor may or may not have been satisfied with the user controls over the issuance of credits to accounts receivable. Using audit software, he can extract a random sampling of credits and also cause all credits above a certain dollar limit to be reported for his review. With this information, the auditor can go back to the documents supporting the transaction to ascertain whether any irregularities might have been involved. (See Appendix I for information on audit software packages.)

The auditor, for one reason or another, may not have been entirely convinced that compliance with controls over name and address changes in a pension system is as it appears to be. Again, using audit software sampling capabilities, the auditor could extract all changes made within the past 90 days and carefully examine the supporting documents for these changes. The auditor may also wish to send registered mail or an investigator out to some of the previous addresses to ascertain whether the pensioner has, in fact, not moved or is not deceased, in which case there would be an indication of fraud.

The auditor may wish to verify price changes on certain classes of inventory and, based on his verifications, satisfy himself that irregular manipulations are an unlikely possibility. In more routine financial records auditing, the auditor may take the payroll master file and, for some or all records, perform (using audit software) gross to net pay calculations, comparing the result with the net pay as shown on the computer record. He may also add up the individual tax deductions for each person on the payroll and compare them with the summary figures and those posted to the company's general ledger.

Audit software can also be employed to assist the auditor in checking on compliance with company and administrative policies. For example, a company may have a rule that no customer may exceed his credit limit by more than 10% without explicit authorization from the credit manager. The auditor could employ his audit software to select those accounts from the file that have receivable balances which exceed 10% of the credit limit in order to verify that the authorization called for in company policy exists. The extraction may be done so that categories are established which will enable the auditor to initially direct his attention to the more significant cases. For example, the auditor might have a category of accounts receivable in amounts $10,000 and up which exceed their credit limits by more than 50%.

Of course, the auditor may also be interested in the rather mundane recalculation of figures to prove that the amounts that appear in the company's financial statements are reflective of the information shown on computer records. For this purpose the auditor may take a master file that was produced as of a certain cutoff date for, say, a quarterly financial statement, and add up the dollar amounts of the accounts receivable, accounts payable, inventory amounts, and so on. He would then verify his results with those that are presented in the statements.

There are many other possibilities employed in the actual auditing of computer records, and their use depends upon what is to be verified and what fact the auditor wishes to prove. Readers will recognize that the chief difference between financial records auditing and the other forms of audit discussed in this chapter is that the records audit is oriented toward discovering what actually happened, whereas the other forms of auditing are oriented toward the prevention and detection of future actions.

EDP AUDITING METHODS AND TECHNIQUES

In 1977 the Institute of Internal Auditors published the *Data Processing Audit Practices Report*, which was based on the Institute's Systems Auditability and Control Study (SAC). The SAC study surveyed the state of the art in the audit and control of computer systems and identified the techniques that we will discuss in this section.

The descriptions of the techniques, which parallel those found in the *Audit Practices Report*, are divided into the following four areas:

- Audit management tools and techniques.
- Computer application audit tools and techniques.

- Computer service center audit tools and techniques.
- Application system development audit tools and techniques.

The four techniques discussed below are directed to the planning and management of EDP audits and are used to select areas for audit and to exercise quality control functions over their performance.

Audit area selection. This is a computerized technique to assist the EDP auditor in determining which locations to audit. Its objective is to optimize the use of limited audit resources by pinpointing potential problem areas, such as those where there is a heavy exposure to risk of fraud or loss of control. The technique involves developing a location profile matrix that contains key financial and control information for each location.

Scoring. In this technique the auditor assigns a numerical value to each of the computer application systems. This value permits the auditor to classify applications in the order of their auditability needs. The scoring may be based on corporate assets involved, the sensitivity of the data bases that are updated, the computer resources that are used, legal requirements, and other factors.

Multi-site audit software. This technique is intended for companies having regional computer centers with centralized systems design and programming functions. The idea behind this technique is to develop audit software at a central location and install it at the regional computer centers. The efficient use of this technique requires that the computer applications run at the various centers be similar in nature.

Competency center. This technique entails the identification of a central data center to run computer audit software. This center receives data files from other locations, executes the audit software, and distributes the output reports to the internal auditors at those locations. Applicable to large multi-location organizations, this technique eliminates many of the problems that may be experienced in using audit software at multiple locations.

The 12 techniques discussed below are used to check compliance with the policies and procedures of an organization and to test the controls designed to enforce that compliance.

Test data method. This method is one of the more common methods used by EDP auditors to test and verify selected processing logic, computations, and application controls. It involves the use of specially prepared sets of input data that produce preestablished results.

Base-case system evaluation. This technique involves running an application system with a comprehensive set of test data sufficient to ensure that all program functions have been exercised. A "base case" is established when examples of all valid classes and many invalid classes of transactions have been introduced into the system and have been correctly processed, and when consistent and valid system output is achieved over repeated iterations of the processing cycle. When system changes are made, their effect can be ascertained by comparing before and after results on the base case. Therefore, this is a system test technique, in addition to being used for EDP auditing.

Integrated test facility. This technique allows the EDP auditor to review the results of application processing in its normal operating environment. It is an audit technique that uses a fictitious entity (such as a dummy vendor or department) within the framework of the regular application processing cycle. The auditor can select the types of data processing functions he wishes to examine and then submit test transactions, intermingled with regular transactions, to be posted to the fictitious entity during normal processing. This technique can be used for validation of test results as well as for EDP auditing purposes.

Parallel simulation. This technique involves the use of one or more special computer programs to process live data files and simulate normal application processing. The special programs normally include the logic, calculations, and controls that are relevant to specific audit objectives, and, as a result, they are typically less complex than their operational counterparts.

Transaction selection. This technique utilizes an independent computer program to monitor and select transactions for review by the EDP auditor. The audit software is not integrated into the production application system, and it can be changed or given new parameters depending upon the auditor's interests.

Embedded audit data collection. This technique uses one or more programmed data collection modules which are embedded in the application programs to select and record data for the EDP auditor's subsequent analysis and evaluation. The criteria for the data extraction can be supplied during system design or at the time of audit, depending upon the flexibility of the particular type of module that is employed. One of these techniques is known as SCARF (system control audit review files).

Extended records. By means of a special program, this technique pulls together all the significant data that have affected the processing of an individual transaction. The technique provides a comprehensive audit trail which can be used to trace transactions from inception to final disposition, or backward from consolidated totals to individual transactions.

Generalized audit software. This is the most extensively used technique for auditing computer applications. It permits the EDP auditor to independently analyze data files, using highly flexible and reliable software to perform such functions as calculation, compare, total, balance, select transactions, prepare a statistical sample, stratify, and foot and cross-foot data files. Generalized audit software is often parameter-driven, meaning that the auditor need not be a programming expert. (See Appendix I for attributes of such software.)

Snapshot. This technique, in effect, takes pictures of parts of the computer memory that contain elements of data that are involved in a particular computerized decision-making process or at times when the status of data is of interest. This technique requires the logic to be preprogrammed into the system and may also require the use of a special code in certain transactions to cause the triggering of the snapshot and printing of the memory area that is of interest. The snapshot technique can be used for system debugging as well as auditing.

Tracing. The purpose of tracing is to show which instructions within specific programs are executed during the processing of a transaction. This enables the EDP auditor to determine which program modules were applied to a particular transaction. Some programming languages have associated support software to accomplish tracing, and this technique is used for program debugging as well as EDP auditing.

Mapping. The original intent of mapping was to assist in the optimization of program execution by counting the number of times that each program instruction is used. A mapping program will typically list any program segments that are not executed, the program steps consuming the most time, and a listing showing the number of times each instruction was executed. The auditor can evaluate the extent of system testing using these reports. He can follow up on any untested steps and recommend additional testing as needed.

Control flowcharting. Flowcharting is a graphic technique to illustrate the controls pertinent to a specific operational system. It

244

aids in identifying both existing controls and needs for additional controls. The flowcharts are drawn based upon a study of the flow of information and processing.

The three techniques discussed below are practices used to evaluate the security, procedures, and controls employed in a data processing operations center.

Job accounting data analysis. Job accounting software is available through computer and independent vendors as an adjunct to the operating system. They provide the means for gathering and recording information to be used for billing computer services to users and for evaluating system use. Examples of information collected are job start and end times, data set usage, hardware usage, and use of invalid passwords. Although designed primarily to serve the needs of EDP management, much of the information provided by these facilities is useful to the EDP auditor.

Audit guide. An audit guide typically consists of a set of questionnaires that include analysis criteria geared to the possible range of answers. Such a guide may be used to conduct a complete audit or just to provide information that narrows the scope of the audit to areas most vulnerable to loss of control and fraud. The effective use of an EDP audit guide will depend on the auditor's knowledge of and experience in EDP.

Disaster testing. If the company has developed an EDP contingency plan, the auditor, on an unannounced basis, simulates a disaster in the computer center to verify the adequacy of the plan. Although this technique is not directly relevant to fraud prevention and detection, one might easily understand how arson could be used to cover up evidence of a fraud and, obviously, create disaster conditions.

The five techniques discussed below are used by auditors during the review and evaluation functions they perform at the time a system is being designed, programmed, tested, and put into production status.

Post-installation audit. This is a formal, standardized procedure to be followed in examining applications after they are in a production mode. It covers all operations from the preparation of the source document through final outputs, and covers all user functions related to the system. In terms of fraud prevention and detection, the audit will focus on whether the system is adequately controlled and whether the data validation, access controls, and other safeguards are functioning at an acceptable level.

Control guidelines for use during system development. These are guidelines that the auditor uses in evaluating the adequacy of system controls (input, processing, and output), data file security, audit trail, data retention, error-control procedures, changes in accounting methods, controls to ensure the accomplishment of objectives, and so forth.

System development life cycle. This technique defines the system development process in terms of phases and identifies quality control checkpoints of interest to the auditor for each such phase. At these critical points, the EDP auditor observes and appraises the status of the system from an auditability and control standpoint. Some of the phases that may be involved include project definition, system design, program coding and testing, system tests, and conversion to the new system.

System acceptance and control group. This technique relies on a group within the EDP department that is independent of the system development team. Its function is to continually review and monitor the development of new systems. The EDP auditor can look to this group to create and maintain effective computer application standards for control and auditability. He may wish to rely on this group for much of his compliance work, reviewing the work and reports produced by such a group.

Code comparison. This technique involves comparing two copies of program coding for a particular application which were made at different times. The purpose of the comparison is to verify that program change and library updating procedures are being complied with. Discrepancies between the two sets of coding which are not supported with change authorizations may be the basis for an auditor to follow up on an irregularity that may involve fraud.

EDP AUDITOR QUALIFICATIONS

The auditing profession has only recently begun to realize how important it is to have EDP internal auditors who are proficient in computer technology as well as auditing. Many companies have instituted crash programs to develop competent EDP auditors. There have been vigorous efforts to acquire the needed skills through intracompany transfers of EDP people into internal auditing, hiring from outside the company, and in-house and outside training of auditors.

Qualified EDP auditors are very much in demand these days, as anyone who has tried to recruit them will readily acknowledge.

Companies have to pay dearly to attract and retain the good ones. For one thing, the auditor's EDP skills are in demand purely from the standpoint of his being a computer systems specialist; so internal audit departments are competing with the EDP community, which pays well and offers good advancement opportunities. The other aspect is that the internal audit function in many companies has been viewed as a dead end from a career standpoint. In the past, the perception of internal auditing by those outside the field was not good; it was characterized as an appendage to the organization, which consisted of poorly paid, marginally competent people who were unqualified for any other type of responsibility. All this is changing rapidly, owing in part to the influx of first-rate professionals in EDP auditing. Additionally, more and more companies are viewing internal auditing as a good tour of duty for their better people who are on a fast track to the executive suite—few other company positions provide an opportunity to see and learn so much in a relatively short period.

It almost goes without saying that companies which encourage professionalism in EDP auditing and which can point to actual examples of career advancement potential will be able to more readily develop and retain a qualified EDP internal audit staff. Companies which do not maintain this posture can expect problems with unplanned staff turnover and an inability to attract people with good EDP audit skills.

EDP internal auditing, as it pertains to computer fraud, is perhaps one of the most advanced areas of the profession. Accordingly, the issues we raised above are doubly important. *Someone who is barely qualified as an EDP auditor cannot be expected to cope with audit implications in matters of computer fraud where clever technical deceptions may be involved.* If you are interested in having EDP internal auditors conduct meaningful audits for computer fraud, they will have to be first-class EDP auditors.

In the following sections, we will discuss the professional qualifications of the EDP auditor in these areas:

- Auditing skills.
- EDP skills.
- Business knowledge.
- Personal characteristics.

Since, in this book, we are primarily concerned with the EDP auditor's competency with regard to preventing, deterring, and detecting computer fraud, the skills and characteristics we will be describing are those needed for assignments pertaining to such matters. Readers should understand that all the basic skills brought out here are needed for EDP auditing, but that computer fraud auditing stresses a greater degree of qualification than many of the other activities with which EDP auditors become involved.

Some individuals on your EDP audit staff may need to have all these skills, depending on the scope of your EDP audit plan. You may also be able to use a team of EDP auditors comprised of people whose combined skills bring the needed expertise to bear. Also, you can supplement your auditors' skills with appropriate outside EDP consulting/auditing skills.

Auditing skills

A good EDP auditor understands the role and responsibility of an auditor as being one that calls for probing and challenging the status quo, rather than being one of advocating a position or accepting the status quo. Although this sounds simple enough, there are plenty of people who cannot do it. Unfortunately, there is some percentage of people who are now auditing who cannot do it and, although whatever they are doing may be of value to their companies, it is not auditing. Perhaps "internal consulting" might describe it.

Whereas the auditor's job is to poke at a system to find its weaknesses and to offer constructive criticism, the EDP practitioner's natural role is to advocate the system and be convinced of its merits. Understanding that this is the auditor's perspective, let us touch on some of the items that pertain to his skills:

- Knows how to audit.
- Is able to apply modern auditing tools.
- Keeps up to date on auditing practices.

Knows how to audit. Auditing often involves verification that a system of control or quantitative representations are what they purport to be. The auditor must first be capable of understanding the system or representation that is presented to him. If, for example, the auditor is given documentation and an explanation of how a computer password security system works, he has to comprehend what is presented. If, to cite another example, the auditor is informed or reads that the company has $4,500,000 in consignment sales, he must understand what this means. Beyond this, the auditor should bring enough experience and training to the job to enable him to challenge what he is told. This will entail, initially, some study of the controls or some tests of the transactions, or both.

The auditor must bring to his work, in this case, a fundamental understanding of the rules governing the posting of a consignment sale to accounts receivable. If the auditor is not aware that sales on consignment may not qualify as sales, he will probably fail to make sufficient inquiries to know whether fraud or misrepresentation is a possibility. Similarly, if the auditor does not know enough to ask about how passwords are developed, assigned, and protected, he will probably fail to note important weaknesses in the system.

The auditor's opinion about controls and representations will often carry a great deal of weight with top management and outsiders. The auditor must recognize that the auditee recognizes this and will typically try to give the auditor the most favorable side of the situation, even to the point of misleading the auditor. The auditor must be alert to these possibilities and conduct his audit with due regard for them.

For example, numerous frauds have gone undetected for years after repeated physical inventory audits that failed to disclose significant discrepancies. In one instance, auditors were observing a physical inventory count where, as a first step, tags (showing item number and quantity) were attached to the items. When this was being done, the auditors failed to note that company personnel altered certain inventory tags and created other tags which were included with actual count tags prior to the computer tabulation of the inventory. Data from fraudulent tags that had been added were printed in the inventory listing as a block in numerical sequence. This fraudulent block showed a quantity measure 10 times greater (50,000 pounds per unit versus 5,000), than anything the company ever manufactured or purchased. Neither the entry of the fraudulent transactions nor the enormously high quantity measure in the computer listing was noticed.

Auditors, without proper regard for what they are doing, are sometimes careless about leaving their work papers and auditing plan where they can be obtained by the auditee. In one instance of an ongoing fraud, the perpetrator was able to find out what·the auditors were doing at every step of the way and thus was able to outmaneuver them. In another case, a computer security consultant, using two paper clips, was able to pick the lock of a bank EDP internal auditor's desk in under 2 minutes. Inside the auditor's desk were all the parameter cards for use with audit software, the complete audit plan, and information about special situations the auditor was tracking. Although the consultant was thoroughly qualified in all aspects of computer security, his locksmith skills were at only the most primitive level. Someone else, a perpetrator of a fraud, could easily have done the same thing.

Knowing how to audit embodies a practical grounding in fundamental characteristics of business and EDP systems in general. We have seen situations where the auditor examined the system of routine controls for a computer application, found them to be adequate, and walked away satisfied without searching for the exceptions—not the routine exceptions, but the exception-exceptions. For example, in a security and control review of an accounts payable system which had come out of prior audit without problems, an experienced

249

EDP auditor knew enough to inquire about "rush" payments where checks had to be produced immediately to pay for certain raw-materials deliveries. The accounts payable supervisor merely explained the system for making up such checks, and it was obvious that the procedures had none of the controls that were in place for the routine operations and normal exceptions. Indeed, the entire system could have been easily compromised by means of the "rush payment" route. Not infrequently, users of computer applications will be able to describe how a system could be manipulated for fraudulent purposes. Often, if the auditor knows enough to ask, these people are only too happy to explain how it could be done.

Auditing know-how is developed from firsthand experience, some of which is gained in situations such as those described above, plus formal education and continuing development of skills through outside and in-house training. Professionalism in auditing also contributes to establishing such know-how. The CPA (certified public accountant) designation has auditing as one of its professional qualification standards. Those standards include accounting, business law, and other disciplines and call for certain formal education and experience requirements as well as passing test grades.

A newer development on the professional front is the CIA (certified internal auditor) designation, awarded by *The Institute of Internal Auditors* (Altamonte Springs, Florida). The CIA also has education and experience requirements and requires a passing test grade. The *EDP Auditors Association* (Hanover Park, Illinois), after making an evaluation, decided in 1978 to establish a certification program in EDP auditing and has been developing undergraduate, graduate, and continuing education curricula for EDP auditing. Readers may be interested in contacting these organizations to learn of the latest developments in EDP auditing, certification, and membership benefits. Another organization whose membership program, literature, and seminars will be of particular interest to EDP auditors is the *Computer Security Institute* (Hudson, Massachusetts).

Knowing how to audit for fraud, it seems to us, is an additional skill that, when acquired, will become integrated into all aspects of the EDP auditor's work. An essential part of this skill is having a real understanding of how computer frauds can be perpetrated and recognizing the opportunities and clues—much of this book is devoted to these matters. Another essential part of the skill has to do with personal characteristics—a subject we shall discuss shortly.

Is able to apply modern auditing tools. Suggested audit tools were covered earlier in this chapter. At this point, we would like to address the matter of how well your internal auditors make use of the available audit tools. One common shortcoming among both internal and external auditors is lack of an adequate grasp of automated techniques for auditing. When this deficiency exists, auditors sample "around the computer" rather than with the computer. Basically, auditing around the computer means that manual input procedures and output are checked but not the actual computer processing. There are two reasons why auditing around the computer is not adequate. First, such an approach may fail to detect certain types of irregularities. For example, in cases where breakage or siphoning off small amounts from numerous computations is employed as an embezzlement scheme, this may not be apparent under auditing around the computer, if overall totals are undisturbed.

Another shortcoming of auditing around the computer pertains to use of on-line and real-time systems. In such environments, source documents may not be available. Unless the auditor can tap the magnetic images stored in machine-readable form, it may be impossible for him to reconstruct an audit trail.

Besides knowledge of audit procedures and computer auditing techniques, the ability to correctly apply statistical methods is necessary. An EDP auditor should be well versed in the use and limitations of statistical techniques. Failure to understand the relevant principles of statistics can result in oversampling, which is expensive. Another possibility is that an auditor who is weak in statistics may draw incorrect inferences and thus either avoid discovering a serious problem or, alternatively, launch an elaborate investigation of a relatively trivial problem. Similarly, an auditor who is weak in statistical sampling theory may fail to make an important test on the application or installation he is auditing.

The statistical terms below are illustrative of the techniques and concepts with which the successful EDP auditor should be acquainted:

- Alpha risk.
- Attribute sampling.
- Beta risk.
- Biased sampling.
- Cluster sampling.
- Coefficient of correlation.
- Discovery sampling.
- Difference estimation.
- Error of estimate.
- Judgment sampling.
- Precision interval.
- Random sample.
- Reliability factor.
- Sampling error.
- Sampling risk.
- Skip interval sampling.
- Standard deviation.
- Standard error of the mean.
- Stop-or-go sampling.
- Stratified sampling.
- Systematic sampling.
- Unrestricted random sampling.

Like fine medical instruments in the hands of a qualified surgeon, statistical techniques can aid the qualified practitioner in drawing valid conclusions. As we indicated earlier, such methods should only be applied by those who understand what they are doing. Or, to put it another way:

251

| Extensive sampling with sophisticated techniques | + | Inability to diagnose and analyze | = | Confusion |

In matters where computer fraud is the central concern, because of the trickery and deception that is often attendant, the analytical and diagnostic abilities take on even more importance.

Keeps up to date on auditing practices.   EDP auditing is a rapidly changing field. If the individuals performing that function for your company do not keep up to date with the field, the usefulness of the services they perform will tend to deteriorate. The following strategies exist for keeping up to date and we recommend that your internal auditors employ all of them:

- Professional books and periodicals.
- Professional associations.
- Personal contacts.
- Professional conferences and seminars.

Professional books and periodicals.   A variety of publications relating to auditing, accounting, and internal auditing exist. Periodicals featuring articles dealing with EDP auditing include:

- *Computer Law and Tax Report* (Warren, Gorham & Lamont, Inc., Boston).
- *EDPACS Newsletter* (Automated Training Institute, Reston, Virginia).
- *The EDP Auditor* (EDP Auditors Association, Hanover Park, Illinois).
- *Internal Auditor* (IIA, Altamonte Springs, Florida).
- *Journal of Accountancy* (AICPA, New York, New York).
- *Management Accounting* (NAA, New York, New York).

EDP Auditing (Auerbach Publishers, Inc., Pennsauken, New Jersey) is a bimonthly updated reference service providing portfolios on EDP auditing matters.

Professional associations.   Professional associations sponsor innovations in auditing as well as conferences, personal contacts, and publications. Associations relating to the EDP audit function, as mentioned previously, include:

- Institute of Internal Auditors.
- EDP Auditors Association.
- Computer Security Institute.

Membership in such organizations is recommended, as is active participation in activities they sponsor.

Personal contacts. Personal contacts with other auditors of the internal, EDP, and public varieties are very helpful in keeping up with the state of the art. They also furnish informal information about computer fraud that may not be publicly available. Where possible, your EDP auditors should lunch or otherwise associate with their counterparts on a regular basis.

Professional conferences and seminars. Professional conferences provide training as well as contact with peers in other companies. Where these conferences and seminars are held locally, your company should make every effort to send a representative. At least once or twice a year all of your key EDP auditors should attend such gatherings, regardless of whether or not they are held locally.

EDP skills EDP skills are absolutely necessary if your EDP auditors are going to do an adequate review job and still maintain independence from individuals whose work is being audited. The chances of obtaining a single individual who possesses all the desirable skills are slim, but somehow these skills have to be represented. Alternatives include use of consultants as well as resident experts. Skills to which your EDP auditors should have access include:

- Applications programming.
- Systems programming.
- Hardware.
- Data base/data communications.

As a practical matter, the most desirable area for those skills to be in depends upon technologies employed by your company.

Applications programming. Knowledge of applications programming is required to understand system design. Individuals with no background in programming are not going to understand documentation well enough to audit your computer systems. Almost any applications programming experience is adequate for that particular purpose.

Review of program source code is not uncommon in EDP audits. Obviously, the individual performing this review must be conversant with the programming language involved. If your company has no standard as to programming language, your EDP audit staff will experience a burden in maintaining staffers with the necessary programming skills.

Another need for applications programming arises from the need to develop, modify, and apply audit software. Much of the software your EDP auditors will need is available commercially. Still, someone will have to develop occasional extra programs, modify the packages, and generally be available when the other EDP auditors run into snags in using available tools.

Systems programming. Some EDP auditors will need systems programming skills to audit systems software and to support audit software. Supporting audit software is by far the simpler of the two requirements. Some very sophisticated and hard-to-detect methods of perpetrating computer fraud exist for individuals conversant with systems programming. Only a systems programmer conversant with the particular software would be able to identify the technical possibilities for the operating systems, data base, and data communications software.

Hardware. Hardware knowledge is necessary to complement systems programming knowledge and to appreciate the special vulnerabilities of each type of hardware employed by your company. Hardware knowledge also facilitates detection of tampering with network equipment and other hardware.

Data base/data communications. Knowledge of data base/data communications complements hardware and operating system programming knowledge. Clearly, your EDP auditors need to be conversant with the same data base/data communications technology as that employed by your company. In addition, they will need an understanding of available means of protecting data communications, such as personal identification technologies and encryption methods.

Business
knowledge Effectiveness in a number of aspects of auditing comes from knowledge of the line of business being audited. The EDP auditor should be familiar with standard practices in the industry and in his particular company. This familiarity aids the auditor in detecting suspicious departures from common practice. It also promotes knowledge of weaknesses in prevailing practices.

If your company opts to obtain EDP auditing from external services, lack of specific business knowledge may be the main trade-off. At best, you may get good auditors with general knowledge and technical expertise but little intimate knowledge of your company or industry.

Personal characteristics   Managers who hire and promote people such as systems analysts, EDP auditors, and so on, frequently set utopian goals for personal characteristics and usually settle for something less. The goals or criteria for EDP auditors should be high, even though they are never going to be fully met. Technical know-how of the type discussed previously is fundamental to the basic job that has to be done. However, readers will recognize that ultimate effectiveness takes much more than just technical abilities. Here, then, are some of the more significant qualities you should be evaluating for EDP auditors in general, and for ones who will be concerned with computer fraud matters, in particular:

- *Above-average general and analytical intelligence.* In a nutshell, this means the kind of intelligence that is needed to both define and solve somewhat complex problems. It also entails an ability to discriminate between degrees of useful and spurious information, fact and opinion, values that are difficult to measure, logical and illogical circumstances, and auditee credibility levels.
- *Superior abilities in oral and written communications.* Much of the auditor's work calls for him to clearly express himself, whether in interviewing an auditee, giving a formal presentation to management, or preparing a written report covering his findings and recommendations. In fact, the written report is often all that remains as evidence and a representation of the auditor's work. It is, you might say, the tangible product of his work, and is used by the auditee and others as the basis for some important decision making. Of necessity, the quality of such communications must be high.
- *Listener and thinker.* Some auditors tend to be gadflys, talk a lot, assume much, and pay inadequate attention to what the auditee says and does. Indeed, it would be fair to say that their work is often superficial for these reasons. These types can be deadly and should be avoided in favor of someone who can draw out responses from the auditee, pay close attention to what is said, and draw valid conclusions in the process.
- *Curious and inquisitive.* The better auditor will enjoy getting to know how systems and other things work—and do not work—in a fair amount of detail. "Big-picture" types are important and have a valid place in auditing but should be avoided as working-level EDP auditors.
- *Polite, firm, and assertive.* The EDP auditor has to be polite and even deferential, initially, to obtain the cooperation of the auditee. If this fails to elicit the desired response, the same

255

auditor should be able to don the hat of a dispassionate, tough-minded investigator and become assertive about his requests. If your auditor thinks he is out there mostly to make friends with auditees, you had better not look to that person to deal with computer fraud matters.

Professional and mature. This is much more a question of the auditor's attitude and bearing than one of age. It is the kind of thing that spurs the auditor to do independent research and study. It is also the ability to command respect and to work effectively with little or no direct supervision. This includes the ability to deal with all levels of auditee personnel. Finally, it means using discretion in handling sensitive information.

Some readers may argue that at least some of the personal characteristics shown above can be acquired skills and are not, therefore, personal. Although this may be true to some degree, what we are trying to emphasize is that these characteristics, irrespective of how they were derived, should be ingrained in the auditor's manner and method of work.

EDP AUDIT ORGANIZATION AND PLANNING

The EDP internal audit function should be an *independent appraisal* activity within the company, having the overall objective of protecting company assets and improving profitability by furnishing directors and management with pertinent recommendations in the areas of computer-related efficiency, effectiveness, accuracy, reliability, integrity, security, and control.

In the following sections we will discuss how to plan and organize the EDP audit function in terms of its charter, reporting relationships, and staffing level.

The EDP auditing charter

Included in the charter for EDP auditing should be a statement of mission and purpose, an example of which might be quite similar to the opening paragraph of the section above. Beyond this, it is useful to indicate, in more detail, the kinds of functions to be performed by EDP audit. Among the responsibilities that should be included are those discussed below.

- Develop and/or acquire audit software, questionnaires/checklists, methods/techniques, skills, training, outside assistance, and other resources needed to accomplish EDP audit objectives.
- Evaluate the adequacy of proposed and enacted corporate standards and procedures, financial policies and procedures, EDP policies and procedures, standards for project control,

program and system design standards, and documentation standards for systems, programs, and operating and user instructions.

- Test and observe compliance with all enacted policies, procedures, and standards.
- Provide information to and work, as necessary, with the company's external auditors.
- Evaluate systems under development as to their proposed features for maintaining accuracy, reliability, integrity, security, and control; as to their auditability when they become operational; as to their efficient use of corporate time, effort, money, and other resources; and as to their effectiveness in achieving the desired results.
- Evaluate operational systems as to the adequacy of and compliance with features for maintaining accuracy, reliability, integrity, auditability, security, and control; as to the efficient use of corporate resources; and as regards effectiveness in satisfying user needs.
- Review EDP management, administrative, and operating practices and controls as they pertain to the accomplishments of corporate and EDP departmental objectives.
- Evaluate the adequacy of and compliance with user and support group functions as they pertain to maintaining accuracy, reliability, integrity, security, control, and auditability of computer systems; and as regards efficiency and effectiveness.
- Audit financial and other EDP records for integrity and consistent, fair presentation.
- Conduct investigations of shortages, mysterious disappearances and destruction, suspected fraud, and losses at the request of corporate management and directors.
- Call to the attention of corporate management and directors situations where significant business, financial, legal, safety, and other risks appear imprudent or excessive and involve grave consequences should they materialize.

Even though it is not explicit in every case mentioned above, all involve EDP audit activities that deal with preventing, detecting, and deterring computer fraud. That the items above seem to be of a sweeping nature is not an oversight, but intentional, the idea being to give the EDP auditor sufficient latitude to avoid piecemeal reviews when desirable and make his examinations as complete as they need to be in the circumstances. This, too, is important in the EDP auditor's ability to deal with matters involving computer fraud—again, because the trickery and deceptions involved could take many different forms and call for pursuing various avenues to discovery and prevention.

When we defined the purpose of the EDP internal audit function, we emphasized the words *independent appraisal*. Before reporting relationships can be discussed in a meaningful way, it is important to understand just what we mean by independent appraisal.

Independent means that the EDP audit function is not controlled by the auditee. Its auditors do not depend on any auditee (audited department or function) for pay increases, promotions, performance evaluations, or political favors. It does not depend on any auditee for budget approval. Its recommendations are not dictated by the auditee's budget.

Independent means that the auditee neither controls nor interferes with the auditor's decisions about what to audit, how to audit, when to audit, where to audit, and whom to audit. This does not, of course, mean that the auditee cannot request and have the auditor agree to look into something of particular interest to the auditee.

Independent means that the auditor conducts himself in such a way as to remain free of influences that may jeopardize or appear to jeopardize his objectivity.

Appraisal means just that. The auditor must not make or appear to make decisions for the auditee. He must not perform functions that are the responsibility of the auditee, as a service to the auditee. This would include everything from programming, to designing controls, to establishing standards, to testing a system, to reconciling a company checking account (except in connection with an audit). When the EDP audit function crosses the boundary between appraisal and the exercise of auditee responsibility, the further value of the audit function with respect to those matters is placed in doubt. This would be the case where an executive has reporting to him both auditors and a staff function that performs these services for an auditee.

Now, let us return to reporting relationships. It may have become obvious that the only place to which the audit function can report, in order to meet the "ground rules" set forth above, is the company's board of directors. Indeed, more and more audit functions have this direct reporting relationship. Typically, it is to the *audit committee* of the board, which is also something that more and more companies are establishing.

Sometimes the audit committee will direct that the internal audit department report *administratively* to the president or another top executive, since the board cannot personally see to administrative matters on a routine basis. However, the *functional or substantive* reporting relationship is directly to the full board or its audit committee. We have seen numerous audit committees go out of their way to emphasize and reemphasize to the internal auditors that they want the bad news, uncluttered by euphemisms and pleasantries. The reason is that in prior years, when the auditors reported to someone such as the company controller, many boards heard very little bad news, and what they did hear was watered down. Although it is certainly not true that many of the controllers were at fault, there was a tendency on the part of the auditor to filter the news before it reached the controller. In these cases, the auditor was simply responding to a human condition of "understanding where his bread was buttered"—inasmuch as much of his auditing dealt with functions that reported to or were influenced by the controller.

If your company's board of directors is not terribly interested in creating an EDP audit function, your company will almost surely be wasting its time and money on establishing one. We say this because the audit recommendations will often fall on deaf ears or the auditee merely pays lip service to them, because they are not supported with clout of the type invested in the board. A good auditor will not stay long at a place where he and his recommendations are unwelcome. In the end, you will have nothing but the drones left. They, in turn, will give the department the kind of reputation that it richly deserves and which will linger for years—a problem that could have been avoided if people made the effort to get the appropriate level of board support in the beginning.

A similar situation can develop in a company where there has been a traditional non-EDP audit function which is run by a person who feels threatened or intimidated by this new breed: the EDP auditor. The insecurity may have its genesis in a lack of understanding. This can be remedied with some education, provided that there is at least a willingness to learn. A worse situation is where the person in charge of the audit function truly believes that EDP auditing serves no useful purpose or, worse, has an EDP audit function for cosmetic reasons and makes sure that superficial EDP auditing is done and that meaningful findings and recommendations never see the light of day. Audit committees would be well advised to watch for these possibilities and, if they exist, have the head of EDP auditing report directly to them and perhaps consider other changes.

Reporting relationships within the EDP internal auditing department may take on several forms, depending on the size of the EDP audit staff, number and type of EDP sites to be audited, and types of applications that are involved. In the larger EDP audit departments, we see a trend toward specialization in staff functions. For example, there may be some auditors whose work is largely concerned with on-line systems. Others may be especially knowledgeable in data base management systems. Others may be specialists in the use of generalized audit software. Still others may be skilled in the evaluation of EDP security and controls. There may also be EDP auditors who tend to specialize in certain kinds of computer applications. Whether these specialties form groups having group leaders depends largely on how many people are involved in a particular activity.

Probably due to the influence of the external auditing profession, we often see internal auditors classified as follows: staff, advanced staff, in charge, senior/supervisor, manager, and director. In many banking and insurance companies, officer designations will start with supervisor. As a general rule of thumb, about 2 years of experience separate each title up through manager. The director designation often takes considerably longer.

Staffing level   Without knowing a great deal about your company, we cannot tell you how large your EDP audit staff should be. Our recommendations would vary widely depending upon conditions. What we can do is to explain the factors affecting the size of the staff and provide some rules of thumb for you to go by.

Factors affecting size of staff required.   Factors affecting the size of the staff include number of applications, size and complexity of each application, frequency with which each application is to be audited, number of installations, diversity of technologies employed, geographic dispersion of installations, system development locations, and data preparation sites.

- *Number of applications.*   The more applications your company has, the more audits will have to be performed.
- *Size and complexity of each application.*   The larger or more complex an application gets, the greater the amount of time that will be required to audit it. Factors affecting size include number of programs, input volume, and master-file volume. Factors affecting complexity include number of distinct types of input transactions, number of interfaces, and number of processing functions performed. If documentation is poor, scanty, or out of date, the result will also be more audit time. More time will also be required if the programs are poorly written, excessively patched, or if controls are weak.
- *Frequency of audit.*   The more frequently an application is audited, the larger the overall staff will have to be. Recommended frequency of audits ranges from once a year to once every 2 years. Frequency should vary with the application, with the riskiest ones getting the most frequent audits.
- *Number of installations.*   Since each installation has to be audited, the more installations you have, the more installation audits will be required.
- *Diversity of technology.*   The wider the range of technologies employed in your company's data processing function, the larger your EDP audit staff will have to be. It is unlikely that any one individual will be conversant with all technologies

employed, so many technicians may be required in order to cover all the technologies. Types of technology to consider in making this judgment include hardware, programming languages, operating systems, data base management systems, data communications software, and data communications networks. In regard to this issue, we urge all EDP auditors to push for hardware and software standards. Too much diversity will make the auditing function get out of hand in terms of size and manageability. Many large companies we are familiar with use several data base managers, several data communications packages, have several networks and a wide range of computers, and use half a dozen programming languages. The end result for the EDP audit department is the need for more individuals in order to cover all the technologies and scheduling difficulties because of the combinations of technologies each application uses.

- *Geographic dispersion.* The more widely dispersed the sites subject to audit are, the more time your EDP auditors will spend traveling rather than auditing. If diversity is extremely great, you may find your company having to staff regional audit departments, with all the redundancy of scarce skills that implies.

EDP auditing time estimation. As a first step, let us determine how many working hours an EDP auditor has in a given year. We will assume that the auditor averages a 7.5-hour workday.

2,737 hours	(365 days)	
− 780	(52 weekends)	
− 75	(10 days vacation)	
− 75	(10 holidays)	
− 30	(4 sick and personal days)	
− 90	(12 days in training and seminars)	
1,687	working hours available	

The 1,687 available working hours *excludes travel to and from the audit site during working hours.* There are so many circumstances that can have a bearing on this travel time that it is impossible to estimate. However, for the sake of discussion, let us assume that rougly 5% of the available working hours are devoted to travel, or about 87 hours. *Thus, we end up with 1,600 working hours available.*

Rules of thumb that can be used to get a general idea of staffing levels are as follows:

Review Area	Audit Hours		
	Small	Medium	Large
Application[a]	150	250	400
Development[a]	300	500	800
Security[b]	350	600	1,000
Financial[a]	200	400	800
Investigation[c]	500	900	1,500
Operational[b]	450	1,000	1,700

[a] Each application.
[b] Each installation.
[c] Each significant incident or fraud.

Readers should recognize that these are merely rules of thumb for small, medium-size, and large installations and applications and, as such, the number of hours may be much larger depending on circumstances and on the person performing the audit or review.

Using the rules of thumb without regard for the levels of staff performing the work, let us calculate what it might take to accomplish an annual EDP audit program for a medium-size installation.

500 hours	(two application reviews at 250 hours each)
300	(a system development review for a small system)
600	(a medium-size security review)
800	(two medium-size audits of financial systems)
200	(a small system financial audit)
1,000	(a medium-size operational review)

3,400 hours in annual EDP audit program

You see here the need for two EDP internal auditors (3,200 hours) plus 200 hours of outside assistance, if all this work is to be started and completed during the company's fiscal year. Of course, this program assumes that everything starts and completes on a tight schedule. In planning, you may very well want to provide some cushion to account for starting delays, overruns, and delays and lost time attributable to auditees. This cushion can be provided by budgeting for more outside consulting assistance which can be used as needed, when there is slippage or a need for specialized know-how.

9

Common Computer Fraud Manipulations and Countermeasures

In many of the computer fraud cases with which we are acquainted, it seems that some of the manipulation schemes recur with ponderous frequency. This chapter examines the manipulation patterns that appear time and time again—the most frequently used modus operandi of perpetrators of computer fraud—and discusses the general types of countermeasures that can be employed to deal with these frequently observed forms of manipulation. Actually, there are surprisingly few common forms of manipulation—in fact, just these three:

- Input transaction manipulation schemes.
- Unauthorized program modification schemes.
- File alteration and substitution schemes.

Readers may be interested to know that, after we had written this chapter of the book, the results of research by Brandt Allen of the University of Virginia appeared in print. One of the things he did was to classify types and frequencies of computer fraud schemes for the 150 cases he studied in his research project. Our less-than-scientific basis for choosing the three types of manipulation shown above produced exceptionally accurate results, when compared with Allen's research, as illustrated in Figures 9-1 and 9-2.

Input manipulation schemes are the most common group of computer fraud ploys. In most cases, the fundamentals of the fraud are simple, even though a series of transactions or input manipulations may be involved. The common varieties of input manipulation are:

- Extraneous transactions.
- Failure to enter transactions.
- Modification of transactions.
- Misuse of adjustment transactions.
- Misuse of error-correction procedures.

Extraneous transactions Making up extra transactions and getting them processed by the system is a rather straightforward form of input manipulation. A perpetrator may either enter extraneous monetary transactions to benefit himself, or he may enter file maintenance transactions that change the indicative data about a master-file entity (customer, vendor, product, general ledger account, salesman, department, etc.) in some way that he will later exploit. Standard methods exist for preventing and detecting extraneous transactions.

METHOD 1. In any system handling customer accounts (accounts receivable, banking, etc.), the perpetrator *enters an extra payment* benefiting his own account or the account of an accomplice. He then converts that payment to cash by drawing down the account—making a cash withdrawal, money transfer, writing a check, charging merchandise or services, and so on. If the amounts involved per transaction are fairly small and processing results are reviewed promptly, simple detection methods will stop this scheme.

By carrying a total of authorized monetary transactions throughout all manual and automated processing steps in a system, it is possible to detect extraneous transactions one step past their point of origin and halt further processing of them. By maintaining similar totals of authorized debits and credits, the amounts of any extraneous transactions can also be established readily. If the number of transactions is rather large, it may be possible to divide them up into smaller batches and maintain totals for all the batches as well as for the number of batches and the total debits and credits involved in all batches. By dividing the work up into batches, the ultimate back-checking that must come when a discrepancy is detected can be limited to a single batch.

Method of Computer Manipulation	Payments to Employees and Other Individuals	Accounting/ Inventory Control/ Disbursements	Billings/ Collections/ Deposits	Miscellaneous
Transactions added or altered	40	44	17	—
Transactions deleted	2	3	2	—
File changes	6	3	1	2
Program changes	2	7	5	—
Improper operation	4	1	—	—
Miscellaneous, unknown	2	11	2	2
Totals	56	69	27	4

Note: Totals do not add up to 150 because some cases are classified in more than one category.

Figure 9-1

Schemes Used in Computer Frauds. (After Brandt Allen, "The Biggest Computer Frauds: Lessons for CPA's," *The Journal of Accountancy,* May 1977, p. 56. Copyright © 1977 by the American Institute of Certified Public Accountants, Inc.)

Method of Computer Manipulation	Corporation	Bank/Savings and Loan	State and Local Government	Federal Government
Transactions added	16	9	9	{48
Transactions altered	8	12	—	
Transactions deleted	3	4	—	—
File changes	5	3	5	—
Program changes	6	8	—	—
Improper operation	4	—	1	—
Miscellaneous, unknown	4	1	1	11
Totals	46	37	16	59

Note: Case totals do not add up to 150 because some are classified in more than one category.

Figure 9-2

Victims of Computer Fraud. (After Brandt Allen, "The Biggest Computer Frauds: Lessons for CPA's," *The Journal of Accountancy,* May 1977, p. 55. Copyright © 1977 by the American Institute of Certified Public Accountants, Inc.)

If use of the batch concept is not practical, there are other approaches that will enable rapid identification of the extraneous transaction(s). By maintaining one or more hash totals of entities such as customer account number, item/part number, or salesman number, it is possible to get a closer fix on the identity of the extraneous transaction. Another method is to maintain subtotals by subledgers —of accounts, products/items/parts/services, departments. These subtotals also accomplish the purpose of reducing the number of transactions that must be checked against paper documents in order to detect the extraneous transactions.

METHOD 2. The addition of an *entirely new master-file record* in an application that involves recurring payments is another means to siphon off funds. By adding another pensioner, welfare recipient, shareholder, salesman, employee, taxpayer, vendor, customer, or whatever, the perpetrator can set himself up to receive regular payments from the system. If the system is one that issues automatic payments, then all the perpetrator has to do is sit back and collect the money. If the system requires additional mechanisms to initiate a payment, the perpetrator will combine this approach with other methods—not necessarily input manipulation methods.

To stop this type of ploy, it is necessary to maintain authorization control over file maintenance transactions. This means that transactions cannot be initiated without suitable authorization and source documentation. It also means that totals of maintenance transactions must be in balance throughout all manual and automated processing steps. Preferably, maintenance transactions should be totaled by type or transaction code. That way, if extraneous file maintenance transactions are detected, fewer transactions have to be researched before the offending transaction is singled out.

METHOD 3. By *adding bogus file maintenance transactions* that change indicative data about an entity (customer, product, department, employee, etc.) a perpetrator can set himself up for substantial gains. The type of indicative data we are talking about includes name, address, Social Security number, credit privileges, account status, applicable discount rate, and so on. Here are some examples:

- Increasing one's credit limit with a view toward using it and not paying the bill.
- Changing the name, address, or active status of a recipient of periodic payments (rent, installment payments, loan payments, annuity payments, pension checks, disability benefits, unemployment payments, welfare checks, payroll, Social Security payments).
- Changing the status of the account in such a way as to obtain special privileges, such as unreported overdrafts, or access to certain programs or data.

Methods of preventing this form of computer fraud are very similar to those we recommend for preventing method 2. Authorization control must be maintained along with totals by transaction type throughout all manual and automated processing steps. Controls should be broken down by type of maintenance transaction to expedite identification of extraneous items. If input volumes make review of all transactions of a particular type when an exception occurs unwieldly, other measures are in order. Secondary measures include subtotals by batch, department, individual, product, and so on, or hash totals by similar entity.

Failure to enter transactions

Perpetrators can obtain substantial benefits simply by failing to enter properly authorized transactions. One of the simplest cases we are familiar with involved action on the part of check-processing clerks who simply destroyed their own canceled checks before they were debited to their accounts. The same thing can happen in a customer billing system. File maintenance transactions can also be excluded dishonestly, with similar benefits. Again, standard methods will stop such abuses. To understand these methods, let us look at some of the specific methods perpetrators use.

METHOD 1. In a customer account situation, a perpetrator may *intercept* charges against his account before they are permanently recorded. Lest you think that this type of caper would involve only small amounts, think about what would happen if the charges involved related to large-dollar items and if the perpetrator were selling these items. Transaction and dollar totals of debits and credits will immediately point out any missing transactions, as well as the amounts of money involved. Still, checking back to manual records can be messy. To alleviate the work involved in checking, we recommend some further controls:

- Use of batches with subtotals maintained by batch.
- Subtotals by type of transaction or by subledger of accounts, departments, products, and so on.
- Hash totals on entity such as customer/vendor/employee identifier.

METHOD 2. The method we are contemplating here can be best described by considering a pension system and then drawing analogies to comparable circumstances. When a pensioner dies, payments are supposed to be terminated. By *interception of status-change transactions* designed to record the death of a pensioner, a perpetrator could cause payments to continue indefinitely. By combining that action with a change to the pensioner's recorded name/

address, the perpetrator could arrange to receive benefits intended for a deceased person, with no one the wiser.

Clearly, it is just as important to assure that all valid file transactions are processed as it is to assure that no extraneous ones are processed. The most elemental controls to accomplish that objective are those that maintain control over the number of file maintenance transactions throughout all stages of manual and automated processing. To begin with, you need a total of authorized file maintenance transactions that is rechecked during each stage of processing. If any transactions are missing, that fact will be noted during the next processing step. If the volume of file maintenance transactions is great, rechecking every transaction against source documents could be burdensome. To simplify matters, we recommend one or more of the following additional controls:

- Use of batch totals.
- Use of subtotals by type of transaction.
- Use of subtotals by subledger, as discussed previously.
- Use of hash totals on identifiers, such as customer, product, department, or general ledger account.

METHOD 3. A variation on method 2 is the *transaction-interception-with-substitution scheme*. For example, in an accounts receivable fraud, even where dollar total and transaction count controls are maintained, a perpetrator could substitute charges to his account with fraudulent charges to other accounts. The other accounts may be selected on the basis that they are dormant or inactive, about to be closed or written off as bad debt, or perhaps in dispute. Sometimes just any account is posted with the bogus substitute. The customer may be slow to complain or the company may be slow to inform customers of their account status, permitting substantial charges to build up before customer inquiries and complaints reach alarming levels.

Substitution of invalid transactions for properly authorized ones can be detected by employing one or more of the following methods:

- Totals of transactions by type or transaction code.
- Batching.
- Use of subledgers.
- Hash totals.
- Monitoring activity by customer, department, product, and so on, with a view toward detecting unusually high or low activity.
- Segregating particularly sensitive entities, such as employee accounts, purchasing department expenses, and so on, for closer scrutiny.

The ways in which a perpetrator can obtain illicit benefits by modifying properly authorized transactions really brings home the need for a variety of input control totals. In a previous example we showed how a perpetrator could substitute a monetary transaction destined to be applied to one account with a transaction of a like amount to a different account. That example could be thought of as a special type of modification, one in which only the account number is altered. Here are some other methods perpetrators may use.

METHOD 1. Fraudulent gains can be realized by *altering the amount* of a properly authorized monetary transaction. Here we are talking about instances in which the perpetrator reduces the amount of charges against a particular account or increases the payments into a particular account, after an actual charge or payment has been made. If a perpetrator uses this method, a discrepancy can be detected in monetary totals, but the total number of transactions and hash totals will be of no help in detecting the incident.

Controls over monetary amounts that break the input volume into smaller subsets are the most beneficial in detecting this type of discrepancy. Here we are talking about the use of batches or subledgers. If both the hash totals and item counts are in order, the only way of tracing a discrepancy in the dollar totals is to match every transaction against source documents until a discrepancy is noted. If the number of input items is great, this checking can be time-consuming.

Business constraints may not permit postponement of processing while this manual check is going on; therefore, the bad transaction might have to be processed along with the other input. If that happens, there is a chance that the perpetrator can be off with the money before the discrepancy is detected. Another possibility is that management will opt to overlook small discrepancies because the time required to straighten them out is more costly than the discrepancy. If that decision is made and the perpetrator is aware of it, he may continue indefinitely exploiting minor discrepancies. The only way to avoid both the potential loss and the cost of rechecking all the work is to provide the capability of breaking down the input into smaller batches or subledgers that will contain fewer transactions each and which can be rapidly verified in case of a discrepancy.

METHOD 2. Another modification scheme that involves *changing indicative data* on file maintenance transactions can also net substantial benefits for perpetrators. Here we are talking about things such as name, address, monthly closing date, account type and status, privileges, and so on. Since errors in indicative data are fairly common and since controls over such transactions tend to be weak in many companies, this method is particularly promising. There can be a variety of schemes:

- Changing the name and address on a credit account so that a new charge card is mailed to the perpetrator instead of to the customer.
- Changing the monthly closing date on an account in such a way that the closing date never occurs.
- Changing the account credit status on a file maintenance transaction to give a "customer" unauthorized privileges.
- Changing the address on a vendor record so that payments destined for that vendor are received by the perpetrator.

In credit card applications, legitimate name changes (e.g., due to marriage) are often accompanied by address changes, and such changes require issuance of a new credit card. There are some reasonable ways of catching the ones that have been manipulated dishonestly. We recommend manual comparison of such changes against original source documents as one method. Another method we recommend is to monitor account activity following such changes. If payments are not received for charges or if the amount of charges is running unusually high, consideration should be given to investigating the account, reducing the credit limit, or possibly closing the account.

Changes to an account's monthly closing date can be controlled best by programmed checks. Dates that will never occur, such as the 32nd of a month, can be caught by editing input for reasonableness and refusing to process transactions that contain unreasonable data. If the billing date is changed repeatedly, but always with reasonable dates, a perpetrator could avoid being billed indefinitely unless the following precaution is taken. Amounts owed before a change to billing date should be billed immediately, before that change is reflected.

Transactions designed to give customers new privileges can best be protected by manual review of such changes and comparison to source documents. If the perpetrator simply changes the account number on the transaction, a discrepancy could be brought to light through the use of a hash total on account number. If no change to the account number is involved—that is, if the account was authorized for some change—a modification can only be detected by a manual review of all changes.

Changes of address on vendor records can be controlled in various ways. First, if the change is being applied to the wrong vendor, a hash total on a vendor number will cause the discrepancy to become apparent. Even more to the point, we recommend manual confirmation of validity of the change with the vendor. A creditor who is concerned with receiving prompt payment will try to avoid sending your company an address change after the fact or even a short time before the change takes place. Accordingly, a phone call to the old location can be a simple way of making sure that each change is valid.

METHOD 3. The most insidious of all transaction modification methods involves *exploitation of blanket file maintenance transactions.* Here we are talking about a transaction that instructs the system to change the corresponding master-file data element for any and all corresponding fields filled out on the input form. Our advice on this matter, very simply, is avoid the use of such transactions. Design systems so that there is a transaction code for each type of change or so that only one change is permitted per transaction. If your system permits blanket changes, only 100% manual verification will detect additional fields that have been added, or even fields that have been removed from a properly authorized file maintenance transaction.

Misuse of adjustment transactions

Misuse of adjustment transactions is a common ingredient in input manipulation schemes. Here we are using the term "adjustment" to refer to monetary corrections of past errors or inaccuracies that have come about in the system through physical loss or spoilage of materials. Often, perhaps out of concern to set things straight as quickly as possible, adjustment transactions are processed with inadequate control. The result can be a computer fraud of massive proportions.

METHOD 1. Perpetrators have taken large sums of money simply by initiating *bogus adjustments.* In those instances, there was no mechanism for monitoring adjustments and checking them for validity. The perpetrator was aware that adjustments were not being checked and found a way to siphon off money through their use. Examples can be found in many applications:

- Perpetrators pad their bank accounts by putting through adjustments to increase the balance.
- Perpetrators put through adjustments to their department store charge accounts to indicate that items charged to that account had been returned.
- Perpetrators adjust their credit card accounts to indicate that a payment made was never recorded or a charge shown was never made.
- Perpetrators put through adjustments to indicate debts to vendors.
- Perpetrators have stolen inventories or supplies and then put through adjustments to indicate that the items had been damaged or lost.

In preventing bogus adjustments, the first step is to require authorization for adjustment transactions, separate from normal input and from output reconciliation processes. Control totals similar to those required for ordinary monetary transactions are necessary throughout all processing steps, from authorization of the adjustment through reconciliation of the output on which it appears. Different individuals must also be responsible for authorizing adjustments, preparing adjustment transactions for the system, and for reconciling system outputs reflecting those adjustments.

METHOD 2. Using *adjustments to inactive accounts*, perpetrators have siphoned large sums. The schemes consisted of an unexplained reduction to the inactive account, offset by an increase in an account to which the perpetrator had access. If the account had been active, the unexplained adjustment would have been subjected to scrutiny and promptly investigated. The inactive accounts include bank accounts, charge accounts, general ledger accounts, and inventory of items no longer in use.

The best protection for inactive accounts is not to permit them to exist. Charge accounts should be closed if they show no activity for an extended period. Inactivity may mean that the customer has died or moved away.

Similarly, when need for general ledger accounts ceases to exist, these accounts should be rendered inoperative. Continued postings to such accounts may be a cover for fraudulent adjustments. Simply by getting rid of inactive general ledger accounts, perpetrators will be forced to make any fraudulent entries to accounts that are scrutinized.

Inactive inventory accounts can arise through changes in production methods, discontinuance of a product, closing of an office, or even through organizational change in which an old function is not covered in the new organization. In the absence of an oversight, the inactive inventory would be sold off for scrap value. One way to guard against the continued existence of inactive inventories is to build into the computer system an automatic reporting feature that will report inactive inventories on an exception basis. In order for this exception reporting to be effective, responsibility for reviewing such reports should be clearly fixed—primarily in user management and secondarily in the internal auditing department. In order to assure that such exception reports, and mechanisms for reviewing them, get built into all applicable systems, these measures should be elevated to the level of companywide system design standards.

Inactive bank accounts require special treatment. By their nature, the bank cannot render them closed simply because they fail to show activity within a reasonable time. To prevent abuse of such accounts, it is necessary first to identify them on an exception basis. Once these accounts have been identified, the capability must exist to flag them within the computer system so that any activity that takes place against them can be subjected to special reporting and review.

There needs to be fixed responsibility for reviewing adjustment transactions that occur against inactive accounts. This responsibility should be totally separate from the ability to authorize transactions for the system—often it lies in the internal auditing department. Procedurally, issuance of customer confirmations should be automatic whenever activity resumes against inactive accounts. Since inactivity in an account may reflect moving or death of the customer, confirmations should be positive (requiring response by the customer in order to confirm) rather than negative (confirmed unless the customer responds by disagreeing).

METHOD 3. A dangerous situation exists when *error rates are high and adjustments to correct errors do not promptly follow detection of errors.* In these instances, records maintained by the output reconciliation clerk do not match those maintained by the adjustment clerk, since not all of yesterday's errors are adjusted for today. When any day's adjustments include not only yesterday's errors but also errors from the day, week, or year before, it becomes impossible to assure that all errors get corrected. Similarly, the output reconciliation clerk loses the ability to double-check the validity of adjustments. In the midst of such confusion, large-scale frauds have taken place.

The best deterrent against this method is for management to take a very hard line against errors. This means setting high standards for accuracy and then monitoring error experience. If errors are too frequent, action needs to be swiftly taken to correct the underlying causes. It may be that users need additional training or increased staffing. If existing staff is too small to handle the work volume accurately, management action is required—to allocate resources to clean up the backlog and also to increase operating staff responsible for correcting errors.

Other control requirements are those generally recommended for adjustment transactions:

- Separation of responsibility for adjustment authorization from responsibility for adjustment preparation and from reconciliation of system output.
- Maintenance of control totals over adjustments, throughout all manual and automated processing steps.

Misuse of error-correction procedures

Millions of dollars have been embezzled by perpetrators under the guise of error corrections. Although many of these abuses are special cases of previously mentioned methods of manipulating input, we feel that error corrections are often a problem and deserve special attention. Ways that perpetrators abuse error-correction procedures include entering extra error corrections, failure to enter necessary corrections, and modification of properly authorized error corrections.

METHOD 1.   A common method of abusing error-correction procedures is to *enter corrections when no error actually exists*.   If monetary corrections can be made outside of procedures for adjustments, the risk is particularly great.   Ordinarily, error corrections are processed in such a way that they do not become part of the permanent record about an account or other entity.   If monetary corrections receive the same treatment, fraudulent error-correction transactions become easy to hide.   The best way to prevent this is to treat all monetary corrections as adjustments and subject them to the controls we recommended for adjustments.

METHOD 2.   Used in the normal course of business, *file maintenance error corrections* can be profitably and dishonestly employed. If no control is exercised to assure proper authorization of error corrections, perpetrators can use error correction as an excuse for entering extraneous file maintenance transactions.   Previous examples have already demonstrated that many types of applications are subject to fraud through entry of extraneous file maintenance transactions.

The first step in stopping use of error corrections as a guise for fraud is to require tangible evidence of an error's existence before a correction can be authorized.   Entry of corrections should not be possible without proper authorization, which means separation of authorization, input preparation, and output reconciliation functions. Control totals such as those previously recommended for file maintenance transactions are also required.   In addition, it is a good idea to maintain separate totals for error corrections and other file maintenance transactions.   By keeping error corrections separate from other file maintenance, it is possible for the output reconciliation clerk to determine whether or not corrections correspond to previously noted errors.

METHOD 3.   Some perpetrators have *exploited program controls that reject transactions* containing invalid data in order to prevent the transactions from being processed.   The method depends on weaknesses in system controls such that no follow-up occurs when input transactions are rejected by the computer system.   Particularly in batch systems, it is common for occasional errors to occur which, for some reason, cannot be corrected on the spot.   For example, a transposition error could occur in a customer/vendor account number and that error could go undetected until computer processing reveals either that the account number is illogically constructed (failure of the check digit, invalid characters, or range) or that no such account exists on the master file.

If controls do not force correction of and reentry for these errors, all the perpetrator has to do is create an error that will cause rejection of that transaction. This type of scheme can be prevented if control totals are maintained throughout all processing steps and if error-detection and -correction responsibilities are separated from input preparation functions.

Summary— reducing the risks of input manipulation

The basic idea of reducing input manipulation risks is to increase the *work factor* for the perpetrator and make the odds of detection sufficiently high. Controls that would require collusion to enable fraud accomplish both objectives. Hence, separation of duties is a primary method of preventing input manipulation. Functions that require separation include authorization of input, preparation of input, posting of input (accomplished by computer), and reconciliation of output to previously established amounts and numbers of transactions authorized for processing. In order to realize the potential benefits of separating functions, maintenance of control totals throughout all stages of processing is required.

When errors are detected, or when discrepancies in control totals become apparent, the ability to find the cause of the error or discrepancy and take corrective action on a timely basis is extremely important. By breaking control totals down, by type of transaction, batch, or subledger, the process of identifying errors can be expedited. The use of hash totals on critical identifiers, such as account number or product identifier, also facilitates detection of errors and discrepancies.

Most applications are equally vulnerable to manipulation of indicative and accounting data. Therefore, file maintenance transactions should not be overlooked in building suitable controls. Some types of file maintenance transactions are particularly risky and should be subject to special verification after the fact. System designs that permit blanket file maintenance transactions are particularly risky and should be avoided.

Transactions that affect account status require particular attention. Here we are talking about transactions that open or close an account, affect account classification or privileges, and transactions that reflect new activity against inactive accounts. Inactive accounts are a special problem, requiring identification of their existence and monitoring of sudden changes.

Employee accounts pose a special risk. We recommend separating employee accounts from others by a reliable method such as use of a special range of account numbers for employee accounts. We also recommend procedures to assure that all employee accounts are coded as such. It is entirely possible that an employee with larcenous intentions might attempt to open an account without revealing the fact of being an employee. To guard against that sort of misrepresentation, we recommend checking a prospective customer's identity before authorizing a new account. Once employee accounts have been specially coded, we recommend careful monitoring, to include periodic audit, as well as records of transaction activity and dollar volumes processed per accounting period.

PROGRAM MODIFICATION SCHEMES

Program modification schemes are the most insidious and difficult to detect. Even though the reported instances of such cases is fairly low, leading auditors and security consultants share a chilling view of reported statistics: reported incidence bears no relation to the actual enormity of the problem.

To explain this commonly held view, consider the following:

- Some program modification schemes are untraceable.
- All program modification schemes are difficult to detect.
- Motivation for perpetrators is great because a single blitz can effect large benefits rapidly with little chance of detection or prosecution.

When we speak of programmers who could potentially commit such crimes, we are not referring only to individuals who are formally classified as such by your company. We are referring to anyone who knows how to program or who has access to programs and knows someone else who knows how to program. This larger group of individuals includes anyone who can get into your computer room or tape library, as well as anyone who can submit a job to your computer system.

With such a large population of potential perpetrators, it may be very difficult to trace the actual perpetrator, even if discrepancies are noted. Keeping tabs on all potential perpetrators is very difficult.

As an alternative, your company can stop fraudulent program modifications by reducing the opportunities to make such changes as well as by applying particular countermeasures that stop the strategies perpetrators use in modifying programs.

Larcenous strategies for modifying programs

These are the strategies used by perpetrators:

- Breakage.
- Undocumented transaction codes.
- Balance manipulation.
- Deliberate misposting.
- File modification.
- Fudging control totals.

276

Breakage. Siphoning off small sums from numerous sources is commonly referred to as breakage. This method is particularly well suited to being implemented via program modification, because a few simple lines of code can bring about repeated theft of a large number of amounts. Breakage can be employed whenever a computation is called for:

- Computation of applicable service charge.
- Computation of discounts.
- Payroll withholding computation.
- Computation of commissions on sales.
- Computation of retirement benefits.
- Computation of interest on savings.
- Computation of welfare, medicare, Social Security, or unemployment benefits.

In any of these situations, all the perpetrator has to do is to instruct the computer to accumulate amounts resulting from rounding, and possibly small additional amounts, and to allocate the sum of all such amounts to a single account to which he has access. This activity will not be readily detected by system controls because the total amount of money involved will agree with any predetermined control totals. The individuals involved are unlikely to notice a discrepancy in their accounts. Even if they do notice a discrepancy, they are unlikely to comment if the amounts involved are small.

Periodic application of a simple auditing technique known as simulation is the best way of stopping breakage. The simulation involves recomputation of amounts to be applied to each account and comparison of those amounts to what was actually applied in each case. Even if the perpetrator only took amounts arising from rounding, there will still be a large discrepancy in the amount applied to one account.

Undocumented transaction codes. By programming the computer to accept undocumented types of transactions, perpetrators can arrange to receive substantial profits in a very short time. Once having made provision for processing of the extra transaction type, there are several means of getting the necessary transactions into the system. One means is to have the computer generate the fraudulent transaction. If evidence of the computer-generated transaction is printed on system outputs, control totals such as dollar amounts or number of transactions will show a discrepancy that can be investigated and will eventually point to the fraudulent transaction.

If evidence of the fraudulent transaction is not printed, detection will be extremely difficult. Remaining means of detecting the transaction include audit review of account or inventory balances vs.

previous balance and historical record of transactions. A spot audit is unlikely to select the entity (account, inventory item, etc.) containing the fraudulent manipulation. A complete audit will reveal the fraud but is not likely to be performed unless other evidence points to the possibility of a problem.

Review of the program, either periodically or following authorized maintenance, would be helpful in detecting the existence of instructions for processing the undefined type of transaction, provided that this review were performed by someone other than the perpetrator and if the review were sufficiently thorough. Program review is not a common practice because it is extremely cumbersome. Nevertheless, it can be facilitated by using automated flowcharting programs and then comparing the computer-generated flowchart to the program specifications. There are also source and object code comparison programs that can help reduce the effort. The amount of work involved can also be limited if review is confined to only those programs that update master files in which large amounts are involved. Program review can be brought about indirectly by rotating programming assignments periodically and by maintaining a work environment in which programmers are encouraged to ask questions.

If evidence of computer-generated transactions is printed, exploitation may still be possible if the output is not reviewed by the individual assigned to do so, or if the programmer is the individual who reviews the output. To make sure that output reconciliation catches the discrepancy, mechanisms are required to ensure that the review takes place as prescribed. The task of reviewing output should be assigned to someone other than the programmer.

If the programmer is able to input transactions, he may be in a position to exploit this method without causing an apparent discrepancy in the output. Organizational controls that separate responsibility for input authorization and preparation from programming are effective here.

A programmer may also exploit his undocumented type of transaction by providing extra input to the system in addition to the authorized input. If he has access to the computer room while the job is being set up, he may be able to slip an extra punched card into the input file. This can be prevented by keeping programmers out of the machine room and out of areas in which input decks are stored prior to processing.

Another way in which a programmer might exploit undocumented types of transactions is to add an extra input file to be read in as part of the processing. This can be prevented if operating instructions are suitably specific regarding which and how many files are to be used as input, and if operators follow the written instructions carefully. Keeping programmers away from the computer room will also help to prevent them from adding extra input files.

A perpetrator might also be able to cause an extra input file to be read following restart or recovery activity. Existence of written and complete restart and recovery procedures should make it possible to keep the programmer out of the computer room when restart is going on. Naturally, someone other than the programmer should review the restart procedures carefully to ensure that the procedures themselves do not contain provision for utilization of extraneous input files.

A programmer might also be able to slip in extraneous transactions if he were called in after his program had failed to run to normal completion. Again, we recommend keeping the programmer out of the machine room. As an additional precaution, we also recommend maintenance and review of a log of all files mounted and other actions taken during emergency program modification.

Balance manipulation. Simple, undisguised balance manipulation is a method that involves assuming that processing results will not be properly reviewed. The output should show a discrepancy in that the sum of all previous closing balances plus the current day's input should equal the sum of all current closing balances. If an account has been manipulated, the sum of current-day closing balances will be off by the amount of the manipulation, even if the total number of input items and the total input dollar amount agree with the totals authorized.

A dishonest programmer can modify appropriate programs so that all totals and balances appear to be correct for any given day. The *work factor* in modifying all programs that are involved is typically high, so the programmer will more often attack just one or two programs. One of the programs will usually be the main posting run, which prints out all totals for the application. Naturally, if you look at just the results emanating from this program, all results will appear to be in order. However, if you check the final totals that showed up on the previous day's run against the opening totals for today's run (these should agree), you will probably see a difference, which will be your first clue to a possible fraud. The programmer's scheme, then, escapes detection as a result of your failure to check the previous day's figures. Clearly, you will want to be sure to incorporate this checking as one countermeasure.

Since applications pass the same data from one program to another, the totals accumulated and printed out at the end of one run should agree with the corresponding totals found in other runs on any given day. We pointed out above that it is unlikely that all programs in an application will be compromised to perpetrate fraud. Hence, you are likely to find differences in the totals where there should be agreement from run to run. By manually posting control totals from the various runs, and visually comparing them, you will have introduced another important countermeasure.

Aside from maintaining run-to-run control totals, it is absolutely necessary to review processing results promptly and without fail. If the discrepancy represents a random occurrence and one day's processing results are not checked, the discrepancy will never be detected. Even so, we have observed laxity in many instances, either because the clerk responsible was overburdened with other work or was absent and no provision had been made for having someone else fill in during the absence. Management involvement is called for here to assure that the necessary checking is done and to take action when it is not. If the responsible manager can be identified and made aware of the importance of checking and if a formal procedure exists for informing management of the results, laxity is unlikely.

Our recommendation as to a formal procedure for communicating results of output reconciliation is as follows. A multiple-part form can be used on which the output reconciliation clerk summarizes the current and previous control totals as well as aggregate changes and errors. If the responsible manager or his designate does not receive a copy by a certain time of day, that is his signal that follow-up action is required. Another copy of the form should go to the individual responsible for authorizing input, along with any discrepancies that may have been detected. Should that second copy not be received, the individual responsible for authorizing input should be instructed to investigate why before authorizing any further input for processing.

If a discrepancy in the run-to-run control totals is detected, its source may not be readily apparent. Possible sources will include past errors, errors in the input, and errors in the computer processing. In order to narrow down the scope of things that have to be checked, we strongly recommend breaking control totals down into smaller units—batches, subledgers, type of transaction, or any other convenient way of isolating the source of the discrepancy to one of a relatively few accounts or transactions. As noted under our discussion of input manipulation methods, there is a greater likelihood that a discrepancy will be simply dismissed if the amount of work necessary to track it down is too great.

Another consideration arises when processing results are received late as the result of difficulties at the data center. If the data center is experiencing hardware or power difficulties, certain jobs may have to be rescheduled or otherwise delayed. This may lead to laxity in reconciling the output simply because the clerk has gone home before processing results become available. It is very important for the relevant management to assure that results are checked at the first possible opportunity rather than overlooking a day's results.

Receiving processing results late may also lead to secondary difficulties if the amount of work necessary to reconcile output is great. Very simply, it may not be possible for the clerk to do a thorough review of two days' work in one day. Here management must take initiative either to authorize overtime or to assign additional manpower on a temporary basis. Allowing a backlog of output reconciliation to become chronic is extremely dangerous.

Similarly, difficulties can also arise if chronic hardware problems are experienced at the data center. Clerical personnel may be unwilling to work overtime, and constant reassignment of other individuals may cause problems in getting other work done on time. Nevertheless, these problems should not be an excuse for laxity in checking output. A clever programmer may, in fact, know of several ways of deliberately causing system "crashes" and may deliberately cause a system crash coincident with manipulation of accounts, in an effort to prevent discovery of that fact.

Deliberate misposting with lapping. A program that has been manipulated to cause misposting either fails to apply a charge to a perpetrator's account (the charge gets applied to another account) or credits a perpetrator's account with a payment (the account that should have been credited is not posted). Either way, certain problems are bound to arise. In the first case, complaints can be expected from those whose accounts now carry unauthorized charges. In the second case, complaints can be expected from those whose accounts were not credited (a salesman who did not get his commission payment, a vendor who is dunned despite the fact he has paid his bill and can prove it, the bank customer whose account fails to show a deposit, etc.). Although it may be possible for a would-be perpetrator to discover certain kinds of accounts (not necessarily customer or vendor accounts) where fraudulent mispostings and failures to post would not raise suspicion and complaints, it is usually necessary for the perpetrator to, in effect, correct the mispostings after some period of time (in a bank account, the period of time could be that which occurs between customer statements—perhaps a month) in order to avoid discovery.

The process of deliberate misposting, correcting the deliberate misposting, and creating another deliberate misposting to continue the fraud (the benefit typically being that the perpetrator gets to use a fixed or constantly increasing sum of money) is known as *lapping*. All lapping schemes of any merit call for masterful time management and meticulous record keeping on the part of the perpetrator in order to perpetuate the fraud. A slipup by the perpetrator, which may arise from a sudden illness that keeps him away from work, could readily lead to discovery of his scheme.

In some systems, the perpetrator may be able to use the computer to keep track of which accounts have been affected and by how much. If there is an unused data field in the master-file record, it could be used to code the fraudulent difference. On reversing the mispost, the perpetrator can reset that field to zero.

If the perpetrator is sophisticated in his selection of transactions for misposting and if he is well aware of system controls and the extent of manual checking, detection of this method may be extremely difficult. Overall control totals will not show any discrepancy. If control totals are maintained on a lower level, perhaps on a subledger basis, mispostings can be detected if they cross subledger boundaries. In that case, the control totals for one subledger would be low and the control totals for another subledger would be high.

Even with application of a subledger concept, a perpetrator may disguise fraudulent mispostings by keeping them within a subledger. Then his only risk would be that sufficient additional transactions destined for that subledger might not come in within a reasonable time period. Although that possibility is remote, it could happen if volume is relatively low in that subledger. Should this happen, and should a customer or other complaint or inquiry ensue, it is important for that issue to be fully investigated.

Hash totals on the appropriate entity (account number, salesman number, vendor number, etc.) are also relevant, in that they may detect misposting. However, we hasten to point out that the programmer may easily fudge the hash total so that it comes out to the expected value.

Complete verification of amounts posted and account number can obviously be helpful in revealing a discrepancy. There are two problems with complete verification. First, there may be too many transactions involved to make this an economically feasible control. That disadvantage can be circumvented by verifying only a portion of affected amounts and by rotating the subset checked every day so that all accounts will be subjected to periodic verification. If the crime is an ongoing one, checking will eventually reveal a discrepancy.

The other problem with verification as a means of detection is that a clever perpetrator may not reveal the misposting on the output. He may show the transaction as though it were posted to the intended account. In that event, the only viable protection measures are audit of the master file and of the program code. If the auditor obtains an independent printout of balances shown on the master file and compares them manually to balances as shown on the normal system output, discrepancies may be noted. If the number of affected accounts is high, chances are good that at least one affected account will be examined. Similarly, if the number of accounts affected is small but the overall dollar amount is great, auditors may detect the misposting by examining all transactions over a certain dollar amount.

Review or audit of the program may also reveal the existence of the fraudulent scheme. As mentioned previously, such review is time-consuming and subject to error, even with the assistance of automated flowcharting techniques. Even so, we recommend periodic review of critical programs.

File modification. Altering programs to effect secret changes in account status is a fairly common programming technique for computer fraud. The types of account status changes we are referring to include: opening an account for subsequent fraudulent manipulation or in order to receive automatic payments (payroll, retirement, unemployment, welfare, etc.); destroying the record of a fraudulent account; inhibition of printing of an account's past-due status; increases to a credit limit on a credit account so that greater charges will be authorized.

The first step in preventing use of this scheme is to maintain control totals, input and run to run, over the number of accounts existing and with various privileges. Existence of such totals, along with provision for manually reconciling processing results, will make things more difficult for the perpetrator. Still, a perpetrator can easily destroy evidence of his work by not having his program print any of the fraudulent changes on the output and by not reflecting these changes in control totals.

Fudging control totals. This tactic is often combined with other programming schemes. Here we are talking about processing that occurs without being properly reflected in control totals. Fudging is a serious problem because it may conceal large-scale fraud and because it is very cumbersome and costly to detect.

One method of detecting fudging is through audits that independently verify aggregate balances and number of accounts on the master file. Other useful forms of auditing include independent simulation of a day's processing and comparison of those results obtained through normal processing and historical reconstruction of an account's balance in order to compare the current balance with the previous balance and records of authorized changes.

Review of program code is another means of detecting fudging. Such review cannot be constantly performed, unless it is computerized, so there may be some delay between initiation of a fraudulent change and detection. The other problem is that the program may be written in incomprehensible fashion, so that adequate review may not be feasible, even with the aid of automated flowcharting.

Existence and enforcement of suitable standards for programming will be helpful in mitigating the latter problem. Along these lines, we would like to make a few suggestions. The first is use of modular system design so that individual programs are not large and complex. The second suggestion is use of structured programming techniques so that program logic is relatively easy to follow. Another suggestion is to review all programs from the standpoint of maintainability before accepting them into production status. This latter review could be accomplished by giving a second programmer copies of the program specifications, a flow chart, and the program source code and having the second programmer determine whether or not the program is easily maintainable.

Miscellaneous limit tests and activity counts might also be helpful in uncovering the effects of control total fudging. It may be possible to estimate an anticipated maximum frequency of activity to an account. If activity runs higher than the anticipated maximum, it would be advisable to audit that particular account. Similarly, it may be possible to anticipate the maximum expected balance for an account in a given category. If the balance of that account surpasses that balance, an audit would again be indicated. By combining these and other logical tests, the chances of detecting programming frauds that depend upon fudging control totals are increased. For example, if the perpetrator is going to take large amounts, he will either be caught because his balance gets suspiciously large, or because, in an attempt to prevent scrutiny of his large balance, he has had to put through a suspiciously large number of transactions.

Methods of accomplishing program modification

By now it should be apparent that detection and prevention of programming frauds are very difficult once the fraudulent program modification has been made. Therefore, prevention of programming fraud schemes must depend heavily upon preventing the fraudulent changes from ever being made. To prevent fraudulent changes, you need to understand how they are made. The following are examples of the most common means used by programmers in making fraudulent program changes.

METHOD 1. The simplest means that programmers use to make fraudulent modifications are to *simply put in the program change* when they feel like it. If there are no controls over program modification, there is no means of detecting or preventing a programmer from using this method. However, relatively simple measures can stop it.

By maintaining a program library and requiring authorization for release of programs from the library, access to the program is made more difficult. If authorization is also required for program modifications, the programmer cannot make changes without management's knowledge. To assure that authorizations are not forged and that the authorization procedures are followed, logs should also be maintained and authorized program changes and access to programs reviewed.

METHOD 2. In situations where control is exercised over program access, it is still possible for a programmer to remove a program from the library and *surreptitiously modify* it. The perpetrator might either remove the program unobserved, or might convince the librarian to release it without authorization, or might get into the computer room while the program was there for an authorized run and then initiate the modification run before the program was sent back to the library.

From this, alone, it is immediately apparent that programmers should not be allowed in the computer room or in the library. All special requests to librarians and operators should be handled by means of written request and authorization forms. Another precaution to consider is logging of access to compilers. Normally, a program change requires recompilation of a program. By maintaining and periodically reviewing all access to compilers, it is possible to identify unauthorized program changes. In some instances programmers have also made changes directly to the machine-usable copy of the program (load module) by using utility programs (for example IBM's Superzap program) that permit direct changes. The latter approach is particularly dangerous, since changes made will not be detected by reviewing program code. We strongly suggest that access to such utilities be stringently controlled and logged, and that the logs be reviewed frequently.

Library control software (see Appendix H) also provides a degree of protection against surreptitious program modifications. With most such software, an historical audit trail of all versions of a program is maintained and new versions of a program are stored under a new name. The combination of having a record of all changes and of using a new name after modification makes surreptitious programming changes easier to detect and therefore less possible.

METHOD 3. Another way of making unauthorized program changes is to sneak them in *as part of an emergency recovery operation* that may take place either following a system crash or following an unsuccessful run of the program. Here, procedural methods can be very effective. In the case of a system crash, the existence of well-documented and tested recovery procedures obviates the need for the programmer's involvement.

In cases in which running of a program is unsuccessful (the program "bombs"), the programmer's presence is required, and action may have to be taken on an emergency basis. Under those circumstances, all actions taken by the programmer should be logged and reviewed immediately thereafter. This means that a record should be kept of all programs modified and all access to files.

METHOD 4. The most difficult of strategies to combat is fraudulent changes made in *conjunction with authorized changes*. Here, the programmer has to wait for an authorized change to be requested before he can carry out fraudulent maintenance. Still, for most systems, authorized changes are so common that waiting for one is not a big obstacle.

Our first recommendation would be for authorization of program changes to explicitly indicate which programs are to be changed and for someone with technical knowledge of the system to review the need for changing each program. Without this proviso, a programmer could change programs that have no bearing on the authorized change, based solely on the existence of an authorization. By explicitly naming the programs that are to be changed, the frequency with which a programmer can make fraudulent changes is limited somewhat.

Another recommendation is that a second individual review changes actually made. This can be accomplished in various ways. One method is to have a second individual review the changes before they are submitted and determine whether they will do what they are supposed to do. Another method would be to have the computer display the program before and after change, highlighting the actual changes. The other method that can be employed is to have the second programmer review before and after computer-generated flowcharts.

In some installations, management would object to having a second programmer review changes on the grounds that maintenance work is too frequent and that the review by a second individual would be too costly. In that situation, we would suggest that programs accessing master files be identified and that only those programs be subject to review after maintenance. If management still feels that review would be too costly, we would like to suggest that those programs are poorly designed and require rewrite. Frequent modification of the basic posting programs may mean either that the programs do not meet user needs very well, or that the programs contain too much built-in data that should be contained in a reference file rather than in the program. Another possible undesirable design feature that may be present is that the programs may not be suitably modular in design—in other words, individual programs may be covering too much of the processing job.

METHOD 5. Another consideration in fraudulent program modifications is the concept of *temporary versus permanent fraudulent changes*. At one extreme, a programmer could secretly slip in a change right before a production run and then remove the change immediately after the run. If the fact that a change had been made was not recorded and if the nature of the change was unknown, it would be extremely difficult, if not impossible, to trace the source of any resulting discrepancy. This possibility argues very strongly for use of access control, formal authorization, and logging of changes, as well as review of all changes.

At the other extreme is a fraudulent change that is put in once and left in. The danger with this type of change is that it can continue indefinitely. On the positive side, if there is a discrepancy, the change will still be in the program and will serve as evidence of the source of the discrepancy.

METHOD 6. Some computer fraud strategies depend upon secret *use of undefined data fields* built into master files. Normally, such fields may have been initially put into the master file as a provision to facilitate future expansion, or they may have arisen when a data element part of the original design was no longer needed. Our advice is to get rid of any unused data fields. As long as they continue to exist, they provide a convenient means for program schemes that depend upon keeping track of previous fraudulent actions.

A closely related consideration arises regarding the possibility that a programmer may have secretly modified a master-file layout in order to provide space to keep track of fraudulent activity. To make certain that this has not happened, a periodic comparison should be made of the file layout and the file description maintained for the computer (contained in job control language, VTOC, or record layout of source code). This type of checking is particularly critical for master files that keep track of monetary matters, although if a system maintains additional reference files, it is also possible that fraudulent information could be hidden in them.

This brings us to another point. A perpetrator could also create an extra "master file" in which he stored a record of accounts that have been manipulated and of how much had to be put back into each account. If the run book contains instructions for use of a file not contained in other system documentation, we suggest that you consider this to be a highly suspicious finding and investigate it promptly.

**Summary—
reducing the risks
of program
modification
schemes**

Program modification schemes are among the most profitable schemes for perpetrators and among the most difficult for management to uncover. Although many methods exist for reducing exposure to this threat, many of the countermeasures are only suitable for periodic application. In the interim, programming frauds may continue for some time and the perpetrator may be long gone with large sums before a loss is discovered.

Input control totals and run-to-run control totals are necessary and are of some help, but most programming frauds can easily circumvent this countermeasure simply by fudging the totals. Access control over programs, combined with good procedures for authorizing, logging, and reviewing program changes are among the most effective means of reducing opportunities for making fraudulent program changes, but these methods do not protect against fraudulent modifications that are slipped in along with authorized maintenance. To guard against the latter possibility, we recommend having a second programmer review all changes to sensitive programs.

Certain auditing approaches are also advisable. These approaches are expensive to implement and so we recommend that you use them periodically and when discrepancies arise. Among auditing approaches recommended are simulation of processing results and comparison of simulated results to results actually obtained, reconstruction of account balances from historical records, use of limit and activity checks, investigation of instances in which these predetermined thresholds are surpassed, and investigation of actual versus documented file layouts and program processing. In conjunction, we also recommend that employee accounts, dormant accounts, and accounts representing high dollar volumes receive special audit consideration.

Maintenance of a certain level of documentation was also implicit in our recommendations. This documentation includes up-to-date program specifications and listings, file layouts and descriptions, run books, record of changes and authorizations, as well as output reconciliation procedures. Absence of specific documents or failure to keep documents up to date indicates a control problem and also presents a barrier for review and audit.

FILE ALTERATION SCHEMES

Most fraudulent file alteration schemes are really variants of input manipulation and program modification schemes. Still, there are a few variants of file alteration with slightly different characteristics. To acquaint you with the methodology and suitable countermeasures, we have compiled the following examples.

METHOD 1. One fairly common form of fraudulent file alteration is to obtain *access to a live master file* and (using either a program specially written for the purpose, a general retrieval program, or a utility) make surreptitious changes to the file. Changes may include modification of monetary amounts or changes to other data. Changes to monetary fields may or may not be detected by run-to-run control totals. Changes to data fields that do not involve monetary amounts will be extremely difficult, if not impossible, to detect.

The primary methods of preventing this approach are authorization techniques and controls governing physical access to files. For starters, we recommend having a data library for live files. Physical access to the library should be limited to the librarian. Files should only be released upon authorization. Release of files for processing should be recorded in a log showing the reason the file was released, who authorized the release, the time of the day released and returned, and the date.

The next step we recommend is recording of all accesses made to live files in the computer room. This log should include, the file name, the job name, the user initiating the job, and the time of day and the date when processing was begun and ended. Both this log and the library log should be reviewed frequently for suspicious or unauthorized access to files.

Another measure we recommend is labeling of files, externally and internally. In their absence, an operator could easily be duped into mounting a live file for an unauthorized purpose, without being aware of it.

Other precautions we recommend include prohibitions against access to live files by other than formally designated production programs and control over which programs get designated as production. In particular, we recommend that programs not be accepted for production status solely on the programmer's word. Management authorization should be required before production status is given, and authorization should be accompanied with information concerning who is to be authorized and charged for running the program, run schedule, and run instructions, as well as backup and recovery procedures.

METHOD 2. Another method of fraudulent file alteration is to obtain access to a live master file and then *substitute a dummied-up version* for the real file. Superficially, it would seem as though creating a believable dummy that would not lead to a large number of discrepancies would be difficult. In fact, this very approach was part of a very large and well-known case.

This scheme depends upon one of two possible sequences of events. In either case, the scheme begins with the perpetrator obtaining access to the master file, possibly under the guise of making a copy for use as test data. Then the file is run against a program, either in house or at a service bureau. The program creates a very similar file, containing only a few modifications. The newly created file is then substituted for the live file and returned to the data library.

The primary means of preventing this is through control over access to the file. That means maintenance of a physically secure data library and release of a master file for processing only upon receipt of a properly signed authorization.

Since authorizations can be forged or created dishonestly by those with the ability to sign them, certain logs are also required to be maintained and frequently reviewed. In the data library, the log should show the file name, person authorizing release, purpose of authorization, date, and time of day. In the computer room, the log should show the same facts plus the program(s) against which the file was run, any other files created, and the user identification of the individual submitting the run request.

METHOD 3. Another form of fraudulent file alteration may occur if *transaction files are accessed and modified prior to normal processing.* Possible fraudulent actions that may be involved in this type of scheme include addition, modification, and deletion of input transactions. Two approaches are recommended for preventing this scheme: physical and authorization controls regarding access and employment of control totals as recommended for prevention of input manipulation schemes.

Summary—reducing the risks of fraudulent file alteration

The primary means of preventing fraudulent modification of live files involves suitable control over access to live files and logging of all accesses made. Access control implies existence of a physically secure data library from which files are released only upon properly signed written authorization. Logging of all file accesses should be made both in the data library and in the computer room. Logs should be reviewed periodically and compared for consistency.

As a further protective measure, only formally designated production runs should be authorized to access live files. Copies made of live files for testing purposes should receive proper respect and attention. Programs should not be accepted into production status without authorization and proper documentation.

In order to protect input files from fraudulent modification, they should be accorded the status of live files. In addition, input controls are recommended for transaction files in order to provide the ability to detect modifications that may be made between the time of their creation and use.

III

LOSS RECOVERY, LEGAL, AND INVESTIGATIVE CONSIDERATIONS

10

Fidelity Bonding and Crime Insurance

This chapter is about special forms of insurance covering fraudulent and dishonest acts by employees and hazards of crimes such as forgery or alteration of checks and similar instruments, wrongful abstraction of money and securities, and burglary. The sections in this chapter that relate to computer fraud aspects cover:

- The role of insurance as a secondary form of protection.
- Types of coverage.
- Conditions and limitations of fidelity coverages.
- Preparing a bond claim.
- Amount of coverage.
- Need for other safeguards.

THE ROLE OF INSURANCE AS A SECONDARY FORM OF PROTECTION

A good system of internal and administrative controls, computer security measures, and internal auditing can make computer fraud difficult but not impossible. Safeguards whose effectiveness depends on segregation of duties can be circumvented by collusion. Changes in business operations, user organizations, and computer systems may not be accompanied by adequate advance consideration of new fraud risks introduced by such changes. Management oversight can become lax for any of a variety of reasons, and a failure to enforce compliance with control procedures can increase opportunities for fraud. So, while a good system of control will serve to deter potential perpetrators and will often detect fraud at an early stage, there is no guarantee of prevention.

A reasonable set of safeguards provides reasonable but not absolute assurance of asset protection. This implies that the cost of a prevention program should be reasonable, as judged against the fraud loss exposure. Since there are risk factors which cannot be anticipated in making this trade-off as well as risk factors beyond the scope of a reasonable program, insurance can be used to offset such risk factors. But, insurance has a price, too, and should be looked to strictly as a secondary line of defense. Remember that:

1. Loss experience will determine your premium for insurance. If you start out paying $1 per $1,000 of coverage and your rate increases to $15 per $1,000 because of your losses, a good system of control may seem cheap by comparison. For example, if you carry $500,000 of honesty insurance on 100 employees, your initial annual premium (at the $1 rate) would be $50,000. When the premium increases to $750,000 (the $15 rate) because of your carelessness, you probably will not be able to afford the protection, supposing that it was even made available.

2. Insurance is for the prudently managed company. An insurance carrier may successfully disallow your claim (i.e., you lose in a court of law your lawsuit to have the carrier make good) because of negligence in providing safeguards that a "reasonable person" would have provided in similar circumstances.

3. You have to be able to prove your amount of loss and that it resulted from an insured cause. The fact that your company suddenly finds itself with a $1,000,000 shortage on a computer system is *not* a proof of loss. A good system of controls and other safeguards, on the other hand, can provide the basis for showing that the fraud occurred, how it occurred, and the amount of loss sustained as a direct result.

In short, you will want to keep insurance in perspective, as it is a secondary form of protection that may not cover an entire amount of loss and which is intended for prudent companies. It should complement fraud countermeasures, and its protection should be seen as beginning where other safeguards fail.

TYPES OF COVERAGE Since most computer frauds occur as a result of employee dishonesty, forms of coverage aimed at this cause will be stressed.

Fidelity bonding (also referred to as "honesty insurance") protects your company against losses that arise from employee dishonesty. In other words, if defalcation occurs, the fidelity bond will reimburse your company for the loss. In order to collect the insurance, the loss must of course be detected and the perpetrator must not have made full restitution. The other conditions are that the perpetrator must have been covered by the bond and the amount of the loss must be no greater than the amount of the bond, in order to receive full repayment for the loss.

Besides protection against unreimbursed losses, fidelity bonding also provides a degree of prevention and investigation. The mere knowledge of being bonded will serve as a deterrent to some employees. In addition, records maintained by fidelity bonding companies on individuals who have caused losses to other insured employers may prevent your company from hiring such an individual into a sensitive position. Finally, if a loss should occur as the result of employee dishonesty, the bonding company will often perform an investigation. If your company lacks experience in investigation, that service can be helpful in identifying the perpetrators, in documenting the extent of the loss, and in gathering evidence necessary for legal prosecution of perpetrators.

Individual bond

This type of bond protects your company against dishonesty by the individual named in the bond, regardless of his geographic location or the job functions performed. Individual bonds are occasionally used by small companies wishing to bond only a small number of individuals. We do not recommend individual bonds to companies with computer installations because of their limitations as to specifically named individuals covered by the bond.

Schedule bonds

Schedule bonds come in two varieties: name schedule bonds and position schedule bonds. *Name schedule* bonds apply to individuals named in the schedule, in the dollar amount listed next to that individual's name. *Position schedule* bonds cover whoever performs a given job function in the dollar amount specified in the bond next to that position. If frequent turnover exists, a position schedule bond reduces the administrative work necessary to assure continuity of coverage.

The main characteristic of a schedule bond is to limit coverage to a specific group of employees. That characteristic may not be desirable for a company using computers, because there may be a large proportion of employees who will have the opportunity to perpetrate a computer fraud. Taking into account the fact that embezzlement can also be non-computer-related, other employees of your company should probably be bonded, and schedule bonds are awkward for covering a large number of employees and positions.

295

Commercial blanket bond	Commercial blanket bonds cover all of a company's officers and employees up to the amount of the bond. New employees are automatically covered by the bond unless a consolidation or merger takes place. The minimum amount of coverage available is $10,000 and there is no maximum.

Commercial blanket bonds cover all of a company's officers and employees up to the amount of the bond. New employees are automatically covered by the bond unless a consolidation or merger takes place. The minimum amount of coverage available is $10,000 and there is no maximum.

Because commercial blanket bonds can be obtained in any amount over $10,000, this is a recommended form of coverage if there is the possibility of catastrophic loss resulting from the actions of one or more employees—a possibility that exists for many companies using computers for processing applications of a financial nature. If your company does not already have this form of coverage, we recommend giving it consideration.

One disadvantage of commercial blanket bonds is their coverage in the event of collusion among employees in perpetrating a fraud. If collusion occurs, recovery will be possible per incident rather than per employee. In other words, if your company had a $100,000 bond and two employees conspired to create a total loss of $200,000, recovery would only be the $100,000 per incident rather than $100,000 per employee involved.

Blanket position bond

Blanket position bonds are similar to commercial blanket bonds in that they cover all employees and officers and in that coverage of new employees (other than those gained through consolidation or merger) is automatic. Blanket position bonds are available in amounts ranging from $2,500 to $100,000. Because of the relatively low maximum available, blanket position bonds do not provide adequate protection against catastrophic loss for large companies.

One particularly desirable feature of blanket position bonds is coverage provided in the event of collusion. If several employees conspire to create a loss, the full amount of coverage can be collected on each employee, provided that the individuals responsible can be identified. In other words, if the amount of the bond is $100,000 and you can identify the two employees that conspired to create a loss of $200,000, the full amount of the loss will be recoverable—$100,000 for each of the two employees involved.

Comprehensive 3-D policy

The comprehensive 3-D (dishonesty, destruction, and disappearance) crime policy is more than a pure fidelity form of coverage. There are five insuring agreements (each with specified dollar amounts) within the basic 3-D policy, and additional insuring agreements can be added by endorsement. The five agreements are:

1. *Employee dishonesty.* This is a fidelity bond and may be either Form A (commercial blanket bond) or Form B (blanket position bond).

2. *Premises.* This covers loss of money and securities within the premises as a result of destruction, disappearance, or robbery.
3. *Messenger.* This covers the loss of money and securities outside the premises while being conveyed by messenger. Loss may result from destruction, disappearance, or robbery.
4. *Money orders and counterfeit currency.* This covers loss resulting from accepting in good faith counterfeit paper currency (U.S. and Canadian) and money orders which are not honored on presentation for payment.
5. *Forgery.* This covers losses resulting from forgery or alteration of the insured's checks and other specified instruments, and covers all premises.

Blanket crime policy

This policy is nearly identical to the 3-D policy except that a single dollar amount of coverage is specified and none of the basic insuring agreements may be eliminated at the option of the insured.

Special forms of crime insurance

Readers will recognize that certain industries have specialized fidelity and crime insurance needs arising from risks peculiar to their lines of business. Examples of this kind of coverage, which is similar to the blanket crime or 3-D forms with additional coverage or endorsements, include:

- Standard Blanket Bond Form No. 22—Savings and Loan Associations (covers cost of outside fraud audit required by regulatory authorities).
- Standard Blanket Bond Form No. 24—Commercial Banks.
- Standard Blanket Bond Form Nos. 25 and 25L—Insurance Companies.
- Standard Blanket Bond Form No. 26—Small Loan Companies.

Excess indemnity coverage

Under the commercial blanket position bond and some other forms of insurance previously discussed, you may wish to have additional amounts of coverage for company officers and employees who hold key positions relative to computer fraud risks. This can be had for an additional premium and will give you an excess indemnity endorsement to the basic coverage.

In order to collect the *excess* amount in the event of a fraud, it will be necessary to identify the specific individuals involved as ones covered in the endorsement.

If a fidelity bond is canceled or terminated, it is generally the case that losses that occurred during the period in which the bond was in force must be discovered no later than 1 year from time of the termination of coverage in order to submit a claim of loss. Since some of the more significant computer frauds have gone on for a period of years prior to discovery, this may prove to be a problem if coverage is simply dropped.

However, if a new bond is purchased to take the place of another which is canceled on the effective date of the new bond, a rider is generally attached (unless the bond itself contains a superseded suretyship provision), agreeing to pay losses that would have been recoverable under the old bond except for the expiration of the discovery period. This, then, gives uninterrupted continuity to the bonding coverage for prior losses, at a dollar amount that is the lower of the present or former bond amounts.

CONDITIONS AND LIMITATIONS OF FIDELITY COVERAGES

A fidelity bond is a legal contract between the insured (your company) and the underwriter (the bonding company). The real meaning of the words in the contract changes according to what the courts decide they mean and according to interpretation of state laws as applied to these contracts. Readers who have a particular interest in this are referred to the Fidelity and Surety Law Committee of the American Bar Association.

From what we have turned up in our research, it appears that, in terms of case law, the court decisions are favoring the insured. In some instances, the courts have interpreted "fraudulent or dishonest act" to mean a negligent act on the part of an employee without intent to cause a loss to an employer or to profit personally. Clearly, this trend means higher premiums, encourages litigation, and results in more and more fine print being put into the insuring agreements.

On the other hand, the courts could start the pendulum swinging in the other direction, requiring more and more from the insured. Either way, we wish to point out several of the more significant conditions and limitations that are found in most forms of fidelity coverage.

Prior fraud Many business people fail to realize that bonding coverage of an employee who has committed fraud is automatically terminated once that fact becomes known. So, if you have a known thief on the payroll, you lose the coverage for that person's fraudulent acts. The wording in the bond goes something like this:

> Coverage shall not apply to any employee from and after the time that the insured or any partner or officer thereof not in collusion with such employee has knowledge or information that such employee has

committed any fraudulent or dishonest act in the service of the insured or otherwise, whether such act be committed before or after the date of employment by the insured.

Notice *"any* fraudulent or dishonest act"; notice also that the time frame is *not* limited to the period of employment. Although courts have not applied as strict an interpretation to these words as they might, you should be alert to this covenant of the contract.

Proof of loss

The fact that a shortage of money, inventory, or other property is discovered does not constitute a proof of loss. Such a shortage could be due to a computer system or human error in record keeping, or it may have been sustained as a result of fraud perpetrated by an outsider. A fidelity bond does not cover losses incurred from such causes. With respect to these matters, here is wording similar to that which you can expect to find in any insuring agreement for fidelity losses.

Coverage is not provided for losses or those portions of a loss, the proof of which, either as to its existence or amount, is dependent on an inventory computation or a profit and loss computation. However, coverage is provided for losses of money or other property which the insured can prove, through evidence wholly apart from such computations, is sustained by the insured through any fraudulent or dishonest act(s) committed by one or more employees (who are covered in the bond).

Loss by
unidentifiable
employees

Under blanket bonds, losses are covered even though it may not be possible to designate which specific employee(s) caused the loss. Evidence of such a loss, however, must reasonably prove that the fraud or dishonesty was in fact perpetrated by an employee(s).

This benefit of the coverage is not intended to enable you to "hide" the identity of the employee if you know it.

Other
Considerations

Bonds normally apply to employees in certain geographical areas, which, in general, include all states and possessions of the United States, the District of Columbia, and Canada. Employees who are not on temporary assignment from such areas but are regularly employed elsewhere (e.g., England) would not be covered.

Ordinarily, a bond insures property owned or held by the insured in any capacity (whether or not the insured is legally liable for its loss).

**PREPARING A
BOND CLAIM**

The preparation of a claim under a comprehensive bond is often more complex than the process for other kinds of insurance. Your bonding company will have trained fidelity claims representatives to assist in preparing a claim, and you should involve the carrier at the outset.

To start with, you will want to document how the loss was discovered. It could have come about accidentally, during the time an employee was on vacation. Or there may have been symptoms, such as a shortage in inventory, a pattern of misposting, or differences in bank accounts. Also, an internal or external audit may have revealed discrepancies of one kind or another.

Next, you will want to conduct an analysis to determine how much is missing, how the loss was accomplished and concealed, and who perpetrated the fraud. Careful, methodical examinations must be made of computer logs, program changes, authorizations on error and adjustment transactions, and so on. Auditors will need to study the appropriate accounts (disbursements, payroll, accounts receivable, etc.) in attempting to determine the extent of loss, and the success of their work will depend on adequate maintenance of accounting records reflecting daily transactions and audit trails. The auditor may wish to use confirmation procedures, physical counts, and other means of verification that call for the use of computer systems.

At some point, one or more employees (acting alone or in collusion) may be implicated. If the employee can be persuaded to cooperate, he may reveal or be able to re-create records that can make the proof of loss fairly easy. This happy situation is not typical; generally, the suspect denies all knowledge of the loss or may confess without being willing or perhaps able to substantiate the amount of loss. Obviously, a significant investigative effort must go forward to close the gap in the claim. Chapter 9 has suggested common types of control weaknesses that the suspected perpetrator may have exploited.

Obligations of the insured

In general, it is the obligation of the insured to do the following things:

1. Promptly notify the underwriter of the loss.
2. Take sensible action to minimize opportunities for further loss.
3. After a loss has occurred, make no statements and take no actions that may prejudice an action for recovery against another party.
4. Help the underwriter's investigator to the fullest extent possible.
5. Prepare and submit a well-documented claim.

The confession

If you are lucky enough to be able to obtain a signed confession, it can be your best evidence of a loss if it is properly prepared. The confession should be as descriptive as possible, reciting in narrative detail how the fraud was accomplished; what use or disposition was made of the stolen money, goods, or services; and the names and addresses of the employee(s) and outsider(s) who are alleged to have participated in the scheme.

You will want to have two witnesses to the confession or, better yet, have the confession notarized; in either case, their signatures should be on the confession as witnesses. Above the confessor's signature, there should be a statement to the effect that the circumstances described are, to the best of his belief and knowledge, true and accurate, that he is giving his statement voluntarily, and that he has read and understands the statement. Any changes to the statement should be initialed by the confessor, and it may be a good idea to have him initial each paragraph of the document.

We, of course, would recommend that legal counsel draw up such confessions. However, as a practical matter, the circumstances under which a confession can be obtained should be exploited when they arise, as it may be impossible to re-create these conditions later.

Sometimes managers get overzealous and attempt to get other forms of agreement from the confessor, such as a promissory note to pay a certain amount of money in order to make restitution. There are several reasons to avoid this: (1) the amount may not be accurate, as may be revealed in subsequent investigation; (2) by taking a note, you may simply create an obligation to pay that may tend to bar further action, and you will have to try to collect the amount due; and (3) such a note could be construed so as to release the bonding company or delay the processing of the benefit claim.

As we have previously pointed out, a bonding claim must be substantiated. It is important to keep in mind that the proof of loss should be prepared so that it will withstand a court test, should litigation be necessary. As the following quotation points out, a confession will ordinarily show that the loss was due to an insured cause (employee dishonesty) but is not taken as the sole proof as to the amount of loss.

> Many lawsuits and the resulting expenses could be avoided if claims were properly prepared, covering only those losses which are covered by the bond. It should be kept in mind that the burden of proof rests entirely on the insured and not on the bonding company. Too often reliance is placed on the confession of the embezzler. A confession is normally accepted as evidence of dishonesty but not as to the extent of the loss. The best type of evidence will usually be found by a searching examination of the records of the company. This requires time, patience and experience, but in the end it is the shortest and least expensive procedure to follow. A bonding company will recognize and promptly pay a valid claim if the loss is incurred under the terms of its bond and sufficient proof is submitted to substantiate the loss.[1]

[1] Lester A. Pratt, *Embezzlement Controls for Business Enterprises* (Baltimore: Fidelity and Deposit Company, 1974), p. 32.

Written internal reports should be prepared by your company covering cases of dishonesty and criminal acts. You may start out with a preliminary version of such a report, to which supplements are added, in order to develop a final version. Items to be included in a report of this nature are:

- Location and date of report.
- Name and position of preparer.
- If known, name of employee. Also, his address, birth date, marital status, number of dependents, position, earnings, level of security clearance, length of service, date of hire and discharge, and Social Security number.
- Date of loss and nature of loss (value and description of property stolen or missing and description of circumstances surrounding discovery of fraud).
- Action taken to avoid future losses.
- Disciplinary action taken against employee.
- Prosecutive action taken or pending (include specific charge, details concerning indictment, arrest, bail, arraignment and trial, continuances, sentence imposed, etc.).
- Loss-computation details (loss sustained, expense to receive or protect stolen property, amount of recovery and restitution secured, net loss for insurance claim).
- Opinion on whether full extent of loss is known and reason.
- Attachments:
  —Confessions.
  —Supervisor, guard, police reports.
  —Copies of evidence (falsified program code, checks, fraudulent adjustments, etc.).
  —Auditor's report and proof of amount of loss.

This report should be kept as a permanent record for reference during claim processing, legal action, and to help defend any legal actions brought against your company in the distant future. (See Appendix J for an irregularities reporting procedure.)

AMOUNT OF COVERAGE

Where inadequate coverage or no coverage exists against employee dishonesty, the victim bears part or all of the loss. It is not uncommon, in situations either of great loss or in situations involving not so great losses but relatively small companies, for the victim to be forced out of business as the result of such a loss. One survey we are familiar with revealed that almost 90% of businesses eligible for fidelity coverage carried no coverage whatsover.[2]   Another survey covering losses over $10,000 among companies carrying insurance revealed that 65% of the losses were not fully covered by the victim's insurance.[3]

For those readers whose companies carry substantial blanket fidelity bonds, we would like to point out that exposures change over time.   If the business grows, exposure will also increase.   Changes in the way your company does business, performs accounting functions, or is organized will also affect your exposure.   Fidelity coverage judged to be generous at one point in time can subsequently become very skimpy.   At the minimum, exposure should be reviewed from that perspective every time you renew your policy.

Guidelines for amount of coverage

The Surety Association of America has devised a formula for computing the minimum amount of insurance advisable.[4]   Before presenting this formula, we hasten to point out that results obtained from applying the formula represent only the minimum advisable and that the precise amount of insurance your company should carry can best be determined in consultation with a qualified broker.   The formula for any size or type of commercial firm operates in the following manner:

(1)   Enter the firm's Total Current Assets (cash, deposits, securities, receivables, goods on hand, etc.) $_____

    (A)   Enter the value of Goods on Hand (raw materials, materials in process, finished merchandise or products) $_____

    (B)   Enter 5% of (A) $_____

    (C)   Enter Current Assets less Goods on Hand, i.e., the difference between (1) and 1(A) $_____

    (D)   Enter 20% of (C) $_____

(2)   Enter Annual Gross Sales or Income $_____

    (A)   Enter 10% of (2) $_____

    THIS TOTAL IS THE FIRM'S DISHONESTY EXPOSURE INDEX $_____

    SUGGESTED MINIMUM AMOUNT OF HONESTY INSURANCE $_____

The suggested minimum amount of honesty insurance is determined from the Exposure Index, using the table (Figure 10-1) or

[2] *Fidelity Bonds* (New York: The Surety Association of America, 1967), p. 2.
[3] *How Much Honesty Insurance?* (New York: The Surety Association of America, 1971), p. 3.
[4] *Ibid.*, pp. 4–6, 13–15.

charts (Figure 10-2). If a separate figure for goods on hand is not available, omit (A) and (B) and insert the total current assets figure in line (C).

The table presents graduated brackets of the Exposure Index and the suggested minimum amounts of honesty insurance for each bracket. Charts A and B arrive at similar conclusions by direct readings. The Exposure Index is plotted along the bottom of each chart and the minimum amount of coverage is the amount shown on the vertical margin. For an Exposure Index of $5,000,000 or less, use chart B. For an Exposure Index above $5,000,000 and up to $250,-000,000, use chart A. The table also projects the Exposure Index and the amount of coverage for values in excess of the figures on chart A.

An instance of how the formula works is shown in the following example for a wearing apparel manufacturer:

(1)	Total Current Assets		$ 950,000	
	(A)	Goods on Hand	600,000	
	(B)	5% of (A)		$ 30,000
	(C)	Current Assets less Goods on Hand	350,000	
	(D)	20% of (C)		70,000
(2)	Annual Gross Sales or Income		3,000,000	
	(A)	10% of (2)		300,000
		TOTAL (EXPOSURE INDEX)		400,000

In the table, the $400,000 Exposure Index falls in bracket 4 ($250,-000–$500,000). The suggested minimum amount of honesty insurance for this insured is between $75,000 and $100,000, or more exactly by interpolation, $90,000.

Using chart B, the suggested minimum amount of honesty insurance, corresponding with the Exposure Index of $400,000, for this insured is directly read as $90,000.

Here is another example, that of a farm machinery manufacturer:

(1)	Total Current Assets		$15,000,000	
	(A)	Goods on Hand	8,000,000	
	(B)	5% of (A)		$ 400,000
	(C)	Current Assets less Goods on Hand	7,000,000	
	(D)	20% of (C)		1,400,000
(2)	Annual Gross Sales or Income		82,000,000	
	(A)	10% of (2)		8,200,000
		TOTAL (EXPOSURE INDEX)		10,000,000

Suggested Minimum Amounts of Honesty Insurance			
Exposure Index	Bracket No.	Amount of Bond	
$ 1,000 – $ 25,000	1	$ 15,000 – $ 25,000	
25,000 – 125,000	2	25,000 – 50,000	
125,000 – 250,000	3	50,000 – 75,000	
250,000 – 500,000	4	75,000 – 100,000	
500,000 – 750,000	5	100,000 – 125,000	
750,000 – 1,000,000	6	125,000 – 150,000	
1,000,000 – 1,375,000	7	150,000 – 175,000	
1,375,000 – 1,750,000	8	175,000 – 200,000	
1,750,000 – 2,125,000	9	200,000 – 225,000	
2,125,000 – 2,500,000	10	225,000 – 250,000	
2,500,000 – 3,325,000	11	250,000 – 300,000	
3,325,000 – 4,175,000	12	300,000 – 350,000	
4,175,000 – 5,000,000	13	350,000 – 400,000	
5,000,000 – 6,075,000	14	400,000 – 450,000	
6,075,000 – 7,150,000	15	450,000 – 500,000	
7,150,000 – 9,275,000	16	500,000 – 600,000	
9,275,000 – 11,425,000	17	600,000 – 700,000	
11,425,000 – 15,000,000	18	700,000 – 800,000	
15,000,000 – 20,000,000	19	800,000 – 900,000	
20,000,000 – 25,000,000	20	900,000 – 1,000,000	
25,000,000 – 50,000,000	21	1,000,000 – 1,250,000	
50,000,000 – 87,500,000	22	1,250,000 – 1,500,000	
87,500,000 – 125,000,000	23	1,500,000 – 1,750,000	
125,000,000 – 187,500,000	24	1,750,000 – 2,000,000	
187,500,000 – 250,000,000	25	2,000,000 – 2,250,000	
250,000,000 – 333,325,000	26	2,250,000 – 2,500,000	
333,325,000 – 500,000,000	27	2,500,000 – 3,000,000	
500,000,000 – 750,000,000	28	3,000,000 – 3,500,000	
750,000,000 – 1,000,000,000	29	3,500,000 – 4,000,000	
1,000,000,000 – 1,250,000,000	30	4,000,000 – 4,500,000	
1,250,000,000 – 1,500,000,000	31	4,500,000 – 5,000,000	

Figure 10-1

Exposure Index—Bond Amount Table

On the table, the $10,000,000 Exposure Index falls in bracket 17 ($9,275,000 to $11,425,000). The suggested minimum amount of honesty insurance for this insured is between $600,000 and $700,000, or about $630,000. Using chart A, corresponding with the Exposure Index of $10,000,000, the suggested minimum amount of honesty insurance is found to be $625,000.

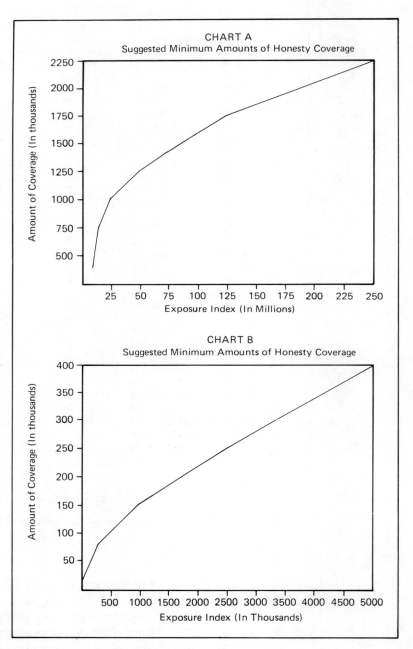

Figure 10-2

Exposure Index—Bond Amount Charts

306

| Role of the risk manager | Your company's risk manager—the person responsible for insurance and the reduction of risk for insured hazards—in cooperation with an insurance broker having computer risk expertise, can develop special forms of coverage (manuscripted policies) that address computer fraud hazards and which have provisions for self-insurance and co-insurance to keep the premium in line with the protection that is really needed. |

NEED FOR OTHER SAFEGUARDS

There are three compelling reasons why your company should not rely solely upon fidelity insurance for protection against losses from computer fraud:

- Size of the premium.
- Possibility of being underinsured.
- Possibility of computer fraud by individuals not in the employ of your company.

Size of the premium

The amount of premium your company will have to pay for fidelity insurance depends upon the amount of coverage desired, upon the type of coverage selected, upon the industry of which your company is a part, and upon your company's past experience with losses. Your company's past loss experience can make a big difference in the amount of premium it will have to pay for a given type and amount of coverage.

A case we are familiar with illustrates this last point. The victim was a financial institution. In one particular year, its fidelity bond premium was about $125,000. During that year, it experienced several cases of defalcation, amounting in aggregate to nearly $1 million. The next time the premium was due, a bill for $325,000 was received. The controller was appalled and called the bonding company, stating that this must be a 3-year premium or it had to be some mistake. The broker agreed to check into the matter and eventually responded as follows: We did make a mistake; your premium should be $425,000 not $325,000—for one year!

Possibility of being underinsured

As indicated by the Surety Association of America guideline, fidelity bonding coverage is normally an amount less than the net worth of your company's business. It is impossible to predict in advance the maximum loss that can occur through employee dishonesty. Therefore, there is always a chance of a loss occurring that exceeds coverage under the bond.

If your company neglects all safeguards besides fidelity bonding, loss experience will be much greater than would be true otherwise. Almost infinite opportunities for embezzlement will exist in the absence of other controls. Since detection mechanisms will be absent, embezzlement will continue and increase for long periods of time. Furthermore, your company may not be able to provide sufficient evidence to prove a claim if other safeguards do not exist.

Fraud from outside   The final reason why fidelity bonding cannot be your company's sole safeguard against computer fraud is the fact that employees are not the only perpetrators of computer fraud. The threat of computer fraud by individuals outside the company's employ exists regardless of the application, but it is particularly acute for systems that utilize telecommunications. Although types of fidelity coverage available commercially vary, they do not, as a general rule, protect against fraud unless the perpetrator is an employee of your company. Some type of crime coverage would need to be considered as an offset to the nonemployee hazards.

11

Legal Aspects
of Computer Fraud

Computer fraud raises a number of interesting and sometimes complex legal issues of which you should be aware in order to protect your company's interests as well as your own personal interests. If computer fraud occurs in your company, you may find yourself having to handle computer evidence and deal with suspected perpetrators. Some knowledge of the law can be helpful to you in these situations. If you are a law-enforcement investigator, these legal considerations will be important in maximizing the chances of successful criminal prosecution of guilty individuals. Your company's directors, officers, and independent auditors can become subjects of a lawsuit should your company be the victim of a major computer fraud. In this connection, we hope to make you aware of the current legal trends.

We are not lawyers, so our perspectives on the legal issues are necessarily those of laymen. Our purpose in presenting these issues is not to make you a legal expert. The law itself changes and evolves and is always subject to interpretation in courts of law. Although detailed knowledge of the law and its interpretation should be left to qualified attorneys, there are certain concepts with which you should be acquainted. In this chapter we have classified these concepts under the following headings:

- Federal criminal laws.

- Federal rules of evidence.

- Search and seizure of computer evidence.

- Preserving the chain of custody of evidence.

- Admissibility of computer evidence.

- State computer fraud laws.

- Lawsuits against independent auditors and company directors.

- Cooperation with law-enforcement agencies.

In our discussion of these topics we will be dealing almost exclusively with legal matters that are pertinent to jurisprudence in the United States. We caution our readers that the legal systems in countries other than the United States may differ significantly.

FEDERAL CRIMINAL LAWS

The criminal laws of the United States are found in *Title 18 U.S. Criminal Code*. Crimes are defined in Part I of Title 18, which consists of about 70 chapters and continuously numbered sections (statutes) running from 1 to over 2500. Part II deals with criminal procedure, has about 21 chapters, and sections numbered in the 3000 series. There are several other parts of Title 18 which are not pertinent to our discussion.

Title 18 U.S. Criminal Code

In general, Title 18 establishes federal jurisdiction in such a way that it is difficult to think of a major computer fraud that could not, in some manner, be construed to fall within such jurisdiction. Several possibilities are:

- Fraud against the federal government.
- Frauds in other governmental bodies and organizations that use or disburse federal funds.
- Frauds that in some manner involve the use of the mails.
- Frauds that involve the use of telephone systems, particularly for interstate communications.
- Frauds that in some manner involve interstate commerce.
- Frauds in any national bank or financial institution that is federally insured.

This list is by no means exhaustive, and Title 18 contains some 40 sections that the federal government can use to prosecute computer crimes of all types. But all 40 statutes were written to combat abuses other than computer crimes and, as such, federal prosecutors have been handicapped because they had to construct their cases on laws that did not envision the technical aspects of computer crime.

For example, a major crime conviction was won in a well-known case only because the perpetrator had used a telephone line to penetrate the computer system of a federal contractor across state lines. Had the telephone been used in intrastate rather than interstate data communications, the Wire Fraud Statute (18 U.S.C. 1343) under which the indictment was brought may have been inadequate. In the same case, a part of the indictment was dismissed because electromagnetic impulses which transmitted valuable data were determined not to be "property" as defined in the Interstate Transportation of Stolen Property Statute (18 U.S.C. 2314).

In another federal case, the government lost because of the definitional difficulties in establishing whether checks issued by a computer on the basis of fraudulent or manipulated data were forgeries. The Congress of the United States, recognizing these difficulties in prosecuting computer crime, is (at the time of this writing) considering passage of a tough new law to deal specifically with it. This is the topic of the following section.

Proposed Federal Computer Systems Protection Act

When enacted into law, the captioned act will add a wholly new section to Title 18, known as *Section 1028—Computer Fraud and Abuse.* It will be found in Chapter 47—Fraud and False Statements of Title 18. We will refer to it as the Computer Fraud Statute (18 U.S.C. 1028).

This statute is specifically designed to give federal prosecutors a weapon against four main categories of computer crime.

1. Introduction of fraudulent records or data into the computer system.
2. Unauthorized use of computer-related facilities.
3. Alteration or destruction of information or files.
4. Stealing, whether by electronic means or otherwise, money, financial instruments, property, services, or valuable data.

It was the intention of Congress to make virtually all unauthorized use of federal computers and computers used in interstate commerce a federal offense, punishable by up to 15 years in prison, a $50,000 fine, or both. This heavy a punishment is unprecedented in federal criminal law for white-collar crime. Congress intended this to be a deterrent to the potential computer criminal and it is a clear warning that a hard line is to be taken with computer criminals.

In drafting 18 U.S.C. 1028, the Congress recognized the risks involved with electronics funds transfer and banking systems, with input manipulation, with program alteration, with clandestine coding in programs, with impersonation to gain access to on-line systems, and with eavesdropping and wiretapping. Readers will recognize all of these as the forms of manipulation that are used in perpetrating computer fraud. The text of 18 U.S.C. 1028—Computer Fraud, as of this writing, reads as follows:

> Whoever knowingly and willfully [attempts to or actually] directly or indirectly accesses or causes to be accessed any computer, computer system, computer network, or any part thereof which, in whole or part operates in interstate commerce or is owned by, under contract to, or operated for, on behalf of, or in conjunction with, any financial institution, the United States government, or any branch, department, or agency thereof, or any entity operating in or affecting interstate commerce, for the purpose of (1) devising or executing any scheme or artifice to defraud, or (2) obtaining for themselves or another money, property, or services by means of false or fraudulent pretenses, representations, or promises, shall be fined not more than $50,000 or imprisoned for not more than 15 years, or both.
>
> Whoever knowingly and willfully, [attempts to or actually] directly or indirectly accesses, alters, damages, or destroys [or causes such acts to be done] any computer, computer system, or computer network described above, or any computer software, program, or data contained in such computer, computer system, or computer network, [or any person related or associated thereto, with intent to cause harm, damage, or destruction] shall be fined not more than $50,000, or imprisoned not more than 15 years, or both.

The technical terms used in the proposed statute are contained within it and the meanings are given as follows:

- *Access*—to approach, instruct, communicate with, store data in, retrieve data from, or otherwise make use of any resources of a computer, computer system, or computer network.

- *Computer*—an electronic device which performs logical, arithmetic, and memory functions by the manipulations of electronic or magnetic impulses, and includes all input, output, processing, storage, software, or communications facilities which are connected or related to such a device in a system or network.

- *Computer system*—a set of related, connected or unconnected, computer equipment, devices, and software.

- *Computer network*—the interconnection of communication lines [or systems] with a computer through remote terminals, or a complex consisting of two or more interconnected computers.

- *Property*—includes, but is not limited to, financial instruments; information, including electronically [processed or] produced data; and computer software and programs in either machine- or human-readable form, and any other tangible or intangible item of value.

- *Services*—includes, but is not limited to, computer time, data processing, and storage functions.

- *Financial instrument*—any check, draft, money order, certificate of deposit, letter of credit, bill of exchange, credit card, marketable security, [or any electronic data processing, representation thereof].

- *Computer program*—instructions or statements, in a form acceptable to a computer, which permit the functioning of a computer system in a manner designed to provide appropriate products from such computer system.

- *Computer software*—a set of computer programs, procedures, and associated documentation concerned with the operation of the computer system.

The financial institutions referred to in 18 U.S.C. 1028 are federally insured commercial banks, savings and loan associations, savings banks, and credit unions. Also included are securities broker dealers registered with the Securities and Exchange Commission, businesses insured by the Securities Investors Protection Corporation, members of the Federal Reserve, and Federal Reserve Banks.

As you can readily see, there is very little in the way of computer fraud that would not come within the purview of this proposed statute, with the possible exception of purely intrastate frauds that in no way involve schemes that utilize federally regulated, funded, or insured services. Cases outside federal jurisdiction may be covered by state laws and possibly even by certain local laws. We would not be surprised to see state laws that are modeled on 18 U.S.C. 1028 and are designed to pick up where federal jurisdiction ends.

Misprision of felony (18 U.S.C. 4)

Readers should be aware that it is a federal crime to have knowledge of the actual commission of a felony (of the type that could be prosecuted in a federal court) and to conceal and not make that felony known as soon as possible to a judge or U.S. law enforcement agency such as the Federal Bureau of Investigation. The penalty is a fine of not more than $500 or imprisonment for not more than 3 years, or both.

With the advent of 18 U.S.C. 1028, computer frauds of nearly every type will be federal felonies (a federal felony is an offense punishable by imprisonment for a term exceeding 1 year). The usual *interpretation* of 18 U.S.C. 4 is that the person with the knowledge of an actual felony must do something to actively hide or cover up the criminal act. Passive knowledge is not generally regarded as sufficient grounds to prosecute, but we hasten to add that the law itself does not seem to read this way. Should you find yourself in a situation like this, you would do well to discuss it with legal counsel.

FEDERAL RULES OF EVIDENCE

Another item of special relevance in federal computer fraud cases is Public Law 93-595 Section 1 which is *Federal Rules of Evidence*, enacted January 2, 1975. These rules are numbered starting with 101 and extend to over 1100 at present. Any given rule may have a number of sections and/or subsections.

Prior to the enactment of these rules, federal computer cases have relied upon the Federal Business Records Act 28 U.S.C. 1732 (a) as the authority for admitting computer materials. Presently, the Federal Rules of Evidence are invariably used because of their more liberalized and explicit language, especially as it pertains to computer records.

Later in this chapter we will discuss, in general, the subject of the admissibility of computer evidence into a court of law. For now, you should understand that the rules of evidence are designed to secure fairness in the administration of justice. Computer evidence is so-called "hearsay," in that it is evidence based not on a witness's personal knowledge but on matters told him by another. In general, hearsay is not admissible in the federal and other courts, in that it is secondhand knowledge. The aim of the court is to get the "best evidence" introduced into the case. There are, however, exceptions to this "hearsay rule" provided that the proponent of such evidence provides sufficient guarantees of its trustworthiness. In terms of the Federal Rules of Evidence, the particular rules pertinent to computer evidence are discussed below.

Rule 803—Hearsay Exceptions (Availability of Declarant Immaterial). This rule states that the following are not excluded by the hearsay rule, even though the declarant is available as a witness:

- *Section (6) records of regularly conducted activity.* A memorandum, report, record, or data compilation, in any form, of acts, events, conditions, opinions, or diagnoses made at or near the time by, or from information transmitted by, a person with knowledge, if kept in the course of a regularly conducted business activity, and if it was the regular practice of that business activity to make the memorandum, report, record, or data compilation, as shown by the testimony of the custodian or other qualified witness, unless the source of information or the method or circumstances of the preparation indicate a lack of trustworthiness. The term "business" as used in this paragraph includes business, institution, association, profession, occupation, and calling of every kind, whether or not conducted for profit. (This particular rule is basically the *business records exception to the hearsay rule* which allows flexibility as to who can authenticate and testify to business records. Hence, an EDP supervisor can testify as to the records produced by the computer, even though data entry operators and programmers other than himself may have been responsible for that particular record being compiled by the computer.)

- *Section (7) absence of entry in records kept in accordance with the provisions of Section (6).* Evidence that a matter is not included in the memoranda, reports, records, or data compilations in any form, kept in accordance with the provisions of Section (6), to prove the nonoccurrence or nonexistence of the matter, if the matter was of a kind of which in memorandum, report, record, or data compilation was regularly made and preserved, unless the sources of information or other circumstances indicate a lack of trustworthiness. (This is the rule that can be used to prove *negative facts*, such as failure to enter authorized transactions into the normal data input stream.)

- *Section (8) public records and reports and Section (10) absence of public record or entry.* These are similar to Section (6) and Section (7), respectively, except that they pertain to records, reports, statements, or data compilations, in any form, of public offices or agencies.

- *Section (24) other exceptions.* A statement not specifically covered by any of the forgoing exceptions but having equivalent circumstantial guarantees of trustworthiness, if the court determines that (a) the statement is offered as evidence of material fact; (b) the statement is more probative on the point for which it is offered than any other evidence which the proponent can procure through reasonable efforts; and (c) the purposes of these rules and the interests of justice will best be served by admission of the statement into evidence. However, a statement may not be admitted under this exception unless the proponent of it makes known to the adverse party sufficiently in advance of the trial or hearing to provide the adverse party with a fair opportunity to prepare to meet it, his intention to offer the statement and the particulars of it, including the name and address of the declarant. (This is a *catchall exception* that is broad enough to cover many kinds of computer records and other evidence, whether or not developed in the usual course of business.)

Rule 901—Requirement of Authentication or Identification. This rule states that the requirement of authentication or identification as a condition precedent to admissibility is satisfied by evidence sufficient to support a finding that the matter in question is what the proponent claims. By way of illustration only, and not by way of limitation, the rule offers a number of examples of authentication or identification conforming with the requirements of this rule. The one pertinent to computer fraud cases is:

- *Subsection(b) (9) process or system.* Evidence describing a process or system used to produce a result and showing that the process or system produces an accurate result. (This basically requires that the proponent explain to the court how the computer functions and why its output is accurate and reliable and, hence, establish that the computer record is authentic and admissible as evidence.)

Rule 1001—Definitions as to the Contents of Writing, Recordings, and Photographs. This rule is defining what kinds of records might be admissible and covers the following four categories, three of which pertain to records of the type one might find in connection with computerized systems.

- *Section (1) writings and recordings.* "Writings" and "recordings" consist of letters, words, or numbers, or their equivalent, set down by handwriting, typewriting, printing, photostating, photographing, magnetic impulse, mechanical or electronic recording, or other forms of data compilation.
- *Section (2) photographs.* "Photographs" include still photographs, x-ray films, video tapes, and motion pictures.
- *Section (3) original.* An "original" of a writing or recording is the writing or recording itself or any counterpart intended to have the same effect by a person executing or issuing it. An "original" of a photograph includes the negative or any print therefrom. If the data are stored in a computer or similar device, any printout or other output readable by sight, shown to reflect the data accurately, is an "original."
- *Section (4) duplicate.* A "duplicate" is a counterpart produced by the same impression as the original, or from the same matrix, or by means of photography, including enlargements and miniatures, or by mechanical or electronic rere-

cording, or by chemical reproduction, or by other equivalent techniques which accurately produce the original.

Hence, under Section (3), a computer printout would be directly admissible without having to offer the magnetic tape or disk on which the data were stored. This is significant in that some direct access storage devices and memories are not portable, and also because certain intermediate computational results may not be permanently stored on other computer media.

A computer printout would appear to qualify as a "duplicate" of the source documents from which computer input was prepared, even though the underlying documents had been destroyed routinely in the ordinary course of business.

Cases involving computer evidence. In addition to the guidelines provided by statute, a number of cases have been decided wherein the issue to be decided was the admissibility of computer records.

The case *United States* v. *DeGeorgia,* 420 F.2d 889(9th Cir. 1969) resulted in the first federal decision to admit computer evidence in a criminal prosecution. In that case, the majority buried its criteria of admissibility in the following footnote:

> While . . . it is immaterial that the business record is maintained in a computer rather than in company books, this is on the assumption that: (1) the opposing party is given the same opportunity to inquire into the accuracy of the computer and the input record used, as he would have to inquire into the accuracy of written business records, and (2) the trial court, as in the case of challenged business records, requires the party offering the computer information to provide a foundation therefore sufficient to warrant a finding that such information is trustworthy [*Id.* 420 F. 2d at 893 (note 11)].

In concurring with the decision, one of the judges in the case emphasized more strongly the responsibility of the trial judge in such matters:

> In order to fully protect the defendant in a criminal case from undue infringement of his right to confront the witnesses, this type of evidence should still be strictly tested. . . . In a day when the pace of our technology threatens to exceed the development of rules for governing human conduct, we must be careful to insure that fundamental rights are not surrendered to the calculations of machines. If a machine is to testify against an accused, the courts must, at the very least, be satisfied with all reasonable certainty that both the machine and those who supply its information have performed their functions with utmost accuracy. Therefore, it is essential that the trial court be convinced of the trustworthiness of the particular

records before admitting them into evidence. And it should be convinced by proof presented by the party seeking to introduce the evidence rather than receiving the evidence upon the basis of an inadequate foundation and placing the burden upon the objector to demonstrate its weakness (*Id.* 420 F. 2d at 895–896).

In this decision, the same concurring judge incorporated into his opinion an excerpt from a decision in the state of Mississippi. The Mississippi case was *King* v. *State ex rel. Murdock Acceptance Corp.*, 222 So. 2d 393 (Miss. 1969). This case produced what may be one of the most widely quoted judicial standards for testing the admissibility of computer evidence. It reads as follows:

> We hold that the printout sheets of business records stored on electronic computing equipment are admissible in evidence if relevant and material, without the necessity of identifying, locating, and producing as witnesses the individuals who made the entries in the regular course of business if it is shown (1) that the electronic computing equipment is recognized as standard equipment, (2) the entries are made in the regular course of business at or reasonably near the time of the happening of the event recorded, and (3) the foundation testimony satisfies the court that the sources of information, method and time of preparation were such as to indicate its trustworthiness and justify its admission (*Id.* 222 So. 2d at 398).

In this case, the plaintiff offered a computer printout which was a record showing the amount the defendant owed on a note held by the plaintiff. Employees of the plaintiff would accept payment at branch offices, making an entry at that office on a receipt card. The card was then transmitted to a central computer at the head office, where the information was fed into a computer and then sent back to the branch office and microfilmed. In this way, the transaction was recorded in order to update the balance owed on the account. The treasurer for the plaintiff provided testimony which stated that the home office used a Burroughs B-280 computer, which is recognized as an efficient and accurate machine. In addition, he described the procedures used to accumulate and record information by the B-280. No attempt was made to call the clerks who had accepted payment. Nor were attempts made to produce either the original records in the branch office or the microfilm copies. The defendant objected to these records on the grounds that the requirements of the "regular-entries-rule" were not met because the accounting manager had no personal knowledge of the entries and none of the clerks who made the original entries at the branch office were called to testify or shown to be unavailable to give testimony. In this case, the court had no problem in extending the regular-entries-rule exception to hearsay to encompass computer records. It, in effect, stated that expedients

318

which the commercial world recognized as safe should be sanctioned by the courts. The court further expressed the view that it was unnecessary to call the original maker of the record, even if identified and available, wherever the inconvenience of calling him outweighed the utility of doing so.

Using the same reasoning as applied in the Mississippi case, a Nebraska court noted that a computerized business entry, if relevant and made in the normal course of business, may be offered in evidence where the court deems its method, source of information, and timeliness of preparation sufficient to justify its admission. The court, in the interest of bringing the realities of business and professional practice into the courtroom, admitted electronic recordings rather than records made in the conventional manner, and storage on tape rather than in bulky files or hard copy reports [*Transport Indemnity Co.* v. *Seib* (178 Neb 253, 132 N.W. 2d 871, 11 ALR 3rd 1368)].

In another decision, *Sears Roebuck and Company* v. *Theresa Merla* [361 A 2d 69 (1976)], the plaintiff intended to rely at the trial on a computer printout of the defendant's account where the plaintiff had destroyed the original invoices when the information they contained was transferred to the computer, and the plaintiff was unable to give a description of the goods sold. However, the plaintiff stated that the computer printout would show dates, costs, and departments from which the various purchases were made, the number of the defendant's credit card, the payments made on account, and the balance presently due. The court allowed the computer printout, holding that as long as the proper foundation is laid, a computer printout is admissible on the same basis as any other business record.

SEARCH AND SEIZURE OF COMPUTER EVIDENCE

Computerized business records present some difficult problems for investigators and law-enforcement people who need such records for evidence of fraud. For one thing, the evidence can be quickly obliterated or altered without leaving traces of physical destruction. People with something to hide can press a few buttons on a terminal or computer console keyboard, enter a special job control card, or have "self-destruct" coding built into programs that will effectively cause potentially incriminating evidence to vanish. Or a reel of tape can be passed through a "degausser," and in a matter of seconds, the contents of an entire reel are erased. Since degaussers are routinely used in a number of EDP centers to erase out-of-date tapes with sensitive information, a perpetrator need not go to the trouble of bringing his own.

The other thing is that due process of law, at least in the United States, often puts the law-enforcement official in the position of tipping his hand when attempting to seize computer evidence. This advance notice tends to provide time for a perpetrator to destroy or impair the usefulness of evidence in the ways outlined above.

During the days just before the Equity Funding scandal came out in the open, some employees reportedly removed incriminating evidence by the armful and erased magnetic tapes in the computer room. It was also reported that one of the masterminds of the Equity Funding fraud ordered his computer operations manager to destroy the library tape and scramble identification codes, at a time when the investigators were hot on the trail of incriminating evidence. The library tape was a master index to some 3,000 reels of computer data and, being recorded on magnetic tape, it was open to quick erasure. As some readers will recall, of the approximately 100,000 insurance policies carried on the computer records of Equity Funding, about two-thirds were fraudulent. It has been said that if the tape library had been destroyed, it would have been virtually impossible to differentiate these bogus policies from the real ones. In the end, investigators did seize the 3,000 reels as computer evidence.

**Legal means of
obtaining
computerized
business records**

Remembering that a legal or illegal business entity may use computers, there are three methods to obtain computer evidence that are generally recognized as acceptable to a court in which the evidence is later presented. The three methods are by:

1. Consent or voluntary.
2. Subpoena duces tecum.
3. Search warrant.

In the following subsections, we will discuss how each of these methods of obtaining computer evidence applies in computer cases.

Consent or voluntary. An investigator may make a polite request of a business to have access to computer data and this consent or voluntary request for permission may be just as politely refused by the business entity, perfectly within the law. If the business entity consents to the search on an entirely voluntary basis, it waives the protection of the Fourth Amendment to the U.S. Constitution. In general, business organizations enjoy the full benefit of the Fourth Amendment, which provides protection against unreasonable search and seizure. In making a polite request, the investigator is under no requirement to advise a company of its Fourth Amendment right to refuse a warrantless search of business premises for computer evidence. However, law-enforcement authorities may not obtain consent under false pretenses, such as by claiming they have a valid search warrant when they do not. A business entity that is, itself, suspected of engaging in computer fraud may very well have some-thing to hide from investigators and, accordingly, a consent search request is likely to be turned down in such a hostile environment. However, the fact that a request for a voluntary search is declined does not automatically mean that the business entity has something to hide. In fact, the business entity may very well wish to cooperate with law-enforcement officials but in doing so wish to avoid possible reprisals by a third party whose records were given up without his (its) consent. The business entity has a better measure of protection for itself if computer evidence is seized on the basis of a search war-rant or is surrendered in compliance with a subpoena duces tecum, as discussed below. Readers would be well advised to check with legal counsel before consenting to a voluntary search.

Subpoena duces tecum. This is a court order to produce certain business records and documents. It means that on the day and time you are to appear in court, as specified in the subpoena, you are to have in your possession the business records indicated so that they might be entered into evidence. This kind of subpoena would be issued to you if you are reluctant to volunteer or prefer the formality of an official request. While you may not refuse to honor a sub-poena, you may be able to obtain a postponement of your appear-ance by explaining the circumstances to the judge who has issued the subpoena. For example, you may need more time to get the requested documents together.

Notice that the subpoena duces tecum is an order for you to ap-pear in court and bring these specified records with you. An in-vestigator may not break down the door to your company to gain admission because the order does not carry with it the weight of a search warrant, as discussed below.

Search warrant. A search warrant is a court order that entitles an investigator to enter your business premises and seize the com-puter evidence and other records named in the search warrant. Before a law-enforcement official can get a search warrant that gives him such permission, he must appear before a judge and swear that he has "probable cause" to believe that certain evidence of a crime will be found in the search. The term "probable cause" has been defined as meaning that his reasons are such as would lead a cau-tious man to take action. He cannot simply be guessing or playing a hunch.

Even with the warrant, the investigator must still follow certain procedures. In general, he must request admittance, identify himself as an officer, and give you time to read his warrant if you want to. If you refuse entry he is legally entitled to proceed with the search.

State and federal courts have typically been consistent that search warrants not be issued to conduct "fishing expeditions." Warrants must impose a meaningful restriction on the scope of the search and upon the items vulnerable to seizure.

The custodian of computer evidence in a nonhostile environment can certainly aid the investigator in identifying the evidence to be described in the search warrant, because of the custodian's knowledge of such records and information. Such would ordinarily be the case where the trustee in bankruptcy has taken over a company that has been the victim of computer fraud or has itself engaged in fraud. On the other hand, in a hostile environment, there can be great difficulty describing narrowly and with specificity the items to be named in the warrant. If a search warrant turns out to be too broad and nonspecific, there is a good chance that it would be quashed by a grand jury on the basis that it is a general warrant—meaning that it is condemned as a general exploratory search.

**Avoiding
suppression of
computer
evidence**

In considering the legal methods investigators can use to legally obtain evidence of computer fraud, readers will recognize that in all instances there is a possibility that computer evidence can be suppressed or obliterated. Consent searches for computer data can be validly refused. A subpoena calls for the custodian of the records to gather up the requested information and bring it to court. In the intervening time, there is usually ample opportunity to rid the records of potentially incriminating data elements or claim that they have mysteriously disappeared. The search warrant, if it is to withstand judicial review, must be rather narrow in terms of the scope and the specific data records that are to be seized. As a practical matter, because of the complexity of many computer systems and their programs, the effective use of a search warrant will require the investigator to have somewhat detailed knowledge of the systems and records before seeking a search warrant. This knowledge could be obtained voluntarily from the company in a nonhostile environment or from informants of one type or another.

As indicated earlier, a consent search will enable the investigator to enlist the aid and advice of company personnel who are most knowledgeable about what records would be most appropriate to the investigator's case. If an investigator has any reason to anticipate the denial of a consent request, he can hold a search warrant in reserve. Then, if the company refuses the polite request, he can pull out his search warrant and enter the premises to seize the records identified in the warrant. The latter approach helps avoid the spoiling of computer evidence that might otherwise result.

Under the *emergency doctrine*, to preclude the destruction of evidence, law-enforcement officers may make a warrantless entry onto business premises and keep the record custodians under involuntary surveillance while a search warrant is sought by a fellow officer or by way of a telephone call. Unless there is a true emergency situation such as where the wrongdoer is about to remove evidence or is in the process of actually destroying it, a warrantless search can easily result in the evidence seized being thrown out of court because it was obtained by unlawful means. If the investigator had reasonable grounds to obtain a search warrant before going to the premises, the fact that he failed to do so and thereby created the emergency situation may very well be grounds for ruling that the evidence obtained is inadmissible.

An exception to the rule against securing the premises while waiting for a warrant can occur during the execution of a lawful arrest procedure. In this context a very limited search is permissible and the investigator is entitled to secure the premises to prevent the disappearance of evidence of the crime.

**Self-incrimination
and the
administrative
search doctrine**

Officers of a collective entity such as a corporation, union, or partnership, when acting in their representative capacities, must produce upon legitimate demand official records and documents of their organization, even though doing so may tend to incriminate them personally.

Under the Fifth Amendment to the U.S. Constitution, an accused is not required to give testimony or evidence that would tend to incriminate him. Such evidence might include personal letters, diaries, and other documents of a highly personal nature. Since computer fraud usually occurs in a corporate setting, the corporate records that might tend to incriminate a perpetrator would not be considered evidence of this general character.

Regulated industries (such as insurance and securities broker-dealers) and government agencies have no constitutional privilege against self-incrimination in any practical respect. Additionally, their protection against unreasonable search and seizure under the Fourth Amendment is practically nonexistent, under the "visitorial powers" of government investigators.

For example, in the Equity Funding fraud, the insurance regulation departments of California and Illinois, because of their statutory authority, did not have to resort to judicial process to gain access to corporate computer records.

As creations of the states in which they are registered, corporations are subject to state supervision and inspection, and this is interpreted to fall within the administrative search or "visitorial powers" doctrine.

This section is based on the work of Edward H. Coughran of the University of California, San Diego, developer of the "Symposium on Computer Abuse for the Prosecuting Attorney" and author of *Computer Abuse and Criminal Law*.[1]

There is nothing unique about a computer tape or magnetic disk. One tape or disk may be physically indistinguishable from any of a thousand others. Nor is there any promise of permanence in the magnetic pattern encoded on the computer tape or disk. The materials are erasable. In normal use, they are used, erased, and reused routinely. They are vulnerable to alteration and spoilage.

If the prosecutor intends to offer computer evidence at trial, it behooves him to maintain careful records of the chain of custody for each of his computer materials:

> When real evidence is offered, an adequate foundation for admission will require testimony first that the object offered is *the* object which was involved in the incident, and further that the condition of the object is substantially unchanged. If the offered item possesses characteristics which are fairly unique and readily identifiable, and if the substance of which it is composed is relatively impervious to change, the trial court is viewed as having broad discretion to merely admit on the basis of testimony that the item is the one in question and is in a substantially "unchanged condition." On the other hand, if the offered evidence is of such a nature as not to be readily identifiable, or to be susceptible to alteration by tampering or contamination, sound exercise of the trial court's discretion may require a substantially more elaborate foundation. A foundation of the latter sort will commonly entail testimony tracing the "chain of custody" of the item with sufficient completeness to render it improbable that the original item has either been exchanged with another or been contaminated or tampered with [McCormick, *Evidence*, 527–528 (2nd ed., 1972)].

In the Equity Funding case, upon receiving the consent of the trustee in bankruptcy, the FBI physically seized and sealed off the computer area. But unless policyholders, shareholders, and bond holders were to be wiped out, the company had to continue its day-to-day operations. Before any tape could be removed, there was a mammoth task of copying a duplicate for every tape on the premises. The trustee hired a recognized computer expert to do the copying. The setting was carefully controlled, and all copying was done on Equity Funding's own computer equipment. The original tapes were transported to an off-site vault.

It is important to have a computer expert participate at every step of the way. To avoid deterioration of the tapes, they had to be

[1] Edward H. Coughran, *Computer Abuse and Criminal Law* (San Diego, Calif.: University of California—Computer Center, 1976).

stored under controlled temperature and humidity conditions. Some 3,000 reels of tape were involved. Here again, with that mass of material an expert was necessary to give advice even as to such elementary matters as stacking the tapes in a way to avoid warpage or other damage that might render them unreadable.

The U.S. Attorney's Office double-padlocked the vault, posted a 24-hour guard, restricted access to the tapes, and utilized a sign-in log for all people entering and leaving the vault area.

At the time of the initial seizure, FBI agents scratched their initials and the date onto each tape canister. Most of the tapes were already numbered serially. The original numbering system was retained, with new numbers assigned to the tapes that had not yet been numbered.

The agents compiled a separate log book to keep track of each tape, the recovery date, and the particular agent who took initial possession of the reel. The log book would have been available to refresh the memory of government witnesses or to serve as "past recollection recorded" in a subsequent trial.

Los Angeles Assistant District Attorney Philip Wynn writes his initials on the tapes, seals the computer tapes into individual envelopes, and labels the envelopes with the location of the source, date, and time. The tapes then go into the evidence room without precautions quite as elaborate as in the Equity Funding case.

Another difference is that Mr. Wynn cannot ordinarily use the owner's equipment to make duplicate tapes because of the enormous cost problem. As a matter of trial tactics, he always prepares an evidence list for distribution to the judge, the clerk, and the defense attorney.

A presumption of regularity attaches to official actions so that the foregoing procedures will almost certainly be sufficient. But out of an abundance of caution we might also suggest the following:

1. Initials should be scratched onto the tape reel, since the tape canisters are readily interchangeable.
2. In marking a magnetic disk, you can scratch your identification initials and date onto the metallic bottom.
3. It might be a good idea to scratch the tape identification number onto the reel or disk as well. Masking tape or gum labels might easily be switched.
4. Some computer centers have perforators that can be used to put a "permanent" marking on the tape itself. This could serve as a safeguard against any suggestion that the tapes had been switched from one reel to another. But perforated labels can always be clipped off and a new perforation substituted. So there is no avoiding some dependence on the presumption of regularity.

5. Be warned that some computer systems do not use inter-changeable tapes or magnetic disks. Their memory core may be a nontransferrable, easily erasable, machine component. If the company is not cooperative, you may have to foot a large bill for computer time in order to run a complete print-out of data stored in the system.

6. If you already identified your potential defendants, and if they have retained counsel, you can probably forestall later objections by inviting the defense to participate as an observer whenever scientific tests are made on the tape and whenever a key evidence tape is used to produce a copy.

Prosecuting a complex computer fraud can be a costly proposition. If you are not budgeted to retain outside consultants, you may be able to borrow a computer expert and/or computer facilities from another agency within your governmental unit.

ADMISSIBILITY OF COMPUTER EVIDENCE

The preceding sections discussed some of the more important laws and procedures that are fundamentally important in the admissibility of computer evidence into a court of law. In this section we would like to recap some of the essential ideas, so readers will have a basic understanding of what is involved. Computer evidence will legally be judged on the following principles:

- Evidence must be relevant.
- Evidence must have a foundation laid for its introduction into court proceedings.
- Evidence must be obtained by legally permissible means.
- Evidence must be properly identified.
- Evidence must be preserved in such a way as to prove that it has not been tampered with or altered because of storage conditions.

Relevance. Relevant evidence includes proof that fraud has taken place, documentation as to the amount taken and the time period over which the loss occurred, identification of the acts or methods used to perpetrate the fraud, proof linking suspects with the acts and methods used, and possibly proof as to the suspects' motives for perpetrating the fraud. Matters unrelated to the fraud are not evidence and neither is documentation that the suspect is generally base or immoral.

Documentation of the facts of the crime would normally result from the investigation. These facts would establish what and how much has been taken, when it was taken, and how. In some cases the crime might consist of entering one big transaction or stealing one particular item. In other instances, numerous transactions over an extended period of time must be identified in transaction journals and other computer printouts. It may be that a program that has been fraudulently altered will have to be discovered and submitted as evidential material.

Evidence linking the suspect with a crime normally comes out as part of the investigation procedure. In computer-related cases, there may be no physical evidence such as fingerprints that would link the suspect with the crime. What you may possibly be able to do is prove that the suspect was able to perpetrate the crime because he was responsible for preparing input, maintaining programs, or because he had access to the means used to enter data and programs onto the computer.

If a forgery of manual documents is involved, analysis of handwriting and typing samples can be legally admissible. Even if the documents have been partially destroyed, scientific methods exist for their authentication. The value of such evidence will be highly dependent upon the professional qualifications of the expert rendering an opinion during his testimony.

Another way of linking an individual with a computer crime is to prove that the individual received financial benefits associated with the crime. This may be proved through the use of what investigators and prosecutors sometimes refer to as the techniques of "follow the dollar" and "follow the paper trail" in order to get to the bottom of the crime. If the perpetrator is doing something like putting money directly into his own account, these techniques will enable that evidence to be traced and authenticated. More often than not, the perpetrator may be committing his fraudulent acts under an assumed name or names. In such an instance, law-enforcement or other surveillance techniques might be used to establish the whereabouts and activities of the suspected perpetrator (see chapter 12).

Legal foundation for computer evidence. Once the computer case comes to trial, you will have to use appropriate witnesses and show that the computer records and materials introduced as evidence are trustworthy.

In the case of *United States v. Russo* [480 F. 2d 1228(6th Cir. 1973), *cert. denied*, 414 U.S. 1157], an appeal was denied, and in doing so the court concluded with this statement:

> The witnesses . . . were qualified as experts by education, training and experience and they showed a familiarity with the use of the particular computers in question. The mechanics of input control to assure accuracy were detailed at great length as was the description of the nature of the information which went into the machine and upon which its printout was based (*Id.* 480 F. 2d at 1241).

In what has been called a veritable bible for trial counsel dealing with computer evidence, Roy N. Freed lists the following elements of proof as the essential foundation for admitting EDP materials (16 *Am. Jur., Proof of Facts*, 273–350):

1. Identity of the record custodian.
2. Familiarity of the record custodian with machine accounting procedures.
3. Description of machine accounting procedures.
4. Precautions taken to prevent errors.
5. Correction of errors discovered.
6. Explanation of the reason magnetic tapes are erased.
7. Establishment of usual and customary business methods.
8. Explanation of the reason for elimination of unnecessary machine operations.

These elements of proof should be presented in such a way so that they are understood by judge and jury. The explanations by experts relative to the equipment and other data processing procedures can and should be presented in a manner that is understandable to laymen.

Legally permissible means. Perhaps the best way to understand legally permissible means of obtaining evidence is to consider some of the methods that are not legally permissible:

- Obtaining evidence in violation of the Bill of Rights (notably procedures that violate Amendments 4, 5, and 14 of the U.S. Constitution).
- Unlawful search and seizure (obtaining evidence under false pretenses, or seizing it without a valid search warrant or the custodian's consent).
- Wiretapping, hidden cameras, and similar secret recording devices (except when the use has been ordered for a specific purpose by a court of law).
- Access to personal data such as bank records (without either a search warrant or the subject's permission) is a procedure that is legally questionable at best.
- Forced confessions and statements given without the "Miranda warning." For law-enforcement officers, it is important that suspects in custody be explicitly informed of their rights. Not so clear-cut is whether this warning applies to interrogation of individuals not in police custody and by private citizens. The Miranda warning explains to someone that he has the right to remain silent, tells him that anything he says can

and will be used against him in a court of law, explains that he can talk to a lawyer and have the lawyer present during questioning, and lets him know that he can get a lawyer, even if he cannot personally afford to hire one. In waiving these rights, the person is asked whether he understands each one of them, and, with these rights in mind, whether he wishes to talk with the law-enforcement official.

Evidence identification. As discussed in an earlier section of the chapter, computer-based evidence such as tapes, printouts, program listings, documentation, source documents, and other forms of evidential material must be properly identified by the law-enforcement official who seizes it. The marking of such evidence should be done promptly, and if there is any volume of evidence, a log should be maintained as an index to all the evidential material seized.

Preservation of evidence. After evidence is seized and properly identified, it is important that, as it changes hands and goes into an evidence storage facility, it be handled under strict control. Under conditions of excessive heat, humidity, or magnetic radiation, tapes are subject to alterations by environmental conditions, so care should be taken as to where they are stored. Needless to say, these items of evidence should be kept under lock and key, and it is a good idea to have a computer expert participate at each step to avoid contamination of the evidence through accidental or possibly even deliberate means.

STATE COMPUTER FRAUD LAWS

With the advent of 18 U.S.C. 1028, the proposed federal computer fraud statute, which will have broad applicability in computer fraud cases, we would expect to see fewer cases prosecuted under state law than had been the case. Of course, it 'is quite possible for a computer fraud to take place within a state in such a manner that it does not violate federal criminal laws, and it would therefore be prosecuted under state laws. Prosecution under state laws varies with the state and locality having jurisdiction and with the nature of the crime itself.

In the following sections we will discuss some of these state laws as well as some principles about computer evidence that we believe are generally applicable under state laws.

In a survey of relevant state laws conducted by Susan H. Nycum,[2] numerous statutes are identified that might provide legal recourse.

[2] Susan H. Nycum, *The Criminal Law Aspects of Computer Abuse: Applicability of State Penal Laws to Computer Abuse* (Menlo Park, Calif.: Stanford Research Institute, 1976).

The relevant law depends upon whether the perpetrator has used a remote access computer terminal or used direct physical access to the EDP installation in order to perpetrate the crime.

State laws pertaining to remote access by way of computer terminal

Where a perpetrator obtains access by way of a computer terminal, there are five types of state offenses that may apply:

- *Trade secret* laws exist in the states of California, New York, New Jersey, and Texas. Each of these states has its own provisions for the applicability of such laws and related penalties.
- *Larceny* statutes provide coverage in some of the states in the survey. The states of Pennsylvania, Massachusetts, and Illinois provide the greatest protection because trade secrets are specifically mentioned in the larceny law. In the states of New York, New Jersey, Texas, and California, prosecution under their larceny statutes would require the ability to prove that the item stolen was a thing of value.
- *Credit card abuse* legislation may provide protection in the states of New York, New Jersey, California, Pennsylvania, Virginia, Florida, Texas, Massachusetts, and Delaware, if the perpetrator used a false account number or identification code.
- *Theft of services* statutes may be applicable in Illinois, California, New York, Pennsylvania, Texas, Delaware, and the District of Columbia.
- *Telephone abuse* statutes of the states of California and Illinois may be applicable if the perpetrator uses a telephone connection in perpetrating the acts. However, the California statute may be generally inapplicable because of a judicially imposed limitation that the message be a false relay.

State laws involving direct physical EDP access

Where the perpetrator uses direct physical access to the computer installation in order to steal computer software or data, there are two types of statutes that may apply:

- *Burglary* statutes may apply in California, New York, Pennsylvania, Massachusetts, Illinois, Texas, Delaware, Florida, Virginia, New Jersey, and the District of Columbia. In many of the states, the statute applies whether or not forced entry was involved and even if the perpetrator had the privilege to enter the EDP installation.
- *Forgery* statutes may be applicable in California, New York, Delaware, Texas, Pennsylvania, and the District of Columbia, provided that the perpetrator used someone else's confidential access code to perpetrate the computer fraud.

Readers will recall that state laws may be passed to the extent that they are not in conflict with the provisions of the U.S. Constitution. In matters of computer fraud, it is the first ten amendments to the Constitution that provide citizens protection against potentially oppressive government. One of the very important protections is the guarantee of "due process of law." Much of this due process has to do with the way in which evidence may be obtained, and is further amplified as the result of court decisions.

In 1974, the National Conference of Commissioners on Uniform State Laws approved a revised version of the Uniform Rules of Evidence. The new uniform rules are very similar to the Federal Rules of Evidence. In general, most American courts that have heard cases involving computer evidence have not found it to be a problem as long as a proper foundation was laid for its admission. Among the common law jurisdictions, Mississippi led the way in admitting computer printouts as evidence, in a case previously cited in this chapter:

> The rules of evidence governing the admission of business records are of common law origin and have evolved case by case, and the Court should apply these rules consistent with the reality of current business methods. The law always seeks the best evidence and adjusts its rules to accommodate itself to the advancements of the age it serves. *King* v. *State ex rel. Murdock Acceptance Corporation* [222 So. 2d 393, 397 (Miss. 1969)].

Robert P. Bigelow, writing in the February 1977 issue of *Computer Law and Tax Report,* points out:

> There is a growing understanding among lawyers that there are many sources of error in computerized records. Anyone relying on computerized records must be prepared to show their accuracy.
>
> In one case a bottled gas manufacturer tried to collect a debt by introducing a computer prepared summary [actually a manually prepared recapitulation] into evidence without either producing or explaining why it did not produce original invoices. The defendant produced a number of cancelled checks in court which he claimed paid all of the bills; the gas company was thrown out of court [*Harned* v. *Credit Bureau of Gillette* (513 P. 2d 650, 5 C.L.S.R. 394–Wyo. 1973)].
>
> The validity of the programming, the security of computer operations, and the other controls that management should exercise, are important factors in determining the admissibility of computer records.
>
> Far more lawyers are learning the weak spots in computer systems and, when representing the defendants, look for opportunities to prove that the records were not properly maintained.[3]

[3] Robert P. Bigelow, "Computerized Accounts Receivable: Can You Prove Them in Court?" *Computer Law and Tax Report,* February 1977.

In the same issue of *Computer Law and Tax Report*, the Evidence Act of South Australia is cited. A section of this statute provides the EDP manager with a good checklist of what his company's lawyer may have to prove in order to get computerized records admitted into evidence. American companies should look at the standards of South Australia, as they are excellent guides that would, it appears, meet the standards of many U.S. courts. These guidelines are set forth below.

- The computer is correctly programmed and regularly used to produce output of the same kind as tendered in evidence.
- The data from which the output is produced by the computer are systematically prepared on the basis of information that would normally be accepted in a court of law as evidence of the statements or representations contained in or constituted by the output.
- In the case of the output tendered in evidence, there is, on the evidence before the court, no reasonable cause to expect any departure from the system or any error in preparation of the data.
- The computer has not, during the period extending from the time of the introduction of the data to that of the production of the output, been subject to a malfunction that might reasonably be expected to affect the accuracy of the output.
- During the period there have been no alterations to the mechanism or the process of the computer that might reasonably be expected adversely to affect the accuracy of the output.
- Records have been kept, by a responsible person in charge of the computer, of alterations to the mechanism and processes of the computer during that period.
- There is no reasonable cause to believe that the accuracy or validity of the output had been adversely affected by the use of any improper process or procedure or by inadequate safeguards in the use of the computer.

LAWSUITS AGAINST INDEPENDENT AUDITORS AND COMPANY DIRECTORS

For the most part, previous sections of this chapter have looked at computer fraud as a crime, punishable under federal and state criminal laws. There are other kinds of laws that may come into play in connection with computer fraud. One type is what may be termed *agency or administrative law*, an example of which would be the Federal Securities Law, which is enforced by the Securities and Exchange Commission (SEC). Another type is *civil law*, involving contracts (not necessarily written) and torts (which enable persons who have been wronged to collect damage from wrongdoers). Lawsuits against independent auditors, members of a company's board of directors, and corporate officers are most often based on agency and civil laws.

Federal securities law

In large-scale computer frauds, it may be that the shareholders of a company whose stock is publicly traded will, in the end, be the big losers. Since there are federal laws designed to protect such shareholders, and which regulate stock exchanges and the conditions under which securities may be sold, these laws have come into play at one stage or another where computer fraud has been involved. Accordingly, we would like to briefly acquaint you with one of the pertinent laws and some of the principles that have evolved from cases.

SEC rule 10(b)-5

This regulation seems to speak for itself (as it applies to independent auditors, directors, corporate officers, and others) and reads as follows:

> It shall be unlawful for any person, directly or indirectly, by the use of any means or instrumentality of interstate commerce, or of the mails or any facility of any national securities exchange,
> (a) to employ any device, scheme, or artifice to defraud,
> (b) to make any untrue statement of a material fact, or to omit to state a material fact necessary in order to make the statements made, in light of the circumstances under which they were made, not misleading, or
> (c) to engage in any act, practice, or course of business which would operate as a fraud or deceit upon any person in connection with the purchase or sale of any security.

A number of other regulations under the Federal Securities Law, in a sense, are amplifications or restatements of Rule 10(b)-5. For example, Rule 14(a)-9 deals with solicitations by proxy, as might be involved in a corporate acquisition, and carries similar requirements.

Cases involving independent auditors

In what has been called a landmark decision, the U.S. Supreme Court in its first decision on an "auditors case" ruled that there had to be proof of a defendant's *intent to deceive* as a prerequisite to the imposition of liabilities under many of the provisions of the Federal Securities Law. This decision was handed down in the *Hochfelder* case, which was decided in March 1976.

However, in a case that was heard in a lower federal court subsequent to Hochfelder, known as the *Standard Knitting Mills* case, the court decided that an auditor's *failure to reveal significant weaknesses in EDP controls constituted a misstatement of material fact,* and therefore found the auditor to be in violation of SEC regulations. This case involved a corporate acquisition where the auditors were asked to give an opinion on financial statements, and failed to *qualify their opinion* regarding weaknesses in the company's EDP and other internal controls as revealed through prior audits. The court concluded that the defendant (the independent auditing firm) acted willfully, with intent to deceive and manipulate, in reckless disregard for the truth. In so doing, the court determined that the failure to fully disclose the significant weaknesses in controls was an intent to mislead users of a proxy statement.

In an informative article on the subject of "Legal Implications of EDP Deficiencies," which discussed the Standard Knitting Mills decision, the authors summarized as follows:

> . . . the federal court took the first steps toward defining these [auditors'] legal responsibilities. If later applied, this decision should affect the auditing profession in two ways. First, the Standard Knitting Mills decision could place severe limitation on the use of "auditing around the computer" as a replacement for adequate evaluation and testing of EDP controls. Second, the Standard Knitting Mills decision should broaden the concept "full financial disclosure" employed by the public accountant in the preparation of audited financial statements. Although this first statement of the courts may have a significant effect on the EDP auditing environment, the public accountant can be relatively sure that this is only a precursor to future legal decisions.[4]

The sequence of events

Whenever a major loss occurs due to computer fraud, there may be a cascading effect to the lawsuits that are brought in connection with the matter.

First, the perpetrator(s) is caught, convicted under criminal law, and goes to jail. Typically, all the embezzled money has been squandered and the perpetrator has no way of making restitution. Or, in a securities fraud such as Equity Funding, the perpetrators use the computer to produce fraudulent data which were the basis for showing attractive earnings, which in turn made the company's stock attractive at higher and higher prices per share. Upon the disclosure of the fraud, the price per share plummets, and shareholders lose money.

Second, the Securities and Exchange Commission looks into the matter to see if Federal Securities Law was violated, and, if so, it prosecutes a case.

Third, the shareholders and or other injured parties (perhaps as a class action) with their lawyers look around for "deep pockets"

---

[4] John O. Mason and Jonathan J. Davies, "Legal Implications of EDP Deficiencies," *The CPA Journal*, May 1977, pp. 21–24.

to sue for damages under civil law, often basing their case on what came out of the proceedings in the criminal case against the perpetrators and in the SEC case against the independent auditors and directors.

The people who are sued are those who might be able to come up with the money if the shareholders' suit against them results in a judgment that they must compensate the injured parties. Independent auditors and directors, by virtue of their ability to pay and the insurance they carry, are typically the targets of such suits for damages. Since the lawyer representing the injured parties may be earning a fee that is contingent on the amount of money actually received and since recovery of money is the real object of the action, the real crooks are seldom defendants. Suing them would not pay, and the use of legal action mainly for revenge is strictly for amateurs.

**The best defense
is offense**

As Roy Freed points out in his article "Computer Fraud—A Management Trap" (*Business Horizons*, June 1969), corporate officers may legally incur *personal* liability both to the company and to its stockholders if, through their neglect or oversight, a major fraud should occur.

As we previously pointed out, the reason directors, independent auditors, and occasionally corporate officers are sued is their ability to make good if a money judgment goes against them. Of course, the plaintiffs in such a case must show that reckless, irresponsible, or grossly negligent acts of the defendants were involved. Some of the issues that may come up in these cases are discussed below.

Application of auditing standards. Independent auditors in the U.S. have auditing standards promulgated by the American Institute of Certified Public Accountants (AICPA). Adherence to these standards must be demonstrated in the auditor's defense of the lawsuit. As you might imagine, the lawyer for the plaintiff will be more or less expert on these standards and will try to show, through vigorous cross-examination, that the standards were not properly applied and/or the audit was inadequately supervised and performed. A number of the newer AICPA standards deal with computer systems, and the auditor who does not take them seriously does so at his own peril. In general, if the plaintiffs cannot show the court convincing evidence that the auditor failed to adhere to the standards, the auditor will ordinarily win the case. Of course, the auditor will have to bear the legal expense to defend himself unless he decides to countersue the plaintiffs to recover his expenses. There have been occasions where auditors have filed a countersuit on the basis that the lawsuit brought by the plaintiffs was capricious, and such cases have been decided in favor of auditors.

Clearly, in the application of auditing standards, we are not talking about cases where it is ultimately shown that auditors conspired with other parties named in the lawsuit to defraud shareholders and others. To such parties who are adjudged guilty of such wrongdoing, we offer no advice.

Materiality. In reviewing the financial statements of a company, external auditors do not undertake to uncover fraud unless it is of such proportions as to have material impact on the fair presentation of the financial statements, which are the representation of management. As you might imagine, the fee charged for an audit depends on its scope and the number of man-hours the auditors have to spend to render an opinion, not to detect fraud.

An experiment conducted by a managing partner of a large public accounting firm illustrates that management would generally be unwilling to pay the price for an audit in sufficient depth to discover frauds of all types. The partner told some of his medium-size clients that his firm would be willing to perform an audit in sufficient depth so that his firm would be in a position to indemnify the clients against undiscovered fraud at any level of their organization. The clients were enthusiastic until they learned that the audit fee would be $1 million as compared with their usual fee of $50,000.[5]

Common practice is to define an amount as material if it affects net income by 10% or more and not material if it affects net income by 5% or less. In the interval from 5 to 10%, careful analysis of the issue under study needs to be performed.[6] Alternatively, a decision on the materiality of a particular fact may also involve a judgment call which centers on whether a reasonable man would have assigned significance to the fact in making his ultimate decision.

Prudence. Prudence is by no means a clear-cut term. A prudent man has been defined as one who exercises *care, skill, and caution.* Although these terms are subjective, some implications can be drawn that apply directly to company directors and officers. Care implies that the prudent man makes decisions based on all the information available, not solely on the advice of others. Skill implies that individuals will be held responsible for exercising special skills they possess that are relevant to the prevention of fraud losses. Caution implies a lack of risk taking, precluding even risks that an individual might take if only his personal assets were at stake.[7]

The typical thinking on prudence is that prudent directors will

[5] John R. Thompson, "The Big 8—the Disclosure Mess," *MBA Magazine,* November 1976, pp. 21–23.

[6] Diane P. Barnes, "Materiality—An Illusive Concept," *Management Accounting,* October 1976, pp. 19–21.

[7] Paul I. Kampner, "When Is a Prudent Man Prudent?" *Management Review,* June 1976, pp. 37–40.

select prudent management, who will, in turn, establish a strong internal control system. In order to monitor management's system of internal control, the board of directors will have internal and external auditors, and other outside experts, make periodic reports regarding the status of internal control and will demand that management act on any significant control weakness cited by the auditors.

The results of financial audits by independent public accountants may be accompanied by a "management letter" which will point out a number of internal control weaknesses that the company should review and determine what follow-up action is needed. If these letters are consistently ignored, as may be determined when lawyers introduce such letters in evidence in order to prove a point, they might be the basis for evidence that management has acted imprudently. On the other hand, evidence to the effect that each and every one of the points was seriously followed up would tend to indicate prudent regard for the weaknesses brought to their attention.

Negligence. Negligence occurs when an individual has failed to exercise prescribed duties or has failed to carry out those duties in a prudent manner. Negligence may arise because of either nonfeasance or malfeasance, and may be the result of an error of commission or omission on the part of the officers, directors, or auditors who are defending a lawsuit.

Directors may be negligent if they fail to require independent audits or if they do not require management to act upon the results of audits. If internal auditors call management's attention to certain weaknesses in internal controls, and the directors fail to heed that warning, they would be negligent. Similarly, if an audit turned up a significant discrepancy and the directors or officers chose to overlook that discrepancy, they would be considered negligent. Independent auditors can be adjudged negligent if they fail to detect material fraud, particularly where it is shown that they failed to follow generally accepted auditing standards.

Courts will be looking at the question of negligence in order to decide whether it was of such a nature as to be considered "ordinary" or "gross." *Ordinary negligence* normally involves an act or a failure to act that resulted from simple carelessness or basic human error. At the other extreme, *gross negligence* involves what the court finds to be a reckless, willful, or wanton act or failure to act in view of the circumstances. As you might imagine, the court will tend to "throw the book" at those who are judged guilty of gross negligence, whereas a somewhat lighter view is taken of ordinary negligence. In computer fraud cases, the existence of *scienter*, or intent, on the part of the defendants may hinge on whether the negligence is adjudged to be ordinary or gross, the implication being that gross negligence translates to intent.

Three areas of cooperation with law-enforcement agencies are suggested:

- Maintaining contact and generally cooperative relations.
- Prosecuting cases of computer fraud.
- Cooperating with legally acceptable requests for assistance.

Maintaining contact

By maintaining contact, we mean that your auditors and computer security people should get to know the state and local law enforcement people who are responsible for investigating white-collar crimes and develop appropriate contacts with the Federal Bureau of Investigation. This will open up channels of communications for an exchange of information and help your company become aware of the latest problems and trends in connection with computer fraud. By maintaining contact when there is no problem, you are also assured of better help when you do need it, in the sense that investigators will be more aware of your problems and concern. This does not involve playing politics in order to get law-enforcement assistance, only that the more they know about your situation, the better able they will be to mobilize resources to protect your interests.

Our experience has been that law-enforcement officials who are specialists in the area of white-collar crime are highly professional, interesting to talk with, and able to provide advice on an informal basis. You should not expect them to serve as consultants to your company, as this would be a violation of their responsibilities as public servants paid by all taxpayers.

Prosecuting detected cases

Your company's role in bringing in law-enforcement officials to prosecute cases of computer fraud provides two benefits. First, your employees and prospective employees will see that your company is not a soft touch or sucker for embezzlers and others intent on committing fraud. The deterrent effect of this is powerful indeed. The second benefit is that of knowing that you have lived up to your responsibility as a citizen and have acted in a manner that preserves the American ideals for this generation and for future generations. Crime, need we point out, is a blight on a society and your role in supporting law-enforcement and judicial efforts is all that stands between democracy and a state of either tyranny or anarchy.

Cooperating with requests

Many companies receive occasional inquiries from law-enforcement agencies regarding customers, vendors, and employees. While it is true that in the recent past, certain investigatory and intelligence agencies have gotten a bad name because of their invasion of personal privacy, cooperation under most circumstances is highly desirable.

In deciding on the manner in which to cooperate, you will want to consider several factors:

- Privacy legislation that might forbid supplying certain information that has been requested.
- An understanding of the purpose for which information is requested or cooperation is sought.
- Whether or not for the protection of all concerned, you should request that law-enforcement officials obtain a search warrant or subpoena before supplying actual information.

12

Investigative Procedures for Computer Fraud

The vast majority of computer frauds are crimes through which the victimized company (1) suffers direct dollar losses, (2) is placed at a competitive disadvantage, and/or (3) experiences a loss in business as a result of diminished public trust and confidence. Some of the investigative methods discussed in this chapter are intended to enable a company to act promptly, on its own behalf, when there are suspicious situations—the idea being to minimize ongoing losses. Virtually all the methods are applicable to law-enforcement officials assigned to investigate computer fraud cases—their objective is to see the perpetrators brought to justice.

Computer frauds, like jigsaw puzzles, may be difficult to solve and can require special approaches to unravel and prove a case. This chapter will show you:

- How to recognize clues to the existence of computer fraud.

- How to plan and organize an investigation.

- How to apply traditional covert methods.

- How to conduct interviews and interrogations of witnesses and suspects.

- Special investigative tools and how to use them.
- Means of tracing money and benefits of doing so.
- How to package a case for successful prosecution.

Part of this chapter was adapted from information found in *The Investigation of White-Collar Crime: A Manual for Law Enforcement Agencies.*[1]

CLUES TO THE EXISTENCE OF FRAUD

There are a number of conditions that can be symptomatic of computer fraud. Only an investigation can determine whether or not fraud actually exists. Some of the more important clues to watch for are:

- Unexplained activities on computer operations logs.
- Unresolved exceptions on exception reports.
- Out-of-balance conditions.
- Customer/vendor complaints.

More information about clues can be found in Chapter 9 and other chapters of this book.

Unexplained activities on computer operations logs

Activities appearing on logs without supporting records of authorization and without being related to scheduled computer production activities may be symptomatic of computer fraud. Many installations have job accounting systems that record every job processed and the time of day and date of processing. If these logs reveal that processing of an application took place at an unscheduled time or more frequently than prescribed, and if no record of an authorized rerun exists for that date, it is possible that an extra run was made for purposes of fraud. Investigation of the integrity of data files maintained by the application is called for. If the system produces negotiable documents, investigation of whether or not extra documents were produced is also indicated.

Many on-line systems have a facility for automatically recording attempted security breaches. If your system has such a feature, all items listed should be investigated. Repeated attempts at security breaches may mean that someone is looking for a trap door into the system. Lack of repetition of security breaches does not necessarily mean that the ones recorded were accidental. Another possibility is that the perpetrator succeeded in finding a way into the system.

Logs of file access are common in many installations. Accesses

[1] Herbert Edelhertz et al., *The Investigation of White-Collar Crime: A Manual for Law Enforcement Agencies, Law Enforcement Assistance Administration,* (Washington, D.C.: U.S. Department of Justice, 1977).

to files stored off-line in a library are normally recorded manually by the librarian. If review of such logs reveals that files were released at unscheduled times or on unusual dates, the situation bears investigation. Similarly, if the logs reveal that files were out of the library for much longer than usual on a given occasion and no supporting record exists to explain the reason—machine problems, scheduling difficulties, or whatever—there is a possibility of fraudulent activity against the file or copying of the file to sell the data.

When files and data bases are stored on-line in the computer, automatic logging of all accesses is fairly common. If such logs are maintained in your installation, they should be reviewed to make sure that all accesses can be explained by production processing or other authorized activity. Any unexplainable accesses may represent file manipulation or attempts to steal confidential data.

When programs are stored on-line, for example in time-sharing systems, logs of all accesses and modification dates may exist. If such logs are maintained for your applications, the entries should be compared to records of authorized processing and maintenance activity. If differences exist and if the supporting records are accurately maintained, the discrepancies may be due to unauthorized processing or modification.

Unresolved exceptions

Unresolved items on exception reports or on transaction journals mean either errors or fraud. In either case, the situation could mean a loss to your company and is a danger signal. Operations in which there are many errors and delays are good places to look for masquerading fraud. Even if the problems do not involve fraud, their continued existence can create a temptation.

Transaction rejects. Transactions may be rejected either because there is no match on account number or because the data items on the transaction reflect unacceptable values or illogical combinations. Most rejects are caused by errors, but they also can be caused intentionally. Some of the reasons why a reject might be caused intentionally include:

- Desire to avoid paying a bill.
- Desire to prevent recording inventory acquisitions so that after the corresponding amount is stolen, the computer record will be in balance with the physical count.
- Desire to prevent recording termination of an employee or death of a pensioner so that payments can be diverted to the perpetrator.
- In a monetary transaction, desire to cover up a fraudulent transaction of equal amount and still have the system appear to be in balance.

Unpaid balances. Most past-due balances reflect either inability to pay or disputes between your company and the customer. Another possibility is customer or employee dishonesty. It is possible to create accounts for fictitious persons and record charges against these accounts in order to cover inventory thefts. The perpetrator may either choose to continue charging against the fictitious account until it is closed, or he may put in a transaction to record an ongoing dispute and continue charging against the account indefinitely.

Consumer credit legislation stipulates that if a customer notifies your company in writing of a disputed item on a bill, there will be a grace period for investigation of the dispute, and, during that grace period, payment is not required. If your billing is automated, chances are that your system keeps track of existing customer disputes. An astute embezzler can exploit that fact by continually advancing the dates involved so that the grace period is never over.

One final tack that an embezzler can take with unpaid balances is to charge them off to bad debt quickly. This matter is covered elsewhere in this book, so we will not dwell on it here.

Unusual discounts/prices. Some systems permit processing of transactions reflecting unusual discounts or prices on the theory that the business environment requires some flexibility for salesmen. If that situation is true for some of your applications, most of the exception items falling in this category are probably valid. Some of the exceptions may be errors and another percentage may be fraudulent. If the exceptions remain unexplained, there is no way of telling whether or not embezzlement is involved.

Incomplete or invalid data on master file. Sometimes transaction rejects are caused by incomplete or invalid data on the master file or data base. The cause may be erroneous file maintenance or account creation, or it may be deliberate activity designed to avoid paying a bill or to cover inventory thefts. Our concern is that these situations should be researched and corrected promptly. Laxity costs your company money regardless of whether the problem is error or fraud.

**Out-of-balance
conditions**

Chronic out-of-balance conditions in an accounting system indicate potentially serious trouble. The underlying cause may be errors or fraud. Either way, if you allow the situation to continue, it will present a strong temptation for employees to steal under the assumption that a slightly larger out-of-balance condition will be tolerated.

Out-of-balance conditions can arise in several ways. One cause is failure to resolve rejected transactions. Another cause is processing too many or too few transactions. Discrepancies in the amount on a transaction can also cause out-of-balance conditions.

Bogus program changes are also a possibility. The perpetrator may have made a program change causing the program to exclude certain transactions from the control totals. Such a change would create an out-of-balance condition between transactions authorized as input versus transactions reported as processed by the computer.

Customer/vendor complaints

Complaints about bills may mean either errors or frauds. Either way, your company stands to lose money. Investigation of all complaints should be done promptly. The volume of complaints can also be a danger signal. If the volume suddenly slips way above historic levels, it may be a signal that employees are manipulating accounts. If the additional complaint volume is due to honest errors, allowing it to continue may create temptation to perpetrate fraud.

Even if there has been no sudden increase in volume of complaints, the magnitude can be a cause for concern. Historically high complaint volumes can mean that fraud has been ongoing or they can mean persistent accuracy problems. Either way, significant levels of complaints should be treated with great concern.

PLANNING THE INVESTIGATION

The first step in an investigation is to formulate a work plan. Computer frauds are sometimes complex crimes, and planning improves the effectiveness of investigative activity. The work plan should include a statement of the facts leading to the investigation, questions to be answered, scope, resources required, and some consideration as to how the case will ultimately be presented to a prosecutor.

Considerations that will be of help in formulating the plan include:

- Common characteristics of white-collar crime.
- Potential perpetrators.
- Sources of information.
- Personnel selection and possible need for experts.

Common characteristics of white-collar crime

If the right mix of characteristics is present, there is a high probability of both a criminal violation and a civil remedy. Although it is not necessary to support every one of the following characteristics with evidence, consideration of each characteristic will help decide the scope and nature of the investigation:

- *Intent*—to commit a wrongful act or to achieve a purpose inconsistent with law or public policy.

- *Disguise of purpose*—falsities and misrepresentations employed to accomplish the scheme.

344

• *Reliance*—by the offender on the ignorance or carelessness of the victim.

• *Concealment*—of the crime.

Of these characteristics, the matter of *intent* is often the most critical in proving a computer fraud case. Since many frauds masquerade as errors, there is a possibility that the perpetrator, when confronted, will claim that there was an error rather than criminal intent. That possibility should be anticipated during the investigation and suitable evidence gathered to disprove such a claim.

Potential perpetrators

Depending on how the case came to light and on how the evidence is being gathered, it may or may not be clear as to just what individuals might be implicated as suspects. Sometimes, the method(s) used to perpetrate the fraud will emerge out of investigative activity, but not be linked to particular suspects. Figure 12-1 indicates some of the possibilities that might be considered in this connection. Readers should be aware that the "opportunity levels" shown in Figure 12-1 may be very different, depending on the size of the computer installation and on the nature of the security and control provisions that exist in the environment. If, for example, the data processing manager, application programmer, and computer operator are the same person (as is sometimes the case in smaller installations), the basic segregation of duty concepts underlying the opportunity levels shown would not exist. Hence, the reader would want to change the entries in Figure 12-1 to reflect such situations.

Sources of information

Two sources of information that should not be overlooked in planning an investigation are the victim's own records and records maintained by third parties.

Victim's records. Both manual and computerized records should be considered as potential sources of information. Although every transaction should be recorded in these records, some relevant records may have been destroyed if the perpetrator is an insider. Even so, it is unlikely that the perpetrator would have been able to destroy both the manual and computerized records of fraudulent transactions.

Third parties. Investigators should bear in mind that both the victim and the perpetrator do business with suppliers and others whose records will reflect what should be in the books of the subjects. Many such third parties are not in as sensitive relationships with their

Method	Data Processing Manager	Systems Programmer	Applications Programmer	Computer Operator	Computer Equip. Maint. Engineers	User Management	User Personnel	Outsiders and Former Employees
• Manipulations of systems software to create error conditions used to conceal fraud	B	A	B	C	C	C	C	C
• Manipulations of systems software to disable security and protective features within operating systems and data base management software	B	A	B	C	C	C	C	C
• Disclosure of security and protective features of the system to outsiders	A	A	A	B	C	B	C	B
• Manipulation of application programs to create error conditions used to conceal fraud	B	A	A	B	C	C	C	C
• Manipulation of application programs to bypass controls and exception reporting that are intended to detect fraud	B	B	A	B	C	B	C	C
• Substitution of application programs that have been manipulated for fraudulent purposes	B	A	A	A	C	C	C	C
• Copying data files containing sensitive information and selling such files to competitors or others	B	A	B	A	C	B	B	C
• Using test or utility programs to examine, alter, or copy data files	B	A	A	B	B	B	B	C
• Disabling security or protective features of computer hardware and terminals	C	B	C	B	A	C	C	C
• Impersonation of a bona fide user	B	A	B	B	C	B	B	A
• Violations and noncompliance with internal control and transaction authorization procedures	C	C	B	B	C	A	A	C
• Falsifying own data files for the purpose of deceiving third parties	B	B	B	C	C	A	A	C
• Penetration of operating systems to alter programs and data files, and to perform unauthorized functions	C	A	B	C	B	C	C	A
• Manipulations of input transactions	C	C	C	B	C	A	A	B
• Alteration or destruction of output containing evidence of fraud	B	C	C	A	B	A	A	C

Figure 12-1

Potential Perpetrators and Opportunities to Use Fraudulent Methods

Method	Data Processing Manager	Systems Programmer	Applications Programmer	Computer Operator	Computer Equip. Maint. Engineers	User Management	User Personnel	Outsiders and Former Employees
• Obliteration of data files containing evidence of falsified information	B	A	B	A	B	C	C	C
• Unauthorized use of computer terminals	B	A	B	C	C	A	A	A
• Abuse of managerial privileges such as control overrides and special adjustments	B	C	C	C	C	A	B	C
(Opportunity to use method: A = good, B = fair, C = poor)								

Figure 12-1 *Continued*

customers as are banks, telephone companies, and so on, and may be persuaded to disclose their own operations and records. Thus, a supplier can show his order and delivery records without being in the sensitive position of a telephone company voluntarily disclosing with whom a customer was talking.

In seeking records from third parties that require a subpoena, as may be the case with respect to banks, utility companies, telephone companies, and others, it is advisable to make contact in advance with an officer of the institution whose records are being subpoenaed. Since the investigator may have to make more than one visit, it is important to develop good relations from the outset. Advance notification may prevent the possible alarming effects that a surprise visit could have.

Investigators who fail to develop a rapport with these institutions will find a negative attitude in response to their requests for records. Even with a search warrant, without this rapport, the investigator will find himself searching through vast, complicated files of records without assistance.

Appendix L is a guide to third-party sources of information and the types of information that can be obtained from each source. Records maintained by banks and credit card companies are rich third-party sources. Further guidance on how to use these sources is contained in Appendix M. An illustration of how third-party records have been used in actual cases is presented later in this chapter.

Specialists in law, accounting, computers, and other fields may be required in a computer fraud investigation. The investigator should not overlook the availability of advice from such specialists in planning the investigation.

Lawyers. Investigators should assume that their grasp of the law as it pertains to computer crime is weak. The law is still being formulated and relatively few cases have been successfully prosecuted to date. For these reasons, the overall effectiveness of investigative teams can be greatly enhanced by having a lawyer serve as a full-time or part-time team member.

Accountants. During the investigation, accountants may be needed to interpret financial transactions and record keeping practices. Accountants may also be needed at a later date as expert witnesses for the prosecution.

Computer experts. Computer expertise will be needed throughout the case. In the early stages, computer experts can often highlight the most promising starting points for an investigation. Later, computer experts can assist in harnessing the computer for investigative purposes, a matter discussed in more detail later in this chapter. Once the case goes to court, computer experts may be required to give testimony on matters pertaining to their speciality.

Others. Where the required special expertise is not readily available to the investigative team, help should be sought from government agencies, independent consultants, private business, and personal contacts. Even if the outsiders are not experienced in investigative procedure, they will be helpful once they understand what is suspected, the kinds of information that will be useful, and the suspect's probable modus operandi. The investigator who operates under the premise that the required expertise must come from within his department stunts his own growth and limits the success of his team.

Computer crime activities sometimes flow across national boundaries, and information and evidence will have to be sought abroad— using the facilities of foreign police agencies. When the trail leads abroad, the unit can call on the services of Interpol, an international criminal police organization that has experience in helping with white-collar crime investigations.

Interpol will help the unit by arranging for *voluntary* cooperation in more than 120 countries abroad. Such assistance covers a broad range, including, but not limited to, criminal history checks, locating suspects, fugitives, and witnesses, and even full investigations that could lead to arrests and extraditions. Where such help is needed, the investigative unit should contact Interpol by letter addressed to the agency at Room 1116, Main Treasury Building, Washington, D.C. 20220.

The letter of request should briefly state the nature of the investigation or assistance required, and from whom assistance is sought. No special form is needed. If the unit is not certain as to who should be contacted abroad, Interpol will advise. If the matter is of great urgency, and delay would render assistance meaningless, or less valuable, Interpol should be telephoned at the U.S. Main Treasury Building in Washington, D.C.

There is no charge for Interpol assistance. The United States office is located within the U.S. Department of the Treasury and is staffed by personnel from federal law enforcement agencies (Customs; Secret Service; Drug Enforcement Administration; Bureau of Alcohol, Tobacco and Firearms).

Another potential source of assistance in investigating abroad is embassies—both U.S. and foreign—who may have law-enforcement specialists-attaches to advise.

Within the United States, state and federal (FBI) experts can be called upon for assistance. Readers who are inclined to be reluctant to call upon law-enforcement agencies for assistance are reminded of the following quote from the late J. Edgar Hoover:

> One effective deterrent to the individual contemplating a fraud is the sure knowledge that his crime will be reported to the authorities promptly upon discovery. Business and professional people can do much to make embezzlement and similar crimes a risky business by cooperating with those agencies whose duties are to investigate these schemes.[2]

Training of law-enforcement investigators may be obtained from the following sources:

California Department of Justice
Advanced Training Center
1771 Tribute Road
Sacramento, CA 95815

Ohio Organized Crime Prevention Council
State Office Tower
P.O. Box 1001
Columbus, OH 43216

Federal Bureau of Investigation
White-Collar Crime Training Program
Washington, DC 20535

[2] John Edgar Hoover, "FBI Investigation of Fraud," *Journal of Accountancy*, July 1965, p. 39.

New Jersey State Division of Criminal Justice
Prosecutor's Supervisory Section: "Investigation of Criminal
Financial Transactions"
Trenton, NJ 08600

COVERT METHODS Many of the covert methods traditionally used by investigators are relevant to computer fraud investigations. Among those are: intelligence, informants, undercover investigations, and surveillance.

Intelligence Traditionally, intelligence has served investigators in three ways:

Identifying suspects through references to known criminals. Although most computer frauds are not perpetrated by known criminals, this could change. Many prisons are giving computer programming and operation instruction to inmates, and experts have voiced concern regarding possible entry of organized crime into the computer fraud field. If the trend changes, traditional systems such as mug shots and fingerprint files may become important for computer fraud investigations.

Applying the experience of old timers as an educational resource for new investigators. Police work has always operated on the principle that seasoned investigators pass their experience on to rookies. This book is designed to accomplish a similar end by acquainting the reader with common computer fraud modi operandi and specialized investigative techniques.

Detecting suspicious activity. Logs, journals, and certain EDP auditing techniques discussed in earlier chapters serve this function. The office grapevine may also be a source of information such as who was asking questions about the check-printing program, who borrowed a copy of its documentation, and who was observed operating a terminal.

Informants Few crimes, except violent crimes in which the perpetrator is caught with the proverbial smoking gun, are solved by law-enforcement authorities without the use of informants. Anyone may be an informant, although informants are sometimes thought of as seedy characters having contact with known criminals. Informants are often paid by law-enforcement officials for any useful information that they provide and, over time, may become dependent upon these payments for their livelihood. Informants should be viewed as a breed of special consultant. Businessmen may have difficulty in using certain types of informants because of the disparity in their social outlook.

350

Undercover investigations

There are situations in which only an insider may be able to crack a computer fraud case. Management fraud is one example of such a situation. Another example is collusion between employees.

Undercover investigations can be risky for the investigator and should not be attempted by amateurs. Professional investigators always begin with a plan for gathering the necessary information. The plan specifically addresses the credibility of the investigator in the assumed role.

Usually, an undercover investigator poses as an employee. To avoid suspicion, employment of the investigator often takes place through the company's usual hiring practices. This means that the investigator needs an elaborate cover, including working experience, credentials, references, and appropriate outward mannerisms. If the investigator's dress or speech is inappropriate, his effectiveness will be impaired by suspicion.

Similarly, an investigator who appears too inquisitive will also arouse suspicion. Since the purpose of an investigation is to obtain information, a great deal of planning and experience are required in order to gather the necessary information without appearing overly inquisitive.

Surveillance

Traditional surveillance of suspects can serve two important purposes. First, it may help to establish a motive on the part of the suspect. For example, if the suspect is a keypunch operator and you observe him driving a luxury car, you may begin to suspect that the individual is living beyond his means.

Surveillance also helps to establish a link between the perpetrator and stolen funds. Consider, for instance, a disbursement fraud in which the perpetrator has set up dummy companies with post office boxes for mailing addresses. If the suspect were identified as the person picking up the checks at the mailbox, there would be a link between the suspect and the dummy companies.

When the investigator is having difficulty tracing the stolen funds, he should consider surveillance of the mail delivered to the suspect. Help from the Postal Inspection Service will be required to do this. The procedure is as follows:

> A law enforcement agency may ask the Postal Inspection Service to institute a mail cover for a 30-day period on all mail addressed to a firm or individual. (The period may be extended under certain circumstances.) The postmark and name and return address of the sender, if any, is recorded from the cover of the mail and furnished to the agent or agency making the request. Mail covers may only be placed with respect to investigations relating to: (a) the protection of national security; (b) efforts to locate a fugitive; and (c) efforts to secure evidence of the commission or attempted commission of a crime. This process can reveal an enormous amount of information

about the suspect, i.e., identity of banks, suppliers, advertising agents, customers and potential customers, and numerous other leads to additional sources of information. There are certain restrictions on its application, however, and it should not be requested routinely but reserved for investigations in which other sources have proved fruitless or impracticable. The local Postal Inspector is the point of contact for mail cover requests.[3]

Surveillance of warehouse or plant premises can pay off in certain kinds of inventory theft cases. A recent case illustrates the need for surveillance. Law-enforcement officials bought clothing items believed to have been stolen from the factory. When the law-enforcement officials took the clothing to factory management, the management confirmed that the items had been produced in the factory, but could find no record of the items in their computer system.

Since management could not prove ownership of the clothing, the chain of evidence was effectively broken and prosecution of the "fence" was impossible. Here, surveillance of the factory premises and exits would have been an appropriate step. Law-enforcement officials had determined that $15,000 worth of clothing from the factory was being sold monthly by the fence. Surveillance could have been used to catch the perpetrators removing the merchandise from the factory.

Photographic and electronic methods—wiretaps, tape recorders, and "bugs"—represent other forms of surveillance that should not be overlooked. In spite of past abuses that have given electronic surveillance a bad name, these methods can be extremely effective. The use of electronic surveillance is restricted legally to criminal cases.

Although wiretaps require a court order and written authorization from the U.S. Attorney General, the U.S. Supreme Court has ruled that federal district courts, on the basis of evidence no stronger than needed for a search warrant, have the authority to order telephone companies to install certain surveillance devices. The devices at issue in this decision, known as "pen registers," record the telephone numbers of outgoing calls but do not intercept the telephone message as wiretaps do.[4]

**INTERVIEWING
AND
INTERROGATION**

The differences between interviewing and interrogation are a matter of the purpose for which an individual is being questioned and the types of individuals involved in each situation. "Interviewing" is the correct term to use when the investigator is questioning witnesses who may have knowledge of events, persons, or evidence. "Interro-

[3] Charles A. Miller, *Economic Crime: A Prosecutor's Hornbook*, a project of the National District Attorneys Association, July, 1974, Note 84, pp. 76–77.

[4] Warren Weaver, Jr., "Justices Relax Rule on Phones in Surveillance," *The New York Times*, December 8, 1977, p. 1.

gation" is the correct term to use when questioning suspects or uncooperative witnesses.

The investigator should bear in mind the guidelines for admissibility of evidence presented in Chapter 11. The distinction between "interviewing" and "interrogation" is not always a clear one. In fact, the situation with regard to an interviewee may change over the course of an interview or an investigation. Because of this possibility, the investigator should always be prepared to stop long enough to give the Miranda warning, should that become necessary.

Interviewing

At the outset of an investigation, the investigator often possesses very little information concerning the crime. Possibly, the fact that a crime occurred has not been established. There may be a complaint, some physical evidence of a crime, or some intelligence suggesting that a crime has occurred.

Objectives of interviewing. The objectives of interviewing are to obtain:

- Information that establishes the essential elements of the crime.
- Leads for developing the case and gathering other evidence.
- Cooperation of victims and witnesses who may be asked to recount their experiences in court.
- Information concerning personal background and personal and economic motives of those to be considered for witnesses at the trial.

Planning an interview. Planning interviews is essential for computer fraud investigations, since the interviewer is likely to find schemes with which he is unfamiliar. Without proper planning, the investigator may neither understand the answers being given nor know what further information to request. Although it may be more convenient for the investigator to conduct interviews in his own office, there are some circumstances in which the interview should take place in the interviewee's office:

- The interviewee is more likely to have papers, appointment books, and so on, available for production if they become relevant to the interview. The interviewee may also be in a position to immediately call on coworkers for additional information and corroborative evidence.
- It may be more convenient for the interviewee, thus making it more likely that he will agree to the meeting for the interview in the first place.
- It may be advantageous to catch the potential interviewee off

guard, before he can have second thoughts, talk to someone else, develop fear, or be contacted by the subjects of the investigation.

Conducting an interview. The investigator's demeanor has significant bearing on the cooperation he receives from interviewees. The following suggestions will be instrumental in obtaining the maximum possible cooperation:

- Never talk down to the person you are interviewing. Never assume that the subject is less intelligent than you. Any hint of disrespect or condescension can quickly turn a cooperative interviewee into an uncooperative one.
- Never use language that disparages the intelligence or competence of the interviewee, even if you may think he acted foolishly in being victimized, in not preventing victimization of a friend or associate, or in failing to notify law-enforcement officers when it would have been common sense to do so.
- Be sensitive to the personal concerns of the victim or witness, especially when these involve perceptions of how the interviewee may be treated because of sex, race, religion, or ethnic background.
- Be businesslike. Conduct the interview in a professional manner. The investigator should be friendly but not familiar. Certain pleasantries are sometimes necessary, but the interview should not become a social occasion.
- Do not become authoritarian or attempt to dominate the interview.
- Make it clear that anyone, no matter how smart or well trained, can be victimized—that there are others who are and have been in the same boat. If possible, cite examples of well-known cases.
- Always be sympathetic and respectful to victims and complainants. Never suggest that a victim is a victim because of something he did. You must be extremely careful not to injure his pride in his own judgment, not to belittle his loss, and not to build up any false hopes as to the possibilities of his recouping all or part of his loss.
- Give careful thought to the language to be employed during the interview to make sure that it is consistent with the approach and understandable to the interviewee. Avoid law-enforcement or other bureaucratic jargon.
- Compliment the victim or complaining witness for taking the trouble to complain and cooperate—that not to complain and cooperate would be playing into the hands of the subject of the investigation.

• End every cooperative interview with thankful, sincere appreciation. Perhaps this will encourage the subject to maintain contact if he acquires or remembers more information.

Investigators should take notes of important names, dates, and monetary amounts during the interview. If a tape recorder is permitted by the interviewee, it should be used as a backup rather than a substitute for note taking. Since computer frauds are often complex and often involve technical details, the use of two investigators should be considered so that one individual can take the lead in questioning while the other takes notes. Since interview notes may eventually result in a memorandum or signed affidavit to be used as evidence, it is important that the notes be clear and accurate.

Interrogation

The purpose of interrogating a suspect is to obtain evidence or admissions that will be useful at trial. The interrogation may arise at the investigator's request or at the request of the suspect or his attorney. There are a number of pitfalls inherent in interrogating a suspect, and the investigator should consider them carefully before making a choice.

If the evidence of guilt is inconclusive, any one of the following may happen:

• Disclosing the fact that an investigation is under way or a prosecution is being considered may stymie the investigation and prosecution.
• The suspect may learn something during the interview or interrogation from which he can figure out how to obscure evidence or manipulate victim and witness attitudes and willingness to cooperate.
• The suspect might flee the jurisdiction before charges are filed and bail set.
• The investigator may be deceived by the suspect and consequently either waste investigative resources on a false lead or allow the suspect more time to put together a scheme to counter the investigation process.

A factor that might make interrogation prior to arrest a waste of an investigator's time is the fact that white-collar criminals are often proficient liars and are therefore unlikely to admit guilt or provide useful information. Some of them thrive on the challenge of their ability to deceive people. Thus, the failure of the interrogation is more likely than not. If such results are expected, the anticipated lies are often useful as evidence against the suspect.

Interrogation of a suspect prior to arrest may be unnecessary or undesirable in cases where the investigation has developed solid comprehensive evidence for a prosecution. What the suspect has to say prior to arrest may not matter. The fact that law enforcement has found it previously unnecessary to confront the suspect may also have a tremendous psychological impact upon him. It is demoralizing for a suspect to believe that the case against him is so strong that investigators found it unnecessary to even inquire into his explanation —and this could be a factor in an ultimate plea of guilty.

Tips for laymen

The following tips on interrogation are intended for individuals who are not law-enforcement officers:[5]

1. If the suspect is guilty, he may experience a great deal of fear during the interrogation. The fear can be used to the interrogator's advantage.
2. If the interrogator is an employee, it is desirable for him to be a more senior employee than the suspect. The interrogator should have had a minimum of personal contact with the suspect prior to the interrogation, and in no case should the interrogator be a personal friend of the suspect.
3. The interrogator should compile the following information before questioning the suspect:
   - A list of facts which the interrogator wants to obtain from the suspect.
   - As much background information about the suspect as possible, including any personal characteristics that might aid him in detecting stress during the interrogation. The interrogator should also try to find out about any personal weaknesses that can be used to start the subject talking.
   - Detailed questions that the suspect will be asked.
   - A plan for the interrogation, including a strategy and the sequence in which questions will be asked.
   - Copies of exhibits the interrogator plans to show the suspect, arranged in the order in which they are to be presented.
4. The interrogation should take place in private with all distracting influences such as telephones and magazines removed from the room. The blinds or drapes should also be drawn.
5. During the interrogation, the suspect should be allowed basic physical comforts such as meals and an opportunity to use the restroom, although the interrogator should accompany

[5] This material was adapted from James Binns, "The Internal Auditor's Role in Questioning Fraud Suspects: Part I," *The Magazine of Bank Administration*, October 1977, pp. 38–40.

the suspect. Failure to allow these basics may later allow the suspect to claim that the confession was obtained under duress.

6. There are several pros and cons of having interrogators work alone or in pairs:

   - Working alone provides greater freedom to select questions.

   - An interrogator may be able to gain the suspect's confidence more rapidly by working alone.

   - In most cases, guilty persons would prefer to confess to as few people as possible.

   - If an oral confession is obtained by an interrogator working alone, there is no one to substantiate the confession.

   - If the interrogator working alone is a man, a female suspect may later claim that the interrogator attempted to compromise her.

   - With two interrogators present, one can ask the questions while the other records answers and watches the suspect's reactions.

   - When two interrogators are present, great care must be taken in making statements that could be interpreted as direct accusations, since the suspect may later sue for slander and use the second interrogator as a witness.

7. The interrogator should appear calm and free from all kinds of pressures when he is questioning the suspect.

8. The suspect should be brought in for the interrogation by his supervisor without being told in advance the purpose of the meeting.

9. The exhibits should be placed in a folder or envelope and presented one at a time.

10. Only law-enforcement officials are required to give the Miranda warning. Other interrogators should refrain from doing so.

SPECIAL INVESTIGATIVE TOOLS AND TECHNIQUES

Detection and investigation of computer crimes often necessitate use of special tools and techniques. Many computer frauds are only detectable through audit. Others require use of the computer to analyze the voluminous files of data stored on magnetic media.

Crimes that can be detected through audit

Consider the case in which a computer is fraudulently programmed to show that an oil company barge is receiving 2,000 barrels of oil each trip, although the barge is actually receiving 4,000 barrels. A physical count of inventory or a spot check of transactions recording the amount of oil delivered would be a common means of detecting the fraud, other than informants or accidental detection. One case of this sort continued for 7 years.

Sometimes audit techniques for detecting fraud can be computerized. In one case, an insurance company created bogus policies and sold them to reinsurers for immediate income. The auditors were shown computer printouts listing the fake policies. They eventually became suspicious and asked to see the original paperwork backing up the computer records. Management stalled long enough for the conspirators to create the backup paperwork. If the auditors had used their own auditing programs and computer operators to print the policy master file, the list would have shown clear indications that policies had been fabricated. Common sense would have then either forced the auditors to closely observe the retrieval of backup paperwork or cast a great deal of suspicion on any stalling on the part of management.

Harnessing the computer

The computer is an ideal tool for uncovering suspicious patterns. Because of its speed, the computer can scan large volumes of data rapidly. Computers can perform relational and validity checks and they can simulate the results of past processing.

Consider the example of a fictitious company unemployment compensation fraud. A perpetrator sets up six companies, each with two fictitious employees, registers with the appropriate state agency, and begins paying taxes. As soon as the minimum period elapses, the fictitious companies "lay off" the employees and the perpetrators apply for unemployment benefits.

In this case the computer could analyze new claims for similarities. Six companies each had two employees who applied for unemployment shortly after the companies were set up. The computer could also be used to analyze the Social Security numbers of new claimants in order to determine whether a suspicious number of identical numbers were applicants during the same time period.

Complex cases

Computer frauds are sometimes complex crimes involving many transactions and many steps. Certain graphic techniques are valuable, both in helping the investigator to comprehend what the perpetrator has done and in communicating the evidence to the prosecutor. These techniques are known as the *link network analysis* and *time flow analysis*. Use of these analyses will be demonstrated with an actual case.

CASE. A classic rip-off of a county's computerized welfare system was perpetrated by a case worker, whom we shall call Ms. Johnson. She was aware that the computer needed two pieces of data to issue a check: her approval and the client's name and address. The name and address were checked for duplicates by the computer to make sure that recipients did not receive multiple checks.

Ms. Johnson persuaded 15 of her clients (welfare recipients) to submit four additional claims each, being careful to use different names and addresses each time. She approved these claims and the computer, after verifying each claim, promptly issued each check, which was then mailed. Each of the clients (we will call one of them Smith) picked up the fraudulent checks at the addresses given on the claim, and paid a "fee" to the individual at the mail drop.

Each perpetrator (Smith, for example) then "endorsed" the checks destined for fictitious individuals over to himself. Smith cashed his regular check at a bank and the fraudulent checks at a credit jewelry store for a "fee." We will call the store's proprietor Ross.

Ross entered the "fees" as payments on debts that had been falsely entered on his books. He then deposited the checks in his account. Meanwhile, Ms. Johnson used the computer to monitor whether or not the checks were cleared and returned to the welfare agency. When the computer reported that the checks had been paid and returned, Ms. Johnson obtained her share of the proceeds from Smith.

Link network diagram. Figure 12-2 shows the link network diagram for Smith in the preceding case. The investigator could use overlays to show the entire case. Notice that persons are represented by circles with their name (or other identifier such as AKA1) enclosed. Organizations are represented by boxes, possibly enclosing the circles representing their members. Entities are linked by solid lines if there is a relationship between them, such as meetings, telephone calls, or transfers of funds. Arrows represent relationships that flow in one direction; for example, the computer sent a check to Smith but Smith sent nothing to the computer.

Time flow diagram. A time flow diagram for the same case is shown in Figure 12-3. The diagram shows the whole scheme as a series of events connected by activities. The events are represented by circles. The lines between the circles represent activities or tasks that must be performed before the subsequent events can occur.

TRACING MONEY AND INVESTIGATIVE ACCOUNTING

Income gained through fraud is not normally declared as income since individuals are reluctant to disclose its illegitimate source. Therefore, it is likely that perpetrators will commit tax violations in respect to the fraudulent income. Furthermore, if the perpetrator attempts to invest income that was fraudulently derived, the failure to report earnings derived from that investment leads to further tax violations.

Methods used by the IRS to detect and prove tax evasion can be

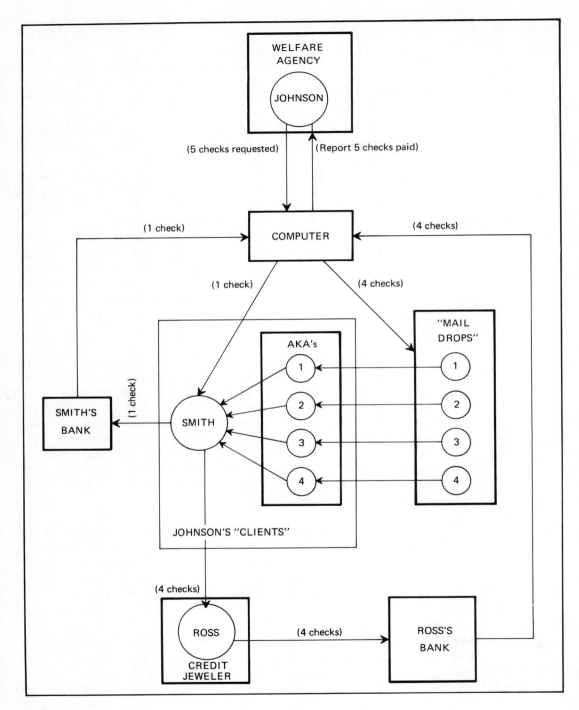

Figure 12-2

Link Diagram Depicting an Actual Welfare Fraud Case

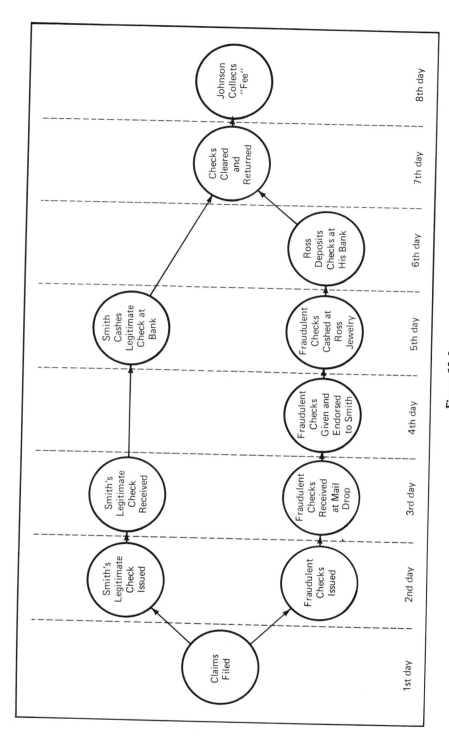

Figure 12-3
Time Flow Diagram

used equally well by computer fraud investigators to identify income derived from illegitimate sources. This method (known as "investigative accounting") consists of tracing all the perpetrator's known sources of income and comparing this to actual expenditures. Expenditures over and above known sources of income represent a measure of the potentially fraudulent income.

To aid computer fraud investigators in applying the principle, we will present a factual situation in which the principle was successfully applied, along with the investigative steps and the means of presenting the results. It was developed by Richard A. Nossen, former Assistant Director of the Intelligence Division, U.S. Internal Revenue Service.[6]

Factual situation   An individual whom we shall refer to as target A was suspected of criminal activity, although authorities had been unable to obtain an indictment. The suspect operated a legitimate business that was believed to be a cover designed to provide a legitimate source of income.

No.

SAFE DEPOSIT-INDIVIDUAL

LESSEE

DEPUTY

DATE OF CONTRACT   RENT $

PASSWORD

LESSEE

DEPUTY

DEPUTY

Figure 12-4

Safe Deposit Box Contract

[6] The material on "Tracing Money and Investigative Accounting" is adapted from Richard A. Nossen's *The Seventh Basic Investigative Technique*, Law Enforcement Assistance Administration (Washington, D.C.: Government Printing Office, 1977).

_____ 19 _____ hereby designate
and appoint _____
as _____ deputy and agent, to have access to the box
covered by this contract. To take and remove from or
add to the contents thereof, and have full and absolute control over the same, hereby waiving any liability of the lessor, arising out of the exercise, by the
said deputy, or any of the powers herein contained.

_____
Lessee

_____
Lessee

_____
Deputy

Witness: _____

_____
Address of Deputy

The Appointment Of The Above Deputy Is Hereby

Revoked _____ 19 _____

_____
Lessee

Witness: _____

_____ 19 _____ hereby designate
and appoint _____
as _____ deputy and agent, to have access to the box
covered by this contract. To take and remove from or
add to the contents thereof, and have full and absolute control over the same, hereby waiving any liability of the lessor, arising out of the exercise, by the
said deputy, or any of the powers herein contained.

_____
Lessee

_____
Lessee

_____
Deputy

Witness: _____

_____
Address of Deputy

The Appointment Of The Above Deputy Is Hereby

Revoked _____ 19 _____

_____
Lessee

Witness: _____

Identification

Name	Name	Name
Residence	Residence	Residence
Phone	Phone	Phone
Firm	Firm	Firm
Address	Address	Address
Phone	Phone	Phone
Mothers Maiden Name	Mothers Maiden Name	Mothers Maiden Name
Color Of Hair	Color Of Hair	Color Of Hair
Color Of Eyes	Color Of Eyes	Color Of Eyes
Height	Height	Height
Weight	Weight	Weight
Remarks	Remarks	Remarks

Figure 12-4 *Continued*

Eventually, an investigator was able to gain the confidence of the suspect's bookkeeper. The bookkeeper told the investigator that the suspect had drawn incomes of $14,000, $16,250, $11,750, and $14,375 for the years 1972 through 1975, respectively; and that the business statements had shown a constant balance of $15,000 in the capital account for the same 4 years.

Investigative steps Through physical surveillance the investigator observed the target enter bank A. Upon making inquiry at the bank, the investigator learned that the target has a commercial account and safe deposit box and that he obtained a BankAmericard through the same bank.

Safe deposit box. The investigator obtained a copy of the safe deposit contract filed with the bank by the target at the time he applied for the safe deposit box rental. The contract, shown in Figure 12-4, contains a physical description of the target, a sample of his handwriting, and other pertinent background information.

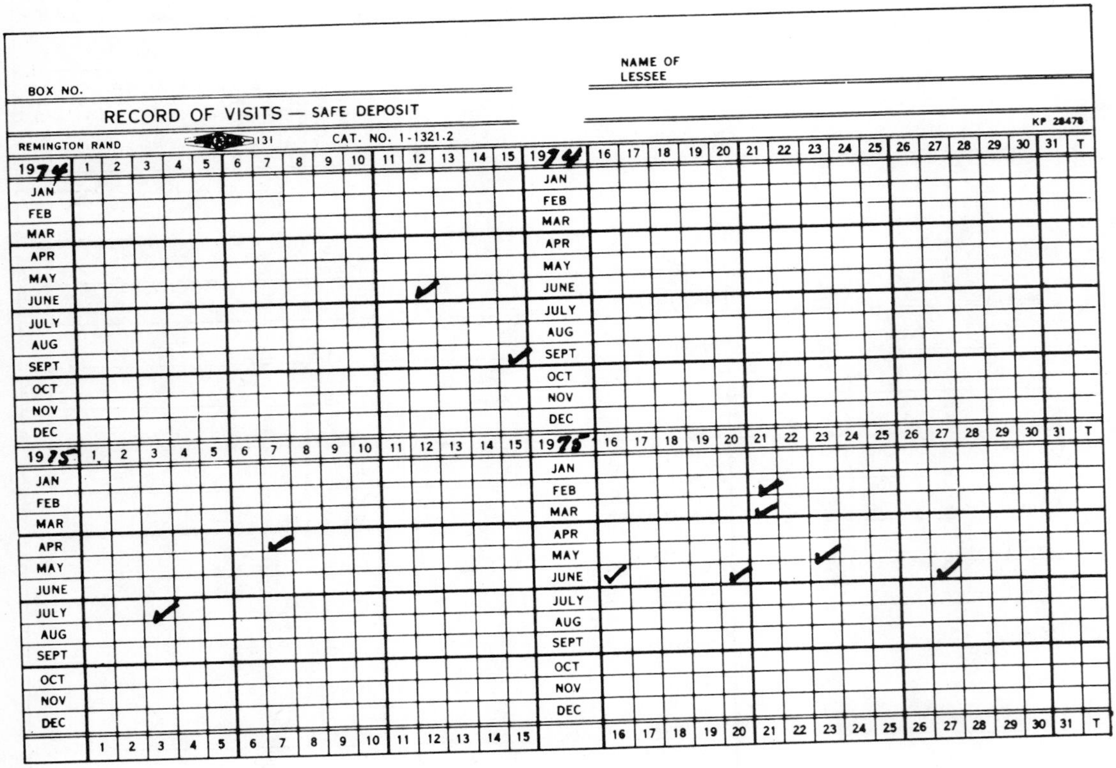

Figure 12-5

Record of Safe Deposit Box Entries

In addition to the contract, each time an individual enters his safe deposit box he is required to sign an entry slip, which is stamped with the date and time of day. This information is particularly valuable since the dates of entry may correspond to dates of other financial transactions. The retention period for safe deposit entries varies among banks. In this case, the record of entries of the target is summarized in Figure 12-5.

PERSONAL DDA SIGNATURE CARD

☐ JOINT
☐ INDIVIDUAL

_____
ACCOUNT NUMBER

Please STAMP Bank Name Here

1	Account Name	SEAL
2	Account Name	SEAL
	Social Security Number	SEAL

I (we) the above-signed, have been provided with and have read the rules and regulations of Bank governing this account and agree to be bound by the provisions thereof, and as they shall, from time to time, be amended by the Bank.

If two or more signatures appear above, each agrees that all moneys, checks and other instruments for payment of money at any time deposited in this account are and will be their joint property during their joint lives and upon the death of either of them the entire right, title and interest therein shall vest absolutely in the survivor; that at any time the balance in this account shall be subject to withdrawal, transfer or other disposition, in whole or in part, by either of them, or the duly constituted attorney of either of them without duty of inquiry on your part; that payment to, or by order of, either of them, or the duly constituted attorney of either of them, shall be full discharge to you for such payment, whether the other be living, incompetent or deceased; that you shall be authorized to make payment in accordance with the terms hereof, not withstanding any notice or demand which may be given by or on behalf of either of them to the contrary. The Bank is authorized to off-set the balance, without notice, against the indebtedness of any one or more of us to the Bank; and to send all statements, notices and vouchers to the address from time to time furnished the Bank.

Date Opened	Opened by	Approved by	Branch
Amount of Initial Deposit	Type of Deposit		Reference Checked

• PLEASE PRINT

	Home Address	City, State, Zip Code		Telephone & Area Code	
☐ SEND MAIL TO ☐	Employer		Position		Yrs. there
	Employer's Address	City, State, Zip Code		Telephone & Area Code	

Bank Reference		Other Reference	
Account Number	Type of Account		Telephone Number
Street Address		Street Address	
City	State	Zip Code	City	State	Zip Code

Personal I.D. Driver's License Number	State
Charge Account Number	Type

Figure 12-6

Signature Card

Checking account. Figure 12-6 illustrates the signature card the target filled out in opening his checking account. The signature card provided additional background information and another specimen of the target's handwriting.

The investigator also obtained copies of the target's monthly checking account statements. The year-end statements for 1972 through 1975 revealed balances of $300, $1,100, $3,600, and $4,300, respectively. Those balances were used in computing the target's net worth for those years.

Figure 12-7 shows the target's checking statement for the month of June 1975. The statement shows that the target made a $25,000 deposit on June 16, 1975. The record of entries by the target into his safe deposit box (Figure 12-4) shows that the target entered his safe

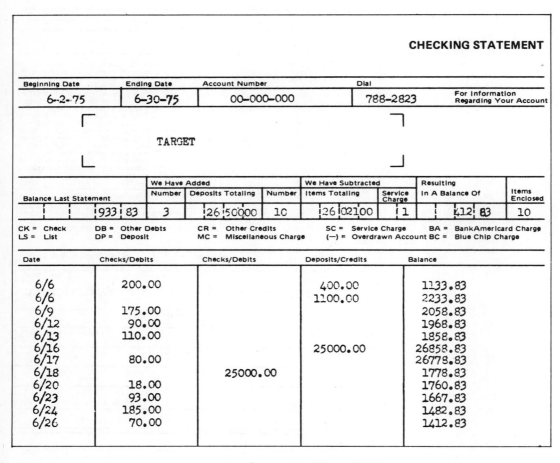

Figure 12-7

Checking Statement

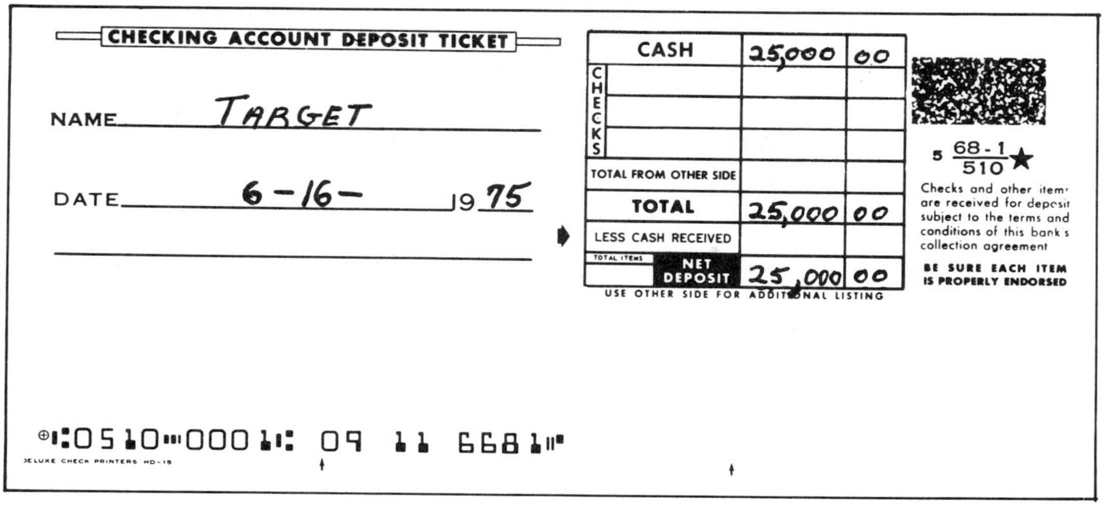

Figure 12-8

Deposit Slip

deposit box on the same day as he made the $25,000 deposit to his checking account. The inference, borne out by examining the bank's microfilm copy of the target's deposit slip, was that the deposit had been made with cash. Figure 12-8 illustrates the deposit slip.

The investigator should always make a schedule comparing the dates of large bank deposits and withdrawals with the dates of other large financial transactions and with the dates of entry into safe deposit boxes. This helps to establish the suspect's pattern in making financial transactions.

In this case, the investigator noted that the target had withdrawn $25,000 on June 18, 1975. Inspection of a microfilm copy of the check revealed that the check had been cashed by the target. The next step in tracing the $25,000 was to examine the bank's cashier's check records. Cashier's checks, which can be purchased from banks, are issued on the bank's own funds and signed by an officer. At the time of purchase, the bank inserts the date and the name of the payee.

By making inquiries, the investigator learned that the target had purchased three cashier's checks, all payable to stockbroker A, on June 18, 1975. The bank teller's proof sheet showed that all three cashier's checks had been purchased with cash. One of those checks is shown in Figure 12-9.

Security account. The endorsements on the three cashier's checks show that they were deposited in stockbroker A's account at bank C in Washington, D.C. The investigator then contacted the Washington, D.C., police and asked them to find out whether the target had an

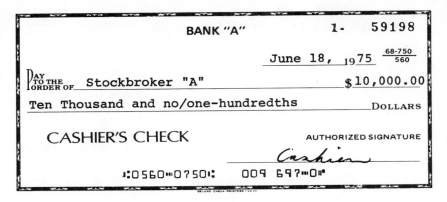

Figure 12-9

Cashier's Check

account with stockbroker A and, if so, to get copies of the target's monthly security statements for the last 4 years.

As it turned out, the target had opened an account with stockbroker A in June 1975 and that had been the only month in which the account had shown activity. A copy of the statement is shown in Fig. 12-10. The statement indicates that the three cashier's checks were used to purchase shares of ABC Corporation and DEF Corporation in three separate transactions.

Purchase of Automobiles. The investigator then checked the state's motor vehicle records to identify the target's automobile. The records showed that the target had purchased a 1975 Cadillac El Dorado and that the automobile was titled in the name of bank B. Inquiries at bank B disclosed that the target had taken out a loan from the bank to purchase the automobile. The investigator also learned that the target also had a savings account and a mortgage loan at bank B.

The investigator noted the target's automobile loan balance as of year end 1975 ($3,000) and then made inquiries at the Cadillac dealership. The dealer revealed that the target had purchased a Chevrolet Caprice for his girl friend in addition to the El Dorado. Copies of the invoices for those purchases are shown in Figures 12-11 and 12-12.

The first invoice shows that the target paid $13,000 for the El Dorado. He also received a $2,500 trade-in on his 1973 automobile, which he had purchased from the same dealer in 1972 for $4,500. Besides the trade-in, the target had made a cash down payment of $5,000 and had financed the balance at bank B.

The second invoice shows that the target paid $6,500 in cash for

PERIOD
ENDING JUNE 30, 1975

YOUR ACCOUNT NUMBER
247630

STATEMENT OF YOUR SECURITY ACCOUNT
WITH

STOCKBROKER "A"

MEMBERS NEW YORK STOCK EXCHANGE AMERICAN STOCK EXCHANGE
TORONTO STOCK EXCHANGE AND OTHER LEADING STOCK AND COMMODITY EXCHANGES

TARGET "A"

KINDLY MENTION YOUR
ACCOUNT NUMBER WHEN
REFERRING TO THIS
STATEMENT OR OTHER
TRANSACTIONS.

DATE	QUANTITY Bought or Received	QUANTITY Sold or Delivered	DESCRIPTION	PRICE OR SYMBOL	AMOUNT DEBITED (CHARGED) TO YOUR ACCOUNT	AMOUNT CREDITED TO YOUR ACCOUNT	BALANCE (BY TYPE OF ACCOUNT)
6 19			Check			10,000.00	10,000.00
6 19	100		ABC Corp.	100	10,000.00		-0-
6 20			Check			10,000.00	10,000.00
6 20	100		ABC Corp.	100	10,000.00		-0-
6 23			Check			5,000.00	5,000.00
6 23	200		DEF Corp.	25	5,000.00		-0-

KINDLY DIRECT INQUIRIES CONCERNING THIS STATEMENT TO THE   OFFICE WHICH SERVICES YOUR ACCOUNT. SEE REVERSE SIDE FOR ADDRESS AND TELEPHONE NUMBER.

LEDGER

FOR DESCRIPTION OF TYPE OF ACCOUNT AND EXPLANATION OF SYMBOLS USED, SEE REVERSE SIDE.

Figure 12-10

Security Account Statement

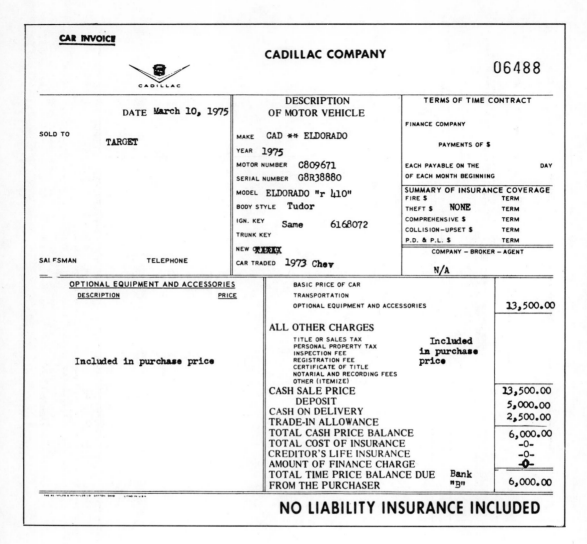

Figure 12-11

Invoice for El Dorado

the Caprice, with no trade-in or financing from the bank. The investigator also showed that the Caprice was titled in the name of a woman later identified as the target's girlfriend. In order to prove continued ownership of the cars, the investigator checked again with the state motor vehicle records and found that the cars were still registered to the target and his girlfriend in 1976.

Savings account. The target's account showed little activity—a few deposits and no withdrawals. The investigator noted the deposit

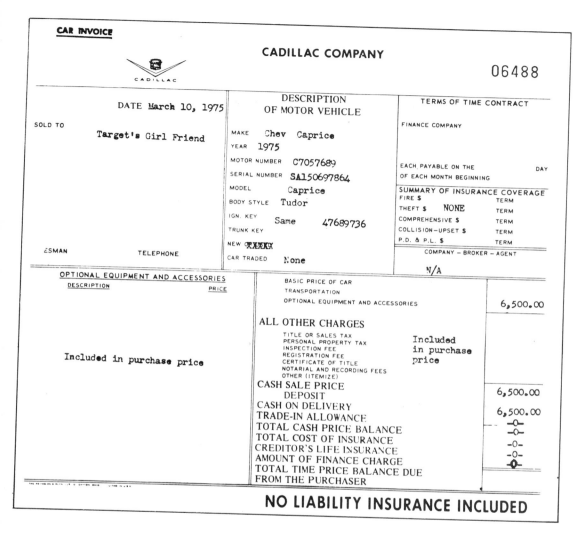

Figure 12-12

Invoice for Caprice

dates and amounts. The year-end balances were $200, $2,100, $7,400, and $9,200 for the years 1972 through 1975, respectively.

Cashier's checks—Bank B. Before leaving bank B the investigator discovered two cashier's checks purchased by the target, each involving significant transactions.

Travelers cheques. The first of the two checks, in the amount of $20,000, was purchased on September 15, 1974, and was payable to, and endorsed by, bank A. (Bank A was the bank where the target maintained his safe deposit box and checking account.) Inquiries at bank A revealed that the target used the proceeds of the cashier's check to purchase 200 $100 American Express Travelers Cheques. Figure 12–13 is a copy of the bank's record for that transaction; from it the investigator obtained the serial numbers of the cheques. The investigator also notes that the record of target's entries into his safe deposit box (Figure 12–4) showed that the target had entered his safe deposit box on the same day he purchased the travelers cheques.

The investigator obtained copies of the canceled travelers cheques from American Express. Review of the payees, dates, and endorsements disclosed that the target had taken two trips with his girl friend in the fall of 1974—to the French Riviera and to Acapulco. The cheques had been used for airline tickets, hotel bills, and restaurants. These expenditures, representing personal living expenses, are summarized later in the net worth and sources-and-application-of-funds computations.

Fur coat. The second cashier's check, in the amount of $5,000, was purchased on March 21, 1975, and endorsed by an exclusive furrier. The furrier confirmed that he had received the check in payment for a full-length fur coat and, from a picture, identified the target's girl friend as the recipient. The investigator also obtained the name of an insurance broker to whom the furrier had mailed an appraisal of the coat.

Diamond ring. A representative of the insurance company confirmed that the insurance on the mink coat was still in effect, proving continued ownership of the coat. The investigator learned that the target had also insured a man's 2-karat diamond ring for $5,000.

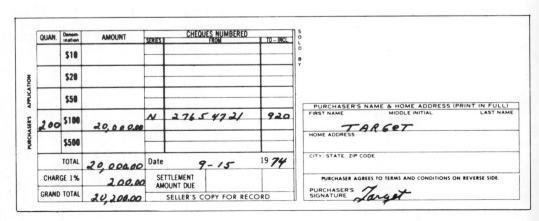

Figure 12-13

Purchase of Travelers Cheques

The insurance on the ring became effective on May 23, 1975, and was still in effect. The appraisal had been received from jewelry store A, known for custom jewelry.

The owner of jewelry store A confirmed that he had sold the target the ring on July 3, 1975. He remembered the sale clearly because the target had paid with fifty $100 bills. A subsequent check on the date of payment revealed that the target had entered his safe deposit box on the same day.

Condominium apartment. Examination of the target's mortgage loan at bank B (discovered earlier in connection with the target's automobile loan at the same bank) disclosed that the target had purchased a condominium apartment in June 1973. The bank's "purchaser's settlement sheet" showed that the target had made a cash down payment of $25,000 and had taken a mortgage for $40,000 on the $65,000 apartment. The record of the target's mortgage balances at year-end showed $37,500, $27,500 and $17,500 for the years 1973 through 1975, respectively. The mortgage records showed that in addition to the required monthly payments of $450 (note that these payments are inconsistent with the income derived from the target's legitimate business) the target had made additional principal payments of $1,750, $8,500, and $8,000 in the years 1973 through 1975.

In order to establish the target's continued ownership of the apartment, the investigator noted that the mortgage had an existing balance as of December 31, 1975, and was being paid in a timely manner. To further corroborate that fact, the investigator checked the county land records, which showed no transfer of the property. If the investigator had not found out about the condominium by other means, he would have discovered it by examining the county records in the county where the target was known to reside. The county records are open to the public and show the date of purchase, description of the property, name of the lender (bank B) and tax assessment. From the tax assessment (which is usually in the range of $10 to $20 per $1,000 of purchase price) the investigator could have deduced the approximate price of the apartment, without ever contacting bank B.

Investigative accounting

The investigator summarized the results of the preceding investigation in two formats, in an effort to determine which format would be most easily understood. Our advice to the reader is to use whichever method seems clearest to him. Both of the following methods are equally correct.

Source and application of funds. This format is shown in Figure 12–14. The target's known expenditures, as determined by the investigation, have been summarized under "Funds Applied." After

SOURCE AND APPLICATION OF FUNDS

FUNDS APPLIED:	1973	1974	1975
Increase in Checking Account Balance	$ 800	$ 2,500	$ 700
Increase in Savings Account Balance	1,900	5,300	1,800
Down Payment on Apartment	25,000		
Purchase of Securities:			
ABC			20,000
DEF			5,000
Purchase of Cadillac (Down Payment)			5,000
Purchase of Chevrolet			6,500
Purchase of Diamond Ring			5,000
Purchase of Fur Coat			5,000
Purchase of Travelers Cheques		20,000	
Reduction of Mortgage on Apartment	2,500	10,000	10,000
Reduction of Loan on Cadillac			3,000
TOTAL FUNDS APPLIED	$30,200	$37,800	$62,000

SOURCE OF FUNDS:			
Income from Furniture Store	$16,250	$11,750	$14,375

INCOME FROM UNIDENTIFIED			
SOURCES	$13,950	$26,050	$47,625

Figure 12-14

Source and Application of Funds

totaling the expenditures for each of the years 1973 through 1975, the investigator subtracted the target's income from his business in order to arrive at the target's "Income from Unidentified Sources."

Net worth and expenditures. This method takes the increase in net worth from one year to the next and adds it to the subject's other personal living expenses in order to arrive at the subject's income from unidentified sources. The two main steps are the net worth computation and the computation of income from unidentified sources. The method is illustrated in Figure 12–15.

Net worth is computed by subtracting liabilities from assets. Note that continued ownership of the assets and continued existence of the liabilities must be established in order to use this method. Once the net worth has been computed, the increase in net worth is obtained by subtracting the current year's net worth from the net worth in the preceding year. More than one year's history is necessary in order to compute the increase in net worth.

Income from unidentified sources is determined by subtracting legitimate income from total expenditures. Income from legitimate

NET WORTH AND EXPENDITURES COMPUTATION

ASSETS	12/31/72	12/31/73	12/31/74	12/31/75
Checking Account — Bank A	$ 300	$ 1,100	$ 3,600	$ 4,300
Savings Account — Bank B	200	2,100	7,400	9,200
Condominium Apartment		65,000	65,000	65,000
Furniture Store — Capital Investment	15,000	15,000	15,000	15,000
Securities:				
200 Shares ABC				20,000
200 Shares DEF				5,000
Automobiles:				
1973 Chevrolet	4,500	4,500	4,500	-0-
1976 Cadillac				13,500
1976 Chevrolet				6,500
Diamond Ring				5,000
TOTAL ASSETS	$20,000	$87,700	$95,500	$143,500
LIABILITIES				
Mortgage-Condominium Apt.		$37,500	$27,500	$17,500
Automobile Loan				3,000
TOTAL LIABILITIES	-0-	$37,500	$27,500	$20,500
Net Worth	$20,000	$50,200	$68,000	$123,000
Less Net Worth Prior Year		20,000	50,200	68,000
Increase in Net Worth		$30,200	$17,800	$ 55,000
Add: Identified Personal Expenses:				
Loss on Trade in of 1973 Chevrolet				$ 2,000
Travelers Checks			$20,000	
Fur Coat				5,000
TOTAL EXPENDITURES		$30,200	$37,800	$ 62,000
Income from Furniture Store		16,250	11,750	14,375
INCOME FROM UNIDENTIFIED SOURCES		$13,950	$26,050	$ 47,625

Figure 12-15

Net Worth and Expenditures

sources, in this case, is the income disclosed by the bookkeeper. Total expenditures are the sum of the subject's increase in net worth and personal living expenses. Personal living expenses in this case included the travelers cheques (spent for vacations) and the fur coat. In other instances, personal expenses may include food, clothing, rent, medical care, entertainment, and travel.

PACKAGING THE CASE

It is common practice for investigators to be in contact with the prosecuting attorney during the course of the investigation. Once the investigation is complete, the investigator must package it for the prosecuting attorney. Even the best of cases may never be prosecuted if it is poorly organized so that the prosecutor does not under-

375

1. Introductory Summary—A brief narrative that explains:

   a. The type of scheme
   b. How it came to the attention of law enforcement
   c. Period of operation
   d. Names, fictitious names, company names, etc. used by perpetrators
   e. Evidence of prior criminal activity
   f. Whether warnings were given
   g. Type and total amount of loss
   h. Possible statutes (criminal, civil, administrative) that were violated

2. Description of Proposed Defendants—A standard identification record can be used, which contains at least the following:

   a. Name
   b. Alias
   c. Addresses (home and business)
   d. Physical description
   e. Place and date of birth
   f. Criminal identification number (FBI or State)
   g. Occupation/employers
   h. Associates/accomplices
   i. Prior record
   j. Identification of those who have cooperated or might cooperate with the prosecution

3. Description of Offenses—A detailed exposition of all pertinent data concerning the who, what, when, where, why, and how of the scheme from its conception through its perpetration. For example, for each occurrence, to the extent possible describe:

   a. How was the scheme conceived?
   b. Who executed it? Who played what parts?
   c. Where was it put into operation?
   d. How long was it in operation?
   e. What was the nature of the scheme, the types of merchandise, service, or concealment involved?
   f. Any information that will provide the prosecuting attorney with a firm comprehension of the magnitude, nature, and characteristics of the scheme

4. Results of Investigation—A narrative description containing the evidence that may possibly be used for development of proof of misrepresentations, fraudulent intent, or other essential elements of the statutes violated.

   a. Any occurrences that might lead to a conclusion of criminal intent. To this should be attached any diagrammatic outlines of the operation that may have been prepared (a link network diagram or a time-flow diagram, for example)

5. Possible Evidence:

   a. List of witnesses (including cooperating subjects of investigation and law enforcement), addresses, telephone numbers
   b. Oral, documentary, and physical evidence associated with each witness
   c. How obtained—interview, surveillance, survey questionnaire, etc.

6. Other Agencies Involved—A brief description of the involvement or interest of other government, law enforcement, or private agencies

stand the issues.   Therefore, the investigator should give careful
consideration to how the case will be presented.

Before organizing the evidence, the investigator should prepare
a checklist of all items.   Oral evidence should be written up in a
memorandum of interview or a signed affidavit.   Physical evidence
should be handled according to the guidelines presented earlier, in
Chapter 11.

As mentioned previously, evidence of repetitious wrongful activity is often the key to proving a computer fraud case.   Therefore,
the investigator should find as many instances of fraudulent transactions as possible.   There is nothing like a long list of fraudulent
transactions to convince juries that an error was not involved.

Figure 12-16 is an outline for packaging the case.

IV

IMPLEMENTING YOUR LOSS CONTROL PROGRAM

13

A Multidisciplinary
Prevention Program

Previous chapters explored, in a more-or-less isolated manner, methods and considerations in preventing, deterring, and detecting computer fraud. We discussed how and why fraud happens; we discussed countermeasures in the form of policies, controls, and techniques; and we indicated general areas of responsibility for the various countermeasures. In this chapter our aim is to tie these considerations together to form what we call a multidisciplinary approach to the prevention program. The sections in this chapter cover:

- Introduction.

- Data processing management.

- Computer security officer.

- Internal auditing.

- External auditors.

- Data administration.

- Personnel department.

- Financial management.

- User management.

- Alternative responsibilities.

INTRODUCTION In some sense, the prevention program may be viewed as a kind of "tug-of-war" between threats and countermeasures, as depicted in Figure 13-1. What we are trying to show here is that people, working through an adequate set of methods and rules, counterbalance the threats. On the other hand, if the methods and rules are ill-conceived or if there are failures to comply with them, the central link in the counterbalancing process is weakened, the implication being that the threats would no longer be kept in abeyance.

People responsibilities Although top management is ultimately responsible for maintaining an effective counterbalancing program, the problem of computer fraud is far too complex and time-consuming to receive daily attention from top management. The solution is for top management to set up a program for preventing computer fraud and delegate responsibility for the implementation and monitoring of that program.

Under the multidisciplinary approach, the most effective means of delegating responsibility is to decentralize it on a functional basis. This means identifying specific responsibilities and tasks, and assigning them to appropriate organizational units. (Because the problem crosses organizational boundaries, centralization of a computer fraud prevention program is just not an effective or economical approach.)

The functional groups to which responsibility should be assigned include data processing management, computer security officer, data administrator, personnel management, internal audit, external audit, financial management, user management, and corporate risk management. Once the role of each of these groups is defined, a highly effective program for preventing computer fraud can be woven into your company's existing organization.

Role of methods and rules A multidisciplinary approach is the logical extension of the principle that no one countermeasure should be relied upon as the sole means of preventing computer fraud. When you have sorted out all the methods and rules—the countermeasures—that should be in your company's prevention program, you are likely to find that implementation will call for specialized knowledge in a number of disciplines, such as: general management policy, organization theory, administrative and internal control practices, personnel policy, computer security, auditing, and operational characteristics of particular applications. Highlights of the roles of each of these disciplines are presented below.

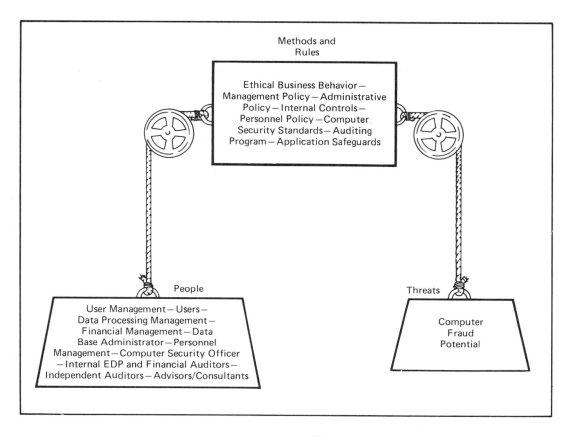

Figure 13-1

Balance Factors in the Multidisciplinary Approach

Role of management policy. Sound management policy helps prevent computer fraud by reducing opportunities for employees to justify dishonesty to themselves. By setting standards for personal honesty and ethical behavior, management forces individuals into the awareness that behavior violating those standards is unacceptable. By setting a personal example of honesty, wise managers remind employees of company standards. By acting to preserve good morale throughout the company, management reduces some of the common motivations for employee dishonesty.

Role of organization theory. Good organization provides two direct benefits related to computer fraud prevention. First, it provides the necessary separation of functions for internal control. Second, it gives key individuals such as internal auditors and com-

383

puter security officers the necessary independence and clout to carry out their missions.

In terms of specific organization layout, these objectives can be met in many different ways, depending on the type of business your company is in and on whether your organization is centralized or decentralized. Because of the number of choices, we cannot prescribe the best approach for your company. But a manager or consultant with a solid understanding of organization theory can provide you with the alternatives for your particular company.

Role of administrative and internal control practices. There are a number of good practices that will reduce your company's vulnerability to computer fraud and increase chances of rapid detection if it should occur. Many of these practices can be stated as general principles for guiding decisions. Formal administrative policy is a vehicle for communicating these general principles.

Role of personnel policy. Acquisition of suitable personnel, management of their career development, and attention to their problems will reduce the likelihood of computer fraud in your company. These activities fall within the provisions of company personnel policy. Review of personnel policy may turn up the need for revisions that are supportive of computer fraud prevention objectives.

Role of computer security. A security-conscious staff in your computer environment will be important to reducing the chances of computer fraud perpetrated by systems personnel as well as outsiders. A good computer security program can create awareness. It also provides for safeguards and controls to help prevent unauthorized access to and alteration of data files and programs.

Role of auditing. Auditing is primarily a discipline to deter and detect rather than prevent fraud. Although, in the sense that prevention may be accomplished as a result of control weaknesses discovered by auditors and prompt corrective action by management, auditors certainly have an important role in giving impetus to the use of prevention measures. Internal auditing, in particular, can be employed to review systems designs and comment on the adequacy of built-in controls before systems go into live operation. And they have an important role in providing an independent verification that other fraud prevention rules and policies are functioning as intended.

Role of application knowledge. When perpetrators manipulate records so that shortages are not apparent, someone with application knowledge is often required to spot the manipulation and uncover shortages. Therefore, user management should bear responsibility for obtaining exception reports capable of revealing manipulation and for reviewing these reports on an ongoing basis. They should also bear responsibility for alerting internal auditors and launching an investigation when evidence of manipulations is found.

Benefits of a multidisciplinary approach

The multidisciplinary approach allows you to build upon existing functions for computer fraud prevention rather than reinventing the wheel. A program in which all affected parties participate has a better chance of acceptance and therefore of success than one imposed externally. Because functions are not duplicated, a multidisciplinary approach is also the most economical.

There are also administrative advantages to the multidisciplinary approach. Preventing computer fraud requires mobilization and coordination of varied and diverse specialized talent. Decentralization of responsibility takes the burden off any one individual. As an added benefit, decentralization of responsibility provides added separation of duties, lest the person in charge of investigation and control also be a perpetrator.

A customized approach

Questions as to creation of new functions or decentralization of responsibility depend upon how your company is currently organized, which of the relevant functions already exist in your company, and who the individuals are in the key positions. The sections that follow depict the ideal assignment of responsibilities as well as alternative ways of assigning responsibility.

DATA PROCESSING MANAGEMENT

Ideally, data processing management should implement computer security policy. As an adjunct to that responsibility, it should also provide for coordination of efforts between systems personnel, the computer security officer, internal auditing, and data base administration. Seeing that other parties do their share is not solely the province of data processing management but should be shared equally by the interested parties.

There are several responsibilities which data processing management should assume regarding computer fraud prevention:

- Providing a secure computer environment either directly or through implementation of policy set by the computer security officer.
- Ensuring that systems professionals have adequate knowledge of security and system control requirements and procedures.
- Raising issues regarding risks or discrepancies that come to its attention.
- Admitting that computer frauds either perpetrated by indi-

385

viduals under its supervision or by means under its functional control are its responsibility to prevent and detect.

Secure environment

If your company has a computer security officer, that individual should determine what constitutes a secure environment and which policies should be stated. In that situation, data processing management ensures that policy is implemented but is in no way relieved of responsibility for raising relevant issues that the computer security officer does not address.

Relevant countermeasures include physical, data, software, DB/DC safeguards, and effective security administration. Data processing management should perform its own studies as to computer security requirements in its environment as well as administer policy set by the computer security officer. Where gaps exist between stated policy measures and computer security needs, data processing management should address those needs by means of policy revisions and additional countermeasures.

Ensuring adequate knowledge

Ensuring that systems personnel have adequate knowledge of control requirements and security procedures is a responsibility of data processing management, regardless of whether the systems development and maintenance functions are centralized or decentralized. In regard to this responsibility, data processing management should determine whether or not adequate knowledge and expertise exist and should see that gaps in knowledge or expertise are corrected through training.

Raising issues

Very often when there is a case of ongoing computer fraud, analysis reveals that interested parties had some inkling of irregularities or control weaknesses but did not raise the issues because circumstances were not deemed to fall within the direct responsibility of individuals noting the problem. Data processing management and other interested individuals should take responsibility for raising such issues as come to their attention, regardless of whether or not it is their explicit responsibility. Examples of such issues include:

- Responsibility for assuring that internal auditors review systems under development.
- Comment if the scope of an internal audit appears to be too narrow or to overlook important factors.
- Action where implementation of computer security appears to be too lenient.
- Pointing out situations where user requests seem to be overlooking security or control considerations.

386

Admission of responsibility

Admission of responsibility for computer fraud that may occur within its control is an essential ingredient for getting data processing management to fulfill its other responsibilities relating to computer fraud prevention. Without such admission, data processing management is unlikely to enforce policy wholeheartedly or to raise issues of which it is aware. Once responsibility is taken, data processing management can be expected to take the prevention of computer fraud seriously.

COMPUTER SECURITY OFFICER

The functions of a computer security officer are to:

- Evaluate computer security risks.
- Articulate policy for minimizing those risks.
- Monitor adherence to security policy.

If your company already has physical security, data administration, and internal auditing functions, the computer security officer will coordinate existing operations and articulate special policies that are not addressed by those other functions. If those functions do not exist, the computer security officer will have to play a much larger role, along with data processing management, user management, and the external auditors.

Evaluating computer security risks

The computer security officer should consider both the applications of your company and the environments in which they are processed. His concern includes automated processing, data storage, and physical security. In general, he is not concerned with factors in the user environment.

Computer fraud risks with which the computer security officer should be concerned include:

- Risks associated with physical access to the data processing installation or the data storage facilities.
- Risks to data while they are within the computer facility in on-line and off-line modes.
- Risks resulting from unauthorized program modification.

Articulating policy

Based upon the nature of applications, the processing environment, and upon his assessment of potential risks, the computer security officer should articulate policy for minimizing those risks. Policy should be articulated in writing, kept up to date, and should be suitable for guiding development of your company's newest applications. As a by-product of this activity, the computer security officer should take responsibility for interpreting policy as applied to a specific situ-

387

ation and for assisting interested parties in setting up appropriate educational programs.

Monitoring adherence

The computer security officer should monitor adherence to computer security policy through ongoing surveillance and through periodic security evaluations. Mechanisms for ongoing surveillance should include checking on log reviews and resulting actions taken as well as spot checks. Security evaluations should include installations and sensitive applications, with priorities set on the basis of potential risk. Computer fraud is one potential risk that should be considered.

INTERNAL AUDITING

Your company's internal auditors should play several roles relative to computer fraud prevention, detection, and determent.

- Review of systems under development for adequate controls and auditability.
- Review of controls and other safeguards for operational systems.
- Installation audits.
- Detection of discrepancies, whether caused by fraud or error.
- Advice to management concerning risks that have not been adequately addressed.

Development review

Ideally, auditing advice and opinion should be easily accessible to both data processing and user management throughout development of a new system. At the very least, internal auditors should comment following system analysis and design as well as in the interval between system testing and cutover to a new system. Auditors should make their comments specific and actionable. Data processing and user management should be under strong pressure to respond to audit recommendations.

Review of operational systems

Auditors should review operational systems on a periodic basis to ensure that prescribed controls are adhered to and remain adequate over time. One argument we have heard against having internal auditors participate in both development and post-implementation reviews is that internal auditors may become biased because they failed to address system weaknesses during development. Such critics go on to say that previously unnoticed weaknesses will not be identified because internal auditors will be protective of their own past oversights. Our response is that the criticism reflects common political problems that top management can take action to ease.

If management actively supports internal auditors and their recommendations, user and data processing management will be under pressure to take appropriate action. If user and data processing management obtain no political benefit from pointing out past oversights of internal auditors, that activity will also die out. The end result will be increased benefits from the internal auditing function. Accomplishment of that end is a function of top management style.

Installation audits

Most EDP internal auditing departments do installation audits. These audits are designed to monitor physical and data security as well as adherence to prescribed operational procedures. Sophisticated internal auditors will also check for integrity of the operating system, data network, hardware, and supporting software such as data base/data communications software and widely used utility programs.

Detection of discrepancies

Detection of discrepancies and discovery of control weaknesses are the most obvious contribution of internal auditors in connection with computer fraud prevention. Application audits review integrity of data in addition to conformance to and adequacy of controls and procedures. The data integrity review aspect of an application audit includes confirmations, review of logs and journals, simulation, file validation, and file reconstruction on a sample basis.

Advice to management

Advice to management concerning risks that have not been adequately addressed should be expected as an outcome of installation, system development, and operational application audits. Internal audit reports should always contain a management highlights section, as a standard practice, that points out significant weaknesses that require correction. Should it turn out that there are no significant weaknesses to be cited, the highlights section should explain why this is so.

A word about attitude

Whatever else he may be, the auditor must be a competent critic. People who cannot do this, and there are many, should not be auditors. We have seen a number of cases where auditors felt their mission was to make friends with auditees and they, sometimes by their own admission, avoided reporting audit findings that were unpleasant. Sometimes this posture was taken because top management was not supportive of internal audit. In other cases, the auditor was anxious to please the auditee in order to secure a position in the auditee's department. And, in some cases, the auditor simply lacked an objective, professional bearing. It goes without saying that your company is wasting money on auditing if such conditions exist.

EXTERNAL AUDITORS The annual financial audit by an external auditor—an independent certified public accountant—is performed to give the auditor a basis for rendering an opinion as to whether the company's financial statements are a fair, consistent representation of the company's financial position as of a certain date and on whether the statements are based on generally accepted accounting principles. The auditor is not searching for fraud as a primary mission, nor is he providing any opinion about fraud.

To be sure, auditors are certainly aware of the possibility of fraud. But the kind of fraud that would cause them to qualify or change their opinions about the financial statements would usually have to be a material fraud; that is, it would have to be big enough to make a significant difference in the financial statements. Where the external auditor fails to detect major frauds of this type, it can be as a result of the auditor's failure to employ generally accepted auditing standards in the situation. These standards are published by the American Institute of Certified Public Accountants (New York) for the United States and by chartered accountant organizations elsewhere in the world.

Despite these qualifications, your external auditors are capable of performing several valuable functions relating to computer fraud prevention and detection, in addition to the fact that auditing is a good deterrent:

- Review of controls as a by-product of the audit.
- Detection of major frauds.
- Optional or discretionary services related to the audit.

Review of controls In performing a financial audit, a standard step taken early in the audit is to review controls for adequacy and compliance. This step enables external auditors to determine how extensive their audit must be in order to be prudently confident of detecting any material misstatements. If controls are weak or conformity is poor, the scope of the audit will be greater than if controls and compliance are good.

Management should avail itself of the information regarding control weaknesses and compliance gathered by external auditors. External auditors may not comment on their findings about controls unless the impact of those findings is material. We believe that external auditors should comment even though the impact is not material.

One way to get external auditors to make such comments is to request that service in advance of the audit. Given such a request, it is a minor effort for auditors to comply. The depth to which external auditors will go in evaluating controls is generally less than the usual depth of an internal audit. Nevertheless, there is the advantage of an added opinion.

A closely related consideration is the matter of discrepancies and questionable items that may be detected by external auditors. Where amounts or items are minor, external auditors may not comment. We feel they should comment. Again, the way to get them to comment on such findings is to request that service in advance of the audit. Investigation of this type of finding has the potential of uncovering computer fraud before it can have material impact.

Detection of major frauds

In an audit of your company's financial statements, as mentioned above, external auditors are responsible for detecting computer frauds of sufficient magnitude as to have material impact upon the validity of those statements. In view of the fact that our readers would want to detect frauds before they reached such proportions as to have material impact upon financial statements, this service is unexciting. Nevertheless, it is a fallback position.

Discretionary services

Besides auditing financial statements, external auditors can perform a variety of other services, if engaged to do so. Examples of discretionary services to consider include:

- Security audits and consulting.
- Audits for fraud detection.
- Investigation of discrepancies and suspected frauds.
- Application and installation audits.

Security audits and consulting. Some of the larger CPA firms have computer security specialists on their management consulting services staffs. Such firms can provide security · audits and other advisory services pertaining to computer systems safeguards. Except for security evaluations sought by top management or your company's board of directors, the outside consultants should coordinate their engagements with the related efforts of your internal auditors and computer security manager, assuming that these functions exist.

Fraud audits. Generally speaking, when a CPA is engaged to perform a fraud audit, its main purpose is to determine the amount of loss. The fact that a fraud has occurred is typically known when the CPA is engaged by the company, a fidelity bonding company, or a trustee in bankruptcy.

Investigative services. During the course of a financial audit, external auditors may come across discrepancies that strongly suggest that a fraud is under way or has taken place. The auditor will call this to management's attention, whereupon management may wish to have the company's internal auditors, a private detective service, and law enforcement officials conduct an investigation. Often, the external auditor is engaged to conduct a probing review of the situation which management can authorize as a special service, over and above the normal audit. These additional services tend to serve the same purpose as a fraud audit, with the additional benefit that the auditor can make recommendations to strengthen safeguards to prevent reoccurrence.

Application control reviews. Computer specialists on the staff of a CPA firm can perform a service similar to the one we have suggested be performed by a qualified EDP internal auditor, known as an application control review. Such a review may be performed on a system design or on a system that is in operation. The purpose in either case is to make recommendations to strengthen controls and security provisions.

DATA ADMINISTRATION

One function of data administration is to determine who should have access to which data elements, and the purposes for which access will be granted. A logical adjunct of this function is to provide mechanisms for restricting access to data and for logging and review of accesses actually made. If your company has a data administrator who performs such a function, you have a good measure of protection against frauds that can be perpetrated through manipulation of machine-readable data.

Access privileges

Formal determination of who can access what data and the purposes for which access is granted is often overlooked. In the absence of a formal determination, ad hoc decisions are made by data processing management or by the media librarian—or access is unrestricted altogether. In the case of a file, this may mean that a perpetrator gets access to the entire file and the opportunity to make changes that may not appear in an audit trail. Uncontrolled access to a data base is even more dangerous because of the concentration of data involved. If your company has a data administrator who determines access privileges, the situations we have just described are less likely to occur.

Access control

Several forms of access control are commonly used by data administrators. For on-line data bases, access control includes passwords, authorization tables, and automatic logging of all actual and attempted accesses. The data base administrator should either review the logs personally or see that this is done by someone who has no access to the data base, the computer, or to data-entry facilities.

In the case of files, the data administrator establishes written procedural rules for removal of the file from the library. The librarian maintains a manual log every time a file is released or returned and the data administrator reviews the log or causes it to be done.

Absence of a data administrator

In the absence of a data administrator, those responsibilities for determining access privileges and for assuring compliance should be borne by the computer security officer. If that function does not exist, the responsibility should be borne jointly by user management, the internal auditor, and data processing management. User management and the internal auditor should prepare a formal statement of access privileges. Data processing management should propose a means of assuring compliance, and the internal auditor should review this proposal for adequacy. Once the access control mechanism is agreed upon, data processing should implement it and the internal auditor should check for compliance.

One dangerous thing about not having a data administrator is that responsibilities get shifted to individuals whose primary responsibilities lie elsewhere and who may neglect this function. Data processing management is likely to be preoccupied with production, system development, and maintenance activity. User management will be concerned with its own responsibilities and internal auditing is likely to be preoccupied with meeting its audit objectives. A computer security officer will be somewhat concerned with access to data but is more likely to be preoccupied with physical security and procedural considerations.

PERSONNEL DEPARTMENT

The personnel department should bear responsibility for assuring that personnel policy and practices are consistent with the objective of preventing computer fraud, and should periodically reevaluate its policies from that standpoint and make any adjustments deemed advisable. Personnel should also bear reponsibility for assuring compliance with its policies. Some specifics that should be addressed by personnel policy are:

- Hiring practices.
- Morale.
- Vacation policy.

Hiring practices

Personnel should take responsibility for establishing hiring practices and for assuring compliance. These practices should include background and reference checks. Another thing personnel should assure is that individuals are not hired for positions materially above or beneath their abilities and qualifications.

393

Morale The personnel department should take responsibility for knowing the prevailing status of morale and for taking action to correct any problems. One means of correcting morale problems is through individual counseling and through transfers. Morale problems can also be minimized if not entirely prevented through personnel practices.

One means of minimizing morale problems is to assure fairness in individual performance evaluations, raises, and promotions. Individuals who cannot qualify for promotions should be given training or the opportunity to transfer into a position in which they can progress.

Vacations Personnel policy should provide for vacations for all employees and protection for employees against loss of vacations because of staffing shortages. Since failure to take available vacations is often found in fraud cases, personnel should also make sure that, at the very least, all individuals in potentially sensitive positions take their allotted vacations and that provision is made for someone else to assume their responsibilities in their absence.

FINANCIAL MANAGEMENT Financial management has several responsibilities related to fraud prevention and detection:

- Review of loss allowances and bad-debt write-offs.
- Establishing limits to the magnitude of financial transactions that individuals at various levels are authorized to approve or initiate.
- Reconciliation of bank records to supporting documentation.
- Review of departmental performance for unexplained changes in sales, net profit, or expenses.

Loss allowances and bad debt One common subterfuge for embezzlement is to offset thefts with write-offs to bad debt or through loss allowances. First the perpetrator takes cash or inventory and then covers the shortage by a credit to the asset account and a debit either to loss allowance or bad debt, thereby keeping the books in balance and eliminating cause for suspicion. A similar ploy is to record a sale to a fictitious customer, send out the merchandise, and later write the receivable off as uncollectible.

Financial management can stop this type of thing through a combination of sound procedures and vigilance. Procedures should require independent and supporting documentation for write-offs. Financial management should review both the write-off and the supporting documentation for agreement and for proper authorization.

Failure to review individual write-offs is a common weakness. Another common weakness is not to review write-offs as long as they fall within a budgeted allowance. The problem is that this, in effect, gives managers the opportunity to budget how much they will steal each year. As long as they keep to that budget, no one will be the wiser.

Transaction approval and initiation limits

Transaction approval and initiation limits serve primarily to limit the number of individuals who can put through large fraudulent transactions. Such limitations are clearly an advantage. Normally, the amount an individual is authorized to sign for increases with rank in the organization. One caution to bear in mind in conjunction with these limits is that there is no reason to presume that upper levels of management are less susceptible to embezzlement than rank-and-file employees. In fact, a recent analysis of large computer frauds revealed that the most common job title for a perpetrator was manager or officer, and that the average loss from frauds by managers and officers was far greater than the average loss for other job categories.

Reconciliation of bank records

Disbursement and bookkeeping frauds may sometimes be revealed through careful review of bank statements and canceled checks. Things to look for include unreconcilable balances and checks that are either endorsed differently than usual, deposited into a bank that differs from the vendor's usual bank, or made payable to a slightly amended form of the vendor's name.

If there is an unreconcilable balance, one possibility is that someone has written fraudulent checks and then destroyed those checks as soon as they came back canceled from the bank. If any such checks have been written, comparison of your company's records with the bank's microfilmed records will identify them.

If the payee, endorsement, or bank of deposit on a check are unusual, the check may have been a fraudulent payment to a bogus vendor, disguised as a payment to a frequent vendor. The appropriate action to take in that instance is to review the related purchase order, invoice, and warehouse receipts for existence and validity.

Departmental performance

Unexplainable changes in departmental sales, profits, and expenses may be a symptom of fraud. Increases in sales without corresponding increases in profit may be symptoms. Similarly, a sudden increase in expenses without a corresponding increase in sales or an explainable increase in acquisition cost of raw materials or inventories should be examined carefully. An effective budgeting system that compares budget to actual and computes variance can be an important aid in detecting these changes.

| USER MANAGEMENT | The responsibilities of user management regarding computer fraud prevention are: |

USER MANAGEMENT

The responsibilities of user management regarding computer fraud prevention are:

- Specification of processing control requirements.
- Authorization, preparation, and conversion of input.
- Review of transaction logs and journals, and researching errors and discrepancies.

Processing control requirements

During development of a new system, user management should be responsible for specifying control requirements. User management has the best grasp of valid combinations of data values and of the potential for fraudulent transactions. Although data processing management and the internal auditor should both take an interest in processing controls, only the user has the depth of application knowledge necessary to envision ways in which the application can be defrauded.

Input authorization, preparation, and conversion

Results of a recent analysis of large computer fraud cases show that the vast majority of cases originated on the input side. Input authorization, preparation, and conversion are particularly sensitive and should be separated from one another.

Formal written procedures for input authorization, preparation, and conversion are also required. User management is responsible for formulating these procedures and for obtaining compliance.

Reviewing logs and journals

User management is responsible for reviewing transaction journals and processing logs and for comparing those results to results anticipated based upon input. If discrepancies or errors become apparent from this review, it is the responsibility of user management to research and resolve them. Another specific responsibility of user management during system development is to request logs and journals that will be suitable for identifying errors and other discrepancies.

ALTERNATIVE RESPONSIBILITIES

In the preceding sections of this chapter we have outlined responsibilities of various groups or functions for preventing or detecting computer fraud. In some instances we stated that if a particular group or function did not exist in your company, the responsibilities could be assumed by another party. In some instances there is no viable alternative, so none was stated. Figure 13-2 summarizes various possibilities for assigning responsibilities.

Party with Primary Responsibility	Nature of Responsibilities	Possible Alternate
Data Processing Management	• Implement security policy and procedures • Ensure adequate knowledge of security and control requirements • Raising issues and concerns • Admission of responsibility	• None • None • None • None
Computer Security Manager	• Evaluate computer security • Articulate policy • Monitor adherence to policy	• Data Processing Management, Internal Auditor, Data Administrator (data only) • Data Processing Management • Internal Auditor, Data Processing Management, Data Administrator (data only)
Internal Auditor	• System development review • Control review of operational system • Installation audits • Detection of discrepancies • Advice to management	• External Auditor • External Auditor • External Auditor • External Auditor (if material), User (if appropriate exception reports and logs provided) • External Auditor, Consultants
External Auditor	• Detection of material fraud • Review of controls • Discretionary services	• Internal Auditor • Internal Auditor • Internal Auditor, Consultant
Data Administrator	• Access privileges • Access control	• Computer Security Manager, User Management-Internal Audit —Data Processing Management (jointly) • Computer Security Manager, User Management-Internal Audit —Data Processing Management (jointly)
Personnel Department	• Hiring practices • Morale • Vacations	• None • None • None
Financial Management	• Review of loss allowances and bad debt writeoff • Establish transaction approval and initiation limits • Reconcile bank records • Review departmental performance figures	• Internal Auditor • None • Internal Auditor, External Auditor • External Auditor (if changes are material amounts)
User Management	• Processing control requirements • Input authorization, preparation, conversion • Review exception reports and logs	• None • None • None

Figure 13-2

Summary of Primary and Possible Alternate Responsibilities

14

Estimating the Costs and Benefits of Countermeasures

One very important question is how much protection you need to have against computer fraud. Overkill is a burden both economically and administratively. Lack of enough or of the right forms of protection can also be costly.

Before you can begin to answer the questions of what and how much protection, you need to be on top of the situation in your company. Earlier chapters tell how you can get there.

Once you are well aware of your company's situation, you will need some kind of basis for selecting countermeasures and deciding which particular ones should be implemented. Armed with knowledge of your own situation and with a theoretical selection basis of the type suggested in this chapter, you can begin to evaluate specific measures. The sections of this chapter cover:

- Theoretical basis.
- Performing the cost/benefit analysis.
- Conclusion.

THEORETICAL BASIS
Theoretically, the objective is to *derive the maximum benefit possible while keeping the cost lower than the benefits*. In practice, both the costs and benefits of countermeasures are difficult to quantify. Cost estimates must consider start-up as well as ongoing operation ex-

penses. Benefit estimates may be derived from risk analysis techniques and other forms of assessments.

Cost estimates   The two factors to consider when estimating the cost of protection against computer fraud are the cost of putting a countermeasure into place and the cost of keeping it going once it is there. Some countermeasures have fairly high start-up costs relative to their operational expenses, especially those that call for a capital investment in electro-mechanical equipment. Others show just the opposite relationship. Items to consider for each are:

- Start-up costs (development manpower, training, program development, and equipment and software acquisition).
- Operational costs (salaries and equipment usage).

Development manpower. Development manpower can be obtained either by temporary assignment of internal staff or by utilizing consulting services. The source of this manpower depends upon the types of skills required and on whether or not these skills are available within your company. Activities involved in development include designing the countermeasure to fit into your environment, preparing administrative procedures for implementing the countermeasure, and assigning responsibility for carrying out the procedures.

If the countermeasure involves technology, design will require some special skills. For example, encryption is a highly specialized discipline for which you need expert advice. Similarly, programmed controls require knowledge of the specific application, means of implementation, and an understanding of control requirements. Countermeasures of an administrative or policy nature require firsthand knowledge of the environment, and an ability to work them into what already exists and gain acceptance.

Once a countermeasure has been designed, means of formalizing its implementation through procedures is usually required. These procedures must be written and clearly expressed. They must also be as simple as possible to accomplish. Otherwise, shortcuts will be devised that may defeat your objectives.

Development of a countermeasure is not complete until responsibility for enforcement and execution have been assigned. Assignment should take into account the existing organization from the standpoints of knowledge, similar responsibility, and need for separation of duties. Assignments need the blessing of affected departments as well as the acceptance by individuals who will be filling those assignments.

Training. The fundamentals of training are "who, what, how, when, and why." All of these fundamentals require thorough under-

399

standing and acceptance for success of the countermeasure. The degree of effort devoted to each of the fundamentals depends on the complexity of the measure and upon how similar or different it is from existing practice.

The objective of communicating understanding of the what, how, when, and why of a countermeasure bears some further examination. Failure to understand "what" will result in the wrong action or no action at all. Failure to understand "how" will have the same effect. Failure to understand "when" will mean either action at the wrong time or no action at all. Failure to understand "why" will lead to shortcuts or total circumvention of the countermeasure.

Training costs include the cost of developing a training program and the time used by the trainer and trainees in the learning experience. Training materials such as written lessons and computer exercises may also be required. Training may also include a period of parallel implementation during which the old and new approaches may be followed simultaneously. Operation of the new countermeasure during that parallel period should also be considered to be a training cost.

Program development. Programs for auditing, edit, validation, encryption, and so forth require software development or modification. The amount of effort varies with the countermeasure and the extent to which it is applied. The programmer time and equipment resources should be considered to be part of program development costs.

Equipment and software acquisition. Some countermeasures require equipment and/or software acquisition for start-up. Encryption may necessitate acquisition of chips or other hardware devices for start-up. Audit tools, if not developed internally, will require software acquisition for start-up.

Salaries. If countermeasures require human resources for their implementation, salaries paid to those individuals are an operational cost. In including salaries, you should only figure that portion of an individual's time devoted to the countermeasure. If the individual performs other useful functions, the entire salary expense should not be charged to the countermeasure.

Included with the salary expense should be any fringe benefits and other overhead related to that individual. If the salary is to be prorated before charging against the countermeasure, the fringe benefits and other overhead should also be prorated by the same factor. Depending upon your company's budgeting plan, you may have to be careful not to double count the fringe benefits and overhead when budgeting for the countermeasure.

Equipment usage. If the countermeasure requires extra computer runs or appreciably more computer time per run, the equipment usage should be added to the operational cost of the countermeasure. Cases in which this expense would apply include runs of audit software and extensive edit and validation checks in an application. Other countermeasures where equipment usage figures in are passwords and authorization tables.

The method of charging equipment usage against a counter-measure should be based upon internal chargeback methods, if they exist. Some methods charge resources based upon CPU resources and time. Some methods include other resources and overhead. In determining the appropriate charge for budgeting purposes, some degree of estimation will be required.

Benefits estimates

The benefits anticipated from a countermeasure include risk reduction and other benefits. Risk reduction can be estimated by risk analysis. Other benefits include any other quantifiable benefit that can be identified; and these sometimes outweigh the fraud-risk-reduction benefits.

Risk analysis. Performing a risk analysis means identifying vulnerabilities of applications and estimating the potential losses associated with vulnerabilities. Earlier portions of this book explain how to identify vulnerabilities. Relevant considerations are listed in Figure 14-1.

Estimating the potential losses is a difficult matter, especially since statistics on the potential loss from a particular risk do not exist. However, the estimation process is fairly straightforward if you take it in steps, as shown in Figure 14-2.

As illustrated, the initial step is to list the specific risks that might materialize. In our examples, the first such risk is having a fraud perpetrated by way of an extra employee on the payroll system.

The next step would be to estimate the occurrences per year for each risk. If, in the absence of appropriate countermeasures, it is estimated that an incident could happen once every 4 years, the frequency would be 0.25.

The third step is estimating dollar loss per incident, generally the figure is what might be an average for such losses. You can, as an alternative, use a somewhat more elaborate approach wherein high/average/low dollar figures are used. In this approach, you would assign, in step 2, frequencies of occurrence for each of the three dollar values.

The last step would be to compute the expected annual losses, simply by multiplying the frequency times the dollar value for an occurrence. The total, then, represents the expected dollar loss from all risks considered. Your countermeasures should cost no more than

Identification and Description

- Name of application
- Description of processing functions
- Users
- Sources of input

Volume Statistics

- Daily dollar volume
- Average transaction amount
- Maximum transaction amount
- Daily transaction volume
- Number of accounts

Installation Characteristics

- Identification and location of installation used to process the application
- Overall security measures
- Organization and policies

Analysis of Fraud Potential

- Input manipulation
- Proprietary data (customer, vendor, product, etc.)
- Program/file modification possibilities
- Length of time before a discrepancy becomes apparent and amount that could be siphoned off in that time

Evaluation of Existing Countermeasures and Safeguards

- Type of countermeasure
- Primary and secondary objectives of countermeasure
- Scope and limitations of effectiveness
- Consistency
- Ease of Circumvention

Figure 14-1

Vulnerability Evaluation Considerations

the total (and hopefully much less), which in this example is $63,750.

Steps 1, 2, and 3 should be accomplished by a group of people who might include representatives from user management, data processing, internal audit, independent audit, security, personnel, and consultants on computer security and controls.

In steps 2 and 3 you may wish to use the *Delphi technique* for developing the occurrence and dollar figures. Delphi is a format for extracting informed guesses from a panel of people. It is an iterative process of obtaining group consensus on values, where the basis is largely speculative.

Step 1	Step 2	Step 3	Step 4
Enumerate the risks	Estimate frequencies of occurrence (occurrences per year) A	Estimate dollar loss per occurrence B	Compute annual expected losses A X B
Extra employee on payroll	3.00	$15,000	$45,000
Breakage in computing taxes	0.25	5,000	1,250
Unauthorized pay rate change	2.00	8,000	16,000
Disclosure of employee data	0.10	15,000	1,500
		Total Annual Expected Loss	$63,750

Figure 14-2

Payroll Risk Analysis Example

Risk analysis, although theoretically appealing, has certain shortcomings that should not be overlooked.

Whereas the mechanics of computation in the risk analysis approach are sound, it can be successfully challenged on other grounds. First, it is difficult to defend the basis of estimation for occurrence frequencies and dollar losses per occurrence. Both factors are developed from guesses, inasmuch as a statistical basis does not exist either in general or for your company in particular (the latter being by far the most important). Second, the approach is better suited to an insurance company's analysis of risks, where such risks are spread across thousands of insureds. Any single insurance premium is computed based on the recognition that many insureds will have no claims, some will have modest claims, and a fewer number will have catastrophic claims. Because the insurance company is in the business of truly spreading the risks, it can cope with the catastrophic claim. Your company cannot spread the risks and there is no way to guarantee that it will be spared a catastrophic loss—it could happen tomorrow and produce devastating results. Thus, the expected loss in the risk analysis, even supposing that the computational factors were accurate, ducks the question of major losses. Third, as a result of the first and second factors cited above, the question of whether the total expected loss provides a sound basis for justifying expenditures on countermeasures is moot.

For the reasons just discussed, an especially perceptive management may throw out the preceding points and seek your response. At this point, you should be prepared with another approach, because there is, as yet, no scientific defense.

Other benefits. Most countermeasures provide multiple benefits. Either they protect against more than one computer fraud threat or they provide other quantifiable benefits, such as error reduction. A sound decision as to protective measures must take into account all the benefits as well as all the costs.

The method of estimating other benefits is more or less the reverse of risk analysis. In risk analysis, you start with the risks, estimate losses if they are realized, and then identify countermeasures. In estimating other benefits, you begin with the countermeasures and then count the dollars they will save in other losses.

Types of other benefits to consider include:

- Reduction of errors.
- Control of sabotage and malicious mischief.
- Productivity increases.
- Protection against other computer fraud threats.
- Information necessary for management information and control purposes.

Errors. Errors are far more common and costly than computer fraud. For every fraudulent transaction, there are perhaps 100 errors that result in losses. Sound administrative practices and controls cut down on errors, aid in detecting and correcting them before they cause serious losses, and also serve as fraud countermeasures.

Sabotage and malicious mischief. Sabotage and malicious mischief are emotionally oriented threats. Their causes often lie in morale problems, which can be controlled through management and personnel policy. Sabotage and mischief can also be made less likely by measures that prevent access to equipment, programs, data, and means of data entry.

Productivity increases. Productivity usually increases when morale is uplifted. In the famous Hawthorne experiments, it was found that changes in the working environment interpreted as improvements in the working conditions led to productivity increases. Management and personnel policy are important determinants of morale.

Protection against other computer fraud threats. When you are considering a countermeasure to protect against one particular threat, you should not overlook the other forms of protection against computer fraud offered by that measure. As an example, control totals carried forward from the point at which transactions are authorized, through all processing to the final computer output, and which are then verified against manually maintained control totals prevent data-entry clerks from adding extraneous transactions. They also prevent data-entry clerks from modifying or deleting transactions. In addition, they protect against similar actions by keypunch operators, messengers transmitting input, crooks with terminals on-line to your system, surreptitious modifications to master files and data bases, and from covert activities by programmers.

Information necessary for management information and control purposes. Information is necessary for everyday business decisions. For example, feedback on volume and cost controls provides information to the decision-making process, as well as for controlling the system and detecting fraud.

PERFORMING THE COST/ BENEFIT ANALYSIS

Evaluating the cost versus benefits relationship for countermeasures is a multistage process. All the steps involve some degree of estimation, but this is inherent in many business activities.

Before the analysis can be accomplished, several preliminary steps and activities must take place:

- Application vulnerabilities must be identified in terms of the possible means for their exploitation.
- Some form of risk assessment is needed to quantify potential dollar losses. The risk analysis approach discussed previously is one such approach.
- Countermeasures that serve to offset the risks need to be identified, and cost estimates need to be associated with each of them.
- Management will need to decide on the minimum annual return that is sought for expenditures on a program of countermeasures (for example, 100%).
- Thought has to be given to defining a general set of countermeasures and safeguards that are common to and needed by all applications (e.g., physical access controls for the entire computer installation).

Having attended to the matters indicated above, you can now commence the cost/benefit analysis.

The worksheet format

Figure 14-3 shows one way to organize cost/benefit data in a convenient format. It is by no means the only way, and your own needs and company may necessitate taking some alternative approach.

In scanning the illustrated format, you will note a detail section and a summary section. The detail section is needed to show how the figures for the various items were apportioned to the application under analysis; in this example it is payroll.

Looking under General Countermeasures, you will see the physical access safeguards. A capital investment and start-up cost of $15,000

COST/BENEFIT ANALYSIS FOR THE *PAYROLL* APPLICATION	Capital Investment & Start-Up Costs (5-year amortization)			Annual Operating Costs		Annual Loss Avoidance & Savings		SUMMARY	
ITEM	Total	Annual	%²	Total	%²	Total	%²	Annual Costs	Annual Loss Avoidance & Savings
Total Expected Annual Loss[1]						63,750	100		63,750
General Countermeasures									
Physical Access	15,000	3,000	10	1,000	10			400	
Librarian				15,000	15			2,250	
Password Administration	10,000	2,000	20	20,000	20			4,400	
Security Supervisor				23,000	10			2,300	
EDP Auditing	12,000	2,400	15	30,000	10			3,360	
.	.	.	.	.	.	.	.	.	.
.	.	.	.	.	.	.	.	.	.
Specific Countermeasures									
Data Segment Access	5,000	1,000	50	9,000	50			4,500	
Journalizing				10,000	30			3,000	
Adjustment Checker	2,000	400	100	9,500	100	4,000[3]	90	9,900	3,600
.	.	.	.	.	.	.	.	.	.
.	.	.	.	.	.	.	.	.	.
Totals:								30,110	67,350

Notes: (1) This value was developed in the risk analysis previously discussed.

(2) These percentages are the pro rata portion devoted to the application (in this example, payroll).

(3) This savings might accrue from error reductions.

Figure 14-3

A Format for Cost/Benefit Analysis

is involved. Using the 5-year amortization, this will amount to $3,000 a year. However, the payroll application's share of the annual amount is 10%, or $300. Also, note that the annual operating costs (electric repair, maintenance, etc.) for the physical access safeguards total $1,000, of which 10%, or $100, is allocated to the payroll application. Since there are no other savings accruing from this countermeasure, there is no entry in the third group. Thus, the apportioned annual cost is $300 + $100, giving a total of $400, which is placed in the summary costs column. Similar computations are performed for all the other items shown.

As was mentioned earlier in this chapter, a countermeasure can and often does serve more than one purpose. The benefits derived from these purposes, if they become significant, are worth noting. For example, one of the Specific Countermeasures in Figure 14-3 called for the use of an adjustment checker. This countermeasure, in addition to dealing with certain fraud risks, also serves to eliminate input errors that would otherwise cost the company money. The supplemental benefit, in the form of loss avoidance or savings, is shown as $4,000 in this example. It was estimated that 90% of this savings was directly related to the payroll application and is therefore shown in the summary as $3,600.

**Computation of
annual return on
expenditure**

More and more companies require an ROI (return on investment) analysis to be submitted with capital expenditure requests in excess of a specified dollar amount. Although capital expenditures are often a part of a proposed system of countermeasures, expense items are typically involved. However, an ROI figure that closely parallels a capital investment ROI may be computed. To avoid possible confusion, we elected to call this measure of investment worth *annual return on expenditure*. This value is expressed as a percentage.

The annual return on expenditure may be computed as follows:

$$\text{Annual Return on Expenditures for Countermeasures} = (100)\ \frac{\text{Loss Avoidance and Savings} - \text{Cost}}{\text{Cost}}$$

Substituting the totals shown in Figure 14-3, we have

$$\text{Annual Return on Expenditures for Countermeasures} = (100)\ \frac{67{,}350 - 30{,}110}{30{,}110} = \underline{124\%}$$

It is usually a good idea to set a minimum acceptable return, as previously suggested. Perhaps a good rule of thumb for expenditures on countermeasures is that at least a 100% return be projected to have the proposal seriously considered for implementation. In our example, then, the 124% would certainly qualify.

Adjusting the mix Suppose that you have just finished the computations, as outlined above, and arrive at a return figure somewhat less than 100%. If your company has adopted the 100% minimum, you have got a problem. However, all may not be lost, unless your figure is well below 100%.

At this point, you will want to go back and reconsider the mix of countermeasures. Perhaps you will be able to come up with alternatives that give about the same protection at a lower cost. Or, it may be that some device which you may have previously rejected as being too expensive may now look attractive in terms of amortized cost as compared with, say, ongoing salary expense.

If further probing is needed, you may wish to consider the elimination of one or more countermeasures, as a last resort. Should you embark on this course of action, you will have to factor down the loss-avoidance value that had been previously used, to reflect the gap in your system of countermeasures. Clearly, your initial pass at eliminating countermeasures should deal with those that are most costly relative to the risk reduction they provide.

Take care not to play with too many numbers and do not fall into the trap of fudging the risk analysis numbers. Those numbers, for whatever validity they may have, should remain untouched.

CONCLUSION In this chapter we have concentrated on a "numbers-oriented" approach to selling a proposition to management. On the surface it looks impressive and may even carry an air of validity. And, as long as you are not challenged, it has much to its credit on a theoretical basis. As we warned previously, however, you should be prepared to back away from the approach if it should turn out that your management is about to tear it to shreds.

Whereas we have found that lower echelons of management are fond of the "numbers" approach, often to the exclusion of anything else, our experience with top management and boards of directors is refreshingly different. We have found, in all but a handful of cases, that men and women at these levels are quite capable and willing to deal with ideas, concepts, and strategies. Perhaps it is due to their relative age and experience in business, but we cannot state this with certainty. We do know that a "hard numbers" analysis is seldom necessary to prove the worth of an investment that calls for locking up the computer room and data files or one that establishes controls for programmer activities. Given the right audience and some reasonable structure and basis for recommending safeguards, we continue to believe that good business judgment is superior to the "numbers game."

15

Successfully Implementing Your Approach

In the other chapters of this book we tried to develop an understanding of the problem. We examined various techniques aimed at preventing, detecting, and deterring computer fraud. We discussed some considerations pertinent to loss recovery. And, in the immediately preceding chapters, we talked about how to formulate a loss control program.

Assuming you have come to grips with these matters in a meaningful way, you have just a few other hurdles to overcome in order to successfully implement your overall approach. To a significant degree, these hurdles are in the arena of *human factors*, such as convincing management that the program is worthwhile and keeping your approach or program alive despite resistance to change and organizational inertia.

Management is unlikely to accept your program without some salesmanship. First, protecting your company is going to cost money, and no management wants to increase costs without good reason. Second, your program is going to require some changes to be made. Human beings and organizations tend to resist changes.

Opposition may be expected from lower levels of management, when these individuals perceive implied criticism of their operations, interference with their prerogatives, or simply see the program as a burden involving added red tape. They may also anticipate difficulties in meeting their budgets, if they comply with the program.

With these considerations in mind and with some advanced preparation, you can develop a strategy to overcome such opposition. We discuss in this chapter a number of strategies which should work for you, provided that you have done your part to size up your company and management.

After you get your program going, steps have to be taken to keep it viable. Good intentions and even aggressive action confined to a discrete point in time are not enough to protect your company against computer fraud. Inertia has a way of eroding the effectiveness of programs. Changes in systems and personnel can be equally deadly unless provision is made for dealing with effects as they arise.

The compliance mechanism in your prevention program will have to take both human factors and the reality of change into account; otherwise, you will face increasing noncompliance. For example, there will be new applications and threats that you cannot explicitly plan for now. Accommodating change will require building special provisions into your compliance mechanisms. In this chapter we offer a number of suggestions regarding compliance mechanisms that you can incorporate in your program.

The sections of this chapter cover:

- Origins of resistance.

- Strategies for selling your approach to top management.

- Presentation tips and approaches.

- Keeping the approach alive in spite of adversaries.

- Policies that ensure enforcement.

ORIGINS OF RESISTANCE

We alluded to some of the problems you may face in implementing your approach. Anticipation and planning will help you to overcome them. Generically, the origins of resistance are:

- Complacency and ignorance of the risks.
- Cost.
- Politics.
- Jacobson's eleven resistance tactics.

Complacency and ignorance of the risks

Ignorance of the risks and resultant complacency on the part of top management are by far the greatest barriers to getting your program going. Once these difficulties are overcome, you will have much less difficulty overcoming other obstacles.

Our experience is that boards of directors and top managements are very much concerned about computer fraud prevention (usually in the context of an overall EDP security program) once they understand what is at stake and why computer-related risks are significant. The degree of responsiveness to these issues drops off sharply as you go down the chain of command, even when there is an appreciation of risks and their significance. We are not saying that all lower echelon managers react this way or that the top people are always positive. But these are, for whatever reasons, the general tendencies. It is also true that top management generally has the decision-making power and clout to make things happen. And, since we have previously pointed out the multidisciplinary nature of the fraud prevention program, it makes sense that top management should provide the guiding hand that brings these disciplines together and mandates unified action.

Another aspect of complacency and ignorance of the risks is top management's confidence in lower levels of management and belief that they must have made adequate provision against risks. This barrier has to be met without directly undermining such confidence. What you have to do is communicate that grave risks do exist without adequate protection but that those risks can only be addressed when a broader view is taken.

Other barriers arise from the viewpoint top management has to take. In order to run a business, top management must take a global view inconsistent with involvement in detail. Top management is going to be too busy to worry for long about computer fraud.

The most favorable of atmospheres you can hope for is related by the following anecdote. The president of a large financial institution read a blood-curdling article about computer fraud and instructed his chief aide to "make sure it doesn't happen here." The aide made a half-hearted attempt, but nothing was ever done. The president never followed up on his request. The moral to be learned is strike while consciousness is raised.

Another problem, both with top management and with most of the lower levels, is lack of understanding of computers. That lack makes it very difficult to fully appreciate the risks. To overcome the problem, you will have to be graphic in describing potential losses, you will have to avoid confusing terminology and examples, and you will have to relate the threats to actual occurrences.

Cost Management resistance to costs that have uncertain payoffs and paybacks difficult to quantify is understandable. When you are trying to make a profit, you cut costs any way you can without reducing profits. As long as computer fraud is viewed as a distant possibility, management may be reluctant to spend money on preventing it.

Management's attitude toward risk taking also figures into the barriers arising from cost. If management is aggressive about taking risks, they are more likely to resist budget items earmarked for preventing computer fraud. A favorable cost/benefit analysis can be helpful here, but, because the estimated losses can be successfully challenged, you should aim for a convincing case-history approach. This is commonly referred to as using "scare tactics."

Politics The political obstacles we are concerned with here are those arising from lower-echelon operating management. In putting your program into place, you are likely to run into a great deal of simple "turf" protection, where individual managers resist attempts to interfere with what they regard as their own internal affairs. One reason for resistance is fear of losing control over their operation. Another factor is a tendency to see recommended changes as personal criticisms. Uncertainty as to how the recommended countermeasures will be covered in their budgets is another cause of opposition.

Wherever you run into political resistance, you can expect a number of problems. One thing they may do is attempt to discredit your factual basis. We have seen instances in which high-ranking managers have blatantly lied about facts that were raised with top management. Another strategy you should anticipate is counterproposals, where the resisting manager attempts to show that his proposal is far better and cheaper than yours. Still another defense is to attempt to show that you did not understand the department and so over or underestimated the risks. The way to deal with this type of resistance is to be prepared in advance and then to sound out managers to find out where they might resist you.

Jacobson's eleven resistance tactics The following material was written by Robert V. Jacobson, Vice President of Information Systems Security, Chemical Bank (New York), and a highly respected authority on computer security. He has graciously consented to let us use this presently unpublished work, which he plans to use for a future magazine article.

These "tongue-in-cheek" guidelines were intended by Jacobson to aid those lower-level managers who wanted to resist computer security measures. As you will see, it also pertains directly to the subject at hand.

It is not uncommon for the DP Manager who is required to respond to a computer security audit or action plan to realize that the reasons he uses to defer action are hopelessly inadequate. His voice lacks conviction and his arguments lack convincing detail. To remedy this deplorable state of affairs we offer here *eleven* solid, convincing responses:

1. *Since the security measure you propose isn't perfect, it's obviously worthless.*

There is no question that the best defense is an offense. Persistent use of this line of reasoning can keep the security planner off-guard and prevent him from ever getting to the central issues. Senior managers cannot but fail to be impressed when you point out how easy it would be for a team of commandos to penetrate the proposed Physical Access Control System. Surely, you can find some string of accidents, no matter how improbable, which will destroy all existing off-site storage of files. The key point is to be persistent in your attention to trivial side issues. With some skill it should be possible to avoid the substantive questions indefinitely.

2. *We can't do that, the cost would be exorbitant!*
Here is another reason that cannot fail to please. Senior management, particularly when dealing in unfamiliar areas, will look for fairly solid cost justifications before approving new programs and can be depended upon to give a good, loud, knee-jerk "No" on general principles. If you can convince your peers that a proposal cannot be cost justified with 100% accuracy (solid numbers), you may be able to block any discussion of its merits. It's sometimes helpful to be able to imply that the same idea was rejected at some earlier time or by some other organization on a cost basis but be careful to avoid specifics.

3. *It won't happen here, or if you prefer, nothing can ever go wrong!*
Undoubtedly, this is an attractive argument for somewhat subtle psychological reasons. No one likes to admit that he is exposed to the same hazards as the common herd. It's nice to be able to think of oneself as under the special protection of the Gods. Finally, you will have placed your opponents in the difficult position of having to "prove" that something that has not, in fact, happened in the past 20 years could happen tomorrow.

4. *But we already have a security program! We keep the grandfather tapes in my bedroom closet, the back door is always locked, etc.*
This is a somewhat different approach. The notion is to switch attention away from what is being proposed. Your opponents will be forced to give an instant appraisal of the value of what you are doing rather than talk about *their* ideas. If you can get them to admit that existing security measures have *some* value, however slight, they will then have the more difficult task of demonstrating adequate incremental value for what they propose to do. If you play your cards right you may be able to convert the discussion into a self-congratulations session regarding the existing security program.

5. *No one could ever steal anything from us because our system is too complicated.*
The implication here is that if, in fact, somebody *did* manage to slip past the locked door, etc., etc., and gain access to your system, he would not be able to do anything because of the complexity of the system. If you plan to use this argument, it's a good idea to invite

one or two programming project managers to join your discussion. They can usually be depended on to make wry comments about the difficulty of getting work done even when you *do* know how the system works. Of course, you will want to make frequent but vague references to the security features of the software. If a potential weakness in a feature appears to be in danger of discovery, switch the conversation to another area. Whatever you do, don't use the full name of anything. Always refer to it by its initials, e.g., NOPW-READ, RETPD, DBCG, DBSG, DDG, and JES. After awhile the security people will stop asking you to translate, leaving you in complete control!

6. *Yes, but not now; we're too busy!*
Truth to tell, this is a commonly used excuse completely lacking in novelty. Certainly there will be ample instances when you can truthfully employ it but it just doesn't have the blockbuster impact as some of the other suggestions. Perhaps it is best reserved for emergency situations when a swift response is required.

7. *Nothing could go wrong here; I trust my people.*
Of course, you do! Play this one for all its worth. If you think you can pull it off, it helps to assume an injured air. No one will have the nerve to suggest that you have hired a gang of potential criminals to staff the DP shop. Don't be put off by the statistics about crime rates, particularly those in your sphere of activity. Force the proponents of the security program to "prove" that your staff is waiting eagerly for an opportunity to pounce on the assets. You can make life particularly difficult for them if you can force them to do it in public.

8. *I have nothing to lose; there is nothing worth stealing, there is nothing confidential here, etc.*
This approach can be used to throw the security people completely off balance. Of course, they have based their thinking on the presumptions that there must be *something* worth protecting in your DP facility. Now they will be in an unexpected and unfamiliar position; proving that their basic premise is, in fact, correct. As they struggle to do so, you should be able to play "yes, but . . ." with them more or less endlessly. For example, if they express concern about theft of proprietary data, you can say "yes, but lots of people already know about it. And, anyway you can't stop people from going to work for our competitor." There are endless possibilities here.

9. *Is anyone else doing this?*
Be careful to use this ploy only when you are reasonably sure that no one else is using the proposed security measure. Otherwise it may backfire on you. However, if your security people have designed a truly innovative system, this approach should work beautifully, particularly if your senior executives tend not to be receptive to new ideas.

10. *We've already tried that.*
This can stop the security planner in his tracks. Presumably he thinks he is proposing something new. Suddenly and unexpectedly he finds himself asking *you* for an explanation of a past attempt. On the basis of what you tell him (or his own knowledge if he is lucky), he will have to explain why it didn't work before and why it will work now. There are all sorts of possibilities. You may be able to put him in the position of going up against a decision made at a senior level. You may be able to show how negligent he has been in failing to review past experience. It's entirely likely that the discussion can stay focused on why the previous attempt failed rather than why the present plan may work. Don't worry about any differences between the two situations, no matter how important they may be. Let the security planner (try to) point out the differences.

11. *Well, sure; but you'll have to take responsibility for the delays.*
It is quite possible that the security people will not be aware of the full impact of a proposed security measure. If you think that this may be the case, hit them with the responsibility for delays they haven't thought about. When asked for an explanation, do so as opaquely as possible. Cite three examples of increasing gravity, don't worry about exaggerating the difficulties a little, and be sure not to give any hint of possible solutions. Cheerfully encourage the security people to "explain" the reason for the delay to whichever of your managers has the biggest clout and the worst temper. If you think this approach will work, wait until the security planner has completely described his proposal, all difficulties have been resolved, and he has decided he has a winner. An unexpected and aggressive attack by you should knock him off balance and keep him out of your hair for weeks to come.

There you have it. With these rich resources at your finger tips you should never want for an effective comeback. Depending on circumstances you can use a new combination each time and interference in your operations should be stopped dead nine times out of ten. Just remember: as long as nothing ever goes wrong, who needs security?

We can assure you that we have seen each and every one of these excuses used, and that Jacobson's list is a faithful representation of reality. You will have to prepare yourself to deal with these responses. Perhaps you can disarm some of the resisting managers by making the list available early on. Here are a few ideas:

- *Use the list to keep score.* Check off the excuses you are given. When the manager asks what you're doing, show him the list. After he reads it, he'll probably feel obligated to come up with original excuses that may force him to seriously reconsider what you had to say.
- *Let the manager keep score.* Pass out the list just before a

presentation or meeting and try to get some agreement, in advance, to ban the 11 known excuses from the meeting. This approach may force the "know-it-alls" and "my-mind-is-made-up, don't-confuse-me-with-the-facts" types to deal head on with the issues rather than their prejudices.

• *Offer modest prizes for new excuses.* Explain to the manager that you are trying to expand your list and so far no one has been able to add to the original 11. You'll buy lunch if he finds a new excuse.

STRATEGIES FOR SELLING YOUR APPROACH TO TOP MANAGEMENT

There is no way to sell a systematic approach to preventing computer fraud unless you have the support of top management. Therefore, they should be your first audience. Once you have their support, you can sell the other levels. The best tack to take depends upon what your management is like and their attitude to risk taking. There are four strategies in particular we recommend. You should select the best one or combination thereof for your company.

• Cost/benefit analysis.
• Case study approach.
• Seek expert advice.
• Factual support.

Cost versus benefits analysis

Regardless of your ultimate strategy for selling your program for preventing computer fraud, a cost/benefit analysis of some type is desirable. Chapter 14 goes into detail about how to prepare such an analysis. Going through that step cannot be ignored if you want to see your program implemented.

One thing a cost/benefit analysis does is to lend credibility to your recommendations. If management sees an expected loss of $100,000, they are going to be alarmed. When you tell them that an investment of, say, $10,000 can prevent that loss, the protection program will seem like a bargain.

For some managements, a cost/benefit analysis is enough to sell your program. For them, you just present the cost and benefits and obtain funding and support. More often, management will be more difficult to convince. One thing they may do is question the validity of the figures in the computation of expected loss and therefore the benefits presented in your analysis. If that happens, you should be ready with another strategy that can be presented.

Case study approach

For many managements, a case study approach can motivate desire for immediate action. As mentioned previously, we know of top executives who have read case study accounts in magazines and requested that their companies take corrective action. There is one hitch. You have to be ready to propose action at the same time management consciousness is high. If you wait days, weeks, or months between consciousness raising and presentation of your plan, you are not going to get the same response.

Case studies will be most advantageous to you if you withhold them until you are ready to present a program along with costs and benefits. If your top management has already reacted once to publicized cases, do not expect the same enthusiasm when you bring them up for a second time. It is effective, however, to present cases (if they are new to top management) when you recommend your program of countermeasures. At that time, you will have a plan and all your numbers together, and you can try for an on-the-spot decision.

There are some winning strategies to selecting the case studies for presentation. They are:

- Industry involved.
- Application.
- Amount of loss.
- Technology.

Industry involved. Presenting cases in your own industry brings the cases closer to home for management. If your company is an electronics supply firm with a computerized accounts receivable system, presenting cases in which bank tellers embezzled millions from computer systems may not help that much. Management may well conclude that large sums can be embezzled from computer systems. Unfortunately, they may also conclude that only banks can have that problem.

If you cannot find good cases in your own or closely related industries, you may have to resort to selecting the closest cases you can find and then explaining how they apply to your company. That sort of fall-back will definitely weaken the impact of the cases. If you do have difficulty in finding relevant cases, we urge you to refer to our bibliography for sources.

Application. The application involved in a case has a definite bearing on its potential impact in convincing management. A case involving receivables fraud against a retail chain may have limited impact upon the management of a company engaged in construction, where there are relatively few receivables. There are also going to be differences in operational details and procedures. Those differences may well be great enough to convince management that the related threat is of little cause for concern in your company. Again, if you cannot come up with a good case in a related application, you are going to have to explain why the case is representative of what can happen in your company. That need for explanation will weaken your presentation.

Amount of loss. The amount of loss experienced in a case is an important consideration in selecting that case for presentation to management. Two factors regarding that amount need to be considered. First, wherever possible, the amount lost in the case should be on a scale relevant to amounts your company could lose in a similar application. If the case involves a much larger company and a loss vastly greater than your company could expect to lose, management may incorrectly conclude that you are exaggerating the risks.

If the amount of loss in the case is much smaller than your company could expect to lose, you may lull management into a sense of relative security. If you project that your company could lose $2 million and the biggest case you can come up with involved $25,000, management is going to think along the following lines: Granted that these things do happen, there is no reason to think it is going to happen here and, even if it does, it won't amount to $2 million.

Along the same lines, case studies involving relatively small amounts should not be selected for presentation. Presenting two or three small cases does not convey the message of potentially great losses. If you present a large number of small cases, your presentation is going to take too long and fail because of lack of attention on the part of the audience.

Technology. Within broad limits, management will be unaware of differences in technology between the cases you present and the way your company's systems are set up. Nevertheless, if you present a case involving an on-line real-time system and your data processing applications are back in the dark ages, management is going to wonder how people using "phone-break" techniques can be a threat. Similarly, if you talk about keypunch operators modifying input and management knows they have terminals everywhere, they are bound to be a bit confused.

Seek expert advice   One dilemma you may be faced with is a general lack of credibility for your assessment of the potential risks. Management may simply think that you are "crying wolf," or someone opposing your program may have a channel to top management and may use that contact to raise skepticism. When that happens, you may need external support for your recommendations.

One way to get that support is to call in an expert respected by your management and have that individual conduct a review and present the risks. If you do not anticipate a credibility problem going into your presentation, you should nevertheless be prepared to say that what you are really planning to do is to call in a consultant to study the problem. If you end up going that route, your presentation should explain what the consultant will do to verify that cost/benefit analysis, how much that study will cost, and why the consultant is reliable, discreet, and knowledgeable.

If you anticipate a credibility problem, the best approach is to call in the consultant before you present your program to management. When the consultant's study is completed, arrange the presentation. You should present most of the material, leaving it to the consultant to present the risks and potential benefits.

There are a number of ways of selecting a consultant. Obviously, competence and reputation are important, and there are a number of such choices. For some managements, being told by consultants from the company's external auditing firm would be most effective. Other managements would be more impressed by someone with experience in their business. Still other managements would be impressed by someone who had found fraud in a competitive company. University professors or researchers may be exactly right for your company or totally ineffective, depending on the tastes and prejudices of your management. No one can respond as to which approach would be best without knowing your management.

You will want to watch for a technical approach that is consonant with your management's orientation. Complex mathematical methods and consultants who speak mostly computerese may not be able to hit a responsive chord with many managements. On the other hand, services in this category, which may be too esoteric for the businessman, can have application elsewhere in your program.

In general, the credentials and experience of the consultant should be impressive. You should expect to pay well for the services of qualified individuals and pay attention to their recommendations. On any other basis, you will end up wasting everyone's time and your company's money.

Factual support

Any factual support you can present concerning instances of computer fraud, or even of possible computer fraud, will be useful in convincing management to endorse your approach. The length to which you should go to obtain examples depends upon what you already know about actual cases in your company and upon how difficult you think it will be to convince top management. If you already know of instances, you should definitely present them as part of your rationale. If you do not have such evidence, you might want to try to find some, if you think it will be needed. If your company uses computers extensively, there is a good chance you will find some examples. However, if your company is fairly clean, you may have to dig deeply to come up with the cases you need. For that reason, an element of judgment is required in deciding whether or not to use factual support for your presentation.

If you do decide to use factual support, there are several types of evidence you might find.   From most effective to least effective, those types of evidence are:

- Ongoing cases of computer fraud.
- Past cases of computer fraud.
- Current situations in which chronic discrepancies exist and in which fraud is a possible, but unproved factor.
- Theft of services.
- Unauthorized disclosure of confidential data.
- Sabotage or malicious mischief.

Ongoing cases of computer fraud.   Few managements will turn down your program if you present evidence of ongoing computer fraud.   If you have such evidence, all you have to say is: "We found this evidence and here is what we are doing about it.   We haven't looked that carefully at every application, but this is our estimate of potential losses if we do not take further action.   Here is the program we propose.   This is what it will cost and this is how much it will save in future losses."

If the first incident you are aware of is not very large, you may want to supplement it with other facts.   Those other facts can be other cases or elements of any of the other strategies we have discussed.   How big a case has to be to be big enough to convince management is a matter of judgment.

Past cases of computer fraud.   Past cases of computer fraud serve to convince management that it can happen in your company.   The greater the loss that was involved, the greater their potential impact will be.

Another factor in judging the potential impact of past cases of computer fraud is what was done as a result of those past cases.   If you are planning to present a program involving significant change, we assume that corrective action taken following the past instances was either minimal or else it was limited to the particular application involved, or possibly there was a brief period of concern followed by a return to laxity.

Current situations involving chronic discrepancies.   Many companies allow chronic discrepancies (out-of-balance conditions, duplicate payments, mispostings, delayed processing, and other problems leading to customer complaints) to continue.   If you know of such a situation and if fraud has not been entirely ruled out, this is the first place to look for it.   Sometimes, you will not have the time, budget, and authority to find out for certain before you present your approach.

Authority to go in and look over the problem can be difficult to obtain. Even if management of the affected area is aware of the discrepancy, they may get very touchy when you ask to look into it. The resistance, if it occurs, will come from the manager's fear that you will expose his loss of control.

Another very real obstacle to investigating current discrepancies can be the amount of work necessary to show whether or not fraud is a factor. We are aware of instances in which it took 6 months for a staff of 20 high-level managers and senior professionals to clear up such a problem. Although such a problem deserves prompt attention, you might not find it practical to investigate it just to prove your point.

If you decide not to investigate current situations involving chronic discrepancies, you may still want to document them in your presentation. They are cases in which a strong possibility of computer fraud exists. Furthermore, even if investigation ultimately shows there was no fraud, the countermeasures you will be proposing will prevent similar situations from arising in the future.

Theft of services. We know of an instance in which a case of theft of services was used successfully to sell an approach to management. You may be able to find instances of it in your company. What we are talking about is programmers that use the company's computer time to play games. You may also find that they can or do run work or develop programs for their own personal customers.

A related piece of evidence you may find is misuse of one of your company's accounts with a timesharing vendor. Available evidence may range from certainty that theft of services occurred to knowledge that unresolvable discrepancies exist between amounts billed and usage that can be documented. In using this type of evidence, a bit of care is advisable. If your support rests solely on minor discrepancies, management will be inclined to believe that your program is overkill. On the other hand, this type of evidence, combined with other forms of factual support, can communicate the idea that a systematic approach is required because so many different types of vulnerabilities exist.

Unauthorized disclosure. Unauthorized disclosure of confidential data can support your argument, whether or not the individual responsible profited. If the individual did realize a personal profit from the disclosure, you have an instance of computer fraud. If the individual did not profit, you still have evidence that confidential data can be stolen from your company.

Sabotage or malicious mischief. Instances of sabotage and malicious mischief will serve to convince management that the environment in which your computer systems operate is not entirely protected. Such cases will demonstrate that your systems are vulnerable and that individuals, whether they be employees or not, have had both the opportunity and motivation to cause measurable losses to your company.

An "unmentionable" strategy

There is one other strategy for selling your approach to management, which you might hear about but we do not recommend your using. Our reason for bringing it up is to explain why we do not recommend your using it. The method we are referring to is sometimes dubbed the "tiger team" approach. The idea is to find out empirically how much your company can lose and then to document it. Put simply, this means committing fraud.

Such an approach could have the effect of disrupting computer operations and data files. In some percentage of circumstances you could end up defending a legal suit (an interesting challenge to our judicial system). And there is a very real possibility that you could be fired on the spot.

PRESENTATION TIPS AND APPROACHES

As we have already mentioned, you will need top management's support to implement a program for preventing computer fraud. Your presentation should propose a course of action and give compelling reasons why that action is necessary.

Recognizing that we are not setting out to give you a complete set of techniques for making presentations, we nevertheless wish to point out key factors that could mean the difference between success and failure.

- *Use an oral/visual approach.* You will want to have a stand-up, face-to-face presentation. Do not expect a written report to have the same impact. The visual aids (slides, posters, flip-charts) should be professional in appearance and uncluttered with busy detail. The visual should support and/or guide the presentation. Never read directly from the visual aid.
- *Outline, rehearse, and revise.* Neither read nor memorize a speech script. Outline all the key points and be sure to rehearse and present using your own natural style. Ask a couple of your associates to be critics when you rehearse, and revise in response to their suggestions.
- *Keep your audience in mind.* Keeping your audience in mind will enhance the impact of your presentation. First, understand that top management usually takes a broad view of the business and cannot afford to devote excessive time to any one particular problem. In this connection, your presentation should be short and pithy. Along the same lines, too much detail or use of technical jargon will also damage your cause.

- *Involve your audience.* Ask that the audience interrupt you at any time to comment or raise questions. Encourage discussion, and allow time for explanations.
- *Give specific recommendations with a defined course of action.* One corollary to the principle that top management will be unwilling to spend too much time on any particular problem is that management may not take action on general principles. Wherever possible, go to management with specific recommendations, even if management agrees in principle. This means that your approach must be well defined before you present it. For example, convincing management that management policy requires revision may not result in action. It is better to propose specific policy revisions and give appropriate management a copy of the proposed policies along with a cover memo for them to sign. During your presentation of specifics, members of your audience may suggest modifications or alternatives. You will want to be open to such suggestions and be prepared to alter your approach. If a suggested alternative would need further study, say so, and avoid accepting or rejecting it until further analysis has been done.
- *Command attention from the beginning.* If you are aware of a compelling instance of computer fraud that has been ongoing in your company, you should begin by describing it and the amount of loss sustained. The next point you should raise is your projection of total losses that could be experienced if your program is not implemented. After that you should go into the reasons why you are projecting that total loss. Those reasons may include other cases in your company, whether present or past, cases that have occurred in other companies, or opinions of independent consultants.

When you have limited factual support regarding ongoing computer fraud in your company, you can project losses if your program is not implemented. That explanation should include any factual support of past incidents available as well as relevant cases from other companies and possibly support from independent consultants. The rationale you choose should have a strong underlying current of "it can happen here." That means that examples should be relevant and significant enough to shock. The next item to present to top management is the program you want implemented. That begins with specific policies you ask them to endorse. After that you should mention organizational changes required. The last item to present includes the equipment, software, and procedural changes you are recommending.

The closing of your presentation should be devoted to asking top management for their support. They will want to know what your program will cost and you should be prepared with a realistic estimate. If you are unsure in advance of the presentation of how willing top management will be to buy off on your program, you may want to segment it into high-, medium-, and low-priority items. That way, if top management is unwilling to buy off on the entire program, you can improve your chances of getting the most critical countermeasures implemented.

KEEPING THE APPROACH ALIVE IN SPITE OF ADVERSARIES

Unless you build in special precautions to prevent it, your company's organization and the changes it undergoes will naturally kill off any program for preventing computer fraud within a few years. Natural enemies of any program to prevent computer fraud include:

- Inertia.
- Changing business requirements.
- Changes to organizational structure.

Those natural enemies can be overcome only if your program has built-in enforcement mechanisms and built-in flexibility to survive change.

Inertia

Inertia will attack your program from two different directions. When you are originally implementing your program, inertia will make compliance difficult to achieve. Once the program has been implemented, inertia will create a tendency for effecting important business or systems changes without considering the computer fraud implications. Both types of inertia can be overcome by making it easier for individuals to comply with your program than it is for them to circumvent it.

For example, suppose that the countermeasure you were recommending was addition of control totals to a computer-based application. There would be the risk that after the initial training period, data-entry clerks would stop computing control totals and output reconciliation clerks would stop comparing totals processed to totals input. Building control total validation into edit programs and having those programs automatically reject data that do not conform to input control totals will force data-entry clerks to prepare control totals and to do it accurately. Similarly, if the output reconciliation clerk is forced to prepare periodic reports of results of reconciliation, that individual is likely to perform the reconciliation as you prescribe.

Once the initial inertia is overcome, the passage of time will bring about new forms of inertia. If provisions for meeting the changes brought by time are *built into your program* and if conformity is again made easier than circumvention, this sort of inertia need not be a serious problem. Ways of accommodating future changes are discussed in following sections.

Changing business requirements

Business requirements can change as the result of competitive pressures, because new products and services are offered to the public or because new technologies provide more desirable computer processing alternatives. These changing business requirements will be translated into changes in your company's computer applications. Unless you are there to supervise those changes, or unless there is a procedure for integrating computer fraud prevention considerations into the new systems, your company will be in trouble. The applications you secure today will be replaced eventually with new ones in which computer fraud threats have not been fully considered. Undesirable effects of changing business requirements can be prevented by reviewing new applications prior to their implementation.

Changes to organizational structure

Your company's organizational structure can be expected to change over time. Those changes are likely to have an adverse effect on computer fraud prevention unless it is a consideration in making the change. Your strategy should, of course, be to force consideration of computer fraud prevention in making organizational changes.

A few examples will illustrate the potential impact of organizational changes:

- Departments are combined, giving one manager complete control over all aspects of an application.
- New departments are created without adequate provision for review and control.
- Staff reduction leads to combining job responsibilities.

Departments combined. If two departments perform interrelated functions, their combination may reduce the effect of dual control over assets and the amount of separation of duties present in specific job functions. It is not always desirable to bar the combination of departments just to provide separation and dual control. However, mitigating or compensating controls can be established, including stepped up internal audit and independent review activities for the newly formed department.

Unless there is a strong procedure for reviewing these organizational changes, combination of departments will take place without adequate provision for newly created threats. The review of all organizational changes, from the standpoint of computer fraud implications, could be performed by someone such as your internal auditors.

One method of forcing review of organizational changes is to require the internal auditor to authorize the resulting entries to your company's budgeting and payroll systems. If new department numbers cannot be added to the payroll or budget without the internal auditor's written authorization, the auditor is certain to be informed of the changes. Similarly, if the auditor's authorization is written and if a record of authorizations is maintained, internal auditors will have a powerful incentive to review changes before approving them.

New departments. Creation of new departments is another organizational change that can adversely impact computer fraud prevention. One thing that can happen is that a new department is set up that is not subject to review by your internal auditor. Another thing that can happen is, in setting up the new department, computer fraud threats may be overlooked. These undesirable possibilities can be prevented by the same means used to protect against undesirable consolidation of departments, discussed above.

Staff reduction. Staff reduction can arise either because personnel turnover causes attrition or as the result of management dictates regarding cost cutting. Whenever staff reduction takes place, some work may be eliminated. The most likely work to be eliminated is that relating to control and cross checking; that is, staff reduction is most likely to take place among individuals assigned to prevent computer fraud.

Another possible impact of staff reduction is that tasks that were formerly performed by separate individuals may now be performed by only one person. If the two individuals formerly served as a cross check on one another, combination of their functions into a single job will result in a control weakness. One way to deal with the possibility of such a control weakness is to prevent the combination of jobs if loss of control will result. Unfortunately, you may not always be able to prevent combination.

If you see that jobs are being combined in a dangerous fashion, one thing you can do is suggest that some other job functions should be combined in place of the ones under consideration. Another approach you can take is to recommend rotation of responsibility for the about-to-be-combined tasks. Although one individual will have a dangerous amount of power, that power will constantly be rotated among several individuals. Unless all those individuals are in collusion with one another, fraud perpetrated by one individual is likely to be detected by one of the others.

Another way to deal with potential combination of duties is to establish an external "watchdog." This may entail having the internal auditor review the application more frequently, possibly giving added emphasis to certain portions of that review. The watchdog does not have to be the internal auditor. It can be a relatively independent department or an individual charged with special responsibility.

POLICIES THAT ENSURE ENFORCEMENT

There are some clear-cut alternatives of a policy nature that will help ensure enforcement of your program over time. Those means are:

- Responsibility and accountability.
- Monitoring.
- Integration of new applications.
- Periodic reappraisal of your program.

Responsibility and accountability

Every countermeasure in your program should be assigned to a specific individual who is to be *responsible* for implementation. He must be *accountable* to another individual for carrying out that responsibility. Responsibility assignment is necessary in order to avoid excuses and "passing the buck," if the countermeasure is not implemented. Accountability helps ensure enforcement and prevents abuse of responsibility.

An example will clarify responsibility and accountability. Assume that the countermeasure affects an input preparation procedure. The individual responsible is the supervisor of the input preparation clerks. He is accountable to his manager for enforcement of that countermeasure and for any consequences that arise if the measure is not enforced. If the responsibility is not clearly assigned, the supervisor can rightly pass the buck to either the clerks or his manager. If accountability does not exist, the supervisor will feel free to ignore the countermeasure and the manager will not check to see if it is being enforced.

Monitoring

Continuous monitoring by the means suggested immediately above is vital to successful program enforcement. There are various other means of accomplishing the necessary monitoring. One means is by means of automation, examples of which have been discussed in preceding chapters: computer-generated logs, passwords and authorization tables, edit and validation programs, and automated auditing tools such as integrated test facilities (ITF) and system control and review files (SCARF).

Another means of monitoring would include the periodic EDP audit reviews of your applications to check on enforcement of countermeasures and data integrity. Such audits should be thorough enough to detect noncompliance and discrepancies. However, since substantial amounts of time may elapse between audits, provisions for monitoring in the interim are also required.

Integration of new applications

If steps are not taken to protect and control new applications, your program is bound to die out at the same rate as old applications are replaced with new ones. New applications should be designed with fraud prevention, detection, and deterrents in mind. Previous chapters examined numerous considerations that should enter into the design process.

Internal controls, applications controls, and computer security standards should be referenced by the system designer. Independent reviews of applications under development are extremely desirable. Appropriate review bodies include the EDP internal auditor and computer security officer. One purpose of the review is simply to ask an uninvolved individual whether or not controls are adequate. Another purpose of the review is to guard against carelessness or incompetency in designing system control methods. In order for the independent review to be meaningful, the reviewer must be independent of the manager responsible for developing the system and comments made as a result of the review must be enforceable.

Periodic reappraisal

Computer technology and business conditions are subject to great changes. Even with responsibility and accountability, monitoring, and integration of new applications into your program, it may become hopelessly out of date in a few years unless you make it dynamic. Periodic reappraisals can be of great value in this regard, the idea being to formally evaluate the adequacy of your program and provide the basis for updating it to keep pace with your company's evolving systems.

Bibliography
An Annotated Selection
of Recent Books

HOYT, DOUGLAS B. *et al.* (eds.). *Computer Security Handbook,* Macmillan Publishing Co., Inc., New York, 1973. 172 pp.

The 12 chapters, written by 12 different specialists, that make up this book, are full of interesting and useful information for those concerned with computer security at the working level.

KRAUSS, LEONARD I. *Safe: Security Audit and Field Evaluation for Computer Facilities and Information Systems.* American Management Associations, New York, 1972. 284 pp.

A manual containing a comprehensive set of questionnaires, the work is a diagnostic procedure to audit and appraise computer security risks and the adequacy of controls and safeguards.

LEIBHOLZ, STEPHEN W., and LOUIS D. WILSON. *User's Guide to Computer Crime.* Chilton Book Company, Radnor, Pa., 1974. 204 pp.

An introductory treatment, the book is intended as a businessman's guide to computer crime threats and protective measures.

MAIR, WILLIAM C., DONALD R. WOOD, and KEAGLE W. DAVIS. *Computer Control and Audit* (2nd ed.). The Institute of Internal Auditors, Altamonte Springs, Fla., 1976. 489 pp.

429

This book provides in-depth coverage of EDP internal auditing subjects, including applications audits, systems development control reviews, and security reviews for computer facilities.

MARTIN, JAMES. *Security, Accuracy, and Privacy in Computer Systems.* Prentice-Hall, Inc., Englewood Cliffs, N.J., 1973. 626 pp.

An extensive treatment of computer security matters, this text is an important reference for those who are concerned with the subject at a working level.

McKNIGHT, GERALD. *Computer Crime.* Walker & Company, New York, 1973. 221 pp.

Written by a British journalist, this book was one of the first addressed to the general public and executive readers on the subject. It is built on a number of interesting case histories that point out the various kinds of dangers.

PARKER, DONN B. *Crime by Computer.* Charles Scribner's Sons, New York, 1976. 308 pp.

A book for the general public and executive readers, this work contains fascinating accounts of some of most newsworthy cases of computer crime in recent times.

PATRICK, ROBERT L. *AFIPS System Review Manual on Security.* American Federation of Information Processing Societies, Montvale, N.J., 1974. 109 pp.

This paperback work poses a considerable number of questions about EDP security matters, and serves to stimulate thinking and an awareness about potential problem areas.

RUSSELL, HAROLD F. *Foozles and Frauds.* The Institute of Internal Auditors, Altamonte Springs, Fla., 1977. 249 pp.

Although there is limited coverage of computer fraud as such, there is much to be gained from the author's many case descriptions and insights on auditing approaches.

Systems Auditability and Control Study (Data Processing Audit Practices Report and Control Report). The Institute of Internal Auditors, Altamonte Springs, Fla., 1977. 219 pp. and (149 pp.).

Consists of two separately bound reports, one on controls and the other on audit practices. The reports are based on field visits and a mail survey to obtain information about the state of the art with respect to controls and audit practices.

APPENDIXES

appendix A

Good Control Practices
for
Funds Disbursement
and
Receipt Applications

On a case-by-case basis, *funds disbursement* computer frauds have the highest losses per incident. Next in line would be *receipts frauds*.

Considering banks, insurance companies, securities brokers, manufacturers, service businesses, government agencies, and thousands of other specific lines of business, it would be impossible, in the framework of any discussion, to deal with all the exceptions that might come into play in any given company. However, the following two sections will cover controls and safeguards that ought to be considered for applications in these two areas. Not included here are the various testing and confirmation procedures that would be included in a financial audit covering disbursements and receipts.

Disbursement applications

The list below indicates how some types of disbursement frauds may take place:

- Pocketing unclaimed wage, dividend, pension, insurance claim, or payables checks.
- Increasing the amount of a creditor's invoice and pocketing the excess or splitting it with the creditor.
- Paying creditors' invoices twice and appropriating the second check.

433

- Padding payrolls as to rates, time, pieces produced, or number of employees.
- Forging checks and destroying them when returned by the bank, then covering up the transactions by forcing the control totals in the accounting records or by raising the amount of legitimate checks recorded on the computer.
- Issuing computer checks for returned purchases, when merchandise was not actually returned.
- Issuing computer checks in payment of bills of fictitious suppliers and cashing them through a dummy corporation or by fraudulent endorsements.
- Withdrawing funds in dormant or inactive accounts.
- Submitting fraudulent claims for insurance and welfare benefits, with forged authorizations for payment.

The following list, which is by no means exhaustive, indicates good practices that you should be looking for in evaluating disbursement applications.

1. Prenumbered checks should be used and securely stored. Have the computer also generate and print a corresponding number that should match the preprinted one when the checks are being computer-printed.
2. Properly deface or perforate voided checks and keep them available for inspection.
3. Signed checks should not be returned for mailing to those who authorized them.
4. Purchase invoices and documents supporting payments should be canceled to prevent their reuse.
5. Custody of the check-signing plate should be the responsibility of a department other than data processing, and the plate should be kept under lock and key when not in use.
6. Checks over a certain dollar amount should require at least one manual signature, and the face of the check should be imprinted to state this.
7. Bank statements and paid checks should be received directly by the accounting department, not by EDP or those who keep payment records and authorize payments.
8. Paid checks should be periodically examined, by a knowledgeable employee, for endorsement, payee, cancellation, and other irregularities.
9. Separate bank accounts, which are limited as to purpose, should be set up for payroll, trade payables, general payables, dividends, and for trade receivables deposits.
10. Transfers from one bank account to another should be supported with properly authorized documentation.

11. Prompt investigations, with written reports as to the findings, should be conducted when there is a sudden or abnormal increase in number of employees, labor costs, materials costs, expenses, vendor complaints about payments, past due notices received, aging payables as reflected on vendors' statements, and so on.

12. When a purchase invoice is received, it should be checked against the original purchase order and receiving reports before a voucher is prepared that authorizes the computer to pay the invoice. The voucher should be signed by the person who checks the documents, and it is a good idea to keep the supporting documents with a copy of the voucher. Vouchers should be prenumbered and issued in groups to preparers, whose names and voucher series are recorded in a log.

Receipt applications

The list below indicates how some types of receipt frauds may take place.

- Pocketing portions of collections made from customers and offsetting them on the computer by improper credits for allowances or discounts.
- Misappropriating cash and receivables checks and charging the amounts taken to fraudulently generated customers' accounts on the computer.
- Charging customer accounts with more than the duplicate sales slips would show and pocketing cash or receivables payments of an equivalent amount.
- Pocketing monies from incoming payments and applying subsequent remittances intended for other accounts to those accounts where the previous payments were not posted. This is known as *lapping*.
- Manipulation of shipment data in collusion with actual or fictional customer (shipment made without computer producing corresponding invoice, altering product code to lower-cost item, substitution of lower price for the higher one of goods actually shipped), resulting in invoicing fraud that may be directly tied to the receipts system.
- Fraudulent adjustments, error corrections, discounts, credits, and so on, that have the effect of reducing what would otherwise be the legitimate amount of the account receivable. Again, this may be tied directly to the receipts system.
- Writing off an account receivable as uncollectible without proper authorization—the account may have been bogus to begin with.

• Sales returns and damaged goods where the amount credited is fraudulent, being higher that the account is entitled to receive.

The following list indicates the kinds of good practices you should be looking for in applications that involve receipts of payments and applications that are often directly tied to such applications. This list is by no means exhaustive, but it should provide the basis for a reasonable initial effort.

1. Statements of open accounts receivable items should be sent to customers monthly, and this should be done by someone other than those involved with accounts receivable payment posting and invoicing.

2. Customer complaints regarding billings should be routed to and resolved by someone other than those who prepared computer input for receivables payments and invoicing.

3. The computer should periodically list delinquent accounts for review by an official other than the credit manager and collections manager.

4. The writing off of accounts as uncollectible should be done by a company official other than the credit manager or collections manager.

5. The computer should produce a special list of account write-offs that should be reviewed by a responsible official, comparing the entries with the authorizing documentation.

6. Credit memo, error corrections, adjustments, and similar transactions should be approved by a responsible official who is not involved in EDP or in the entry of routine receipts and billing data. Authorizing forms should be prenumbered, issued in series groups with a log maintained as to the receiver and series issued. File copies of such forms should be filed with supporting documentation for the transaction attached (receiving reports, inspection reports, etc.).

7. Records of cash receipts produced on the computer should be compared to duplicate bank deposit slips.

8. Bank statements for trade receivables should not be reconciled by those involved with billing, payments posting, bank deposits, and cashier functions.

9. Payments against receivables should use a distinctive address, and this mail should be opened by a responsible person other than those involved in billing, posting, credit, collection, and EDP functions. This person should make a list of receipts, showing account number and amount of payment. The list should be on a prenumbered form and signed

by the preparer and the cashier, after the cashier makes his own count.

10. Incoming checks should be promptly endorsed restrictively and deposited promptly and intact. A cash application form or photocopy of the payment check can be used for subsequent data entry, not the check itself.

11. Accounts reported as uncollectible should be investigated to determine whether the customer actually exists.

12. The sale of scrap, salvage, damaged goods, and so on, should be closely supervised, and receipts from such sales should be scrutinized as to amount and sales support documentation.

appendix B[1]

Application Control
Evaluation Table

The controls identified in this appendix are explained in Appendix C.

[1] Reproduced with special permission. © Touche Ross & Co. Published in *Computer Control and Audit* (2nd ed.), The Institute of Internal Auditors, 1976.

APPLICATION CONTROL EVALUATION TABLE

APPLICATION CAUSES OF EXPOSURES

PREVENTION CONTROLS	INPUT							PROCESSING									OUTPUT						OTHER		
	LOST	DUPLICATED	INACCURATE	MISSING DATA	TRANSACTIONS NEVER RECORDED	BLANKET AUTHORIZE	INITIATED INTERNALLY	WRONG FILE	WRONG RECORD	INCOMPLETE	INCORRECT	UNTIMELY	INAPPROPRIATE	FILE LOST	PROGRAM LOST	PEOPLE LOST	IMPROPERLY DISTRIBUTED	LATE OR LOST	ERRONEOUS BUT PLAUSIBLE	OBVIOUSLY ERRONEOUS	EXCESSIVE ERROR CORRECTION	UNSUPPORTABLE	SHADOW SYSTEM	UNLIMITED ACCESS	MANAGEMENT OVERRIDE
Definition of responsibilities	1	2	2	2	2	2	2	1	1	2	2	2	1	1	1	1	2	2	1	1	2	2	2	2	2
Reliability of personnel	1	1	1	2	1	2		1	1			2	2	2	1	2	2	1	2	2	2	2	2	2	1
Training	1	1	1	2	2	1		1	1	2	2	2	2	2	1	2	2	1	2	2	2	2	1	2	
Competence	1	1	1	2	1			2	1	1	2	2	2	2	1	2	2	1	2	2	2	2	1	2	2
Mechanization	2	2	1			3	3	1			2	3	2	2	1		1	1	1	1	1	2	1	2	2
Segregation of duties																									
Rotation of duties	1	2	1	2				1	1	2	2	1	1	1	1	2	2	2	1	1	1	2	2	2	2
Standardization	1	2	1	2	2			1	1	1			2	1	2	2	1	1	1	2	1		2		1
Authorization	2	2	2	2			2	2	2	2			2	2	2	2	2	1	2	1	1	1	2	3	
Secure custody	1				1				1					2	2	2	1	1				1	1	3	
Dual custody			2	2										2	2	2		1				1			
Forms design	2	2	2	2	1			2	1	2	2	2										1			2
Prenumbered	2	2		2						2	2	2								1	1				1
Preprinted	2	2	2	2							2	2									1				1
Simultaneous preparation	2	3	2		3						2	2													
Turnaround document		2	2	1							2	2	2									3	1		1
Drum card										2	2														
Endorsement	2	2																				2		2	
Cancellation	2	2	2	2	2		2	2	2	2	1	1	2	2	2	2	2	2	1	2	2	3	1		2
Documentation								2	2									1	1	1	2		2	2	
Exception input						1			2	2															
Default option										2			2												
Passwords	3	3	3	3	3	2	2	3	3	3	3	3	2	3		2	2	2	3	2	2	3	1	3	2

EXPOSURES	LOST	DUPLICATED	INACCURATE	MISSING DATA	TRANSACTIONS NEVER RECORDED	BLANKET AUTHORIZE	INITIATED INTERNALLY	WRONG FILE	WRONG RECORD	INCOMPLETE	INCORRECT	UNTIMELY	INAPPROPRIATE	FILE LOST	PROGRAM LOST	PEOPLE LOST	IMPROPERLY DISTRIBUTED	LATE OR LOST	ERRONEOUS BUT PLAUSIBLE	OBVIOUSLY ERRONEOUS	EXCESSIVE ERROR CORRECTION	UNSUPPORTABLE	SHADOW SYSTEM	UNLIMITED ACCESS	MANAGEMENT OVERRIDE
Erroneous record keeping	3	3	3	3	3	2	2	3	3	3	3	3	3	3	2	2	2	2	3	2	2	2	1	3	1
Unacceptable accounting	1	1	1	1	2	2	2		2	1	2	2	3	2	2	2	2	2	2	1	2	1	1	1	1
Business interruption	2	2	2	2	1	1	1	2	2	1	1	1	1	2	3	2	2	2	2	1	2	2	1	2	2
Erroneous management decisions	1	1	2	2	1	1	1	2	1	2	2	1	2	2	2	2	2	2	3	1	2	2	1	1	1
Fraud	2	1	1	1	1	1	1	2	2	1	1	1	1	1	1	1	2	2	1	1	1	2	1	2	1
Statutory sanctions	2	2	2	2	1	1	1	2	2	1	1	2	2	2	2	2	1	2	1	1	2	3	2	1	1
Excessive costs/deficient revenues	2	2	2	2	2	2	1	2	2	2	1	2	2	2	3	3	2	2	2	2	3	2	3	1	1
Loss or destruction of assets	2	1	1	1	1	1		2	1	1	1	1	2	2	1	1	1	2	1	1	1	1	1	2	1
Competitive disadvantage	1	1	1	1	1	1	1	1	1	1	1	1	1	1	1	1	1	1	1	1	1	1	1	2	1

Warning: Reliance and impact relationships must be tailored to individual circumstances.

APPLICATION CONTROL EVALUATION TABLE

APPLICATION CAUSES OF EXPOSURES

DETECTION CONTROLS	INPUT							PROCESSING									OUTPUT						OTHER		
	LOST	DUPLICATED	INACCURATE	MISSING DATA	NEVER RECORDED	BLANKET AUTHORIZE	INITIATED INTERNALLY	WRONG FILE	WRONG RECORD	INCOMPLETE	INCORRECT	UNTIMELY	INAPPROPRIATE	FILE LOST	PROGRAM LOST	PEOPLE LOST	IMPROPERLY DISTRIBUTED	LATE OR LOST	ERRONEOUS BUT PLAUSIBLE	OBVIOUSLY ERRONEOUS	EXCESSIVE ERROR CORRECTION	UNSUPPORTABLE	SHADOW SYSTEM	UNLIMITED ACCESS	MANAGEMENT OVERRIDE
Anticipation	3	2			3					3		1		2	2	2	3	3							
Transmittal document	2	2	2							2				3			2								
Batch serial numbers	3	3	2		2			2		2															
Control register	2	2	2							3				2											
Amount control totals	3	3						3		3	1														
Document control count	3	3						2	2	2	1														
Line control count	3	3	2					3	2	2	1														
Hash totals	3	3	2					3	2	2	2														
Batch totals	3	3	2					3	2	2	2														
Batch balancing			3					2		2	1			1						3					
Visual verification	2	1	1	2					2	1	1		1								2				
Sequence check		2	2		2				2	2	2		2												
Overflow check			2	2					2	2												1			
Format check										2			2							3		3	2	3	
Completeness check			2					2		2		1	2						1		2	3	2	1	
Check digit		3						2												2				2	1
Reasonableness	1	2	2	2	2	2	2	2	2	2	2	2	2	2	2	2		2		2	2	1	1	2	1
Limit check		2	2		2		2	1		2	2	1		1	2					2	1		1		1
Validity check		2	2	2				2		2		2												1	1
Readback	2			2	2			2		2		2	2			2	2	2	1	2	2		1	2	1
Dating		1		2	2	2	1	2	2			2	2				2	3	3	3	2	3	2	1	1
Expiration	2	2	2	2	2	2	1					2	2	2	2	2	2	2	2	3	2	1	1	2	1
Keystroke verification				1	1	1	1	1	1	1	1	1	1				1	2	1	1	1	1	1	1	1
Approval	1	1	2	2		1		1	2	1	2	2	2	2	2	2	2	3	3	2	2	2	1	2	1
Run-to-run totals	1	2	2	2	3		1	2	3	2	1	1	2	3	3	3	2	2	3	3	3	3	3	1	1

RELIANCE ON CONTROLS
3 — Reliably controls applicable cause
2 — Controls cause but should be accompanied by additional controls
1 — Useful but not especially effective
Blank — No significant contribution

EXPOSURES
Erroneous record keeping
Unacceptable accounting
Business interruption
Erroneous management decisions
Fraud
Statutory sanctions
Excessive costs/deficient revenues
Loss or destruction of assets
Competitive disadvantage

IMPACT OF CAUSES
3 — Very likely to occur
2 — Likely to occur
1 — May occur
Blank — Generally little effect

Warning: Reliance and Impact relationships must be tailored to individual circumstances.

© Touche Ross & Co. Permission expressly granted for reproduction not for sale.

APPLICATION CONTROL EVALUATION TABLE

APPLICATION CAUSES OF EXPOSURES

DETECTION CONTROLS (continued)	INPUT							PROCESSING										OUTPUT					OTHER		
	LOST	DUPLICATED	INACCURATE	MISSING DATA	NEVER RECORDED	BLANKET AUTHORIZE	INITIATED INTERNALLY	WRONG FILE	WRONG RECORD	INCOMPLETE	INCORRECT	UNTIMELY	INAPPROPRIATE	FILE LOST	PROGRAM LOST	PEOPLE LOST	IMPROPERLY DISTRIBUTED	LATE OR LOST	ERRONEOUS BUT PLAUSIBLE	OBVIOUSLY ERRONEOUS	EXCESSIVE ERROR CORRECTION	UNSUPPORTABLE	SHADOW SYSTEM	UNLIMITED ACCESS	MANAGEMENT OVERRIDE
Balancing	2	2	2	1				3	3	3	2									3					1
Reconciliation	2	2	2	2	2			3	2	3	2	2	1						2		2	2			
Aging	2	2	1	1	2				2	2	2	2	1								2	1			
Suspense file	2	2		2	2				2	2	2	2	1									1			
Suspense account	2	2	3	2	2			3		2	1	2	1									1			
Matching	3	3	3	2	2			3	3	2	2	2	1									2			
Clearing account	2	2	2	2	1					2	2	2	2												
Tickler file	2	2	3	2	2		3	3	2	2	2	2	2	2	2	2		2	2	3	2	3	2	3	1
Periodic audit			2	2		2				3	1	2	2	2	2		2				2			1	
Redundant process	1	1	1	1				2	2	3				2	2										
Summary process	2	2	1					3	2	3				2	2										
Label																									
Trailer record																									

CORRECTION CONTROLS

CORRECTION CONTROLS	LOST	DUPLICATED	INACCURATE	MISSING DATA	NEVER RECORDED	BLANKET AUTHORIZE	INITIATED INTERNALLY	WRONG FILE	WRONG RECORD	INCOMPLETE	INCORRECT	UNTIMELY	INAPPROPRIATE	FILE LOST	PROGRAM LOST	PEOPLE LOST	IMPROPERLY DISTRIBUTED	LATE OR LOST	ERRONEOUS BUT PLAUSIBLE	OBVIOUSLY ERRONEOUS	EXCESSIVE ERROR CORRECTION	UNSUPPORTABLE	SHADOW SYSTEM	UNLIMITED ACCESS	MANAGEMENT OVERRIDE
Discrepancy reports	2	3	2	2	2			3	3	3	3		2												1
Transaction trail		3	2	2				3	3	2	3	2	2												1
Error source statistics	2	2	2	2					2	2	2		2								3				1
Automated error correction				2							2		2								3				
Upstream resubmission				2							2		2												
Backup and recovery	3								2				2	3	3	3	2	3	3	2		2	1	2	1

3 — Very likely to occur
2 — Likely to occur
1 — May occur
Blank — Generally little effect

RELIANCE ON CONTROLS
3 — Reliably controls applicable cause
2 — Controls cause but should be accompanied by additional controls
1 — Useful but not especially effective
Blank — No significant contribution

EXPOSURES
- Erroneous record keeping
- Unacceptable accounting
- Business interruption
- Erroneous management decisions
- Fraud
- Statutory sanctions
- Excessive costs/deficient revenues
- Loss or destruction of assets
- Competitive disadvantage

Warning: Reliance and impact relationships must be tailored to individual circumstances.

© Touche Ross & Co. Permission expressly granted for reproduction not for sale.

appendix C[1]

Application Control
Characteristics

The explanations and examples in this appendix are for the controls shown in Appendix B.

[1] Reproduced with special permission. © Touche Ross & Co. Published in *Computer Control and Audit* (2nd ed.), The Institute of Internal Auditors, 1976.

DEFINITIONS OF APPLICATION CONTROLS

Preventive Controls:	Explanation:	Example:
Definition of Responsibilities	Descriptions of tasks for each job function within an information processing system. These indicate clear beginning and termination points for each job function. They also cover the relationship of job functions to each other.	The cashier disburses petty cash and prepares deposits but does not sign checks or maintain accounting records.
Reliability of Personnel	Personnel performing the processing can be relied upon to treat data in a consistent manner.	The cashier has a record for regular attendance, few errors, and keeping sober.
Training	Personnel are provided explicit instructions and tested for their understanding before being assigned new duties.	All tellers attend a one-week school before starting work.
Competence of Personnel	Persons assigned to processing or supervisory roles within information systems have the technical knowledge necessary to perform their functions.	The controller is a CPA.
Mechanization	Consistency is provided by mechanical or electronic processing.	Calculation of gross and net pay is performed by computer.
Segregation of Duties	Responsibility for custody and accountability for handling and processing of data are separated.	The cashier does not maintain the cash accounting records.
Rotation of Duties	Jobs assigned to people are rotated periodically at irregularly scheduled times, if possible, for key processing functions.	Payroll clerks are always rotated within two years.
Standardization	Uniform, structured, and consistent procedures are developed for all processing.	A controller's manual describes the processing of all financial applications.
Authorization	Limits the initiation of a transaction or performance of a process to the selected individuals.	Only the timekeeper may submit payroll-hours data.

443

Preventive Controls:	Explanation:	Example:
Secure Custody	Information assets are provided security similar to tangible assets such as cash, negotiable securities etc.	The general ledger is locked in a safe every night.
Dual Access/Dual Control	Two independent, simultaneous actions or conditions are required before processing is permitted.	A safe deposit box requires two keys to open it.
Forms Design	Forms are self-explanatory, understandable, concise and gather all necessary information with a minimum of effort.	The form to establish a new account has instructions for each space and spacing indicated to assist in keypunching.
Prenumbered Forms	Sequential numbers on individual forms printed in advance so as to allow subsequent detection of loss or misplacement.	Checks are provided with preprinted numbers.
Preprinted Forms	Fixed elements of information are entered on forms in advance and sometimes in a format which permits direct machine processing so as to prevent errors in entry of repetitive data.	The MICR encoding of bank and account number on checks.
Simultaneous Preparation	The one-time recording of a transaction for all further processing, using multiple-copies, as appropriate, to prevent transcription errors.	A payment form having check, check copy, and voucher.
Turnaround Document	A computer-produced document which is intended for resubmission into the system.	A utility bill.
Drum Card	Automatic spacing and format shifting of data fields on a keypunch machine.	The tab key on a typewriter is replaced by a drum card on a keypunch.
Endorsement	The marking of a form or document so as to direct or restrict its further use in processing.	Endorsing a check "for deposit only."
Cancellation	Identifies transaction documents to prevent further or repeated use after they have performed their function.	Punching "PAID" into invoices.

Preventive Controls:	Explanation:	Example:
Documentation	Written records for the purpose of providing communication.	Standard forms for journal entries.
Exception Input	Internally initiated processing in a predefined manner unless specific input transactions are received that specify processing with different values or in a different manner.	A salaried employee must submit a separate request for payment of overtime.
Default Option	The automatic utilization of a predefined value in situations where input transactions have certain values left blank.	Salaried employees receive pay for a 40-hour week automatically.
Passwords	The authorization to allow access to data or processing by providing a "password" known only to authorized individuals.	Computer access by a time-sharing terminal requires a user identification and a secret code word.
Detective Controls:		
Anticipation	The expectation of a given transaction or event at a particular time.	Every employee expects his paycheck at 3:00 P.M., Friday.
Transmittal Document (Batch Control Ticket)	The medium for communicating control totals over movement of data, particularly from source to processing point or between processing points.	Receipts for deposit are accompanied by a deposit slip indicating the account, listing the currency and checks, and total.
Batch Serial Numbers (Batch Sequence)	Batches of transaction documents are numbered consecutively and accounted for.	Daily receipts are batched together and numbered, using the Julian date.
Control Register (Batch Control Log)	A log or register indicating the disposition and control values of batches or transactions.	A logbook records the time and batch number of receipts picked up by the armored-car service.
Amount Control Totals	Totals of homogeneous amounts for a group of transactions or records, usually dollars or quantities.	The receivables file totals $1,237,629.53.
Document Control Count	A count of the number of individual documents.	The receivables file contains 3,721 accounts.

445

Detective Controls:	Explanation:	Example:
Line Control Count	A count of the individual line items on one or more documents.	The December invoices had 4,261 line items.
Hash Totals	A meaningless, but useful, total developed from the accumulated numerical amounts of non-monetary information.	The hash total of account numbers is 47,632,177.
Batch Totals (Batch Control)	Any type of control total or count applied to a specific number of transaction documents or to the transaction documents that arrive within a specific period of time.	The December 17 invoices total $44,755.68.
Batch Balancing	A comparison of the items or documents actually processed against a predetermined control total.	A teller will compare currency and checks with the list and total on the deposit slip.
Visual Verification	The visual scanning of documents for general reasonableness and propriety.	A quick scan revealed that the printer's ink roll was dry.
Sequence Checking	A verification of the alphanumeric sequence of the "key" field in items to be processed.	Account number A16352 precedes account number A16567.
Overflow Check	A limit check based upon the capacity of a memory or file area to accept data.	The product of 10,736 $\times$ 37,667 = (404,392,912) cannot be displayed on an 8-digit calculator.
Format Check (Form)	Determination that data are entered in the proper mode—numeric or alphanumeric—within designated fields of information.	The characters 4 H 6 1 are not an acceptable invoice amount.
Completeness Check	A test that data entries are made in fields which cannot be processed in a blank state.	The computer will not print the check if the payee is all blanks.
Check Digit	One digit, usually the last, of an identifying field is a mathematical function of all of the other digits in the field. This value can be calculated from the other digits in the field and compared with the check digit to verify validity of the whole field.	$\begin{array}{ccccc} 1 & 2 & 3 & 5 & \underline{6} \\ \times 2 & 1 & 2 & 1 & \underline{2} \end{array}$ 2+2+6+4+10 = 24 $-$30 $\underline{6}$ (absolute value)

Detective Controls:	Explanation:	Example:
Reasonableness	Tests applied to various fields of data through comparison with other information available within the transaction or master records.	A male patient should not receive charges from the obstetrics ward.
Limit Check (Range Check)	Tests of specified amount fields against stipulated high or low limits of acceptability. When both high and low values are used, the test may be called a "range check."	A paycheck should be between zero and $900.
Validity Check	The characters in a coded field are either matched to an acceptable set of values in a table or examined for a defined pattern of format, legitimate subcodes, or character values, using logic and arithmetic rather than tables.	375-44-006 is not a proper social security number. They all have nine digits.
Readback	Immediate return of input information to the sender for comparison and approval.	Information transmitted over the phone is repeated back to the sender.
Dating	The recording of calendar dates for purposes of later comparison or expiration testing.	A date is placed on all paychecks.
Expiration	A limit check based on a comparison of current date with the date recorded on a transaction, record, or file.	The paycheck is marked "void after 90 days."
Keystroke Verification	The redundant entry of data into keyboards so as to verify the accuracy of a prior entry. Differences between the data previously recorded and the data entered in verification will cause a mechanical signal.	A punch card verifier closely resembles a keypunch.

447

Detective Controls:	Explanation:	Example:
Approval	The acceptance of a transaction for processing after it has been initiated.	The controller approves the journal entry prepared by the payroll clerk.
Run-to-Run Totals	The utilization of output control totals resulting from one process as input control totals over subsequent processing. The control totals are used as links in a chain to tie one process to another in a sequence of processes or one cycle to another over a period of time.	Beginning receivables plus invoices and minus receipts and adjustments should equal the ending receivables balance.
Balancing	A test for equality between the values of two equivalent sets of items or one set of items and a control total. Any difference indicates an error.	The detail of accounts receivable differs from the general ledger by $326.11.
Reconciliation	An identification and analysis of differences between the values contained in two substantially identical files or between a detail file and a control total. Errors are identified according to the nature of the reconciling items rather than the existence of a difference between the balances.	The bank reconciliation indicates an unrecorded service charge as well as outstanding checks and deposits in transit.
Aging	Identification of unprocessed or retained items in files according to their date, usually transaction date. The aging classifies items according to various ranges of dates.	Receivables are aged "current, 30, 60, 90, over 90."
Suspense File	A file containing unprocessed or partially processed items awaiting further action.	The receivables file contains invoices on which neither payment nor partial payment were received.
Suspense Account	A control total for items awaiting further processing.	The total value of the receivables file should agree with the general ledger balance for receivables.

Detective Controls:	Explanation:	Example:
Matching	Matching of items from the processing stream of an application with others developed independently so as to identify items unprocessed through either of the parallel systems.	The payables clerk matches purchase orders to receiving reports and invoices.
Clearing Account	An amount which results from the processing of independent items of equivalent value. Net control value should equal zero.	Intercompany accounts should eliminate upon consolidation.
Tickler File	A control file consisting of items sequenced by age for follow-up purposes. Such files are usually manual.	Copies of invoices filed in invoice-date sequence.
Periodic Audit	A verification of a file or a phase of processing intended to check for problems and encourage future compliance with control procedures.	The Accounts Receivable Department confirms all of its accounts every June 30.
Redundant Process	A repetition of processing and an accompanying comparison of individual results for equality.	A second payroll clerk recalculates each gross pay multiplication.
Summary Process	A redundant process using a summarized amount. This is compared for equality with a control total from the processing of the detailed items.	Total straight-line depreciation can be calculated for each asset class (where everything in an individual class has the same useful life). This balance is compared to total net book value of the property file.
Label	The external or internal identification of transaction batches or files according to source, application, date, or other identifying characteristics.	
Trailer Record	A record providing a control total for comparison with accumulated counts or values of records processed.	The trailer record indicates 373 blocks, which agrees with the actual count.

Corrective Controls:	Explanation:	Example:
Discrepancy Reports	A listing of items which have violated some detective control and require further investigation.	Each month, a list of delinquent accounts is sent to the Credit Department.
Transaction Trail (Audit Trail)	The availability of a manual or machine-readable means for tracing the status and contents of an individual transaction record backward or forward, between output, processing, and source.	A list of property additions and retirements supports changes to the property file.
Error Source Statistics	Accumulation of information on type of error and origin. This is used to determine the nature of remedial training needed to reduce the number of errors.	The Keypunch Department keeps track of the number of errors made by each operator and detected by key verification.
Automated Error Correction	Automatic error correction of transactions or records which violate a detective control.	A debit memo is automatically produced and sent to vendors whose invoices exceed purchase order terms.
Upstream Resubmission	The resubmission of corrected error transactions so that they pass through all or more of the detective controls than are exercised over normal transactions (e.g., before input editing).	All rejected inputs are resubmitted the next day after correction as if they were new inputs.
Backup and Recovery	The ability to recreate current master files using appropriate prior master records and transactions.	Prior day's master files and transactions are retained in case the current master file is destroyed.

appendix D[1]

Advanced Systems
Control Evaluation Table

451

ADVANCED SYSTEMS CONTROL EVALUATION TABLE

Warning: Reliance and Impact relationships must be tailored to Individual circumstances.

RELIANCE ON CONTROLS
3 — Reliably controls applicable cause
2 — Controls cause but should be accompanied by additional controls
1 — Useful but not especially effective
Blank — No significant contribution

CAUSES OF EXPOSURE

Controls	REMOTE BATCH — Loss of Data	REMOTE BATCH — Distortion of Data	REMOTE JOB ENTRY — Loss of Data	REMOTE JOB ENTRY — Distortion of Data	REMOTE JOB ENTRY — Unlimited Access	REMOTE JOB ENTRY — Computer Abuse	SWITCHING SYSTEMS — Loss of Data	SWITCHING SYSTEMS — Distortion of Data	SWITCHING SYSTEMS — Delay of Data	SWITCHING SYSTEMS — Misrouting of Data	REAL-TIME INQUIRY — Invasion of Privacy	REAL-TIME INQUIRY — Information Not Current	REAL-TIME INQUIRY — Distortion of Data	REAL-TIME UPDATE — Unlimited Access	REAL-TIME UPDATE — Hardware/Software Failure	REAL-TIME UPDATE — Unsupportable Results	REAL-TIME UPDATE — Human Data Entry Errors	REAL-TIME PROGRAMMING — Unlimited Access	REAL-TIME PROGRAMMING — Hardware/Software Failure	REAL-TIME PROGRAMMING — Unsupportable Results	REAL-TIME PROGRAMMING — Human Data Entry Errors	REAL-TIME PROGRAMMING — Computer Abuse	REAL-TIME PROGRAMMING — Destruction of Programs	DATA BASES — Unlimited Access	DATA BASES — Destruction of Files	DATA BASES — Software Failure	DATA BASES — Slow Response
PREVENTION CONTROLS																											
Electronic security					2	2					2			2				2					2	2	2	2	
Passwords:																											
Cyphers					2	2					2			2				2				2	2	2	2	2	
I.D. Cards					2	2					2			2				2				2	2	2	2	2	
Device identification					2	1					1			1				1				1	1				
Physical scanners					2	2					2			3				2				2	2	3			
Physical terminal security			2		2	2					2			2				2				2	2				
Authorizations			2		2	2					2		1	2				2				2	2		2		
DETECTION CONTROLS																											
Line protocol	2	2		2	2		2	2					2		1				1		3						
Up-front edits	2	2		2	2		2	2							2		3		2			2		2			
Access logs					2	2					2			2				2				2	2		2		
Authorized user file					2	1					2			2				2				2			2		
Read-back	3	3		3			2	2					2		2		2		2		2						
Redundancy checks (vertical or longitudinal)	2	2		2			2	2					2		2				2								
Line control hardware	2	2		2			2	2		2																	
CORRECTIVE CONTROLS																											
Rotation of access controls					2	2					2		2	2				2				2		2			
Transaction log					2	2					2			2		3		2		3		2				2	
On-line instruction												1					1				1						
Recovery journal	1	1			2		2	2				1			2		2		2		2			2	3	2	1
Graceful degradation	3	3		3			3	3	2				1		2		3		2		3			3	3	2	1

EXPOSURES

Exposure	RB-LD	RB-DD	RJE-LD	RJE-DD	RJE-UA	RJE-CA	SW-LD	SW-DD	SW-Dly	SW-MR	RTI-IP	RTI-INC	RTI-DD	RTU-UA	RTU-HSF	RTU-UR	RTU-HDEE	RTP-UA	RTP-HSF	RTP-UR	RTP-HDEE	RTP-CA	RTP-DP	DB-UA	DB-DF	DB-SF	DB-SR
Erroneous record keeping	3	3					3	3		2	1	1	1	2	2	2	3	2	2	2	3	2	2	1	3	2	1
Unacceptable accounting	1		2	3			1		2							1	1	2		1	1	2	2	1		2	
Business interruption	2	2		1			2	2	2	1			2	2	2	2	2	2	2	2	2	2	2	1	2	2	1
Erroneous management decisions									1	1	2	1		1		1	1	1		1	1	3	2		2		2
Fraud			2	1	2	3			1	1				1		2		1		2		3		2	1		
Statutory sanction			1	1	1	1				1	2			1		1		1		1		2	1	1	1		
Excessive costs	2	2		2	2		2	2		1		1		2	2	2	2	2	2	1	2	2	3	1	3	2	
Loss or destruction of assets	2	1		1	1		1	1		1	1			1	1	1	1	1	1	1	1	3	3	1	3		
Competitive disadvantage	1									1	1	1		1	2	1		1	2	1		1	2	1	1	1	1

IMPACT OF CAUSES
3 — Very likely to occur
2 — Likely to occur
1 — May occur
Blank — Generally little effect

452

appendix E[1]

Computer Abuse
Control Evaluation Table

[1] Reproduced with special permission. © Touche Ross & Co. Published in *Computer Control and Audit* (2nd ed.), The Institute of Internal Auditors, 1976.

COMPUTER ABUSE CONTROL EVALUATION TABLE

REFERENCE	OBJECT					TOOL		SYMBOL	ENVIRONMENT				
	SERVICES THEFT	INFORMATION THEFT	HARDWARE THEFT	MALICIOUS DESTRUCTION	MISCHIEVOUS DESTRUCTION	DESIGN ACT	IMPLEMENT ACT	FRAUD	EMBEZZLEMENT	FRAUD	INVASION OF PRIVACY	DESTRUCTION OF MEDIA	UNCORRECTABLE ERRORS
PREVENTION CONTROLS													
Personnel screening	1	1	1	1	1	1	1	1	1	1			1
Definition of duties	1	1	1			1	1		2	2	2	2	
Segregation of duties	1	1	1			2	2		2	2	2	3	
Dual access		2							3		2		
Professional ethics	1	1	1			1	1	1		1	1		1
Licensing													1
System design controls (a)	3	1	3	3	3	3	3			2	2		3
Physical access security	2	2	3	3	3	2	2		2	2	2	3	
Electronic access security	2	2	2	2	2	1	2		2	1	2	2	2
Fear of detection	2	2	2			2	2	1	2	2	1	2	
DETECTION CONTROLS													
External controls		1						2		2	2		2
Application controls (a)	2	2			2	1	2	2	3	2	2		3
Physical detection	2	2		2	1	1	1		1	1	1	2	
Bait records	2	3			1	1		1	1	1		2	
Auditing	2	1	3			1	2		2	2		2	3
CORRECTION CONTROLS													
External controls		1				1	2	2	2	2	2		
Legal actions	2	2	2		2	1	2	2	2	2	2	1	3
Application controls (a)			1	2	2			2	1			2	
Contingency plans		2	2	3	3	2	2	3	1			2	3
Backup and recovery	3	3	2	3	3	3		3	3		3	3	
Discharge personnel	3	3	3	3		1	1	2	3	3			2
Fidelity insurance	3	3	3	3	3	1		2	3	3	2	3	2

RELIANCE ON CONTROLS
3 — Reliably controls applicable cause
2 — Controls cause but should be accompanied by additional controls
1 — Useful but not especially effective
Blank — No significant contribution

EXPOSURES
Erroneous record keeping
Unacceptable accounting
Business interruption
Erroneous management decisions
Fraud
Statutory sanctions
Excessive costs/deficient revenues
Loss or destruction of assets
Competitive disadvantage

IMPACT OF CAUSES
3 — Very likely to occur
2 — Likely to occur
1 — May occur
Blank — Generally little effect
(a) Refer to detailed controls on applicable control evaluation table

Warning: Reliance and impact relationships must be tailored to individual circumstances.
© Touche Ross & Co. Permission expressly granted for reproduction not for sale.

appendix F[1]

Systems Development
Control Evaluation Table

[1] Reproduced with special permission. © Touche Ross & Co. Published in *Computer Control and Audit* (2nd ed.), The Institute of Internal Auditors, 1976.

SYSTEMS DEVELOPMENT CONTROL EVALUATION TABLE

RELIANCE ON CONTROLS
3 — Reliably controls applicable cause
2 — Controls cause but should be accompanied by additional controls
1 — Useful but not especially effective
Blank — No significant contribution

CAUSES OF EXPOSURE

	REFERENCE	INCOMPLETE ECONOMIC EVALUATION	MANAGEMENT ABDICATION	INADEQUATE SPECIFICATIONS	SYSTEM DESIGN ERRORS	INCOMPETENT DESIGN PERSONNEL	TECHNICAL SELF-GRATIFICATION	POOR COMMUNICATIONS	NO PROJECT KILL POINTS	TEMPTATIONS TO COMPUTER ABUSE	UNMAINTAINABLE APPLICATION	INCOHERENT DIRECTION
PREVENTION CONTROLS												
Appropriate methodology		2	3	2				2	2			2
Project management			2				3	3	2			3
Staff hiring and training		1		2	2	2	1				2	
Checklists		2		1	1	3					3	1
Documentation		2		2		1		3		2	3	
DETECTION CONTROLS												
Technical reviews and approvals				2	2	3	2	2	2	2	3	3
Management and user reviews and approvals		3	3	2	2	2		2	2	2	2	2
Audit participation		3	2	2	2	2		2	2	2	3	3
System test				3	3	3				2	3	3
Post-implementation review		2	2	2		2	2				2	3
Documentation					3		2					3
CORRECTION CONTROLS												
Documentation					2	1		3			3	

IMPACT OF CAUSES
3 — Very likely to occur
2 — Likely to occur
1 — May occur
Blank — Generally little effect

EXPOSURES

Application Exposures (if project implemented)

	INCOMPLETE ECONOMIC EVALUATION	MANAGEMENT ABDICATION	INADEQUATE SPECIFICATIONS	SYSTEM DESIGN ERRORS	INCOMPETENT DESIGN PERSONNEL	TECHNICAL SELF-GRATIFICATION	POOR COMMUNICATIONS	NO PROJECT KILL POINTS	TEMPTATIONS TO COMPUTER ABUSE	UNMAINTAINABLE APPLICATION	INCOHERENT DIRECTION
Erroneous record keeping		2	2	3	3		3		2	2	3
Unacceptable accounting		2	2	2	2		2		2	2	2
Business interruption		1	1	1	1		1		1	1	1
Erroneous management decisions		3	3	2	3		2		2	2	2
Fraud			1	1	1		1		2	1	1
Statutory sanctions		1	1	1	1		1	1		2	1
Excessive costs/deficient revenues		2	3	3	3	3	2	2		1	2
Loss or destruction of assets		1	1		1		1	2	2		1
Competitive disadvantage		2	2	2	2	1	1	1		2	2
Project Exposures											
Erroneous management decisions		3	3		3		3			3	3
Excessive costs	2	2	3	3	3	3	3			3	3
Competitive disadvantage	2	2	2	2	2	1	2	1		2	2
Business interruption (delay timetable)	2	2	2	2	3	2	2			2	2

Warning: Reliance and impact relationships must be tailored to individual circumstances.

appendix G[1]

Information Processing Facility, Control Evaluation Table

[1] Reproduced with special permission. © Touche Ross & Co. Published in *Computer Control and Audit* (2nd ed.), The Institute of Internal Auditors, 1976.

IPF CONTROL EVALUATION TABLE

CAUSES OF IPF EXPOSURES

PREVENTION CONTROLS	HUMAN ERRORS				HARDWARE/SOFTWARE FAILURES			COMPUTER ABUSE							CATASTROPHE			
REFERENCE	DATA ENTRY	CONSOLE ENTRY	WRONG FILE OR PROGRAM	FILE DAMAGED	INTERRUPT OPERATION	LOSS OF DATA	LOGIC ERROR	THEFT	EMBEZZLEMENT	FRAUD	ESPIONAGE	INVASION OF PRIVACY	MALICIOUSNESS	MISCHIEVOUSNESS	FIRE	WATER	WIND	CIVIL DISORDER
Definition of duties	1		1						1		2	2						
Segregation of duties	2	2	2					2	2	2	2	2						
Reliable personnel	2	2	2	2										2				
Competent personnel	2	2	1	1										2				
Job rotation																		
Housekeeping			1	1					2						1			
Equipment maintenance					2	2	1											
Air conditioning					1	1												
Scheduling			2															
Limited physical access								1			2	2	2	2				3
Restricted knowledge			2						2	2	2	2	1	2				
File custodian				1		1		1	2	2	2	2	2	2		1		2
Physical security			2	1				1	2	2	2	2	2	2	2	2		
External labels			2															
Internal labels		1	2						1	1	1	1	1	1				
Protect rings		2	2			1							1	1				
Disk enable		2	2			1												
Containerized operations				2							1	1			1			2
Training	2	2	2		1		1	1	2	2	2	2	1					
Authorization	2				3	2	1							1				
Manufacturer design					2	2	3						2	1	2	3		
Physical structure															2	3	3	
Physical location															1	2	2	1
EXPOSURES																		
Erroneous record keeping	2				1	2	1							1	1			
Unacceptable accounting		1											1	1				
Business interruption			1	2	3	2	1	1					3	1	3	3	2	3
Erroneous management decisions				1	2				3	3			1	1				
Fraud	1							2	3	3	2	3	2					
Statutory sanctions												3						
Excessive costs	2	2	2	2	2	2	2	2	3	2			3		3	3	2	3
Loss or destruction of assets	2	2	2	2	2	2	2	2	3	2	1		3		3	3	2	2
Competitive disadvantage	2		2	2	2	2	2	2	2		2		1		2	2		2

RELIANCE ON CONTROLS

3 — Reliably controls applicable cause

2 — Controls cause but should be accompanied by additional controls

1 — Useful but not especially effective

Blank — No significant contribution

EXPOSURES

Erroneous record keeping
Unacceptable accounting
Business interruption
Erroneous management decisions
Fraud
Statutory sanctions
Excessive costs
Loss or destruction of assets
Competitive disadvantage

IMPACT OF CAUSES

3 — Very likely to occur

2 — Likely to occur

1 — May occur

Blank — Generally little effect

Warning: Reliance and impact relationships must be tailored to individual circumstances.

© Touche Ross & Co. Permission expressly granted for reproduction not for sale.

IPF CONTROL EVALUATION TABLE

CAUSES OF IPF EXPOSURES

Controls	Data Entry	Console Entry	Wrong File or Program	File Damaged	Interrupt Operation	Loss of Data	Logic Error	Theft	Embezzlement	Fraud	Espionage	Invasion of Privacy	Maliciousness	Mischievousness	Fire	Water	Wind	Civil Disorder
DETECTION CONTROLS																		
Supervision	2	2	2	2				2	2	2	1	1	2	2				
Budgets	2	2	1	2				2	2	1	1	1	2					
Management reporting	2	2	2	2	1	2	1		1	1	1	1	1	1				
Operator logs		2	2	1	2	1	2	1	2	1	2	1	1	2				
Console logs (job journal)	1	2	2	1	2	1	2	1	2	1	2	1	1	2				
Library logs	2	2	3	2		2	1		1	1	1	1	1	1				
Control logs	2							1										
Keystroke verification	2			2		2	2											
Hardware checks	1	2	2	2	2	2								2				
Operating system checks	1	1	1					1										
Scan output	1														3			2
Fire detectors													2	2				2
Application controls	3	2	3	2	2	3	2	2	2	2			2					
CORRECTION CONTROLS																		
Recovery plan					1	2	1	1		2	1	1	2	1	2	2	2	3
File histories	2	1	2	2	1	2	1	1	2				2	2				
Error statistics					1		1											
Fire extinguishers													2	2	2	2	2	2
On-premises backup	2	3	1	3	1	3		2	2			3	2	2	2	2	2	
Off-premises backup				3				2	1		2		2	2	3	3	3	3
Discharge personnel	1				2			2	2	2	1		2	1	2	2	2	2
Insurance								2	2	2			2	1	2	2	2	2
Uninterruptable power	2				2	2	2											
EXPOSURES																		
Erroneous record keeping	2	2	1		1	2	2	1	2	2	1	1	1	1				
Unacceptable accounting	2	1	1	2	3	1	1	1	3	1	1	3	3	1	3	3	2	3
Business interruption			2	1	2	2	2	2				2	2	1	2	3	2	
Erroneous management decisions	1	2	1			3	2	2	3	3	3	3	2	2				
Fraud	2	2	2	2	2	2	2	2	3	2	2	2	3	1	3	3	3	3
Statutory sanctions	2	2	2	2	2	2	2	2	3	2	1	3	2	1	3	2	2	2
Excessive costs													1	1	2	2	2	2
Loss or destruction of assets																		
Competitive disadvantage																		

RELIANCE ON CONTROLS

3 — Reliably controls applicable cause
2 — Controls cause but should be accompanied by additional controls
1 — Useful but not especially effective
Blank — No significant contribution

IMPACT OF CAUSES

3 — Very likely to occur
2 — Likely to occur
1 — May occur
Blank — Generally little effect

Warning: Reliance and impact relationships must be tailored to individual circumstances.

appendix H[1]

Sources
of Software Aids
for Systems Development
and Operations Control

This appendix lists and identifies vendors of four types of software aids that were mentioned elsewhere in the book: (1) test data generators, (2) tape library management systems, (3) disk space management systems, and (4) program library management systems. Although these lists show many of the better-known aids, no attempt was made to prepare exhaustive lists.

In addition to audit software, shown in another appendix, there are a variety of other software aids that can be used to facilitate the investigation of computer frauds, including flowcharters, mapping and data set utilization analyzers, error and interrupt analyzers, diagnostic monitoring and trapping software, data file comparison software, and operating statistics extraction and reporting software (to, for example, collect information about system usage, tampering attempts, and so on, and prepare meaningful routine and exception reports on such activities).

For more information about all types of software and software aids, readers should refer to such comprehensive sources as:

ICP Catalogs
International Computer Programs, Inc.
Carmel, Indiana

Datapro Software Catalog
Datapro Research Corporation
Delran, New Jersey

Test data generators prepare data files for testing and validating the correct operation of computer programs and systems. Some of the more common test data generators, and the companies from which they can be purchased or leased, are identified below.

ALLGEN/EXTRACT-II
Michael E. Quihillalt Associates
San Francisco, California

DOS FILE GENERATION
UTILITY
IBM Corporation
White Plains, New York

SYMDATA
Computer Associates, Inc.
New York, New York

TUG
Technalysis Corp.
Minneapolis, Minnesota

DATAMACS II
Management and Computer Services,
Inc.
Valley Forge, Pennsylvania

PRO/TEST
Synergetics Corp.
Bedford, Massachusetts

TEST FILE GENERATOR FOR
COBOL
Sperry Rand Corporation (Univac Div.)
Blue Bell, Pennsylvania

Tape library management systems provide a means for controlling the retention, rotation, use, scratching, and maintenance of magnetic tape files. They produce a variety of reports: physical inventory, back-up storage inventory, reports on tapes sent to and returned from back-up storage, picking lists and stocking lists for tapes, and status reports showing activity. Some of the more common tape library management systems, and the companies from which they can be purchased or leased, are identified below.

AUTOLIB
Quality Data Products, Inc.
Atlanta, Georgia

SUN LIBRARY SYSTEM
Solar Systems, Inc.
Eugene, Oregon

TAPE LIBRARY CONTROL
First Computer Corp.
St. Paul, Minnesota

TFAST/VS
Oxford Software Corp.
Fort Lee, New Jersey

VALU-LIB II
Value Computing, Inc.
Cherry Hill, New Jersey

EPAT
Software Design, Inc.
San Mateo, California

SUPERLIB
Quality Data Products, Inc.
Cocoa Beach, Florida

TAPE LIBRARY CONTROL
SYSTEM
International Data, Inc.
Miami, Florida

TLMS
Gulf Computer Services, Inc.
Houston, Texas

UCC-1
University Computing Co.
Dallas, Texas

Disk space management systems allocate file space, control the retention and expiration of disk files, perform cataloging functions, and keep records concerning back-up files. They produce various reports, such as inventory lists showing file name, characteristics, size, and record count; utilization reports; and activity logs. Some of the more common disk space management systems, and the companies from which they can be purchased or leased, are identified below.

ADAM
Kraftco Corporation
Glenview, Illinois

DFAST
Oxford Software Corp.
Fort Lee, New Jersey

DISCLOSE
Programart
Cambridge, Massachusetts

DISPLAY
Boole & Babbage, Inc.
Sunnyvale, California

DSM
MHT Services, Inc.
Englewood, New Jersey

PAN*DA
Pansophic Systems Inc.
Oak Brook, Illinois

TSO VTOC SPACE LIST
Gabrielle Wiorkowski
Richardson, Texas

Program library management systems work with or are included in operating system software, and are often an integral part of routine computer operations activities. For example, the library system will often have the "production" version of the programs, which is the only authorized version for live operations. The operating system will fetch only the authorized version for production. The library of production programs can only be changed using special procedures and passwords in some of the systems. Such systems also maintain source programs, which may be for production or be under development. Various reports and directories are produced pertaining to library back-up, activity, and program change histories. Some of the more common program library management systems, and the companies from which they can be purchased or leased, are identified below.

CATALR
Marcus Powell Associates
Oakland, California

SOURCE PROGRAM LIBRARIAN
SYSTEM
Florida Software Services, Inc.
Orlando, Florida

MAXI-LIBE
Maxima Systems Group
Alameda, California

THE LIBRARIAN
Applied Data Research, Inc.
Princeton, New Jersey

PLMS
Gulf Computer Sciences, Inc.
Houston, Texas

DOS COBOL SOURCE
STATEMENT LIBRARY
MAINTENANCE—SYSTEM/370
IBM Corporation
White Plains, New York

PANVALET/PANEXEC
Pansophic Systems, Inc.
Oak Brook, Illinois

SLICK
National Computing Industries
Atlanta, Georgia

SUPERLIB
Generic Systems, Inc.
Jacksonville, Florida

appendix I [1]

Attributes of Fifteen Audit Software Packages

[1] From *Advanced Technology Newsletter*, March 1977, © 1977 by The Institute of Internal Auditors, Inc. 249 Maitland Avenue, Altamonte, Florida 32701 U.S.A. Reprinted with permission.

	A	B [15]	C	D	E [16]	F	G
Vendor:	Arthur Andersen Company	Computer Audit Systems	Cullinane Corp.	Ernst & Ernst	Citibank, N.A.	Informatics, Inc	Program Products Inc.
Package:	AUDEX 100	CARS 2	EDP-Auditor	AUDITRONIC 32	PROBE	MARK IV Auditor	AUDIT ANALYZER
Trial Period	Demonstration	90 days	3 months	N/A	N/A	N/A	60 days
Trial Cost	Free	N/A	$1,500	N/A	N/A	N/A	$500
Price - Purchase	Lease only	$12,500	$15,000	N/A	$12,000	$12 to $18 M	$15 - $16 M
Price - Lease/Year	$7,500 perpetually; per year: $2,500/1, $1,000/2+	Installment 50%	$15,000/1 $2,000/2+	$2,400	N/A	$1,395	$7,700/1
Price - Maintenance	Incl.	(2)	(2)	Incl.	N/A	Incl.	(2)
Price - Installation	Incl.	N/A	Incl.	None	Incl.	Incl.	Incl.
Price - Training	Incl.	N/A	Incl. but travel ex.	$800 and travel exp. (9-day course)	Incl.	Incl.	Incl.
Man-hours of Training (Min.=Minimum number of hours)	25	40 (Min.)	35 (Min.)	64	21	16	40
Manuals Supplied	Incl.	10 Incl.	2-installation 2-sys. 10-user Incl.	1/User Incl.	Incl.	Incl.	10 incl.
Forms Supplied	Starter set incl.	20 sets	Initially yes	Starter set yes	Initially yes	Initially yes	10 sets yes
Consultation Service	Incl.	Yes	Incl.	Maintenance/free, spec. applica- tions/per diem	Incl.	Incl.	Telephone/free, on site/per diem $300
User's Group Meetings	No	$50/Year	Yes	No	Yes	Yes	Yes
Number of Users	N/A	50 & 100 installations	400(7)	35 +	85	400(9)	220
Years in Use	6[3]	7	5[3]	2	6	10	2[3]
Age of Supplier	>10	7	8	>10	>10	>10	5
Accessibility of Supplier	International	Very	Very	Very	Very	Very	Moderate
Periodic Package Updates (Current=New Modifica- tion to be announced)	Current	2 free years	Semiannual incl.	Current + / free	Yes	Current	1 to 2 / year
Number of Coding Sheets (av.) per request	6-10	2-16	2-4	5-7	1	1-6	1
PACKAGE REQUIREMENTS:							
Hardware	360/370	360/370(12) + others + European	AUDAK/IBM 360/370	360/370	All	360/370 + others	360/370
Special Hardware Options	None	None	None	None	None	None	Floating point
Core	60-140K	64K	80K	100K	50-64K	64K	80-120K
Operating Systems	DOS/OS/VS	Various	DOS/VS	Various OS/DOS	Std.	DOS/OS/VS	DOS/O S/VS
Sort Utilities	No	Incl.	IBM SORT	Incl.	Incl.	IBM SORT	Incl.
Output Utilities	No	System	System	System	System	System	System
Dedicated System	No	No	No	No	No	No	No
Runs in Multiprogram- ming Environment	Yes	Yes	Yes	Yes	Yes	Yes	Yes
Runs in Time-Sharing Environment	Yes	Yes	Yes	Yes , but not interactive	Yes	N/A	Yes
Self-Generated J.C.L.	No	No	No	Yes	No	No	No
Written in (language)	BAL	(4)	BAL	(4)	COBOL/BAL	MARK IV	BAL
Special Program Language (MACRO)	No	No	No	No	No	No	No

466

H	I	J	K	L	M	N	O
Informatics, Inc.	Touche Ross & Co.	U.S. Department of Commerce	Computer Audit Systems	Coopers & Lybrand	Dylakor Software Systems, Inc.	Computer Audit Systems	Peat, Marwick, Mitchell & Co.
SCORE IV	STRATA	AUDIT	CARS 3	Audit PAK II	Dyl-260	SYS3AUDIT	P M & M 2170
30 days	N/A	No	90 days	N/A	30 days	90 days	None
$1,000	N/A	N/A	N/A	N/A	Free	$430	N/A
$14,000 (1)	$3,500 (average) perpetual lease	$97	$12,500 + interfaces	Lease only	$8,000	$2,000-$4,700	None
$6,000/1	N/A	No	Installment	$1,000 1st yr. & $500 subt.yrs.	N/A	2 year-6% of total per month Long Term-installment 50%	None
(2)	Incl.	No	10% after 2 yrs.	(2)	W/purchase -- $175 per yr. W/lease -- no charge	10% after 2 years	None
Incl.	Incl.	Users	N/A	Travel exp. only	None	$100 plus cost of disk pack	None
Incl.	2 students incl.	No	N/A	Variable	$250 per day if needed	Optional $200/day plus expenses	Depends on amt. of trng. req; is chgd. at stand. rates of instr.
24-32	40	No	40	15 hours	1	Optional	24 hrs. classroom instr. followed by hands-on proc. that varies with skills of participant.
Incl.	2 incl.	$4.25/2	10	Yes	1 set	5	1 per participant in training course
Initially yes	Initially yes	No	Pads	Yes	1 set	Pads	Coding forms
Incl.	Incl.	No	Yes	Yes	Incl.	Yes	Yes, technological and use to meet audit object.
Yes	No	No	$50/year	None	None	Yes	No
25(8)	170	N/A	100 & 300 installations	N/A	$1,000 +	19	Over 200
7(3)	8	N/A	7	1	4 +	1	Six
7-10	>10	>10	7	>10	8 +	7	>10
Very	Very	N/A	Very	International	Phone/mail	Very	Very
$1,000/2nd year on	Yes	None	2 yrs. free	Yes	$15 per lease	2 years free	Cost of reproducing tape
1	7	N/A	2 - 16	7	1 sheet/4 sides	2	5-7
360/370 + others	IBM 360/370 Burroughs 2500 to 4700 and 678 to 7700; IBM Systems 3 (see note 11)	360/370	360/370 + others + European(13)	360/370	360/370	IBM SYS/3	IBM 360/370 Burroughs 2500 thru 4700
None	None	None	None	None	None	None	None
88K	65-100K	Equal compiler	118K	DOS-50K,OS-76K	50K	16K	64K
OS/VS + others	DOS/OS/VS	Various	OS/VS/DOS	OS/VS/DOS	All	N/A	OS/DOS/MCP
Incl.	IBM SORT	User SORT	Incl.	Yes	IBM & DYLSORT	Mfg.	Mfg.
System	System	System	System	No	No	None	None
No	No	N/A	No	No	No	No	No
Yes	Yes	N/A	Yes	Yes	Yes	Yes	Yes
Yes, with TSL exit	Yes	N/A	Yes	Yes	Yes	No	No
$15,000 option	Yes	No	No	For compilation only	Yes	No	Yes
(4)	COBOL/BAL	BASIC and COBOL	(4)	BAL generates COBOL	Assembly load and go	SYS/3 Assembler	COBOL
No	No	BASIC	No	Yes	Yes	No	No

467

	A	B [15]	C	D	E [16]	F	G
Vendor:	Arthur Andersen Company	Computer Audit Systems	Cullinane Corp.	Ernst & Ernst	Citibank, N.A.	Informatics,Inc.	Program Products Inc.
Package:	AUDEX 100	CARS 2	EDP-Auditor	AUDITRONIC 32	PROBE	MARK IV Auditor	AUDIT ANALYZER

ABILITIES:

	A	B [15]	C	D	E [16]	F	G
Can Handle Data Base Structures	Yes (5)	Yes (6) $1.5 to $4M	Yes (6) $5,000 per	Yes (5)	Yes (5)	Yes	Yes (6), $4-5,000 per interface
Contains User Exits	Yes	Yes	Yes	Yes	Yes	Yes	Yes, 70
Min/Max Input Files	1-2 (match, merge)	1-2	1-256	1-2	User control	1-11	No limit, 1-6 drives
Min/Max Output Files	0-6	1-2 with confirmations	0-100	0-98	User control	1-13	No limit, 0-6 drives
Max Reports on One Pass of File	6	11 plus confirms	100	98 plus 5 Frequency distributions	50	255	80
Source Program Utility (tape, disk, card, CRT)	Not CRT	Not CRT	Yes, incl. CRT w. non-equal MACRO	Not CRT	Not CRT	Not CRT	March 1977
Output Utility (tape, disk, card, CRT, print)	Not CRT	Not CRT	Yes	Not CRT/Card	Not CRT	Yes, CRT w/TSO	Not CRT
Degree of Required Programming Knowledge	Min.	Min	None	None	Min.	Min.	Min.
Can Be Catalogued on-Line	Yes	Yes	Yes	Yes	Library only	Yes	Yes
Is Package Portable	Yes	Yes	Yes	Yes	Yes	Per contract	Yes
Only Selected Modules Read in * = Yes	Yes	Generates COBOL*	Yes	Generates COBOL*	Overlayed *	Yes	Yes
Compile and Diagnostic Routines	Yes	Yes, program + COBOL	Generates machine codes directly- Yes	Yes, 2	Not at user level	Yes	Yes
Option to Limit Record Selection for Tests	Yes	Yes	Yes	Yes	Yes	Yes	Yes, read/ select
Conditional Changes on Extracted Fields	20 Compound	Essentially no limit	No limit	No limit	50	Yes	No limit
Max. Number of Logic Levels for Selection	9	99	No limit	9	Data controlled	9	No limit

I/O CAPABILITY; FILE STRUCTURES:

	A	B [15]	C	D	E [16]	F	G
Tape/Disk-Sequential	Yes	Yes	Yes	Yes	Yes	Yes	Yes
Tape/Disk-Index Sequential	Yes	Yes	Yes	In only	Yes	Yes	Yes
Tape/Disk-Random Organization	With user exits	Yes	Yes	In only	Yes	Yes	Yes
Tape/Disk-Fixed Record Length	Yes	Yes	Yes	Yes	Yes	Yes	Yes
Tape/Disk-Variable Record Length	Yes	Yes	Yes	In only	Yes	Yes	Yes
Tape/Disk-Mixed	Yes	Yes	Yes	With exits	Yes	Yes	Yes
Tape/Disk-Variable Number Fixed Length Trailers	Yes	Yes	Yes	With exits	Yes	Yes	Yes
Tape/Disk-Blocked	Yes	Yes	Yes	Yes	Yes	Yes	Yes
Tape/Disk-V/S Randomized Files	In only with ISAM interface	Yes	Yes	In only with ISAM interface	Yes	Yes	Yes
File/Record Labels-Standard	Yes	Yes	Yes	Yes	Yes	Yes	Yes
File/Record Labels-User	In only	Yes	Yes	In only	Yes	Yes	Yes
File/Record Labels-None	In only	Yes	Yes	In only	Yes	Yes	Yes
Min/Max - Field Lengths (bit - byte)	8-99	Mfg.	1-999	1-99 in 8-30 out	Std.	IBM conventions	1-256
Min/Max - Record Lengths (bit - byte)	10K	Mfg.	1-inf.	1-10K in inf. out	Std.	IBM conventions	No limit
Min/Max - Block Sizes (bit - byte)	10K	Mfg.	1 -inf.	1-100K in inf. out	Std.	IBM conventions	No limit
Min/Max - File Lengths	No limit	Mfg.	No limit	No limit	Std.	IBM conventions	No limit
Maximum - SORT Levels	IBM SORT limit	3	20-45	IBM SORT limit	50/run, 6/report	9	30

H	I	J	K	L	M	N	O
Informatics, Inc.	Touche Ross & Co.	U.S. Department of Commerce	Computer Audit Systems	Coopers & Lybrand	Dylakor Software Systems, Inc.	Computer Audit Systems	Peat, Marwick, Mitchell & Co.
SCORE IV	STRATA	AUDIT	CARS 3	Audit PAK II	Dyl-260	SYS3AUDIT	P M & M 2170
Yes (5)	Yes	No	Yes, $1.5 to $4M	Via user exit	TOTAL	No	Yes
Yes, 90	Yes	N/A	Yes	Yes	Yes	Yes	Yes
1-8	1-6	N/A	1-7	1-2	1-4	1-2	1-2
0-8	>10	N/A	1-2 with confirmation	0-9	1-4	1-3	Unlimited
99	20	N/A	11 + confirmation	9	1	3	5
Not CRT	Not CRT	Not CRT	Not CRT	N/A	Yes	N/A	No
Not CRT	Not CRT	Not CRT	Not CRT	N/A	Yes	N/A	N/A
Min.	None	Min.	Min.	None	Min.	None	None
Yes	Yes	No	Yes	Yes	No	No	Yes
Per contract	Yes	Yes	Yes	Yes	Yes	Yes	Yes
Generates COBOL*	Yes	N/A	Generates COBOL*	Generates COBOL*	Yes	N/A (load and go)	N/A (COBOL program executed)
Yes, 2	Yes	N/A	Yes, program + COBOL	Yes	Yes	Yes	Yes
Yes	Yes	N/A	Yes	Yes	Yes	Yes	Yes
90	No limit	N/A	Essentially no limit	N/A	Yes	No	Unlimited
Within level supported by ANS/COBOL	No limit	N/A	99	N/A	No limit	No limit	No limit
Yes	Yes	Yes	Yes	Yes	Yes	Yes	Yes
Yes	Yes	N/A	Yes	Yes	Yes	Yes	Yes
Yes	Yes, with exits	N/A	Yes	Yes	Yes	Yes	No
Yes	Yes	N/A	Yes	Yes	Yes	Yes	Yes
Yes	Yes	N/A	Yes	N/A	Yes	Yes	Yes
Yes	Yes	N/A	Yes	Yes	Yes	Yes	Yes
Yes	Yes	N/A	Yes	Yes	Yes	Yes	Yes
Yes	Yes	N/A	Yes	Yes	Yes	N/A	No
Yes	Yes	N/A	Yes	Yes	Yes	Yes	Yes
Yes	Yes	N/A	Yes	Yes	Yes	No	Yes
Yes	Yes	N/A	Yes	Yes	Yes	Yes	Yes
COBOL limit	1-256	N/A	Mfg.	1-999	IBM Conventions	Mfg.	Mfg.
COBOL limit	1-800	N/A	Mfg.	1-999	IBM Conventions	N/A	N/A
COBOL limit	Std.	N/A	Mfg.	1-999	IBM Conventions	Mfg.	Mfg.
No limit	No limit	N/A	Mfg.	No limit	IBM Conventions	No limit	No limit
9	5	N/A	Input at 3 levels, 3 internal	9	IBM Conventions	5	Use vendor's utilities

469

Vendor:	A Arthur Andersen Company	B (15) Computer Audit Systems	C Cullinane Corp.	D Ernst & Ernst	E (16) Citibank, N.A.	F Informatics, Inc.	G Program Products Inc.
Package:	AUDEX 100	CARS 2	EDP-Auditor	AUDITRONIC 32	PROBE	MARK IV Auditor	AUDIT ANALYZER
Maximum - SORT Key Size	IBM SORT limit	15	No limit	IBM SORT limit	12 bytes	IBM SORT limit	254
Maximum - Control Break Levels	5	3	20-45	3 merge, 1 summary	50/run, 6/report	9	9
Maximum - Accumulator Buckets	10/input, 20/report	15 plus control	998 +	40/run, 20/report	300/run, 6/report	No limit	100/report
Contains a Table-Driven Interpreter	Yes	No	Yes	No	N/A	Yes	No
Size * = Not a Limiting Factor	*	N/A	*	N/A	N/A	*	N/A
Dynamically Allocates Core	DOS, yes	Yes	Yes	N/A	N/A	Modified yes	Modified yes
Compresses/Decompress File and Record Lengths	No	Through user code	N/A	With user exits	No	Option	No
Must Input File Be Presorted	No	No	No	No	No	No	No
Must Input File be Predefined in a Glossary	No	No	No, however, generally done	No	No	Yes	Yes
Must Input File Be Reformatted	Yes, internally	No	No	Internally for output	No	No	No
Must Input File Be Free of Field Errors	No	Auto-Edit	No, but data exceptions could occur	No	No, but may cause data exceptions	No	No
Has Automatic Line-Folding Capability	No	No	Yes	Yes	User coded	Yes	Yes
Has Automatic Control/ Grand Totals	Yes	Yes	Yes	Yes	Yes	Yes	Yes
Has Automatic Report Formatting	No	Partial	Yes	Yes	Yes	Yes	Yes
Has Automatic Page Counts	Yes	Yes	Yes	Yes	Yes	Yes	Yes
Has Automatic Carry-Forward Totals	No	Yes	Yes	No	Yes	Yes	Yes
Has Special Print-Suppress Options	Yes	Yes	No limit	Yes	Yes	Yes	Yes
Maximum Calculations Per Field	40	No limit	No limit	No limit	No limit	No limit	No limit
Can Flag Input Errors Without Halts	Yes	Yes	Yes	Yes	Yes	Yes	Yes
Can Compare Total Field to Detail Fields on DASD Files	No	Yes	Yes	No	No	Programmable via MARK IV	Yes
Has Option to Check Parameters via Intermediary Totals	Yes	Yes	Yes	No	User routine	Yes	Yes
Has Option to Generate Test Data with Flags	No	Yes	Yes	N/A	No	No	Yes
Has Option to Print Confirmation Requests	Yes	Yes	Yes	N/A	Yes	Yes	Yes
Maximum Fields Extractable per Record	60	No limit	No limit	50 in 12 numeric out 15 alpha out	N/A	No limit	No limit
Maximum Number of Aging Levels	8	7	No limit	9	5	20	6
Can Simulate an Application Program for Timing Tests	No	Yes	Yes	No	No	Yes	Yes
STATISTICAL SAMPLING ABILITIES:	Limited	Yes	Elaborate	Yes	Limited	Extensive	Limited
Can Handle Known and Unknown Universe	Yes	Yes	Yes	N/A	N/A	Yes	Yes
Generates Minimum of 3 Random Starts	No(14)	1 + user code	Yes	Yes, 10	User specified	Yes, 9	Yes
Contains Random Number Generator	Yes	Yes	Yes	Yes, 10 seeds	Yes	Yes	Yes

H	I	J	K	L	M	N	O
Informatics, Inc.	Touche Ross & Co.	U.S. Department of Commerce	Computer Audit Systems	Coopers & Lybrand	Dylakor Software Systems, Inc.	Computer Audit Systems	Peat, Marwick, Mitchell & Co.
SCORE IV	STRATA	AUDIT	CARS 3	Audit PAK II	Dyl-260	SYS3AUDIT	P M & M 2170
Operating system limit	IBM SORT limit	N/A	15	256	IBM Conventions	15 bytes each	Use vendor's utilities
6	6	N/A	3	9	7	5	4
20	15	N/A	28 + control	No limit	Unlimited	10	30
Yes	Yes	N/A	No, but possible	No	N/A	Yes	Yes
*	*	N/A	N/A	N/A	N/A	Depends on available core	Depends on available core
No	No	N/A	Yes	Yes	Yes	Yes	Yes
No	No	N/A	Through user code	No	Yes, optional	No	Yes
No	No	N/A	No	No	No	No	No
No	No	N/A	No	No	No	No	No
No	No	N/A	No	No	No	No	No
Yes	No	N/A	Auto-Edit	Yes	No	Automatic Edit	Automatic edit
No	No	N/A	No	No	No	No	No
Yes	Yes	N/A	Yes	Yes	Yes	Yes	Yes
Yes	No	N/A	Partial	Yes	Yes	No (partial)	No
Yes	Yes	N/A	Yes	Yes	Yes	Yes	Yes
Yes	No	N/A	Yes	Yes	Yes	No	Yes
Yes	No	N/A	Yes	No	N/A	Yes	Yes
No limit	No limit	N/A	No limit	No limit	No limit	No limit	No limit
Yes	Yes	N/A	Yes	No	Only totalled	Yes	Yes
With user exits	Yes	N/A	Yes	Yes	Yes	No	No
Yes	Yes	N/A	Yes	Yes	Yes	No (future)	Yes
No	No	N/A	Yes	No	Yes	No	Yes
Yes	Yes	N/A	Yes	N/A	N/A	Yes	Yes
No limit	99	N/A	No limit	No limit	No limit	No limit	50
15	Programmable	N/A	7	2-9	No limit	7	Unlimited
Yes	Yes	N/A	Yes	Sometimes	Yes	No	Yes
Limited	Yes (10)	No	Yes	Limited	Limited	Yes	Yes
N/A	Yes	N/A	Yes	Yes	N/A	Yes	Yes
No	No	N/A	1 + user code	1 per report	User specified	No	N/A-uses unrestricted random sampling(stratified for variables) Yes
Option	Yes	N/A	Yes	No	Option	Yes	

	A	B (15)	C	D	E (16)	F	G
Vendor:	Arthur Andersen Company	Computer Audit Systems	Cullinane Corp.	Ernst & Ernst	Citibank, N.A.	Informatics, Inc.	Program Products Inc.
Package:	AUDEX 100	CARS 2	EDP-Auditor	AUDITRONIC 32	PROBE	MARK IV Auditor	AUDIT ANALYZER
Contains Random Number Table	No	No	Yes	No	No	No	Optional
- Size	N/A	N/A	Up to 21K	N/A	Repeat after 500K	N/A	N/A
Can Select Every Nth Item	No	Yes	Yes	Yes	User coded	Yes	Yes
Sample Size Can Be Specified	Yes	Yes	Yes (or) calculated	Yes	Yes	Yes	Yes
Calculates and Option to Print - Mean	No	Yes	Yes	Yes	Yes	User coded	Yes
- Standard Deviation	No	Yes	Yes	Calculates, no print	Power 10 residual method	User coded	Yes
Accepts Desired Precision Factor	No	Yes	Yes	Yes	Table lookup	Yes	Yes
Accepts Confidence Level and Factor	No	Yes	Yes	Yes	Table lookup	Yes	Yes
Accepts Expected Error Rate	No	Yes	Yes	Yes	N/A	Yes	Yes
Generates Bargraphs	No	User exit	Yes	Yes	No	User coded in MARK IV	Yes
Generates Histograms	No	User exit	Yes	Yes	No	User coded in MARK IV	No
Solves and Displays Graphic Analysis	No	User exit	Yes	No	No	User exit	No
Solves Linear Programming	No	No	Yes, limited	No	No	User exit	No
Does Trend-Line Analysis	No	User exit	User exit	No	No	User exit	No
Does Correlation Analysis	No	User exit	User exit	No	No	User exit	Yes
Does Multiple-Regression Analysis	No	User exit	User exit	No	No	User exit	User coded
Does Matrix Analysis	No	User exit	User Exit	No	No	User Exit	Yes
Has Capability for Interval Sampling	No	Yes	Yes, incl. with library of audit routine supplied with package	Yes	Yes	Yes, 60 strata	Yes
Has Capability for Stratification Sampling	5 Strata	Yes	Yes, incl. with library of audit routine supplied with package	Yes	Yes	Yes, 60 strata	Yes
Has Capability for Cluster or Multistage Sampling	No	Yes, proportionally	Yes, incl. with library of audit routine supplied with package	No	Yes	Yes	User coded
Has Capability for Attributes Sampling	No	Yes	Yes, incl. with library of audit routine supplied with package	Yes	Yes	Yes	Yes
Has Capability for Variables Sampling	No	Yes	Yes, incl. with library of audit routine supplied with package	Yes	Yes	Yes	User coded
Has Capability for Stop-or-Go Sampling	No	No	Yes, incl. with library of audit routine supplied with package	Yes	Yes	Yes	User coded
Has Capability for Discovery Sampling	No	Yes	Yes, incl. with library of audit routine supplied with package	Yes	Yes	Yes	User coded
Has Capability for Judgment Sampling	No	No	Yes, incl. with library of audit routine supplied with package	Yes	Yes	Yes	User coded
Has Capability for Probability Sampling	No	Planned	Yes, incl. with library of audit routine supplied with package	Yes	No	Yes	User coded

	H	I	J	K	L	M	N	O
	Informatics, Inc.	Touche Ross & Co.	U.S. Department of Commerce	Computer Audit Systems	Coopers & Lybrand	Dylakor Software Systems, Inc.	Computer Audit Systems	Peat, Marwick, Mitchell & Co.
	SCORE IV	STRATA	AUDIT	CARS 3	Audit PAK II	Dyl-260	SYS3AUDIT	P M & M 2170
	No	No	N/A	No	N/A	4-byte binary	No	No
	N/A	N/A	N/A	N/A	N/A	2(31)	N/A	No
	Yes	User coded	N/A	Yes	Yes	Yes	Yes	Yes
	Yes	Yes	N/A	Yes	No	Yes	Yes	Yes
	Yes	No	N/A	Yes	Yes	No	Yes	No
	User exit	No	N/A	Yes	No	No	No	Yes, by stratum-no option
	User exit	++	N/A	Yes	No	No	Yes	Yes (stated in $)
	User exit	++	N/A	Yes	No	No	Yes	Yes
	User exit	++	N/A	Yes	No	No	Yes	No
	User exit	No	N/A	User exit	No	No	No	No
	User exit	++	N/A	User exit	No	No	No	Yes
	User exit	No	N/A	User exit	No	No	No	No
	User exit	No	N/A	No	No	No	No	No
	User exit	No	N/A	User exit	No	No	No	No
	User exit	No	N/A	User exit	No	Nc	No	No
	User exit	No	N/A	User exit	No	No	No	No
	User exit	No	N/A	User exit	No	No	No	No
	User exit	++	N/A	Yes	Yes	No	Yes	Yes
	User exit	++	N/A	Yes	Yes	No	Yes	Yes
	User exit	No	N/A	Yes, proportionally	No	No	No	No
	User exit	++	N/A	Yes	No	No	Yes	Yes
	User exit	++	N/A	Yes	No	No	No	Yes
	User exit	No	N/A	No	No	No	No	No
	User exit	No	N/A	Yes	No	No	Yes	Yes
	User exit	No	N/A	No	No	No	No	Yes
	User exit	No	N/A	Planned	No	No	No	Yes

As the internal auditor required pads, pencils, and an adding machine 25 years ago, the modern internal auditor now requires audit software to effectively examine the voluminous data in today's computer files. Audit software has been available from both public accounting firms and commercial software houses since the early 1960's.

The current products, unlike their early predecessors, are powerful data-retrieval and manipulation tools. The software packages enable the auditor to retrieve, summarize, and analyze large amounts of data within a relatively short period of time for formulating meaningful and timely audit recommendations.

Surveys show that less than half of the organizations having internal auditors use audit software packages. Those organizations currently trying to select an audit software package may choose from a wide variety of packages with different capabilities. The auditor selecting the package must analyze these capabilities in order to determine which package will fulfill the needs of the Internal Audit Department.

Charles M. Laier, CIA, developed 117 attributes of audit software packages. He examined 18 packages and compared 11 of these packages in detail.

IIA updated the attributes, and added more packages to the survey.

This *Advanced Technology Newsletter* lists the attributes of some of these packages. Subsequent newsletters will include characteristics of additional audit software packages. We would like organizations with audit software packages used by internal auditors to contact Bill Perry, the editor of this newsletter. He will include the attributes of other packages in future issues.

NOTES AND EXPLANATIONS FOR USE WITH SOFTWARE ANALYSES:

1. Special prices to current customers (free or 20% discount)
2. Included in lease, extra if purchased
3. Original product exclusive of significant periodic modifications. However, most recent versions are being compared
4. A preprocessor which generates an error-free COBOL program ready to compile and to run.
5. With user exits
6. Package option
7. Include CULPRIT
8. 400 for SCORE
9. 1,000 for MARK IV
10. Statistical sampling beyond basic techniques may be done by using exits or using a separate statistical package available for a one-time cost of approximately $800.
11. An IBM System 3 version of STRATA is available for approximately $1,100 — a one-time charge
12. Available for Univac, Honeywell, Burroughs, ICL, NCR, Sieners and COC.
13. Available for Univac and Burroughs (others to follow)
14. A "no" answer in this section (statistical sampling) indicates these functions may be accomplished with user exit coding
15. See also columns K and N
16. See also column H
N/A Not applicable or information not available
++ With separate statistical system package, $800 additional one-time cost

appendix J[1]

Illustrative Procedures Manual Section Covering Irregularities, Reporting, Investigating, and Restitution

[1] From *Foozles and Frauds* by Harold F. Russell, © 1977 by The Institute of Internal Auditors, Inc. 249 Maitland Avenue, Altamonte, Florida 32701 U.S.A. Reprinted with permission.

PROCEDURE MANUAL		Subject	Manual No.
Issued 1/1/	Effective 1/1/	IRREGULARITIES	1234-0001
☐ Complete Revision	Supersedes	REPORTING	
☐ Partial Revision		INVESTIGATING	
(see asterisk)		RESTITUTION	
☐ No Change			Page No.
Distribution			

PURPOSE

To provide a uniform procedure for investigating, reporting, and resolving acts of dishonesty, fraud, or theft which involve employees or nonemployees of the company. Unless unusual circumstances surround a loss of $1,000 or less, local management will handle it and will not be required to submit a report to corporate headquarters.

REFERENCES

1234-0002, Insurance and Self-Insurance
1234-0003, Fidelity Bond — Irregularities
1234-0004, Audit Shortages

DEFINITIONS

Employee — The term "employee" as used herein is as appearing in fidelity bond. (**Note:** These are for bond purposes only and do not necessarily reflect actual, legal, "employee" status.) This includes regular or temporary employees, wholesale commission consignees, commission truck agents, commission truck consignees, retail contract managers, and all other similar agents or consignees who are covered by fidelity bond.

Nonemployees — This includes dealers and all others while acting on behalf of the company or while in possession of money or property belonging to the company or in which the company has an interest, whether or not a contract or bond exists.

Irregularity — This means any loss to company of money or property which results from an apparently fraudulent or dishonest act of an employee(s) or nonemployee(s) either acting alone or with others. The term "fraudulent or dishonest act" is to be interpreted as an intentional act which results in the diversion of money or property and which is admitted or can be proved.

476

EXCLUSIONS

A. Any loss occurring while products are in transit in commercial carriers' equipment unless an employee, insured agent, or insured consignee is involved. (Irregularities involving commercial carriers will be handled by accounting and regional traffic offices as determined in *Procedure Manuals 1001-0001, 0002, and 0003.*)

B. Any loss of product, cash, or other shortage which is based solely on an inventory or audit computation and procedure deviations which do not involve dishonest acts and where there is no factual evidence of fraud which is admitted or can be proved. Such losses are defined as audit shortages with reporting requirements as outlined in *Procedure Manual 4321-0010.*

RESPONSIBILITIES

Local management — The unit manager/controller or his appointed representative is responsible for promptly preparing and distributing required initial notices and subsequent reports, undertaking investigation, requesting headquarters' assistance, if necessary, and arranging for restitution and/or filing for payment under fidelity bond coverage.

Local Office of General Counsel — When a suspected irregularity exists, the nearest representative of the Office of General Counsel should be consulted before embarking upon any contact with the employee(s), distributing the initial or final written notification, and preparing the *CO-0012 — Proof of Loss Claim* or any other written communication relating to irregularities which implicate specific individuals. If any attempted contact with local management is made by a legal representative of the employee(s), he should be referred directly to the local representative of the Office of General Counsel.

North American Division:	Controller's — Coordinate headquarters' reporting and undertake any investigation this department deems necessary under the circumstances.
	Respective functional management — Review reports submitted to headquarters and assist field management as requested.
Corporate Department:	Undertake any investigation and other required action as deemed necessary under the circumstances.

PROCEDURE

1. **Notification of Irregularity** (whether covered by fidelity bond or not)
   A. All employees are responsible for bringing irregularities or suspected irregularities to the immediate attention of their supervisor or manager.
   B. Local managers or their designated representatives should undertake an immediate investigation of the situation reported as an irregularity and determine the need for immediate telephone notification to the Corporate Security and Safety Department.

C. *Initial report* — Depending on the circumstances and in the judgment of local management, immediate telephone notification may be required. This will depend upon the value of the property involved, the number or level of employees, the method used to commit the irregularity, or possible exposure which may prove detrimental to the company. Headquarters' management, upon receipt of the telephone report, will contact the other departments as deemed necessary. *Whether or not a telephone notification is made, a confidential letter must be mailed within ten days after the discovery describing the irregularity.* All subsequent correspondence relating to the irregularity is also to be marked "confidential." *Distribution of a report is limited, and a recipient should not prepare nor distribute additional copies.*

The initial report should cover the following points:

1. Name(s) and address(es) of the individual(s) involved, if known, and any allegations or implications of dishonesty relating to such individual(s) should be documented with incriminating information or admissions from them
2. Location of the office, plant, site, terminal, etc., where the irregularity occurred
3. Type of operation
4. Actual or estimated amount involved
5. Explanation of the circumstances of the irregularity
6. Action taken, including method of investigation, facts uncovered, present status of employee, and steps taken to protect company assets from further loss
7. Indications whether the most recent audit of the location uncovered any circumstances which might have indicated that an irregularity was in progress

D. *Interim reports* — It is anticipated that final reports will be issued within ninety (90) days of the initial report. Where this is not possible, an interim report is to be issued and then each six months thereafter, indicating the current status and the forecast of progress.

E. *Final report* — After the investigation and all the actions within the control of local management are completed, a final report (identified as such) is to be submitted as soon as possible.

The final report should cover the following points:

1. Amount involved exclusive of insurance or other recoveries
2. Name and position of employee(s) and nonemployee(s) involved
3. Methods used to effect the irregularity
4. Time period over which the irregularity occurred
5. Means of disclosure
6. Statement as to whether there was:
   a. An absence of internal control
   b. A circumvention of internal control through collusion
   c. Effective internal control

478

7. Steps taken to prevent recurrence in instance 6a and 6b above
8. The names of the insurance companies and other persons from whom recoveries were made and amounts recovered

F. Local management's responsibility for reporting irregularities under the provisions of the subject manual is in no way relieved by the fact that reports and other correspondence are or will be issued on the same subject either by local management or others. *Irregularity reports must be distributed in accordance with paragraph 1G of this manual and must satisfy all requirements listed in paragraphs C and E with respect to the initial or the final reports as the case may be.* Local management must submit a report which in all cases provides management with comments on all the items above and other items as applicable.

G. Distribution of *Initial Report* and *Final Report:*
Original: Manager, Corporate Security and Safety Department
Copies:
  Corporate Insurance Department
  General auditor
  Manager, North American Division Operations Audit
  Respective North American Division Functional Management
  North American Division Controller, attention of respective functional accounting department's manager
  Local Office of General Counsel
  Local management as determined by the unit manager/controller responsible for reporting
  File

2. Investigation

Investigation must be conducted discreetly to protect innocent individuals and to preclude, insofar as possible, any basis for claims of defamation.

A. Provided the employee(s) does (do) not resign, the individual(s) suspected of being involved in an irregularity may be transferred to another position, continue on present position under strict surveillance, or be suspended until an investigation of the irregularity is completed. Termination of the employee is not recommended during the initial investigative stages. Action taken will depend on attendant circumstances. Appropriate final action will be taken during or after the investigation.

B. Pending results of the investigation, the employee's(s') salary or wages should be continued provided he did not resign. Depending on attendant circumstances and with the Office of General Counsel's approval, an employee(s) may be suspended without pay.

C. The fidelity bond coverage ceases to cover an employee(s) immediately subsequent to the discovery of the irregularity. Should management retain the employee(s), any further losses incurred as a result of an additional irregularity by this same employee(s), if not reinstated by the bonding company under the company's blanket policy, will be charged against the affected North American Division or field unit.

D. Written reports containing any implication of dishonesty on the part of the employee(s) should be prepared and released only after consultation with the Local Office of General Counsel.

3. Restitution

A. Cases involving possible restitution should be pursued by local management with direction from the local Office of General Counsel familiar with the relevant laws of the particular area.

B. It is most important that no expressed or implied assurance be given that the company, its agents, or employees will not testify, initiate, nor assist in legal action where restitution is sought from an employee(s) or from someone on his behalf. Before restitution is accepted, a written disclaimer should be prepared by the company supporting this position and signed by the respective employee(s).

The recommended format of this disclaimer is as follows:

Dear _____ :

In accepting restitution due this company by reason of handling of certain property of the company, it is understood that neither the company nor any of its agents or employees has given or is giving any promise or assurance to conceal any facts or not to institute or to assist in penal proceedings. We wish you to confirm this understanding by your endorsement below.

C. Although not essential, a handwritten confession in the employee's(s') own language should, if possible, be obtained. Where practical, General Counsel should be present when a confession is obtained.

4. Insurance Claims

A. Notify the Corporate Insurance Department (see paragraph 1G) as soon as an irregularity is suspected.

B. Local management should file form *CO-0012—Proof of Loss Claim* in quadruplicate with support documentation when the amount of loss exceeds the $1,000 deductible and when there appears to be no reasonable chance of recovery. It is expected that bond claims will normally be filed within 90 days after detecting an irregularity.

Distribution:
    2 copies: Corporate Insurance Department
    1 copy: (as applicable)
      Manager, Marketing Accounting
      Manager, Manufacturing Accounting
    1 copy: File

C. After a claim is filed, any further settlement with the defaulting employee(s) must be coordinated with the Corporate Insurance Department for routing to the insurance carrier.

appendix K[1]

Illustrative Form
for Confessions

[1] From *Foozles and Frauds* by Harold F. Russell, © 1977 by The Institute of Internal Auditors, Inc. 249 Maitland Avenue, Altamonte, Florida 32701 U.S.A. Reprinted with permission.

The following format of a confession was devised for our use by a Law Department, and it is suggested that this format be followed in obtaining confessions. Any deviations from this format should be cleared with the manager of internal auditing prior to its use. Our experience has also proven that a confession is of extreme importance when filing a claim with our bonding insurer for the amount of the loss.

STATE OF _____

    : SS:

COUNTY OF_____

BEFORE ME, the undersigned, a notary public, in and for the state and county aforesaid, personally appeared _____ , who being duly sworn according to law, did depose and say as follows:

1. My name is _____ , and I reside at _____

    _____

2. I have been employed by the ABC Company, Inc. since

    _____ , most recently as _____ at

    _____

3. Before making any statement I was advised by _____ , a representative of the ABC Company, Inc. that:

    a. I am not obligated to make any statement whatsoever with respect to matters hereinafter set forth.

    b. I am entitled to consult with and be represented by an attorney before and during the making of any statement by me.

    c. Any statement I make may be used in evidence in any civil or criminal proceeding which may be commenced against me.

4. I am making this statement of my own free will without threat or coercion made or offered directly or indirectly and with a full understanding of my rights as aforesaid, and I hereby expressly waive my right to remain silent and to consult with or be represented by counsel in connection herewith. I have not been offered or promised, directly or indirectly, anything of value in connection with the making of this statement, including, without limiting the generality of the foregoing, any promise on the part of the ABC Company from instituting any criminal information or proceeding under applicable state or federal law.

5. The facts relating to this matter are as follows:

6. This statement was given by me orally in the presence of _____ , representative of the ABC Company, Inc., and was reduced to writing by _____ .

7. I have read the foregoing; and the same is true, correct, and complete and is adopted and affirmed by me. I have further initialled each page for identification.

SWORN TO and subscribed before me this _____ day of _____ , 19 _____

_____
Notary Public
My Commission Expires:

appendix L[1]

Sample Guide
to Sources
of Personal Information
for Investigators

Part 1 contains types of information sought, followed by a number(s). This number(s) directs the reader to the sources listed in Part 2.

This guide does not purport to be a complete source reference. It merely indicates where information can be found and does not mean that the information will be automatically given to an investigator. In many instances, information can only be obtained by use of legal process such as a subpoena.

[1] From Herbert Edelhertz et al., *The Investigation of White Collar Crime: A Manual for Law Enforcement Agencies*, Law Enforcement Assistance Administration (Washington, D.C.: Government Printing Office, 1977).

PART 1

TYPES OF INFORMATION DESIRED

Type of Information	Refer to Part 2 Item Number
1. Full name	1,2,4,5,6,10,11,16,17,24, 31,34,35,36,56
2. Address	1,2,4,5,6,10,11,16,17,24, 31,34,35,36,56,62
3. Date of birth	2,3,8,13,24,34,35
4. Description	2,3,13,56
5. Photograph	2,3,13,22,62
6. Occupation	6,13,31,34,35,37,55,62
7. Marital status	12,23,34,55,56
8. Prior addresses of a subject; names of persons previously living at the same address	35,36,62
9. Addresses, present and former, whether renting or buying; credit references; personal and business associates; names of relatives; locations of banks and finance companies	34
10. Telephone numbers and addresses; how long has the suspect had service; record of long-distance phone calls; number of extensions in residence	5
11. Sources of income; expenditures; personal and business references; net worth of subject; handwriting exemplars	31
12. Information as to credit charges that have been made; what hotels are being used; where the suspect has been buying gasoline; employment and credit references	15
13. Registered owners of vehicles; legal owners of vehicles; description of vehicles; previous owners of vehicles; operators' license numbers; signatures; photographs; thumbprints; abstracts of traffic citations	56
14. Application for bonds that give personal and business references; former addresses; former places of employment	32

Type of Information

Refer to Part 2
Item Number

15.	Records of stocks bought or sold, profits and losses	33
16.	Recorded deeds, grants, mortgages, wills admitted to probate, notices of mechanics' liens; powers of attorney	61
17.	Record of registration for securities offered for public sale; record of individuals and firms who have violated state or federal regulations in securities traffic	50
18.	Information concerning reputation of a business; back issues of city directories	51,52,62
19.	Businesses' worth; associates; family holdings and ratings	34,55
20.	Information on persons involved in a medical or dental practice, pharmacists, barbers, funeral directors	47
21.	Names of post office box holders; return addresses on mail received at post office; mail covers	4
22.	To find a forwarding address	4,38
23.	Marriage license applications; addresses, dates of birth; signatures	12
24.	Names of the bride and groom; maiden name of bride; ages	23
25.	Information on divorces (e.g., place and date of marriage); date of divorce/legal separation; ages of children; community property; signatures; income; places of employment	9,62
26.	Information on parents of a child (e.g., occupations, ages, mother's maiden name, name of physician)	20,24
27.	Disposition of monies from an estate; value of estate; inventory of all assets of deceased	30
28.	Name and description of the deceased; property found on deceased and its distribution; cause of death	25,29,30
29.	Where death occurred; birthplace; how long deceased lived in the county, state, or United States; names of relatives; whether or not deceased was a veteran	25,62

PART 1 (continued)

Type of Information

		Refer to Part 2 Item Number
30.	Civil suits—changes of name; liens; description of property involved; name of court reporter, if any, who recorded the testimony	10
31.	Political party; physical disabilities that would prevent marking a ballot; name of spouse; when and where married; last place of registration to vote	6,62
32.	Ship, boat, and yacht registrations	41,42
33.	Names and addresses of owners of ships, boats, or yachts	41,42,59
34.	Ownership of aircraft	60,64
35.	Background on horse owners, jockeys, trainers, and people employed at race tracks	7,62
36.	Case histories of persons on welfare (usually good background information)	21
37.	Student records, past and present; teachers' records, past and present	22
38.	List of all county employees; occupations and rate of pay; records of all financial business for the county	26
39.	Presidents and secretaries of all county medical associations; names of hospitals and sanitariums, number of rooms and beds; doctors' names by street and city; doctor's year of birth, medical school and year of graduation, office address	39
40.	Bar owners' fingerprints, marital status, home addresses, employees, associates	48
41.	Information relative to articles of incorporation, giving businesses, associations, records of election returns; descriptions of seals used by various state officers; papers filed by candidates for election to state offices	43
42.	Names of associates of a person involved in organized crime and which law enforcement agencies have information	27,62
43.	Transcripts of preliminary hearings; probation officer's reports; subpoenas issued in the case; names of attorneys concerned	11

Type of Information

44.	Parole reports; inmate contacts; visitors; correspondence; work and training assignments	53
45.	Copies of telegrams and money order information; possibly handwriting exemplars	37
46.	Record of all warrants drawn on the state treasury; accounts of all persons indebted to the state	44
47.	Legal description of property; amount of taxes paid on real and personal property; former owners of property	17
48.	Amount of cost of construction; blueprints of construction; information regarding location of plumbing and wiring	19
49.	Dimensions of property and taxable income of real property, and improvements, if any, on the property	16
50.	Maps of streets; locations of drains; location of utility conduits; rights of way; old names of streets	18
51.	Maps having elevations, base lines; landmarks; important sites	28
52.	Sources of information in foreign countries	57,58
53.	Information as to anticipated travel of a person in a foreign country and vital statistics	13,62
54.	Addresses of aliens	14,49
55.	Alien information; date of entry; manner of arrival; addresses; occupation; age; physical description; marital status; children; signature; photograph	14,49
56.	A guide to newspapers and periodicals printed in the U.S. and its possessions; thumbnail description of every city, including population, county, and location with respect to the nearest large city	40
57.	Information on cattle and dairies	45
58.	Mining information, petroleum and gasoline, fish and game	46
59.	Arson information and thefts of valuable insured items	54,63

PART 2

SOURCES OF INFORMATION

1. Telephone directories
2. State of California, Department of Justice, Bureau of Identification (CII)
3. FBI
4. Post office
5. Telephone company
6. Registrar of Voters
7. California Horse Racing Board
8. County Clerk's Office, Vital Statistics
9. County Clerk's Office, Divorce Records
10. County Clerk's Office, Civil Files
11. County Clerk's Office, Criminal Files
12. County Clerk's Office, Marriage License Applications
13. State Department, Passports Division
14. County Department of Naturalization
15. Credit card companies
16. County Assessor's Office
17. County Tax Collector's Office
18. Highway Department
19. Building Department
20. Health Department
21. Welfare Department
22. School Department
23. County Recorder's Office, Marriage License Section
24. County Recorder's Office, Birth Certificate Section
25. County Recorder's Office, Death Certificate Section
26. County Auditor's Office
27. Law Enforcement Intelligence Unit (LEIU) (if your department is a member)
28. County Surveyor's Office
29. County Coroner's Office
30. Public Administrator's Office
31. Banks and finance companies
32. Bonding companies
33. Stock brokers
34. Credit reporting agencies
35. Gas and electric companies
36. Water companies
37. Telegraph companies
38. Moving companies
39. American Medical Directory

40. *Directory of Newspapers and Periodicals,* N. W. Ayer & Sons, Philadelphia
41. Lloyds Register of Shipping
42. Lloyds Register of Yachts
43. Secretary of State, Corporate Division
44. State Controller
45. State Department of Agriculture
46. Department of Natural Resources
47. Consumer Affairs
48. Alcohol Beverage Control
49. Federal Immigration and Naturalization Service
50. Securities and Exchange Commission
51. Better Business Bureau
52. Chamber of Commerce
53. Department of Corrections
54. American Insurance Company
55. Dun and Bradstreet
56. Department of Motor Vehicles
57. Treasury Department, enforcement agencies
58. Interpol
59. Harbor patrol
60. Airport security
61. County Recorder's Office
62. Newspaper library or newspaper "morgue"
63. Insurance Crime Prevention Institute
64. Federal Aviation Administration

appendix M[1]

Characteristics
of Bank Checks
and Other Sources
of Financial Information
for Investigators

Recognizing
"cashed" checks

All banks use a series of codes or symbols to indicate on the face of the check the nature of its disposition. Of particular interest to the investigator are those checks, either drawn on the target's checking account, or received by a target from others, which have been cashed. Figure M-1 shows the "cashed" code used by a major bank.

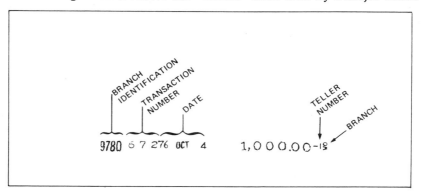

Figure M-1

[1] This material is adapted from Richard A. Nossen, *The Seventh Basic Investigative Technique*, Law Enforcement Assistance Administration (Washington, D.C.: Government Printing Office), 1977.

491

It is one of the most commonly used codes, and is usually stamped on the face of cashed checks. Other examples of "cashed" codes used by banks are shown in Figure M-2. These codes are usually

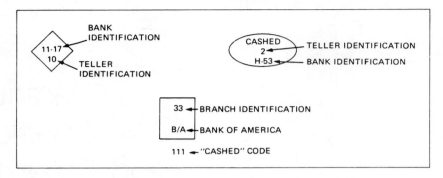

Figure M-2

found on the face of the check. Owing to the variety of codes used, no attempt has been made here to include "cashed" codes of all banks.

Bank identification symbols

Checks printed for banking institutions contain a series of numbers in the upper right-hand corner on the face of the checks. These numbers represent an identification code developed by the American Banker's Association and are usually referred to as the "ABA Transit Number" or routing and transit number. The number is shown in the circle in Figure M-3. The portions of the ABA number are indicated in Figure M-4. A complete listing of the ABA Numerical System Identification Codes is shown in Figure M-5 on pages 494–95.

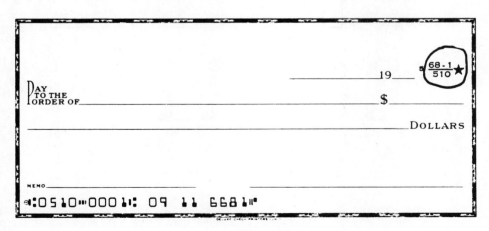

Figure M-3

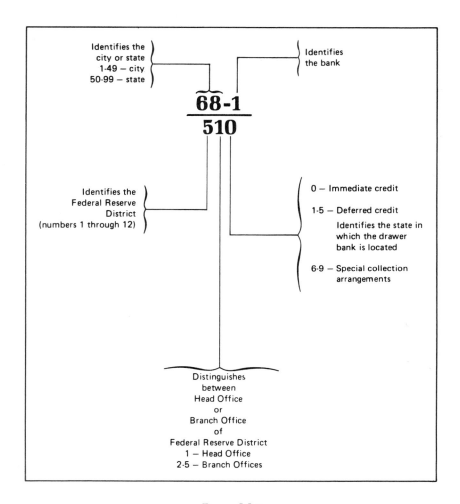

Figure M-4

THE NUMERICAL SYSTEM
of The American Bankers Association
Index to Prefix Numbers of Cities and States

Numbers 1 to 49 inclusive are Prefixes for Cities.
Numbers 50 to 99 inclusive are Prefixes for States.
Prefix Numbers 50 to 58 are Eastern States.
Prefix Number 59 is Alaska, American Samoa, Guam, Hawaii, Puerto Rico, and
    Virgin Islands.
Prefix Numbers 60 to 69 are Southeastern States.
Prefix Numbers 70 to 79 are Central States.
Prefix Numbers 80 to 88 are Southwestern States.
Prefix Numbers 90 to 99 are Western States.

Prefix Numbers of Cities in Numerical Order

1. New York, N. Y.	18. Kansas City, Mo.	35. Houston, Texas
2. Chicago, Ill.	19. Seattle, Wash.	36. St. Joseph, Mo.
3. Philadelphia, Pa.	20. Indianapolis, Ind.	37. Fort Worth, Texas
4. St. Louis, Mo.	21. Louisville, Ky.	38. Savannah, Ga.
5. Boston, Mass.	22. St. Paul, Minn.	39. Oklahoma City, Okla.
6. Cleveland, Ohio	23. Denver, Colo.	40. Wichita, Kan.
7. Baltimore, Md.	24. Portland, Ore.	41. Sioux City, Iowa
8. Pittsburgh, Pa.	25. Columbus, Ohio	42. Pueblo, Colo.
9. Detroit, Mich.	26. Memphis, Tenn.	43. Lincoln, Neb.
10. Buffalo, N. Y.	27. Omaha, Neb.	44. Topeka, Kan.
11. San Francisco, Calif.	28. Spokane, Wash.	45. Dubuque, Iowa
12. Milwaukee, Wis.	29. Albany, N. Y.	46. Galveston, Texas
13. Cincinnati, Ohio	30. San Antonio, Texas	47. Cedar Rapids, Iowa
14. New Orleans, La.	31. Salt Lake City, Utah	48. Waco, Texas
15. Washington, D. C.	32. Dallas, Texas	49. Muskogee, Okla.
16. Los Angeles, Calif.	33. Des Moines, Iowa	
17. Minneapolis, Minn.	34. Tacoma, Wash.	

Prefix Numbers of States in Numerical Order

50. New York	64. Georgia	82. Colorado
51. Connecticut	65. Maryland	83. Kansas
52. Maine	66. North Carolina	84. Louisiana
53. Massachusetts	67. South Carolina	85. Mississippi
54. New Hampshire	68. Virginia	86. Oklahoma
55. New Jersey	69. West Virginia	87. Tennessee
56. Ohio	70. Illinois	88. Texas
57. Rhode Island	71. Indiana	89. . . . .
58. Vermont	72. Iowa	90. California
59. Alaska, American	73. Kentucky	91. Arizona
Samoa, Guam,	74. Michigan	92. Idaho
Hawaii, Puerto	75. Minnesota	93. Montana
Rico & Virgin	76. Nebraska	94. Nevada
Islands	77. North Dakota	95. New Mexico
60. Pennsylvania	78. South Dakota	96. Oregon
61. Alabama	79. Wisconsin	97. Utah
62. Delaware	80. Missouri	98. Washington
63. Florida	81. Arkansas	99. Wyoming

Figure M-5

ROUTING SYMBOLS (IN ITALICS) OF BANKS THAT ARE MEMBERS OF THE FEDERAL RESERVE SYSTEM

ALL BANKS IN AREA SERVED BY A FEDERAL RESERVE BANK OR BRANCH CARRY THE ROUTING SYMBOL OF THE FEDERAL RESERVE BANK OR BRANCH

FEDERAL RESERVE BANKS AND BRANCHES

1. Federal Reserve Bank of Boston Head Office — $\frac{5-1}{110}$

2. Federal Reserve Bank of New York Head Office — $\frac{1-120}{210}$

   Buffalo Branch — $\frac{10-26}{220}$

3. Federal Reserve Bank of Philadelphia Head Office — $\frac{3-4}{310}$

4. Federal Reserve Bank of Cleveland Head Office — $\frac{0-1}{410}$

   Cincinnati Branch — $\frac{13-43}{420}$

   Pittsburgh Branch — $\frac{8-30}{430}$

5. Federal Reserve Bank of Richmond Head Office — $\frac{68-3}{510}$

   Baltimore Branch — $\frac{7-27}{520}$

   Charlotte Branch — $\frac{66-20}{530}$

6. Federal Reserve Bank of Atlanta Head Office — $\frac{64-14}{610}$

   Birmingham Branch — $\frac{61-19}{620}$

   Jacksonville Branch — $\frac{63-19}{630}$

   Nashville Branch — $\frac{87-10}{640}$

   New Orleans Branch — $\frac{14-21}{650}$

7. Federal Reserve Bank of Chicago Head Office — $\frac{2-30}{710}$

   Detroit Branch — $\frac{9-29}{720}$

8. Federal Reserve Bank of St. Louis Head Office — $\frac{4-4}{810}$

   Little Rock Branch — $\frac{81-13}{820}$

   Louisville Branch — $\frac{21-59}{830}$

   Memphis Branch — $\frac{26-3}{840}$

9. Federal Reserve Bank of Minneapolis Head Office — $\frac{17-8}{910}$

   Helena Branch — $\frac{93-26}{920}$

10. Federal Reserve Bank of Kansas City Head Office — $\frac{18-4}{1010}$

    Denver Branch — $\frac{23-19}{1020}$

    Oklahoma City Branch — $\frac{39-24}{1030}$

    Omaha Branch — $\frac{27-12}{1040}$

11. Federal Reserve Bank of Dallas Head Office — $\frac{32-3}{1110}$

    El Paso Branch — $\frac{88-1}{1120}$

    Houston Branch — $\frac{35-4}{1130}$

    San Antonio Branch — $\frac{30-72}{1140}$

12. Federal Reserve Bank of San Francisco Head Office — $\frac{11-37}{1210}$

    Los Angeles Branch — $\frac{16-16}{1220}$

    Portland Branch — $\frac{24-1}{1230}$

    Salt Lake City Branch — $\frac{31-31}{1240}$

    Seattle Branch — $\frac{19-1}{1250}$

Figure M-5 (*Continued*)

National credit cards

Bank Americard (now VISA Card, except for those issued by Bank of America). Records of purchases made by Bank Americard holders are retained on microfilm by participating banks. The record retention period varies according to the record retention policies of the member banks. It should be noted that *all* records relating to customers who have used their accounts, or those of others, in a fraudulent manner, are retained *permanently.*

Since the records of purchases are stored in facilities maintained by each of the member banks, no attempt is made here to list the location of Bank Americard storage centers, owing to the large number of participating banks. This information can be readily obtained on a local basis.

Figure M-6 is a sample monthly statement issued to cardholders by Bank Americard.

Master Charge. Records of purchases made by Master Charge Credit Card holders are also retained on microfilm by participating banks. The record retention period varies according to the record retention policies of the participating banks.

As with Bank Americard, record storage facilities are maintained by each of the member banks. Again, there are a large number of such facilities, so no attempt is made here to list them.

BANKAMERICARD STATEMENT

NOTICE: SEE REVERSE SIDE FOR IMPORTANT INFORMATION

BANKAMERICARD ACCOUNT NUMBER	STATEMENT CLOSING DATE	CREDIT LIMIT	AVAILABLE CREDIT	FOR YOUR RECORDS	DATE PAID	CHECK NUMBER	AMOUNT PAID
4368 110 388 839	05-03-76	1000	930				

NOTICE- SEE ACCOMPANYING STATEMENT FOR IMPORTANT INFORMATION REGARDING YOUR RIGHTS TO DISPUTE BILLING ERRORS

TYPE OF TRANSACTION	[illegible]		DESCRIPTION OF CHARGES AND CREDITS			AMOUNT	BILLING ITEM NUMBER
PREV BAL			PREVIOUS BALANCE FROM LAST STATEMENT			.00	
PURCHASE	04	10	JAMES RIVER BRASS SHOP	RICHMOND	VA	44.20	4368041661173550
PURCHASE	04	17	HOFHEIMERS 40	RICHMOND	VA	9.35	4366042601341648
PURCHASE	04	20	DRUG FAIR 161	RICHMOND	VA	15.67	4366042701788163
NEW BAL			***** NEW BALANCE *****			69.22	
			MINIMUM PAYMENT DUE			10.00	

TYPE OF CREDIT	PERIODIC RATE(S)	[illegible]	BALANCE ON WHICH FINANCE CHARGE WAS COMPUTED	FINANCE CHARGE
NEW CASH ADVANCES (INITIAL BILLING)	1.00 %	12.00 %	0.00	0.00
PREVIOUS CASH ADVANCES	1.00 %	12.00 %	0.00	0.00
OTHER EXTENSIONS OF CREDIT	1.50 %	18.00 %	0.00	0.00
	%	%		

[illegible]	[illegible]	ANNUAL PERCENTAGE RATE FOR THIS BILLING PERIOD
0.00	05-28-76	0.00 %

STATEMENT NUMBER	PAGE NUMBER
5-21010	1 OF 1

® Servicemarks owned and licensed by BankAmerica Service Corporation

BAC 4368-23-0311

Figure M-6

The Master Charge company has converted most of its record-keeping systems to provide cardholders with a monthly statement similar in format to that of Bank Americard. It replaces the system in which copies of the charge tags are returned to customers.

American Express Card. Records of purchases made by American Express Credit Card holders are retained on microfilm for at least 6 years. Requests for copies of monthly statements, if circumstances require making a formal request, should be directed to the American Express Company, Box 13779, Phoenix, Arizona 85002.

The monthly statement issued to card holders by the American Express Company is similar in format to the statement issued by Bank Americard.

Travelers checks

American Express. Canceled American Express Travelers Cheques are retained for a period of 6 years and 1 month in storage facilities located in Piscataway, New Jersey. The checks are filed serially by date of redemption, not by issue date. Requests for copies of paid checks should be directed to the American Express Company, American Express Plaza, New York, New York 10004.

Citibank of New York. Cancelled Citibank Travelers Cheques are also filed, serially, by date of redemption rather than by issue date. Requests for copies of paid checks should be directed to the Citibank Travelers Cheque Refund Department, P.O. Box 2202, F.D.R. Station, New York, New York 10022.

Bank of America. Canceled Bank of America travelers checks are also filed, serially, by date of redemption rather than by issue date. Requests for copies of paid checks should be directed to the Bank of America Check Corporation, Attention: Claims Department, Fifth Floor, 1 Powell Street, San Francisco, California 94102.

Security broker–dealer customer statements

Referring to Figure M-7, the following rules are applicable to analyzing a target's security account statement.

When a target purchases stock there would be entries in all of the following columns:

1. "Bought or Received" column.
2. "Description" column, where the name of the security would be listed.
3. "Price or Symbol" column, where the purchase price per share would be listed.
4. "Debit" column, the amount of the purchase charged to the target's account.

PERIOD ENDING *June 30, 1975*

TARGET "A"

STATEMENT OF YOUR SECURITY ACCOUNT
WITH

STOCK BROKER "A"

MEMBERS NEW YORK STOCK EXCHANGE   AMERICAN STOCK EXCHANGE
TORONTO STOCK EXCHANGE AND OTHER LEADING STOCK AND COMMODITY EXCHANGES

YOUR ACCOUNT NUMBER
247630

KINDLY MENTION YOUR ACCOUNT NUMBER WHEN REFERRING TO THIS STATEMENT OR OTHER TRANSACTIONS.

DATE	QUANTITY Bought or Received	QUANTITY Sold or Delivered	DESCRIPTION	PRICE OR SYMBOL	AMOUNT DEBITED (CHARGED) TO YOUR ACCOUNT	AMOUNT CREDITED TO YOUR ACCOUNT	BALANCE (BY TYPE OF ACCOUNT)
6 19			Check			10,000.00	10,000.00
6 19	100		ABC Corp.	100	10,000.00		-0-
6 20			Check			10,000.00	10,000.00
6 20	100		ABC Corp.	100	10,000.00		-0-
6 23			Check			5,000.00	5,000.00
6 23	200		DEF Corp.	25	5,000.00		-0-

KINDLY DIRECT INQUIRIES CONCERNING THIS STATEMENT TO THE OFFICE WHICH SERVICES YOUR ACCOUNT. SEE REVERSE SIDE FOR ADDRESS AND TELEPHONE NUMBER.

LEDGER

FOR DESCRIPTION OF TYPE OF ACCOUNT AND EXPLANATION OF SYMBOLS USED. SEE REVERSE SIDE.

Figure M-7

When a target sells stock, there would be entries in all of the following columns:

1. "Sold or Delivered" column.
2. "Description" column, where the name of the security would be listed.
3. "Price or Symbol" column, where the sales price per share would be listed.
4. "Credit" column, the proceeds from the sales credited to the target's account.

When a target purchases stock, he has the option of taking "delivery" of the certificates from the broker or leaving them in the broker's custody.

If he takes delivery of the certificates, the number of shares would be noted in the "Sold or Delivered" column and the date column would show the date of delivery. In addition, there would be *no* entry in the "price or symbol" column. If there was a price in the "price or symbol" column, the entries would reflect a sale rather than a delivery.

If there are no entries indicating "delivery" of the securities, they are, in fact, being held by the broker and the target is in what is commonly referred to as a "long" position. Usually the broker will list at the bottom of the target's December statement a summary of his "long" position (i.e., a listing of the number of shares of each stock being held for the target).

Index